GEEK
WISDOM

EMBRACING
THE
SACRED TEACHINGS
OF
POP CULTURE

GEEK
WISDOM

EMBRACING
THE
SACRED TEACHINGS
OF
POP CULTURE

EDITED BY STEPHEN H. SEGAL

With commentary by Zaki Hasan, N. K. Jemisin,

Eric San Juan, and Genevieve Valentine

ILLUSTRATIONS BY MARIO ZUCCA

Hallmark
gift books

QUIRK BOOKS
PHILADELPHIA

This edition published in 2012 by Hallmark Gift Books,
a division of Hallmark Cards, Inc.,
Kansas City, MO 64141
Visit us on the Web at Hallmark.com.

Designed by Doogie Horner and Steven DeCusatis
Illustrations by Mario Zucca

ISBN: 978-1-59530-545-9
BOK1220

Printed and bound in China

A Gift For: _____

From: _____

TABLE OF

CONTENTS

INTRODUCTION

I wish I could remember who asked me the question. Because I know for sure that my answer is what set me on the path that has brought me here, to you, on this page. The question was: "What was your religion when you were growing up?" And my answer was: "Uh, science fiction, pretty much."

I meant it as a joke. I was poking fun at myself, saying that I'd been such a freaking *geek* as a kid, watching *Star Trek* and reading Tolkien and writing computer programs and building TARDIS models, you'd think that stuff was my religion. But as soon as it came out of my mouth, I immediately understood that this was no joke. It was absolutely 100 percent true in a way that I'd never thought of before—and, furthermore, it was a good thing.

What *is* religion? Never mind all the trappings, all the ceremonial garments and the prayer rules and the fish on Friday. What is religion really for? It's a framework of ideas—a body of thought shared by a community, written and handed down through literature—that's intended to guide us toward maturity by helping us ask and answer the big, cosmic questions about existence. Who are we? Where did we come from? Is there anyone else out there in realms of being we can't see? Here on earth, why can't we get along with one another better than we do? And how can we possibly find any redemption for the mess we tend to make of things?

The Bible tells stories answering these questions. So does the Quran. So do the Upanishads. So do the sacred books of every other religion. The stories in each tradition vary a lot in the details, but they all make their way around to more or less the same points that, in turn, ultimately boil down to this: hey, show some respect for the universe, because it's a whole lot bigger than you.

You know what? Religion isn't the only place to find those kinds of stories. The modern scientific world tells them, too. In fact, geek culture is built on them.

Look at the Bible. In the beginning, God gave Adam and Eve a couple simple rules, and they didn't obey them, and we got to see how that affected the rest of their lives and what it implies for us. Then Moses brought down ten divine algorithms from the Mount for everyone to live by—don't kill, don't bear false witness, do honor your parents, etc.—and we got to spend the rest of the Bible tagging along as generations upon generations of slaves, peasants, merchants, and kings alternately followed and broke these commandments and tried to learn how to live with the consequences.

And now look at Isaac Asimov, scientist and novelist. He was not, obviously, God. He didn't create the universe, humanity, and everything in between. But he did imagine that someday humanity would create artificial beings—mechanical intelligences—and would have to give *them* rules to live by. And thus, after school, while my best friend John was in catechism class reading from the Gospel of Matthew, I could be found at home reading from Asimov's book *I, Robot*, watching cybernetic Abrahams and Jobs with "names" like SPD-1 and NS-10 do their damnedest to make it through situations where the rules of life seemed just impossible to cope with.

Does that sound strange? That robots, as envisioned as realistically as possible by a scientifically trained futurist, should suffer from existential angst? In fact, it makes tremendous sense. Because when Asimov sat down to codify his Laws of Robotics— the practical operational rules that would make it possible for these new intelligent beings to live in harmony with one another and their creators—what he came up with was startlingly similar to the moral code outlined by most every religion and philosophy throughout human history. Oh, sure, it looks different—

1. A robot shall not harm a human being or, through inaction, allow a human being to come to harm.

2. A robot shall obey the orders given by a human being, except where this would conflict with the First Law.

3. A robot shall protect its own existence, except where this would conflict with the First or Second Law.

—but when you put that in plainer, more casual language, what it amounts to is this:

It's important to take care of yourself, but it's more important to spread happiness, but it's even more important to hold life sacred.

You don't have to be a robot, or even a sci-fi geek, to under-stand that's a pretty straightforward description of being a good person. And, you know, being a good person is hard. So if geek culture can offer fresh, new, alternative paths to all the eternal truths that religion and philosophy have managed to discover over the past few thousand years—paths that welcome those who've been turned away from the more traditional routes—then I say, let there be geekery.

The realm of geekdom, of course, is much bigger than just science fiction. Geeks are passionate fans of stuff, and particularly of stuff that lies somewhere along one of two cultural axes: *math* and *myth*. The love of math stuff gives us science geeks, computer geeks, chess geeks; the love of myth stuff gives us theater geeks, literary geeks, ancient-Greek geeks. This is why science fiction and role-playing games make up the enduring popular image of modern-day geekdom, mind you, because those are the places where math and myth intersect: literature built on the infinite possibilities of science, improv sword and sorcery shaped by the numerical output of 20-sided dice.

Hence *Geek Wisdom*: the first compendium of sacred teachings from the wide-ranging "holy scriptures" of geekdom, that weird mass of pop culture and high art ranging from blockbuster mov-ies to esoteric novels to cult-classic T-shirt slogans. *Star Wars*. *The Princess Bride*. Albert Einstein. Stan Lee. From such sources we've gathered (and mused thoughtfully upon) the deepest, purest, most profound ideas and sayings to be found. The ones that cut right to the heart of life in the twenty-first century. The ones we quote as if they'd come from the Bible, or from Shakespeare. The ones that, increasingly, have emerged from the underground to form the cellular structure of a true new culture canon.

Our culture canon. And thus does the geek inherit the earth.

A NOTE ON SPOILERS

GEEK WISDOM features quotes from many classic movies, books, and television shows. Some of the points we necessarily address will, technically, be spoilers to anyone who hasn't experienced these works directly. We have avoided, however, ruining any big surprises or twist endings; the spoilers found within are the kind of thing you'd pick up from general cultural discussion of the stories in question. In other words: a few bits may be *spoiled*, but don't worry—none of them are *ruined*.

I.
MY NAME IS
INIGO MONTOYA

(WISDOM ABOUT THE SELF)

"WITH GREAT POWER COMES GREAT RESPONSIBILITY."

—STAN LEE, MARVEL COMICS

S PIDER-MAN'S UNCLE told him this, and that's why he became Spider-Man. George Washington realized it, too, and that's why he decided eight years was long enough for anyone to be president of the United States. Tim Allen tried to dodge around it, and that's why his dishwasher exploded. King David said to hell with it and had his lover's husband killed, and that's why he had epic family problems for the rest of his life. Paris Hilton seems oblivious to the very concept, and that's why animal lovers have long been inclined to worry about her poor, poor dog. And Albert Einstein realized the full, inhuman horror of it—that's why he wrote to Franklin Roosevelt to explain the possibility of an atomic bomb. Sure, the seed of the truism can be found in Luke 12:48 ("To whom much is given, much is expected"). But although the word of that young Jewish carpenter from Nazareth may be eternal, it took an young Jewish comic-book writer from New York City to put it in terms that ring true to the modern ear.

The original quote, from *Amazing Fantasy* #15 (1962), actually said: "With great power there must also come—great responsibility!" Subsequent references rounded off the portentous edges.

"DESTINY! DESTINY!
NO ESCAPING THAT FOR ME!"

—DR. FREDERICK FRANKENSTEIN, *YOUNG FRANKENSTEIN*

THE ODDS ARE EXCELLENT that your grandfather did not dig up corpses, stitch them together, and reanimate them into a murderous, shambling monstrosity. And yet the same inexorable force of genetic history that drove young Frederick to follow in Victor's footsteps is at work in all our lives. Maybe you realize one day, washing your hands for the fourth time since dinner, that somewhere along the line you picked up the same obsessive germaphobia that always made your mom's aunt seem so crazy. Maybe you've just chosen between three different neighborhoods to live in, and you can't figure out *why* you picked the one with the longest commute, until it finally hits your conscious mind that standing outside your new window is a willow tree like the one Dad planted in your backyard when you were nine. Maybe, after a lifetime of gorgeous hair, you're staring down the barrel of a .22-caliber bald head. Whatever it may look like, there is definitely a monster with your family's name—and it's coming for you. It's up to you whether you'll chase it with a burning torch or sing it a sweet lullaby of love.

Filmmaker Mel Brooks has called *Young Frankenstein* (1974) his favorite of all his movies.

"I'M NOT FINISHED."

—EDWARD, *EDWARD SCISSORHANDS*

IT'S HARD FOR ANY SENSITIVE adolescent to have a reasoned, distanced approach to *Edward Scissorhands*. That's because it's one of film's most heartbreaking portrayals of the experience of being a teenage outsider. The horrors of suburban conformity are distilled to their pure essence in the people who surround Edward, all of whom are pretty shells over darker selves. The movie makes several salient points about how this microcosm behaves toward someone who's physically different; even Edward's adoptive mother, who loves him dearly, often treats him more as a cause célèbre than as a person. And even after he finds someone to love, he has to leave her to avoid retribution from those who don't understand him. When Edward whispers, "I'm not finished"—referring to his very self, that is, "My creator didn't give me all the necessary bits"—it's as though he's speaking directly to every uncertain kid who ever longed to be accepted without having to conform. Luckily, growing up "unfinished" can make geeks the very best people to guide and nurture the next generation of outsiders: we know you don't have to be finished to be awesome.

Goth-geek favorite filmmaker Tim Burton is a master of moody visuals first and a narrative storyteller only second. But he has called *Edward Scissorhands* (1990) semiautobiographical, which may explain why the plot is among Burton's strongest.

"THE LIGHT THAT BURNS TWICE AS BRIGHT BURNS HALF AS LONG . . . AND YOU HAVE BURNED SO VERY, VERY BRIGHTLY, ROY."

—DR. ELDON TYRELL, *BLADE RUNNER*

D R. TYRELL WASN'T TALKING about rock and roll, but he might as well have been. See, when Neil Young told us it was better to burn out than to fade away, he wasn't being sincere; his own status as the elder statesmen of grungy rock is proof of that. He was talking about an all-too-common phenomenon, though: often, our most monumental cultural icons, in music or otherwise, are monumental in part because they were taken from us too soon. Whether through their own recklessness (Jimi Hendrix, Jim Morrison), by their own hand (Kurt Cobain, Ernest Hemingway), or at the hands of another (John Lennon, Abraham Lincoln), the life lived in the clouds above mere mortals is frequently doomed to the fate of Icarus, who flew too close to the sun and in his folly perished. *Is* it better for a superstar's legacy if, like *Blade Runner*'s wild-eyed Roy Batty, they burn out rather than fade away? Or should the next wave of ambitious, creative visionaries buck this trend and stick around for their own third acts? The geek takeover of popular culture just may mean a shift in this unfortunate tradition; unlike rockers and replicants, one thing geeks are *not* is reckless.

After decades of proudly gleaming Hollywood spaceships and robots, *Blade Runner* (1982) offered an alternate version of the future, full of grimy streets and corporate advertising. It's a future that's looked more like the present every year since.

"BY GRABTHAR'S HAMMER, BY THE SONS OF WARVAN, YOU SHALL BE AVENGED."

—ALEXANDER DANE, *GALAXY QUEST*

SOMETIMES IT'S HARD to accept one's inner weirdo. In *Galaxy Quest*, jaded actor Alexander Dane finds his thespian career ruined by sci-fi typecasting, and thus spends most of the movie trying to distance himself from his TV character's most famous catchphrase. In the end, though, he learns that some situations call for those very words to be wielded sincerely, in the name of justice. It's not hard to find oneself in this position. The world is frequently cruel to those earnest souls who take "corny" ideas like truth and justice seriously or aren't afraid to wear their hearts on their sleeves—just look at how often the wondrous power of the Internet is used for callous, drive-by snark when commiseration is really what's called for. Folks are eager to point and laugh at the latest online meme making the rounds. After we saw a photo of Keanu Reeves looking genuinely sad get Photoshopped into a thousand comedic punch lines, it was only to be expected that the video clip of that random dude getting excited about a double rainbow was going to be mocked a millionfold. Yet expressing oneself passionately is nothing to be ashamed of. It's a way to clearly communicate the things that, deep down, are most important to us. In fact, *someone* had better do it, or, by Grabthar's Hammer, who shall bother avenging you?

Sometimes, parody or pastiche shows a deeper love for the original source material than a hundred official sequels ever could. In forty years, has there really ever been a better *Star Trek* movie than *Galaxy Quest* (1999)—or a better *Fantastic Four* movie than *The Incredibles*?

"ALL THAT IS GOLD DOES NOT GLITTER / NOT ALL THOSE WHO WANDER ARE LOST."

—J. R. R. TOLKIEN, *THE LORD OF THE RINGS: THE FELLOWSHIP OF THE RING*

TOLKIEN may have been able to more easily sum up his verse description of Aragorn by saying, "Don't judge a book by its cover," but that wouldn't have been very poetic, would it? Like his belief in huge and unexpected good fortune—he coined the term *eucatastrophe* to describe such sudden turns for the good—Tolkien believed in finding virtue in unexpected places, often wrapped in a cloak the modern world would deem ugly. Gnarled tree creatures, road-weary travelers, and grumpy old men in grey rags are just a few of the guises taken by the benevolent powers of Middle Earth. There may be a degree of simple wish-fulfillment fantasy hidden in there, the old cliché of the ordinary person who secretly has amazing abilities, but it's more than that. It's a lesson in judging people—or, rather, *not* judging them. It also speaks to appreciating simplicity in one's life and not underestimating the inner strength of the downtrodden. Despite Tolkien's staunch Catholicism, there is an almost Taoist spirit to the sentiment. Divinity is not labeled as such; you have to look below the surface.

We finally met Aragorn onscreen forty-seven years after his literary debut in 1954; few could fault Viggo Mortensen's performance as the exiled heir to humankind's throne, but some did grumble that, even scruffy, he was more handsome than Aragorn's epigraph should allow.

"I'M NOT EVEN SUPPOSED TO BE HERE TODAY!"

—DANTE HICKS, *CLERKS*

JUST READING that makes you want to slap someone, doesn't it? And yet, at the same time, you totally get it, don't you? Most of us are well acquainted with the sting of being abruptly summoned to spend our off-day working; still, it's not pretty when on-the-job complaints turn into life-sweeping disclaimers. Whiny retail employee Dante Hicks drops this gem approximately eight hundred (thousand) times in this classic slice-of-slacker-life film; specifically, he seems to drop it whenever he's made an error of judgment, as if uttering the words will both send him home and erase his mistakes. Unfortunately, suffering injustice doesn't excuse you from responsibility for your own choices, and Dante spends the day forcibly coming to terms with this fact—or, at least, being dressed down about it by Randal. (Please note that we recommend taking stock of your choices and trying to get closure, instead of just arguing about whether contractors on the Death Star were innocent victims or not.) But don't worry—as long as you're not using it as a catch-all excuse, if you're called in to work on your day off, you're totally still allowed to complain.

It's rarely commented on, since the name Dante experienced a trendy baby boom a couple decades ago, but we do think the idea of naming the protagonist of *Clerks* (1994) after the poet who famously toured all the torments of Hell is a pretty funny bit of hyperbole.

"WAX ON . . . WAX OFF."

—MR. MIYAGI, *THE KARATE KID*

NO ONE ENJOYS ROTE LEARNING. Memorizing a list of facts and figures may pave the way for a passing grade, but as much as we may love books and trivia, we take little true pride in such mental drudgery; we're just glad to have passed. Real learning comes when we get our hands dirty: endless hours of building Legos teaching us about structural engineering; summer jobs at the cash register teaching us how to interact as an adult with strangers; college internships at the office showing us how different our chosen field looks in practice than it did on paper. Through the knuckle-rapping pains of experience, we absorb knowledge in a tangible, useful way, not simply learning how things are done but how to do them—and then, how to do them *better*. If we're paying attention, then before long, we start trying to innovate; we break down walls and change our piece of the world while we're at it. We become not just *smart*—that and a quarter will buy you a gumball—but *competent*. And if there's one thing geeks strive for, it's to be more capable than the norm. Thus, we wax.

Mr. Miyagi, the guru in *The Karate Kid* (1984), was portrayed by Pat Morita, who went on to delight geeks by lampooning the role in the cartoon *Robot Chicken*.

"THAT IS MOST OF IT, BEING A WIZARD—SEEING AND LISTENING. THE REST IS TECHNIQUE."

—SCHMENDRICK THE MAGICIAN, *THE LAST UNICORN*

EVEN A STOPPED CLOCK is right twice a day, and in *The Last Unicorn*, Schmendrick the Magician manages to hit on more than one home truth amid his self-doubt and suspicion. His struggles to channel and control his magic form a through-line of the novel, though he sums them up in this single throwaway comment that strikes at the heart of the problem for many of us: knowing when to listen, and then—when the time to talk arrives—how to be really heard. Of seeing and listening, too much praise cannot be said (one need only look at any YouTube comments section to understand the value of restraint). When you're setting out to learn a new skill, attentive observation will do you more good than any other single training tool. The patience to absorb information before acting is the real art; once you've mastered that, Schmendrick's right—what remains is just details.

Peter S. Beagle's *Last Unicorn* is one of the handful of fantasy classics that's simultaneously considered a classic in a second genre: the pony book. It's as often found on a shelf next to *Black Beauty* and *Misty of Chincoteague* as it is alongside *The Hobbit* or *A Wrinkle in Time*.

**"EVEN A MAN WHO IS PURE IN HEART AND
SAYS HIS PRAYERS BY NIGHT MAY BECOME A
WOLF WHEN THE WOLFBANE BLOOMS AND
THE AUTUMN MOON IS BRIGHT."**

—ANCIENT GYPSY PROVERB, *THE WOLF MAN*

THAT COUPLET at the start of 1941's *The Wolf Man* begins our brief,* tragic sojourn in the brief, tragic life of Larry Talbot, a good man whose pure heart wasn't enough to stop an unfortunate encounter with the business end of a werewolf from saddling him with a very hairy problem. So effectively did writer Curt Siodmak weave the mystery and mysticism of extant werewolf lore into his tale that, even today, many viewers fail to realize that he conjured the proverb entirely from his imagination. What Siodmak's poem signifies is the omnipresent fear we all carry deep inside us that, regardless of the person we've tried to be or the life we've tried to lead, circumstances outside our control might force us to do or be something terrible—and we might ultimately be powerless to stop it.

---

*Brief, that is, until the first of several sequels came along two years later.

"THAT RUG REALLY TIED THE ROOM TOGETHER."

—THE DUDE, *THE BIG LEBOWSKI*

I F YOUR HOUSE WAS ON FIRE and you could grab only one thing before running to safety, what would it be? Tough decision? Not for the Dude. For him, that rug is a talisman as powerful and mythic as Luke Skywalker's lightsaber or Indiana Jones's fedora, and his stalwart devotion to that artifact provides some insight into why the character resonates. We've been conditioned to think of our movie heroes as quick thinking, forceful, and otherwise action-oriented, but the Dude represents a pointed inversion of the classic heroic paradigm. He's our unfettered id brought to bedraggled, beer-bellied life. There's a primal simplicity to the Dude's personal code of honor that we all can relate to—and many of us wish we could embody. Even when offered a cut of the stolen money he's found, he says, "All the Dude ever wanted was his rug back. Not greedy." He remains utterly, defiantly true to himself even in the face of an increasing unhinged, nonsensical modern world. Now that's some good stuff, Dude.

Jeff Bridges may not be the cultural signifier that Johnny Depp's presence in a film is, but his offbeat selection of roles—The Dude, *Tron*'s Kevin Flynn, *Iron Man*'s Obadiah Stane, *Starman*'s titular alien—definitely marks him as a geek star.

"WORST. EPISODE. EVER."

—COMIC BOOK GUY, *THE SIMPSONS*

"BAZINGA!"

—SHELDON, *THE BIG BANG THEORY*

I F GEEKS ARE ANYTHING, WE ARE OPINIONATED. We wield our views like +1 spiked clubs, casting judgment upon throwaway entertainment as if we were debating scripture *(ahem)*. Those of us who've prowled Internet forums and chat rooms don't just know people like *The Simpsons*' infamous Comic Book Guy, we've *been* them. We walk a fine line between commendable passion for that which we love—starships, superpowers, costumes, fantastic stories—and an almost frightening militancy about the Right Way to Enjoy Them. It's part of what makes us who we are. The Comic Book Guy is revolting not simply because he's loathsome—though he is—but because in our worst moments we, too, can be blindly critical and socially inept. Thankfully for the modern geek, those moments are rarer than they used to be. We long ago crawled out of the basement, took hold of popular culture, and developed the ability to laugh at the image of who we collectively once were.

And yet—sometimes we backslide.

One of geekdom's most visible ambassadors this decade, *The Big Bang Theory*'s Sheldon Cooper is a theoretical physicist who has mastered everything from a prepuberty PhD to the rules of that classic game, Rock, Paper, Scissors, Lizard, Spock. Lifting the old stereotype of the asexual braniac to new heights, Sheldon is a derisive, hygienic, methodical academic who nonetheless benefits greatly from the company of his friends. On paper, he's exactly the person many geeks would point to as a flag-bearer. But as the show's ongoing narrative evolved, the other characters' jabs at Sheldon's expense became something he increasingly played into: his fastidiousness became infantilization, his wry observations started to sound like full-on pompous taunts, and his inside jokes turned into shorthand punch lines to any scene the writers couldn't end coherently. (Lookin' at you, "Bazinga.") Geeks of the world, don't let this happen to you. We know you love to revel in your geekiness, but it's easy to slip to the dark side; try hard not to turn into a caricature of yourself. And if you *must* have a signature catchphrase, for God's sake, try to keep an eye on how often you're saying it.

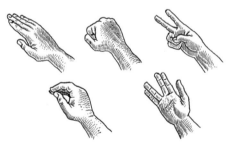

TV producers, take note: geeks know when you're laughing with us and when you're laughing at us. Sheldon and Comic Book Guy: with us. Steve Urkel: at us.

I. My Name Is Inigo Montoya **29**

"FEAR IS THE MIND-KILLER. FEAR IS THE LITTLE-DEATH THAT BRINGS TOTAL OBLITERATION."

—BENE GESSERIT LITANY AGAINST FEAR, *DUNE*

S HE'S THERE, across the room, and her hair is long and it's lovely, and so is she, and you keep stealing glances, you can't even control them, and every time she glances back you avert your gaze because, dear lord, if her eyes were to meet yours. If she could see into yours, she'd know. She'd know what you're feeling and thinking, and that would be so unbearably embarrassing. Your friends nudge. *Go, go*, they say. You can't. Your limbs are frozen, your tongue fat and heavy and swollen. *Go talk to her*, they say. But you won't. You are afraid, and in your fear you've already failed. You know she is already lost to you—or. *Or*. Or maybe you can suppress that fear. Can think, act, do, *talk*; can embrace reason and confidence over raw emotion. Can just go ahead and talk to her, so then maybe, maybe, she'll talk back to you. And you can smile.

Frank Herbert's groundbreaking science-fiction classic, *Dune* (1965), was rejected twelve times. Herbert did not let fear of failure prevent him from continuing to send the book out until he found a publisher who believed in it.

"IF MY DOCTOR TOLD ME I HAD ONLY SIX MINUTES TO LIVE, I WOULDN'T BROOD. I'D TYPE A LITTLE FASTER."

—ISAAC ASIMOV

THAT ASIMOV meant what he said is plain to see in the immense library of knowledge and wisdom he imparted to us during his extraordinary lifetime—a library we'll likely continue to benefit from for time immemorial. But you don't have to be Isaac Asimov to understand his broader point. From the moment we're born, the clock begins to tick, daring us to accomplish all that we need to before that last grain of sand drops through the hourglass. Whether, per Asimov's hypothetical, we know how much time we have left, the knowledge that we're engaged in a race we've been engineered to lose can become reason for despair or a clarion call to action. For anyone who's ever been driven by the creative impulse—by the all-encompassing need to take what's inside and put it out there—Asimov's words don't merely ring true; they carry the weight of gospel.

During the 1960s and '70s, Asimov's huge output as popular science writer, best-selling novelist, and futurism lecturer made him a particularly high-profile ambassador for geekdom. In today's splintered media world, that role may never again be so thoroughly captured by a single person.

"SNOZZBERRIES? WHO EVER HEARD OF A SNOZZBERRY?"

—VERUCA SALT, *CHARLIE AND THE CHOCOLATE FACTORY*

BRATDOM. The four kids adventuring alongside Charlie Bucket in Roald Dahl's masterpiece were part of it, and when spoiled-rotten-girl Veruca famously uttered this sneering inquiry, it epitomized an idea that recurs regularly in the sacred texts of geek wisdom: being a know-it-all isn't smart; it's a sign of closed-mindedness. What the brats in life fail to grasp is that the trails of history are blazed not by those who cling to what *is*, but by those who dare to seek out what *might be*. We could offer examples of such folks, the ones who proclaimed their righteousness most belligerently, but history's ultimate judgment can be found in the fact that their names have largely been forgotten—whereas the names of Copernicus, Galileo, and other such curious truth seekers will be enshrined for eternity. As Veruca Salt is hoisted by her self-possessed petard, she reminds us of the simple lesson that believing your own press is dangerous. Despite her loud mouthings to the contrary, there really *were* snozzberries in Wonka's world—just as there really did turn out to be planets and atoms and quarks in ours. We just have to be open to finding them.

There are four Veruca Salts: the one in Roald Dahl's book (1964), the one in the classic movie (1971), the one in the remade movie (2005), and the Chicago indie-rock band who borrowed her name in 1993 and are still making music today.

"TO ERR IS HUMAN; TO REALLY SCREW UP REQUIRES THE ROOT PASSWORD."

—COMPUTER GEEK TRUISM

POOR WIL WHEATON. He came back from a post adolescent slump as a seemingly over-the-hill child actor to have a triumphant second act as one of the most popular bloggers on the Internet. He spent years rebuilding his mojo at wilwheaton.net. And then, one day in September 2005, he decided to climb down into the code and fiddle with his database—and in an instant, his digital world was kaplooey. Borkded. *Over.* Fortunately for Wil, Google can be most forgiving, and although wilwheaton.typepad.com may not glide off the tongue as euphoniously as his original website did, it's easily found. However, unlike our virtual existences online, a human life has no reset button. In real life, things can be broken irreparably and irreplaceably—a treasured heirloom, a marriage, a nation. So before yielding to the impulse to poke at the soft underbelly of things, it's worth asking: do you know how not to break that? Are you *sure*?

The root is the all-access user account that can control all the files in a Unixlike computer operating system. Wil's database snafu involved a different system, MySQL. Lest you think we're fake geeks, we point out the technical difference while making the fundamentally sound analogy.

"WHY, HELLO, CLARICE."
—HANNIBAL LECTER, *THE SILENCE OF THE LAMBS*

"IF YOU ONLY KNEW THE POWER OF THE DARK SIDE."
—DARTH VADER, *THE EMPIRE STRIKES BACK*

"STEP INTO MY PARLOR, said the spider to the fly." What did Clarice Starling feel as she set down that dank prison hallway to her first encounter with Hannibal Lecter? Probably the same thing we felt as we accompanied her: terror, revulsion, and . . . curiosity. That's always the appeal of evil. It's the temptation of the forbidden, the allure of the illicit, and even though our rational side knows that no good can come from that path, there's another side that longs to push the boundaries to see what happens. The slippery slope is a cliché because it's real: one moral compromise can easily lead to another, and another. And whether we're talking about fictional characters like Lecter and Anakin Skywalker or real-life scenarios like the animal-torturing child who grows up to be an abusive parent, history is replete with the testimonials of those who've taken things one step too far. Yet still we persist in looking the devil in the eyes—perhaps to prove to ourselves that we can. That's why Agent Starling keeps going back even as Lecter pulls his knot of terrifying mind games ever tighter. And let's be honest: it's also why we keep watching. The sequel to *The Silence of the Lambs* wasn't called *Clarice*, after all.

In *The Silence of the Lambs*, the interrogation scenes were filmed in the bowels of Pittsburgh's Soldiers and Sailors Memorial building, just up the road from the geek mecca of Carnegie Mellon University.

"NO, I NEVER DID IT!"

—CLAIRE, *THE BREAKFAST CLUB*

CLAIRE THOUGHT SHE WAS HOT STUFF, didn't she? That is, until she was finally worn down and had to admit to being the inexperienced, insecure girl she'd tried to conceal. Whether we cheered at seeing Ms. Perfect taken down a peg or sympathized with the persona she felt forced to put on doesn't matter. What does matter is that Claire, along with the other misfits of *The Breakfast Club*, showed us that we weren't alone in seeing through the phony BS that was high school. Sure, we all had our cliques and circles and groups—and heaven forbid they should ever intersect with another—but hell, if the hot, rich, redheaded darling was in truth an insecure, awkward teen, too, where does that leave us losers who felt lucky to get to second base by sixteen? It leaves us realizing that those people in school we thought were so, so, so much cooler and hipper and more with it than we were . . . weren't. Because Claire? She never did it.

The Breakfast Club (1982) costarred Judd Nelson, whose geek credentials were further enhanced when he starred as Hot Rod in *Transformers: The Movie* (1986).

"NO MATTER WHERE YOU GO . . . THERE YOU ARE."

—BUCKAROO BANZAI,
THE ADVENTURES OF BUCKAROO BANZAI ACROSS THE 8TH DIMENSION

A S NOTED IN THE INTRODUCTION, statements uttered as jokes can be taken far more seriously than ever intended. Heroic polymath Buckaroo Banzai, while taking a break from his duties as a nuclear physicist-brain surgeon-action hero to play some piano-bar ballads in his alternate guise as a rock star, offered up this little gem to settle down an unruly crowd. Screenwriter Earl Mac Rauch employed it for humor, befuddling the audience both onscreen and off with what sounded like a semantically empty phrase, a sorta–Zen-shaped existential tautology that seems hilarious in its unhelpfulness. But it does mean something real—which is easier to grasp if, in the second clause, you remove the emphasis from the word *there* and put it on the word *you*, instead. The saying isn't intended to mean "Everyplace is a place" but, rather, "*You* can't run away from yourself." You are the single common factor in every situation—so perhaps the best way to improve your surroundings is to improve yourself.

Buckaroo Banzai (1984) may be the ultimate achievement in deadpan storytelling: even dedicated science-fiction fans often call it an awful mess on their first viewing, only to watch it again and realize that the filmmakers were engaged in subtle comedy all along.

"THERE ARE VOCAL QUALITIES PECULIAR TO MEN, AND VOCAL QUALITIES PECULIAR TO BEASTS; AND IT IS TERRIBLE TO HEAR THE ONE WHEN THE SOURCE SHOULD YIELD THE OTHER."

—H. P. LOVECRAFT, *THE CALL OF CTHULHU*

IS THERE ANYTHING that can strike fear into our hearts more effectively than seeing, experiencing, or even just hearing someone's humanity stripped from them? The very idea of uncontrollable fear chills us, because it underscores just how tenuous our grasp on our humanity truly is. We tell ourselves we are not beasts—we are human beings. Fear, though, is a primal thing. Civilized as we may be, fear has a way of worming under our skin and burrowing into the soft, fleshy parts of us we pretend aren't there. Your childhood poison may have been the dark, or heights, or spiders, or clowns, but the results were always the same. Loss of control. The feeling that even when you *knew* you had nothing to fear, your body and mind could paralyze you. In those moments you were not human, you were beast. And more than any darkness or clown or spider, that's what frightened you the most: the terror of losing yourself to something hidden within.

H. P. Lovecraft had lots of friends and interacted with them mostly through written correspondence; he also wrote horror stories featuring thinly disguised versions of his own childhood imaginary characters. In short: he was the original emo geek.

"THE DANGER MUST BE GROWING FOR THE ROWERS KEEP ON ROWING AND THEY'RE CERTAINLY NOT SHOWING ANY SIGNS THAT THEY ARE SLOWING!"

—WILLY WONKA, *WILLY WONKA AND THE CHOCOLATE FACTORY*

THE EXTERNAL FORCES that shake up our lives and plunge us headlong into trouble are often far less worrisome than the trouble we cause for ourselves. That's because we're often our own worst enemy, accelerating trouble or worsening a coming train wreck by making poor (and often selfish) decisions. It almost seems to defy common sense. With foreknowledge of growing danger, you'd think our instinct would be to be more cautious, more careful, more mindful of the things we do. Instead, humans do the opposite. We're rash. We're reckless. We're selfish. Even knowing that bad times are ahead offers little protection against this self-sabotage. Willy Wonka knew it, teasing the children in his chocolate factory about the mounting danger in front of them, taunting them with looming troubles ahead—and ultimately confirming his suspicion that most of these kids would be sunk not by the depths of his wondrous chocolate river, but by the foolishness of their own actions. The rowers can keep on rowing and the danger may be growing, but the biggest dangers we face are often our own poor choices.

Geek-war alert: we hereby declare that this scene in 1971's *Willy Wonka and the Chocolate Factory* proves that—our fondness for Johnny Depp aside—Gene Wilder will never be supplanted as the one true Wonka.

"BUT I WAS GOING INTO TOSCHE STATION TO PICK UP SOME POWER CONVERTERS!"

—LUKE SKYWALKER, *STAR WARS*

"WHY ME?"

—GARION, *PAWN OF PROPHECY*

OH, WHINY SUBURBAN TEENAGERS. Can you not just shut up and do what needs doing? If you could, you would be heroic romantic figures; just look at Westley from *The Princess Bride* (p. 72), who, like you, was just a poor boy from a rinky-dink farm right outside of town. But instead you spend half your time moping, and, we have to tell you, it's not particularly attractive. Hey, Luke, you know why you didn't get the girl? It's not because she's your sister. No, George decided to *make* her your sister because it was painfully obvious that the ladies were hot for Han Solo, who, for all his problems with dodging the collection agencies, at least didn't bitch about it. Likewise your medieval-fantasy counterpart Garion from David Eddings's *Belgariad*, whose sword was just as big and glowy, whose princess was just as opinionated, and who let grownups tell him what to do even while he complained every step of the way. Here's the deal, teenagers: if you have real problems in your life, then of course yes, call for help. But if you're just *bored*? If you just don't feel like doing your chores? Quit your yapping.

Unlike lots of 1980s epic fantasy that ripped off Tolkien, Eddings's *Belgariad* reads more like a fuller, richer *Star Wars* saga dressed up in Arthurian drag.

"YOU KEEP USING THAT WORD. I DO NOT THINK IT MEANS WHAT YOU THINK IT MEANS."

—INIGO MONTOYA, *THE PRINCESS BRIDE*

HERE'S WHY WE LOVE INIGO MONTOYA: there is not a cynical bone in his body. When the mercenary boss Fezzini kept screaming that it was "inconceivable!" his schemes could be defeated, the little loudmouth knew precisely what the word meant—he was simply such an irrepressibly arrogant ass that he was determined to insist the word was warranted when it really, really wasn't. Inigo could have pointed that out. But he didn't. He gave Fezzini the benefit of the doubt and suggested that perhaps, just possibly, the pompous Sicilian was confused about his dictionary definitions. Whether Inigo was being sincere or incredibly subtly sarcastic, he sounded sincere—thus graciously giving Fezzini a chance to step back from his idiocy and rethink things. That Fezzini didn't take that chance meant his fate was inevitable; that Inigo offered it meant he was willing to consider all things possible. Until proven otherwise, of course.

William Goldman, writer of *Butch Cassidy and the Sundance Kid*, wrote both the novel and the movie version of *The Princess Bride*; it may be the most perfectly cross-medium-rendered story in history and, not coincidentally, one of the most frequently quoted.

"CAN IT BE DONE, FATHER? CAN A MAN CHANGE THE STARS?"

—WILLIAM THATCHER, *A KNIGHT'S TALE*

THIS QUESTION, THE CENTRAL THESIS of the romantic jousting comedy *A Knight's Tale*, gives us an excellent example of (a) how easy it is to conflate the modern science of astronomy with the archaic practice of astrology and (b) how poetically satisfying it can be to do so as long as you're not taking it too seriously. When the motif is first introduced, a grizzled old squire tells the young peasant boy William that he can no sooner become a nobleman than he can change the stars— a clear reference to the astronomical fact that the stars, a fact of nature, will be as they are and do as they do, with no relation to the actions of humans muddling along on earth. The boy's father then tells him that if a man is brave and determined enough, he can accomplish anything he sets his mind to. William takes this advice to heart and dedicates his life to "changing his stars"; with that possessive pronoun added, the stars cease to be a metaphor for the implacable universe and become a reflection of the would-be knight's personal destiny. William, in all his lack of education, takes for granted the astrological model of the heavens as our controlling power—and then, at the same stroke, turns it upside down, insisting that he'll master his own fate and the heavens be damned. It's an elegant lesson in the power of myth and metaphor in shaping a narrative—whether that story is the one you're watching or the one you're living.

"WHAT'S THE POINT IN BEING GROWN UP IF YOU CAN'T BE CHILDISH SOMETIMES?"

—THE DOCTOR, *DOCTOR WHO*

"SECOND STAR TO THE RIGHT, AND STRAIGHT ON TILL MORNING."

—PETER PAN, *PETER PAN*

A T SOME UNDEFINED POINT in time between 2006 and 2010, *Doctor Who* became the new *Star Trek*. Which is to say, it ceased to be that goofy British sci-fi show with the laughable special effects that even most American nerds had never really watched, and instead it became the new geek pop-culture touchstone, general knowledge of which marks someone irrefutably as one of the tribe. Why did this happen? In part, it was because there was a void—J. J. Abrams notwithstanding, *Trek* ran out of steam years back—and, in part it was because the Internet-fueled ease of viewing a BBC show in real time, instead of months or years later on PBS, finally made the show widely accessible in the States. But there's something deeper at work, too: the Doctor is a hero for our times. Where latter-day *Trek* gave us an engineer's vision of the future, *Doctor Who* and its semianarchic, semiabsurdist mad-genius time traveler in a galaxy-hopping police telephone box reflect a present era so casually insane that it often feels like the best we can do to overcome our sticky dilemmas is to take a deep breath, think hard, giggle nervously, and try something crazy from the weird part of our brains while crossing our fingers and swearing love and good wishes to the world at large. The Doctor represents not only "the triumph of intellect and romance over brute force and cynicism," as Craig Ferguson so eloquently put it, but, more specifically, our unsullied, childlike vision of a universe where all things ought to be possible. He's a grown-up Peter Pan, always collecting new young friends and teaching them to fight the good fight on Earth rather than in Neverland. That's a pretty great feat for a 900-year-old alien.

"I'M CRUSHING YOUR HEAD!"

—MR. TYZIK, *THE KIDS IN THE HALL*

IT'S ALL ABOUT PERSPECTIVE. Can you crush some-one's head between your thumb and forefinger? Of course not . . . unless you stand ten feet away and hold your hand up to your own eye, in which case, yes, their head is *clearly* a mere grape to be squashed between your massive, unstoppable digits. It's an illusion, naturally, but illusion is a powerful tool. Geek tales often consciously use this kind of Escheresque frame-of-reference shift—for instance, when *Doctor Who*'s TARDIS can fit an end-lessly huge spaceship interior inside the door of a four-foot-by-four-foot-by-seven-foot box, because, you see, the inside dimen-sion is in a realm far distant from the outside dimension. Or when Obi-Wan Kenobi told Luke that his earlier assertion that "Darth Vader betrayed and murdered your father" wasn't a *lie* so much as a spiritual interpretation of the truth. Getting a different perspective on things is one of the best ways there is to kick your imagination or your problem-solving brain into high gear; that's why compa-nies hire outside consultants or take the staff out of the office on retreats to ponder the challenges that lie before them. And it's just as helpful in your daily life—so, today, why not walk a different route? Maybe you'll see something you've been missing. And that something probably won't crush your head—but, you know, it might just blow your mind.

"THIS MUST BE THURSDAY. I NEVER COULD GET THE HANG OF THURSDAYS."

—ARTHUR DENT, *THE HITCHHIKER'S GUIDE TO THE GALAXY*

I N ARTHUR'S CASE, Thursday began with the demolition of his house, continued with the demolition of the entire planet Earth, and eventually culminated in him getting tossed into deep space without a spacesuit. Most people's Thursdays can't compare . . . and yet it's not hard to relate to what Arthur was going through. Because every day of the week presents its own unique problems. Monday, obviously, is the beginning of the work week—*ugh*. Tuesday is almost worse, because it's practically as far away from Friday night as Monday is, but without the satisfaction of being able to complain about it being Monday. Wednesday is the day when you realize that the glorious things you intended to accomplish this week probably aren't all going to happen. Thursday we've discussed already. Friday might be the very worst, because you have a sense that people are having huge amounts of fun on Friday evening, and if you're not, something must be wrong with you. Saturday is wonderful, unless you have chores that need to be done—and you do. And Sunday? Sunday is the Wednesday of the weekend, except that on Wednesday at least half the week is over, and on Sunday it's all ahead of you. Let's face it: Arthur was doomed no matter what day the Vogons blew up the Earth.

II.
FORM FEET AND LEGS

(WISDOM ABOUT RELATIONSHIPS)

"YOU—YOU'VE GOT ME? WHO'S GOT YOU?"

—LOIS LANE, *SUPERMAN: THE MOTION PICTURE*

PEOPLE GREATER THAN ourselves do what they do with no wires and no safety net. They fly free, able to accomplish things that we not only can't do, but that we can't even *imagine* doing. But this doesn't just apply to those who perform astonishing feats of derring-do. Think of a parent—maybe your own, maybe a single mother, maybe a struggling couple. On a daily basis, they swoop up beneath their children, holding them aloft, saving them from hitting the ground too hard when they fall off one of those metaphorical skyscrapers whose edge they hadn't seen coming. Quietly, parents are all Supermen and Superwomen holding up their Lois Lanes and Jimmy Olsens—and the same truth applies to anyone whose efforts support another. Enter Lois's question: if all these people have got her covered, who's covering them? When it comes to the unsung heroes of the world, the answer all too often is, "Nobody." In the real world, they don't have a Superman of their own. That they persevere nonetheless makes them superheroes by any measure.

Superman: the Motion Picture (1978) marked the introduction into the Superman mystique of such concepts as the cold and sterile planet Krypton (in the comics it had been a colorful civilization) and businessman Lex Luthor (in the comics he was a scientist).

"FACE IT, TIGER, YOU JUST HIT THE JACKPOT!"

—MARY JANE WATSON, *THE AMAZING SPIDER-MAN*

ONE OF THE MOST dramatic entrances in comic-book history was more than the introduction of a vivacious, sexy redhead—though it certainly was that!—it was also a lesson in the nature of expectations. For months Peter Parker's elderly aunt had been nattering on about her friend's niece, Mary Jane Watson, but Peter just rolled his eyes and brushed off the old bird's ham-fisted attempt at matchmaking with nary a second thought. He never expected that Mary Jane would be so WOW. That's the thing about life: we find gems in the most unexpected places. Always down on his luck, confused and confounded by the opposite sex, and burdened with personal problems that never seemed to go away, a guy like Peter Parker doesn't expect much good to come his way. Do any of us? Experience teaches us young the danger of being eternal optimists. Yet there she was. The famous comic-book panel of Mary Jane standing in the doorway, a cat-who-ate-the-canary grin on her face while Peter reels, stunned at seeing such a knockout, has come to define having your pessimistic expectations shattered. The jolt of something so happily vibrant is a jackpot, indeed.

One of the bitterest comic-book flamewars of the decade was prompted when Marvel Comics decided to retroactively undo Peter and Mary Jane's two-decade-long marriage via a literal deal with the devil to save Aunt May's life.

"I ASK FOR SO LITTLE. JUST FEAR ME, LOVE ME, DO AS I SAY AND I WILL BE YOUR SLAVE."

—JARETH THE GOBLIN KING, *LABYRINTH*

"YOU HAVE NO POWER OVER ME."

—SARAH, *LABYRINTH*

GIRLHOOD IN GEEKDOM HAS NEVER BEEN EASY. Apart from the usual difficulties of growing up geeky—fitting in, finding oneself, learning that it's okay to be smart and that "eccentric" is in the eye of the beholder—geek girls who are so inclined also have to deal with geek guys. Who are, shall we say, works in progress at that age. Which may be why David Bowie's androgynous, seductive, and artful Goblin King won the hearts and fantasies of so many geek girls. He was a bad boy . . . and yet, a pretty good babysitter. He had a castle inspired by Escher and suggestively talented fingers. And, yeah, he was old enough to be Sarah's grandfather and kind of creepy to boot—but as teen girl fantasy objects go, it could've been

worse. Perhaps most important of all, Sarah found that he *had no power over her, other than what she gave him*. It's fascinating to consider just how few fantasy heroines have been able to assert themselves and remain single in the face of a romance. Bucking the trend of the typical Hollywood epic, *Labyrinth* showed a young woman learning to take responsibility for her actions, persevere in an unfair world, and own her sexual identity. She wasn't just a babe—she was the babe with the power.

David Bowie has been an alien (*The Man Who Fell to Earth*, 1976), a Goblin King (*Labyrinth*, 1986), and a human superscientist (*The Prestige*, 2006). His fans were lobbying hard for him to play Elrond in *The Lord of the Rings*, too.

"ELEMENTARY, MY DEAR WATSON!"

—SHERLOCK HOLMES

N O OTHER QUOTE so quickly puts poor Watson in the hot seat, does it? And it's really not fair. The general public perception of Watson as a bumbling oaf couldn't be further from the character who narrates Arthur Conan Doyle's stories, who's both a clever doctor in his own right and more socially perceptive than the genius with whom he keeps company. But sidekick syndrome can be a big damper on any circle of friends. All it takes is one socially unaware friend who's better-versed in something to put the group rudely in their place. That friend has likely explained to you the detailed virtues of, say, shiraz, or Jonathan Demme's film career, or how your iPod *really* works—snidely and at great length, thus killing forever any interest you might have had in it. It can be a lot to take, but Watsons of the world can take heart: popular culture is beginning to realize that, for all his genius, Sherlock Holmes still didn't know that the earth revolved around the sun, and that Watson saved his pal's bacon more than once. And if you recognize yourself more in Sherlock than in Watson, it might be time for a round of apologies to your social circle.

Testifying once again to the power of mass media, the well-known phrase quoted above is a formulation of the 1929 movie *The Return of Sherlock Holmes*, not of Arthur Conan Doyle's original stories.

"YES. YES, I DID IT. I KILLED YVETTE. I HATED HER, SO . . . *MUCH* . . . IT—IT—THE F—IT—FLAME—FLAMES. FLAMES, ON THE SIDE OF MY FACE."

—MRS. WHITE, *CLUE*

THIS IS HOW LIFE WORKS: we all want to be the butler, but really we're all Mrs. White. Betrayed by the people we trust, sabotaged by those we don't expect, patronized by houseguests, and always on the verge of boiling over—and, finally, feeling as though our feelings are palpable. Of course, few of us ever give in to our darker sides quite as murderously as Mrs. White did; that doesn't mean it's not tempting to tell people exactly what you think of them. That urge for brutal honesty can threaten to overcome all the hard-won social graces we acquire over the years. The good news is, once in a while, that scorched-earth approach can be just what we need to separate ourselves from a bad situation. We recommend, however, that you keep your revenge limited to a few scathing e-mails. These days, not a lot of people buy the "Why don't you come with me to this remote British manor where we can be alone?" approach.

There is hardly a line of dialogue in the entire movie *Clue* (1985) that has not become a cult-classic quote. Kudos to filmmaker Jonathan Lynn.

THE GOONIES isn't the greatest search-for-treasure adventure movie ever made (that's *Raiders of the Lost Ark*), nor is it the greatest group-of-friends-has-their-final-adventure-together movie (that's *Stand by Me*), but it might be the greatest we're-misfits-and-we-belong-together movie. It all comes down to Sloth. He's big, ugly, and maybe a little slow. But he's also loving, and in need of love, and someone who has seen far too much abuse at the hands of others. So when Sloth bellows his proud greeting and jumps into the fray with his newfound friends, it's not just an awesome movie moment, it's a celebration of acceptance for someone who has never before been accepted. Because when you're an outcast crew like the Goonies, you just can't pull the same dirty tricks of shunning and snubbing that other cliques have pulled on you—it would be like stabbing yourself in the heart.

The Electric Company (1971), which Sloth was quoting, may have been one of the most eclectic geek TV shows ever, featuring a PBS version of Spider-Man and launching the career of Morgan Freeman.

"THIS JOB WOULD BE GREAT IF IT WASN'T FOR THE F—ING CUSTOMERS."

—RANDAL GRAVES, *CLERKS*

A S NERDS AND GEEKS, we are often teased in childhood for being so damned smart. As a defense mechanism to help us cope with the accusation that we're not like other people, we come to embrace the idea that most everyone else is dumber than we are. And we grow up sneering at our peers who seem to have an easy time fitting into society, which we declare is because they're *mundane*—even as we secretly resent *them* for how comfortably they all seem to get along with one another. Here's the thing: none of it is true. Those non-nerds? Most of them feel like outsiders, too; they're all just faking it as best they can and trying not to let their insecurities show. So chill out, Randal. The customers in your store only seem so damn stupid because you've spent so long nurturing your own identity as a smartypants. Take a moment to remember the last four stupid things you did, and then be nice to the lady who doesn't understand what it says on the box.

Kevin Smith, writer/director of *Clerks*, may have been the first writer to formally canonize science fiction as the scripture of pop culture, referring to Star Wars as the "Holy Trilogy" in *Chasing Amy* (1997).

"WONDER TWIN POWERS, ACTIVATE!"

—ZAN AND JAYNA, *THE SUPERFRIENDS*

THE PRINCIPAL MESSAGE of the superpowered siblings in this classic cartoon was obvious: we're better when we work together. However, the underlying subtext of the Wonder Twins was more telling: sometimes, one of you is going to have the ability to turn into every awesome animal ever, and one of you is mostly going to turn into a pail of water and spill all over the place. It's a hard lesson. We all want to think that things even out in the end, and that if someone is more talented in one arena, we'll outdo them in another. Often, that's the case.

But sometimes it's not, and it's then that you have to do the work to realize that friendship—or mystical twin-ship, whatever—builds on the work you do together, rather than on one of you standing out. Besides, sometimes it's a bucket full of water that saves the day. And really the best part of being a Wonder Twin isn't even having the powers. It's sharing a secret with your closest friend.

The Superfriends was TV's original adaptation of DC Comics' *Justice League of America*. But unlike past radio/TV creations, like Jimmy Olsen and Kryptonite, that made their way to the comics page, the Wonder Twins have never become a major part of DC's print mythos.

"FEAR LEADS TO ANGER; ANGER LEADS TO HATE; HATE LEADS TO SUFFERING."

—YODA, *THE PHANTOM MENACE*

YODA was paraphrasing the first great African American geek, George Washington Carver, who said a century ago: "Fear of something is at the root of hate for others, and hate within will eventually destroy the hater." Carver, a scientist plying his trade in a time when the intellectual inferiority of black people was simply assumed, knew something about suffering. Born into slavery, kidnapped as an infant, threatened repeatedly with lynching throughout his life, and rejected from school after school due to his race, Carver eventually went on to become one of the best-known American researchers in the biological and agricultural sciences. Widely rumored to be gay, Carver spent his life confronting and overcoming the fears of others, earning an iconic place in geek history. Yoda might be the fictional guru we like to quote, but Carver is the real one whose life reverberates through our culture.

Look, we all know that *The Phantom Menace* (1999) is not a great movie. But the trailer *was* a great trailer, and this quote was in the trailer. Can't we just pretend that the trailer had a different movie attached to it?

"FORM FEET AND LEGS! FORM ARMS AND BODY! AND I'LL FORM THE HEAD!"

—KEITH, *VOLTRON*

THE WORD *organization*, at its root, means "to make people function like organs." When you're a member of an organization, you and your fellows all fit into a larger system like parts of a body, your individual efforts combining to serve a single specific purpose. *Voltron*, and similar Japanese sci-fi shows such as *Super Sentai* (aka *Power Rangers*), took this concept literally, depicting the adventures of five space-warrior squadron-mates. Each one drove a color-coded combat vehicle that could reconfigure itself into a robotic arm, leg, torso, or head, and all five could then combine into one giant, ass-kicking gestalt of a robot. It's a premise that makes sense coming from a nation famous for its cultural focus on collaboration rather than individualism. The United States, on the other hand, tends to mythologize solo accomplishment, in the arts as well as in business and politics. Heck, even our sports teams win fame mostly for their standout superstars. A lot of American kids don't even play sports—and for them Voltron was a powerfully concretized metaphor for the incredible power of teamwork.

Obscure geek trivia: acclaimed artificial-organ engineer James Antaki, PhD, is also the inventor of an electric harmonica—an entirely different kind of "artificial organ."

"SOMETIMES, I DOUBT YOUR COMMITMENT TO SPARKLE MOTION!"

—KITTY, *DONNIE DARKO*

IT SAYS SOMETHING about the power of geek that in a movie about a pessimistic teenage boy who time-travels through parallel universes beside a monstrous seven-foot rabbit, the film's most immortal line is about his little sister's dance troupe. The same geeks' dedication brought this film from the verge of direct-to-DVD obscurity to cult classic; they should be duly proud. Of course, part of this quote's perfection is its perfect storm of relevance to the postmodern era: dead-on suburban satire, overdramatic in-character sincerity, and the comic payoff by the troupe itself. However, the other aspect of Sparkle Motion's enduring popularity is its meme-friendly resilience out of context. Kitty's cry of anguish has been neatly appropriated by geeks to become facetious Internet shorthand for the accusation that someone isn't invested enough in an admittedly frivolous pursuit; it's a beautiful example of how postmodern geekdom can be self-aware enough not to take everything seriously.

Bonus: Sparkle Motion is also the gift that keeps on giving for anyone who wants to take shots at the *Twilight* franchise's glitter-heavy bloodsuckers.

"PINKY, ARE YOU PONDERING WHAT I'M PONDERING?"

—THE BRAIN, *PINKY AND THE BRAIN*

MOST GEEKS have non-geek friends. Inevitably, they sometimes don't know what the heck we're talking about, so most of us have learned how to break down our thought processes for their sakes—to flawlessly translate even the geekiest of concepts into introductory language. This is a variation on the "double consciousness" concept first described by W. E. B. Du Bois (who wrote science fiction as well as activist commentary) in reference to African Americans' need to move between two worlds. In many ways, it's a requirement of any minority population that wants to be accepted by the majority—or at least to be left in peace. But sometimes we get tired of simul-translating our own conversations. Sometimes we just want to relax and be ourselves, even around our non-geeky friends, and sometimes, justified or not, we feel as though *we're* the ones who always have to do the interpreting. That's why so many of us loved it when the Brain didn't bother, blurting out theories and plans so byzantine no one could possibly follow them—and we loved even more that Pinky didn't demand an explanation. It's nice to have a friend who'll meet you halfway.

The Brain was voiced by Canadian actor Maurice LaMarche, who's also *Futurama*'s Kif Kroker and *The Real Ghostbusters*' Egon Spengler. Fans are divided on the question of whether he or Vincent D'Onofrio does a better Orson Welles impression.

"MY NAME IS SAYID JARRAH, AND I AM A TORTURER."

—SAYID JARRAH, *LOST*, "ONE OF THE THEM"

I N A SHOW that survived and thrived for six labyrinthine seasons by asking viewers to question long-cemented notions of "us" and "them," no character was a better exemplar of this than Sayid Jarrah. The Iraqi. The Muslim. The self-proclaimed "torturer." Although a Manichean media culture of prefigured heroes and villains could easily have conditioned us to hate and fear such a figure, over the course of the show's run we also came to know Sayid the technician, Sayid the soldier, Sayid the lover, and even Sayid the poet. All added facets to the character, and all illuminated for us the fluid nature of identity. In the end, "us" and "them" are arbitrary labels, but it was through the specificities, the complexities of Sayid's character that he achieved a kind of universality, painting a portrait of an individual driven by his own demons trying to do right by himself and others—in other words, someone just like "us."

The editors would like to take this space to ask anyone who has not yet watched *Lost* to do so . . . but only the first couple seasons. Don't be a sadist like we were and watch to the bitter end. You'll regret it. Really.

"I'M SORRY, DAVE, I'M AFRAID I CAN'T DO THAT."

—HAL 9000, *2001: A SPACE ODYSSEY*

THE most famous computer malfunction in cinematic history saw HAL, the artificial intelligence running the fictional American spacecraft *Discovery*, go crazy and murder most of the astronauts on board before they reached Jupiter. The sequel revealed that HAL's psychotic break was caused by an irreconcilable conflict between contradictory instruc-  tions: "his" basic purpose of accurately analyzing information for the crew, and his top-secret government directive to conceal *Discovery*'s true mission from them. You have to feel sorry for HAL—he was experiencing the same ominous dread that infects any of us when someone puts us in the uncomfortable situation of having to lie on their behalf. The classmate who wants to use you as an alibi to cover her misbehaving ways; the spouse who invents a fictional emergency to get out of visiting the in-laws; the friend who doesn't want you to tell his wife he's leaving her, never mind that she's your friend, too. What do you do when your loyalty is at odds with your sense of what's right? HAL's story doesn't offer an answer, but it does illuminate what a good idea it is to avoid such situations in the first place.

In the book version of *2001*, *Discovery*'s mission is to reach Saturn by way of Jupiter; in the film, the ship is simply headed to Jupiter. Author Arthur C. Clarke yielded to the film's popularity for the sequel novel *2010* and just went with Jupiter.

"I STAYED UP ALL NIGHT PLAYING POKER WITH TAROT CARDS. I GOT A FULL HOUSE AND FOUR PEOPLE DIED."

—STEVEN WRIGHT

S TANDUP COMEDIANS don't just stand on a stage a few nights a week; they stand apart from humanity every day. Though we think of professional funnymen as a breed all their own, at heart they're pretty much like all the other people who become writers, whether novelists or news reporters. They are outside observers, watching and taking notes on all this fuss the rest of us engage in, all while preparing to turn around and show us something so deeply true about ourselves that we just have to react. Steven Wright is the ultimate exemplar of this kind of emotional detachment; his voice during performance as he mumbles his way through one pithy ten-second joke-concept at a time is distant, muted—almost robotic. But when he delivers this one, you can hear surprise register as he hits the punch line, as if with a simple rising inflection he wants to convey: *hey, this isn't all a theoretical exercise, after all; I really am connected to the rest of the world!* In an era when Internet socializing allows us to reduce our mental picture of our fellow human beings to nothing more than a name and a postage-stamp–size picture on a screen, it's a lesson well worth remembering.

Tarot cards formed the mythic centerpiece of comic auteur Alan Moore's 1999 science-fantasy series *Promethea*, about a superheroine conjured from the realm of pure narrative imagination.

"SUGAR. SPICE. AND EVERYTHING NICE. THESE WERE THE INGREDIENTS CHOSEN TO CREATE THE PERFECT LITTLE GIRLS. BUT PROFESSOR UTONIUM ACCIDENTALLY ADDED AN EXTRA INGREDIENT TO THE CONCOCTION . . . *CHEMICAL X.*"

—OPENING NARRATION, *THE POWERPUFF GIRLS*

GEEK WOMEN—*real* geek women, that is, not the booth babes or big-eyed anime schoolgirls who dominate the imaginations of heterosexual geek men—are built of strange stuff. Consider what it takes to resist the pervasive sexism of American society, which pressures all women to value themselves on appearance alone. Geek women, however, demand to be recognized for their brains. They want to be admired for their l33t skills in gaming, their clever code constructions, their solid engineering designs. In other words, they're not all that different from geek guys . . . which makes things awkward when they turn on a video game or open a comic book to find female characters with size 44F breasts and waists so tiny there can't possibly be functioning organs in there. That's why the Powerpuff Girls are such a viciously ironic thrill. The Girls don't look human; they don't have the same proportions as the other characters in the cartoon, or even fingers and toes. It's basically a juvenile twist on the way adult women are generally depicted for men's viewing pleasure—and yet, the Girls *kicked ass*. They whomped jerks and monsters. They looked out for one another. And for the few men in their lives who saw them as individuals and valued them for their personhood, they made the world a better place.

The Powerpuff Girls ran for six years (1998–2004)—longer than the age of the titular characters.

"UNTIL A MAN IS TWENTY-FIVE, HE STILL THINKS, EVERY SO OFTEN, THAT UNDER THE RIGHT CIRCUMSTANCES HE COULD BE THE BADDEST MOTHERF—ER IN THE WORLD."

—NEAL STEPHENSON, *SNOW CRASH*

THE MALE GEEK has largely made it a point of pride to distance himself from the stereotypical tough guys of the world. But the male geek is deluding himself. Fact is, we're not all that far removed from each other, geeks and jocks. Stephenson nails why: the notion that, if circumstances were right, we could be "The Man" is the impulse that fuels male fantasies, from Mickey Mantle to Batman, from Muhammad Ali to Casanova. Nerd or not, men dream of inspiring awe in those around them—and by "awe" we mean "adoration," and by "those around them" we mean "mostly women." What separates male peer groups is the form these dreams of prowess take. The athlete dreams of attainable feats of athleticism; the geek, lacking such physical agency, just goes ahead and fantasizes much bigger. Win the playoffs? *Pffffft.* We're here to save the universe! Even if that's just our own self-doubt pushing us to overcompensate in the realm of imagination, one thing is clear: there are times when, no matter how outlandish it seems, we're determined to believe that maybe, just maybe, we truly are capable of becoming the badass we dream of.

Stephenson's *Baroque Cycle* has become known as his magnum opus, but *Snow Crash* (1992) made his name as one of the icons of cyberpunk.

"I HAVE BEEN, AND ALWAYS SHALL BE, YOUR FRIEND."

—SPOCK, *STAR TREK II: THE WRATH OF KHAN*

S POCK'S DYING WORDS, uttered upon sacrificing his own life to save the lives of his friends Kirk and McCoy and all their crewmates, are a favorite quote used to express geek camaraderie. But here's a question that's rarely asked: what made these guys such great friends, anyway? It wasn't just their shared experiences on the *Enterprise*; after all, you probably have coworkers you wouldn't give your life for. No, what brought Star Trek's trinity together was that, though all three were men of great passion and great intellectual achievement, they channeled those impulses differently. Scientist Spock carried the flag for the rational approach to life; "just a country doctor" McCoy championed the empathic approach; and Kirk their captain mediated the two, navigating the right blend of emotion and critical thinking to make their way through any situation. We should all have friends who are similar enough to relate, but different enough to challenge us— who respect our thoughts and opinions even while they're telling us how wrong we are.

Daily Show correspondent and "PC Guy" John Hodgman quoted this line to President Obama while grilling him on his geek knowledge at the 2009 Radio and Television Correspondents Dinner.

"DO NOT MEDDLE IN THE AFFAIRS OF WIZARDS, FOR THEY ARE SUBTLE AND QUICK TO ANGER."

—GILDOR, *THE LORD OF THE RINGS*

O N THE SURFACE, this warning to the hobbits of *The Lord of the Rings* appears to be another manifestation of Tolkien's views on social and class structure (most notably on display in Sam's subservience to Frodo). Gildor implies that the wise and great cannot be understood by the merely ordinary, who would do best not to interfere with their betters. Yet look closer: by the end of the story, Gildor and the elves have departed Middle Earth, and the very affairs the hobbits were warned not to meddle in would have gone badly were it not *for* their meddling. The warning, then, is not to avoid crossing paths with your betters—in fact, it's not about one's "betters" at all. Gildor may have meant it that way, but Tolkien clearly didn't. Rather, the point is that to get involved with those who carry the weight of responsibility on their shoulders is to take on a measure of that responsibility ourselves. Meddle in the affairs of wizards at your own peril, lest you find yourself carrying a similar burden.

This saying has spawned a favorite geek parody: "Do not meddle in the affairs of dragons, for you are crunchy and taste good with ketchup."

"NO, MR. BOND.
I EXPECT YOU TO DIE!"

—AURIC GOLDFINGER, *GOLDFINGER*

THERE'S JUST NO TALKING TO SOME PEOPLE. Oh, you can try. You can form your arguments, bring your evidence, and go in with as open a mind as possible. But at some point you have to realize the other person isn't interested in a meeting of the minds. For James Bond, that realization probably hit when he was strapped to a solid gold table by the dastardly Goldfinger with a laser beam inexorably advancing toward his unmentionables. We may never be in a similarly precarious position against a similarly implacable foe, but at some point in our lives we'll likely square off against a rival who doesn't believe in fair play, can't be appealed to or reasoned with, and doesn't just want to win but wants you to lose. While Agent 007 finessed some very quick thinking to stay the hand of his erstwhile executioner, sometimes the quickest thinking of all is to simply recognize the Goldfingers in our lives before we end up staring at that laser.

The laser in *Goldfinger* (1964) was a clever atomic-age updating of the tension-filled threat found in Edgar Allan Poe's *Pit and the Pendulum* (1842).

"AS YOU WISH."

—WESTLEY, *THE PRINCESS BRIDE*

"IT WAS BEAUTY KILLED THE BEAST."

—CARL DENHAM, *KING KONG*

WHY DO WOMEN love *The Princess Bride* so much? Here's a thought: because its hero, Westley, is able to simultaneously fill the roles of dashing romantic adventurer and seriously devoted (maybe even borderline henpecked) fiancé. Buttercup first knows him as her subservient farmhand, and his response to her every request is, "As you wish." Every woman loves to have minions, of course, so having such an eager and handsome one tickles Buttercup's fancy no end. But Westley knows he's got to go make an independent person of himself before they marry, else he'll never have his love's true respect. So off he goes and doesn't come back until he's a world-renowned man of action. Buttercup can't believe that this self-possessed pillar of macho resolve is her farm boy—until she realizes that he will *still* do anything she wishes. To have the power of another entire human being at your disposal: that's an overwhelming gift for one person to give to another, and if trust and respect are to flourish, it demands utter reciprocation. Otherwise, you end up with a power imbalance that can't be sustained—just look at Ann Darrow and poor King Kong. But Buttercup and Westley *had* that kind of mutually trusting relationship, and that's ultimately what made it, famously, "true love."

III.
WE ARE
ALL INDIVIDUALS

(WISDOM ABOUT HUMANKIND)

"KNEEL BEFORE ZOD!"

—GENERAL ZOD, *SUPERMAN*

"CRIMINALS ARE A SUPERSTITIOUS, COWARDLY LOT."

—BATMAN, *DETECTIVE COMICS*

ET'S FACE IT: the thing about villains is that we all hear the call. We all, eventually, reach that point where we'd like to cut loose and tell the world what to go do with itself. The villains are the ones who get to do all the cool stuff: dream up ingenious plans, show off superweapons, and command minions to fight and die on their behalf. More to the point, good villains are the ones determined to be the protagonists in a story of their own devising. Their actions motivate the hero, their intelligence drives the plot, their declarations make the world dance to their tune. Or so they think. But there's a catch: what looks like strength really isn't. Villains are people too weak to master their own interactions with the world, so they're determined to hand off their problems to everyone else. In fact, it doesn't take bravery to steal from another; it doesn't take balls to mess with someone else's life. Doing these things is easy. Those who succumb to the lure, who can't commit to accomplishing the truly difficult—learning to weave their own thread into life's pattern rather than tearing a hole through the bits they don't like—take the coward's way. And for this, they live a life of unease. They see enemies in every shadow, because human beings are predisposed to see ourselves in others. The casual racist assumes others are equally small-minded. The white-collar criminal thinks everyone else is gaming the system, too. And the common street criminal, low man on the totem pole of wickedness? He assumes everyone else is out to get him, just as he is out to get others. If you've ever done something you knew was wrong, no matter how small, you've taken a taste of how the villain lives every day. Yet any person, no matter their status or place in society, need only assert responsibility for their own fate to rise above the gutter. Bravery is in living well regardless of your circumstances.

Batman's scorn for criminals was articulated in his very first story: *Detective Comics* #27 (1939).

"IT'S PEOPLE. SOYLENT GREEN IS MADE OUT OF PEOPLE."

—DETECTIVE THORN, *SOYLENT GREEN*

W HEN CHARLTON HESTON'S THORN makes this dire proclamation at the close of 1973's *Soylent Green*, the ramifications of what he's uncovered become clear: in a world stricken with ever-scarcer resources and an ever-growing population, the bodies of the recently dead are being processed into the wafers that serve as the food supply for the citizenry—a necessary evil for the world to continue on its path without a care for the consequences of our consumption. It's the ultimate expression of dystopic paranoia, and the truly frightening part is that it's not too far removed from the age we're living in right now. That doesn't mean you need to give that potato chip you're about to eat a closer look in case it's actually the remains of your buddy. But perhaps you should consider how, whether children in sweatshops or migrants working under substandard conditions, the lifestyle of comfort that we likely take for granted has been built on a foundation of systemic dehumanization. It's made out of people.

The climactic revelation of *Soylent Green* might be considered a spoiler, but it was seared indelibly into the public consciousness by a hilarious parody from Phil Hartman on *Saturday Night Live* in the late 1980s.

"IDEAS ARE BULLETPROOF."

—V, *V FOR VENDETTA*

I F THERE'S ONE THING Alan Moore is good at, it's anarchist characters who get to the heart of the matter. (And then perish.) In *V for Vendetta* both the principled cause and the willingness to die for it are necessary to effect change in a totalitarian regime. Though one hopes that our own society hasn't quite reached that point, there's certainly no shortage of legitimate threats today to freedom of ideas. The Internet, the closest thing we have to an utterly free exchange of information, is under so much threat of censorship—from both governments and tele-communications companies—that hacking around institutional firewalls has become a cottage industry. However, it's individual privacy that's coming under real fire. Bloggers are harassed for breaking controversial stories, and Facebook, one of the most ubiquitous social networks on the planet, has become little more than that guy who sits in the bushes outside your house. Ideas are bulletproof, yes, but they're only as strong as the protections granted to those exercising them.

Cory Doctorow, one of our generation's übergeeks, achieved that status by simultaneously undertaking one career as a science-fiction novelist and another as an Internet-rights activist with the Electronic Frontier Foundation.

"THERE ARE 10 KINDS OF PEOPLE IN THE WORLD: THOSE WHO UNDERSTAND BINARY, AND THOSE WHO DON'T."

—THINKGEEK T-SHIRT

I F YOU'D NEVER heard of the digits 2 through 9, you could still count from 0 to 10, you'd just have to write the numbers differently: 0, 1, 10, 11, 100, 101, 110, 111, 1000, 1001, 1010. That's how a computer does it, in the harsh, unflinching 1-0/on-off/yes-no of binary notation, and that's why computer-science nerds find this T-shirt hilarious—the "10" actually means "two." Rarely has an epigraph engaged in such vigorous dialogue with its own subtext. On the one hand, it's incredibly self-reinforcing: *there are only two kinds of people in the world—us, who perceive the world correctly in strict, black-and-white, binary opposition, and them, who don't.* You can practically hear the dogma giving itself a high five. But the spirit lurking a bit deeper beneath the sentiment sings a different tune: *there are alternate ways to see the world that reveal hidden possibilities.* Surely, if there can be one alternative to common wisdom on something as fundamental to life as numbers, it's not much of a leap to realize there's probably another, and another, and another. Heck, that holds true even in computer science itself; just ask the thousands—excuse me, the 3E8s—of people who laugh at binary while figuring in hexadecimal.

ThinkGeek.com sells this T-shirt. May all the gods bless ThinkGeek. Who else brings us a plush killer rabbit from *Monty Python*, canned unicorn meat, and a TARDIS USB hub, all at the same online store?

"MR. AND MRS. DURSLEY, OF NUMBER FOUR PRIVET DRIVE, WERE PROUD TO SAY THAT THEY WERE PERFECTLY NORMAL, THANK YOU VERY MUCH."

—J. K. ROWLING, *HARRY POTTER AND THE PHILOSOPHER'S STONE*

AHHH . . . GOOD OLD "NORMAL." It's an idea that clings to us with bewildering tenacity. The implication is that there's a baseline human standard of everythingness that represents how we "should" live—yet half a second of considering what life on earth truly looks like shows that, of course, that's not true. Still, note that Mr. and Mrs. Dursley were pointedly proud to be normal, proud not to be noticed, proud not to be special. Oh, my! Geeks understand that spending your time trying to "act normal" is a special kind of hell. Not because we want to be different just for the sake of being different—that's as bad as militant normalcy, if not worse—but because, in the end, happiness means accepting who you are, even if it turns out that who you are involves standing out like a tattooed, costumed, dice-rolling, blue-haired sore thumb. And because, well, normal is a fantasy far more ridiculous than a secret school of wizards. Nobody's normal—and those who insist they are *are broken people.*

Harry Potter and the Philosopher's Stone was published in 1997. The seven-novel series that ensued soon became the publishing phenomenon of the century, encouraging millions of children worldwide not to worry so much about being "normal."

"THE CAKE IS A LIE."

—PORTAL

GLaDOS, THE ARTIFICIAL INTELLIGENCE who serves as the primary antagonist in Valve's critically acclaimed video game, possesses a rare and unexpected trait for a computer. She lies. When she tells you, "There will be cake," what she really means is there will be death. But hey, doesn't cake sound a lot better? This hypothetical serving of non-existent dessert is *Portal's* understated way of symbolizing the lies told to us in any oppressive and deceitful system. The cake is the promise of safety from enemies that's used to excuse intrusive government policies. It is the "I love you; I promise it won't happen again" of the abusive spouse. It is the advertisement for terrific new stuff to buy that will surely make tomorrow happier than today. We've all been offered the cake. Some of us, the hundredth or thousandth times we've reached for the cake, have noticed what's actually being served on our plates and have tried to tell people what we've seen. The trouble is getting them to listen. Because, well, who doesn't like cake?

Portal (2007) is the first true science-fiction classic written in the medium of video games. If you've played it, you know this. If you haven't, go play it.

"THE SPICE MUST FLOW."

—DUNE

ECONOMIC SYSTEMS are bigger than people. That's why distribution of the precious mind-expanding spice, mélange, that is the lifeblood of galactic society in Frank Herbert's *Dune* must continue unimpeded. That's why, when Paul Atreides—the young nobleman who finds himself hailed as a prophesied savior—asserts his messianic will over the hitherto-powerless throngs of poor wretches living amid the spice mines of Arrakis, he causes commerce to grind to a standstill across a thousand planets, bringing the entire universe to heel. Just as the spice is Herbert's thinly veiled stand-in for oil, gold, or any commodity that greases the wheels of earthly progress, its necessity highlights the inherent danger of linking *any* one such commodity with the maintenance of a particular status quo—whether cheap gas for our cars or cheap clothes at Wal-Mart. "He who controls the spice controls the universe," says the evil Baron Harkonnen elsewhere in Herbert's epic, and it's a lesson that Paul takes to heart, bringing an entire monolithic structure of ingrained corruption down on the heads of those whose only real job was maintaining it. Economic systems are bigger than people . . . except when they're not.

The *Dune* saga becomes extremely amusing if you imagine that the spice was, in fact, coffee.

"FACTS DO NOT CEASE TO EXIST BECAUSE THEY ARE IGNORED."

—ALDOUS HUXLEY

HUMAN BEINGS are very good at ignoring reality. We've had renaissances and ages of reason, but even at our most rational we are a superstitious, irrational species. We are set in our ways. We too often celebrate outmoded ideals and cling to ways of doing things that have long since been revealed as pointless or even detrimental. Even when there's overwhelming evidence that our sincere intentions lead to more harm than good—for a perfect example, just look back at Prohibition in America—we do our best to pretend otherwise and repeat those same mistakes. Maybe it's a collective inability to admit when we're wrong, and we're all just exhibiting the stubborn pride of the know-it-all writ large. Maybe despite what we tell ourselves, we remain an emotional species rather than a rational species. One thing is clear, though: facts are our friends. The longer we as a society insist on ignoring them when they get too uncomfortable, the more we erode our potential to be truly great.

Aldous Huxley's 1932 novel *Brave New World* was an early science-fiction classic that endures as high school recommended reading. But his most fundamental geek truism, quoted here, is from his essay collection *Proper Studies* (1927).

"THE WORLD IS ONLY BROKEN INTO TWO TRIBES: THE PEOPLE WHO ARE ASSHOLES AND THE PEOPLE WHO ARE NOT."

—SHERMAN ALEXIE, *THE ABSOLUTELY TRUE DIARY OF A PART-TIME INDIAN*

SOMEHOW, GEEKS ARE ASSHOLE MAGNETS. There's something about being sincerely attached to a nonmainstream pursuit that traditionally brings the jerks out of the woodwork sniffing for scapegoats. Often these same assholes are avid fans of something themselves and just can't make the connection that one man's fantasy sports team is another man's online RPG. Luckily, the Internet's ability to connect geeks has given us a community that helps combat our tendency toward solitude. That's not to say that geeks can't be assholes to one another, too. Racism, for instance. Consider the assholishness on display with many publishers' continued practice of taking books starring black characters and giving them covers that depict those characters as white, because "it'll sell better that way." Sure, and buses were better organized when African Americans had to sit in the back. Here's hoping we speed up the process of dealing with such questions, because it behooves all of us to work toward a better understanding of one another. We have enough trouble with outside assholes to be dealing with ones of our own.

The "whitewashed" cover-art issue blew up in 2009, when author Justine Larbalestier found that the African American tomboy protagonist of her novel *Liar* had been pictured as a white girl on the cover of the U.S. edition.

"THERE ARE WEAPONS THAT ARE SIMPLY THOUGHTS. FOR THE RECORD, PREJUDICES CAN KILL AND SUSPICION CAN DESTROY."

—ROD SERLING, *THE TWILIGHT ZONE*,
"THE MONSTERS ARE DUE ON MAPLE STREET"

THIS CLASSIC *TWILIGHT ZONE* EPISODE hinges on an alien invasion that employs human beings' own fear and distrust of one another—easy to arouse, even easier to enflame—to turn an otherwise ordinary neighborhood against itself and do the invaders' job for them. As he did so often from his *Twilight Zone* pulpit, Serling uses the epigraph above to express frustration with an unfortunate reality of the human condition. The essential truth at the heart of Serling's dark fable is equally applicable regardless of which "other" we choose to point our finger at; it has manifested at least enough times to allow Japanese Americans to be herded into camps for fear that they were the "enemy" and for countless law-abiding citizens to lose their livelihoods after being labeled Communists during the Red Scare.

The wisdom of Serling's sentiment makes it easy to see why "Maple Street" was crowned the all-time best episode of the series by *Time* magazine. Like all great science fiction, it succeeds by pointedly asking its audience: "What would *you* do?"

Some of the greatest science-fiction writers of the century contributed stories to *The Twilight Zone*: Ray Bradbury, Richard Matheson, Jerome Bixby. This one was written by series creator Serling himself.

"LIFE'S A BITCH. NOW SO AM I."

—CATWOMAN, *BATMAN RETURNS*

RARELY HAS THERE BEEN so loaded a feminist statement in the middle of the boy's club comic-movie genre. When Selina Kyle delivers it, she's just thwarted her boss's attempt to murder her, trashed all the trappings of her traditionally feminine home, and violently constructed a threatening new identity. And yet: that identity involves a skintight leather catsuit and a full face of makeup, which doesn't scream "empowered, outspoken feminist" so much as it does "dominatrix wet dream of a million teenagers." What's more, Catwoman is hardly a bitch; she strikes out against her enemies, sure, but that's no bitchier than any stunt the Penguin pulls. This two-faced social construct—of angry woman as vengeful bitch, and of angry woman as secretly lusty sex object—is a common and problematic one. In the film, though, director Tim Burton gives a nod to the cinematic tradition of cheesecake femmes fatales while taking care to show us the tormented individual behind the mask. We can only hope that general perceptions will shift similarly, so when we look at a woman—angry or not, sexy or not—we see a person rather than a stereotype.

Catwoman has been played by a different actor every year she's been adapted into film and television. Michelle Pfeifer was as different from Eartha Kitt as Halle Berry was from Julie Newmar. Still, the character endures.

"THANK YOU, MARIO! BUT OUR PRINCESS IS IN ANOTHER CASTLE!"

—SUPER MARIO BROS.

IF PINT-SIZE PLUMBER Mario is anything, he's persistent. Time and again he trudges through strange lands peopled with creatures out to get him, and time and again he appears to have accomplished his goal only to have the rug pulled out from under him. Mario might as well be a blue-collar guy trying to get through the workweek. For him the end of the week isn't the end, it's just a brief pause before setting off for the next castle, chasing a princess he'll never rescue because the game is designed to keep her perpetually out of reach. Yet Mario doesn't seem to mind. He doesn't even appear to notice. Neither do the Marios of the real world. They chase their princesses, navigating pipes and pitfalls and creatures only to find she's always in the next castle. The cycle is unbreakable. And so we've got to ask, is Mario depressingly oblivious to his circumstances, or is he the admirable embodiment of working-class perseverance? And is there even a difference?

Mario was first introduced as the hero of *Donkey Kong* in 1981, at which time he was called "Jumpman." Because, you know, he jumped. He only got his name the following year in *Donkey Kong Junior*, the only game in which he's been depicted as the villain.

"LISTEN TO THEM. CHILDREN OF THE NIGHT. WHAT MUSIC THEY MAKE."

—*DRACULA* (1931)

DRACULA'S WISTFUL INTERJECTION has long been the rallying cry of goths worldwide; there's something about the reverential way Dracula mentioned the wolves outside his door that speaks to the heart of every geek who's ever been well acquainted with the night. Among geeks, goths are often a breed unto themselves, situated between horror fans and theater nerds. Goths are aesthetically oriented and have a seemingly endless appetite for dark-spun fairy tales and other subtle horrors. They also have the honor of being some of the most misunderstood of all geek-kind by those who don't seem to grasp the difference between a role-playing goth and an actual vampire. (It takes all kinds, we guess.) However, most goths are able to shake it off and revel in one of geekdom's earnest and most active communities, where they can mingle with others who sincerely share their passions. Bonus: the goth music scene is pretty killer, so even the casual-geek passerby can find out just what music they *do* make.

A lot of kids in today's steampunk scene used to identify with the goth aesthetic—and are pleasantly surprised to discover that normal adults seem intrigued, rather than alarmed, by this new thing. Well, *yeah*. People think of goths as weirdoes who take vampires too seriously, and therefore they can't help being worried on some level that a crazy goth might, you know, want to make them bleed. Whereas steampunks are—what? Weirdoes who take pocket watches too seriously? What are they gonna do, vehemently tell you what time it is?

"THE TRUTH IS OUT THERE."

—FOX MULDER, *THE X-FILES*

PROFESSIONAL INVESTIGATORS: detectives, reporters, intelligence agents. They're incredibly important to us, both in reality and in our belief structures, because we know we've gotta be able to rely on *someone* to uncover the nasty little secrets the world is keeping from us. Specific investigative types have come in and out of vogue over the years; for example, it's not au courant to trust reporters these days, because large numbers of shitty ones on television have dragged down the standard by which we measure them all. But there will always be hidden truths, and there will always be people who are determined to shine a light on them. The trick is figuring out: which of these seekers after revelation are really interested in helping you understand what matters *to you*? Because we've all got our agendas, and there's no definitive guide to them. That fact—not men-in-black conspiracies—is what makes the truth so darn hard to sort out.

Mulder was great, but our favorite TV journalist remains Jack McGee from *The Incredible Hulk*. In the beginning, he was just after a scoop that would make a great story; by the end of his pursuit, he was deeply invested in uncovering the truth, no matter *how* far out there.

"I'M NOT ANTI-SOCIAL,
I'M JUST NOT USER-FRIENDLY."

—T-SHIRT

L OOK, SOME PEOPLE JUST SUCK. Most geeks grow up enough on the fringes to be able to identify a problem crowd when they see one. Those same geeks have gotten pretty good at entertaining themselves. The combination can often result in a group of people with common life experiences enjoying themselves together—and a geek sitting nearby, frowning at their dance moves and tweeting furiously. Dear non-geeks: if you see any geeks wearing this shirt in public, they have come from a long day at the IT mines trying to explain to people how to double-click on something. Leave them be. And to be fair: dear geeks, we understand where you're coming from, but every once in a while, if you look closely, there will be someone in the crowd with whom you have something awesome in common. (Hint: +1 for anyone not dancing the Macarena.) Don't be any more alienated than you really need to be.

Only in the tech world can you call someone a "user" and not mean it as a put-down.

"I LOVED IT. IT WAS MUCH BETTER THAN *CATS*. I'M GOING TO SEE IT AGAIN AND AGAIN."

—HYPNOTIZED THEATERGOERS, *SATURDAY NIGHT LIVE*

FOR THOSE OF US whose interests lie outside the mainstream—and if you're reading this book, yours almost certainly do—most of the people who consume a steady diet of American mass-media culture might as well be hypnotized, droning on and on about how much they like the latest bit of predictable blandness that passes for entertainment in the twenty-first century. Even as we yearn for something better, something smarter, something that engages muscles in our brains and souls we haven't flexed before, we see our neighbors doing little more than repeating what they've heard others saying. *The Truly Real Superstar Babysitters of Orange County*? They loved it. It was much better than whatever was cool last month. They're going to see it again and again. And they really will, because mass culture is built to frown upon anything that isn't conformity. Meanwhile, one thing that has always separated the geek from the pack is that the geek scoffs at conformity. Rest assured, we didn't love it. We're not going to see it again and again. And we like it that way.

Though the quote endures, not many people remember that the "it" referred to was a performance by the hypnotist known as "The Amazing Alexander," portrayed by Jon Lovitz (1986). We think that counts as irony.

"I CAN HAS CHEEZBURGER?"

—INTERNET MEME

TAKE TWO NEWS STORIES. One is a horrible crime, maybe a double murder. Throw in some arson for good measure. The other involves a YouTube video of an adorable kitten being slapped by a thoughtless teenager. Two dead people and a burned-down house later, there will be ten, twenty, a hundred times more outrage about the slapped kitten. The fact is, we recognize ourselves for the really smart yet often cruel apes we are—and are drawn to what we see as innocence in our cats and dogs. One might call that self-loathing, but it's more than that. It's a manifestation of our sense of justice. Humans are victims? Sad, but then, people suck. Kittens are victims? Utterly outrageous! Grab the pitchforks! So when a cheeseburger-loving cat spawned an Internet explosion of grammar-impaired cat pictures, geek culture was doing more than having a laugh. It was putting its protective arms around the very embodiment of the innocence we as a species lack.

While icanhascheezburger.com has become a time-tested favorite, let's not forget that it all started in 2007 at somethingawful.com.

"*LIKE* AND *EQUAL* ARE NOT THE SAME THING AT ALL."

—MEG MURRY, *A WRINKLE IN TIME*

O N THE DISTANT PLANET CAMAZOTZ, human-like aliens are ruled by an authoritarian dictator in the form of a giant, pulsating brain that mentally directs all their actions. Visiting Earth girl Meg Murry discovers this horrific state of affairs when she sees all the kids who live on a Camazotzian suburban block step out of their homes simultaneously and start bouncing their balls in unison—a form of "play" that looks more like the children are mere flesh-colored pistons pumping away in a big machine. In this one freaky image, Madeleine L'Engle made crystal clear the difference between fascism and progressive democracy—a difference that the argumentative rhetoric of today's political pundits, sadly, has sometimes sought to obfuscate. The "all men are created equal" that is the basis of American civil rights doesn't mean we think our lives should all follow the same paths. What it means is that no one else can claim a right to take away our shoes and hobble us along the way.

A Swiftly Tilting Planet, the second sequel to *A Wrinkle in Time,* prefigured the basic premise of the sci-fi television classic *Quantum Leap*—the hero entering the body of a person in the past to set right a glitch in destiny—by a full decade.

"A CONCLUSION IS THE PLACE WHERE YOU GOT TIRED OF THINKING."

—STEVEN WRIGHT

BEING A GEEK can be mentally exhausting; we totally get it. However, the collective short attention span we've inherited from the Internet age means that it's all too easy to answer a pressing question by glancing at Wikipedia and calling it a day. Occasionally that's all you need; it doesn't take too many sources to corroborate the orbital period of Venus, for example. On the other hand, it seems vaguely disheartening that, with access to more information than ever before, so many Internet fights boil down to two people with violently opposing viewpoints attacking each other based on incorrect and incomplete data sets. It's our responsibility as geeks to make sure we never stop learning, that we take little for granted, and that we look at every statement not as a conclusion, but as an invitation to more research.

For all his geek cred, standup comedian Steven Wright has only one clear-cut geek-themed performance to his credit: the 2005 comic-book movie *Son of the Mask*.

"WE'RE ALL MAD HERE."

—ALICE'S ADVENTURES IN WONDERLAND

FEW LITERARY HEROES have the universal, all-ages appeal of Lewis Carroll's rabbit-hole-investigating young miss. In her day, she's been held up as a model of whimsical childhood, as a surrealist pioneer, as an extended metaphor for the society of her contemporaries. (There really is something about a dodo race that's so very open to interpretation.) However, throughout the myriad adaptations of this iconic tale, its core has remained intact: a world that makes no sense, and a girl who's stuck in it with no way out. It's a telling arc, quite different from many of the other coming-of-age stories that pit their young protagonist against an evil that can be defeated. Alice is more world-

weary than that, and it's that perspective—the misunderstood, often-frustrated outsider—that makes her such a hero in the lit-geek circle. Because let's face it: sometimes the only way to face the world is to go a little mad.

Alice's Adventures in Wonderland (note the proper title) was published in 1865; the sequel, *Through the Looking-Glass, and What Alice Found There*, in 1871.

"THERE'S JUST SOMETHING ABOUT AN ANATOMICALLY CORRECT RUBBER SUIT THAT PUTS FIRE IN A GIRL'S LIPS."

—POISON IVY, *BATMAN AND ROBIN*

THERE ARE TWO WAYS to look at Batman. For the past decade or so, pop culture has approached him as the down-and-dirty antihero whose Gotham City is a gritty chaos. This interpretation was a pretty direct backlash against the 1997 movie *Batman and Robin*, which had more color than a box of Crayola and all the dramatic tension of a blooper reel. However, Batman's always been as much high camp as high noir, even when the line between the self-referential and the markedly unaware is thin. Believe it or not, this offers a valuable lesson: multiple readings of a text can be equally valid—a fact that can be easy to forget in an era when Internet comment sections often read like the transcript of the weekly debate of the Extremists' Society.* Some interpretations might be less successful, which this movie outing certainly was, but just disliking an interpretation doesn't invalidate it. Worth remembering, the next time you encounter someone who's wrong on the Internet. (There's also a second lesson to be found in this quote: don't wear an anatomically correct rubber suit unless you want to put fire in a girl's lips. More specific, but equally handy.)

---

*This is a joke. There is no such thing as the Extremists' Society. And if you disagree, you are a Nazi who should die in a fire.

"THERE'S NO CRYING IN BASEBALL!"

—JIMMY DOUGAN, *A LEAGUE OF THEIR OWN*

SOME GENERALIZATIONS are just more immortal than others. When reluctant Girls' League coach Jimmy Dougan berates weeping right-fielder Evelyn with this gem, it's both hilarious and patently untrue—I mean, sports were basically invented so men can fight one another and then cry, right? In context, the tirade says more about Dougan's still-lingering misogyny than anything else. However, it's been neatly co-opted by geeks, and as such has become a go-to response for anyone that's taking something too much to heart. It's equally untrue every time (if something's worth caring about, someone has cried over it), but there's a *je ne sais quoi* about the vast and epic sweep of the generalization involved that's reclaimed this phrase to be almost encouraging—the sort of suck-it-up advice one gives to a fellow soldier in the trenches. So, geeks, keep on caring enough to cry, even when people tell you there's no crying in . . . well, anything.

Things in which there definitely is crying include comic books, *Star Trek*, *Buffy the Vampire Slayer*, and, of course, *I Love Lucy*.

"I WILL NOT BE PUSHED, FILED, STAMPED, INDEXED, BRIEFED, DEBRIEFED, OR NUMBERED. MY LIFE IS MY OWN."

—NUMBER SIX, *THE PRISONER*

WHEN PATRICK MCGOOHAN'S Number Six angrily defies his captors with this litany in the seminal British secret-agent series' opening installment, he crystallizes everything we need to know about the battle of ideas, ideology, and identity that spans the show's all-too brief run. The premise, featuring the dogged, dogmatic Six bedeviled at every turn in his attempts to escape from mysterious captors and reclaim his identity, hinges on the idea that we're all boxed in by a system—whatever that system is—that controls us at every step, and any notions of breaking free from that box are themselves just one more level of control. This makes for one big puzzle of positively Kafka-esque proportions. Although *The Prisoner* goes to great lengths to hold any definitive answers at arm's length, the mere fact that McGoohan's character clings so desperately to his individualism, yet is never more than a number to us, is ample testament to the ultimate futility of his struggle.

The free will-versus-determinism debate embodied by Number Six in *The Prisoner* (1967) also lies at the heart of the character of the Cylon Number Six in *Battlestar Galactica* (2005). Coincidence? We think not.

"SO IT GOES."

—KURT VONNEGUT, *SLAUGHTERHOUSE-FIVE*

S TRANGE AS IT SOUNDS, the most disturbing and tragic part of Kurt Vonnegut's meditation on war, inhumanity, and suffering isn't the violence and horror he shows us, it's the impassionate distance at which the narrator puts himself from it all. Men are born. They suffer. They slaughter one another before dying themselves, often horribly, often at the hands of another human being. So it goes. If we can embrace such coldness, are we then empty shells or are we merely protecting our psyche from deep emotional damage? Cynical as Vonnegut was, it's nice to think he wanted us to take away the latter rather than the former. We can neither take part in the horror of man's violence nor give in to it, but we *must* acknowledge it. In some way we must come to grips with what we're capable of doing to one another. We are a beautiful, terrible, sleepless species. And sometimes we're still animals. So it goes.

Slaughterhouse-Five (1969) is often grouped with several other geek novels from the 1950s and '60s: Ray Bradbury's *Fahrenheit 451* and Joseph Heller's *Catch-22*. Lesson: brainy satire and titles with numbers work well together.

"SPECIALIZATION IS FOR INSECTS."

—ROBERT HEINLEIN, *TIME ENOUGH FOR LOVE*

THINK ABOUT your favorite handheld device. Dollars to donuts says it doesn't just serve as a phone, or a camera, or an automatic coffee stirrer. It probably does a whole bunch of these things. You love it for that very reason. After all, if electronics are capable of doing so many incredible things, why shouldn't one device be able to handle them all? Robert Heinlein thought the  same should apply to human beings—and he was right. Heinlein was a boot-strappy Libertarian amid liberal peers decades before it became trendy, and he took his fair share of criticism for those stringent beliefs. But one thing he can't be accused of is underestimating the human ability to achieve. Excel at many things, he told us. Be capable. Be adept. Be smart and strong and focused. That is our mandate as human beings, and Heinlein's stories are littered with people who show us how. We can say what we will about his views on, say, war, but few can argue against aspiring to be a well-rounded, multitalented person. So go forth and learn how to fix a bicycle, and how to understand ancient history, and how to vacuum corners, and how to calculate a number sequence. You'll be happier.

The rest of the quote from *Time Enough for Love* (1973) is long but worth memorizing: "A human being should be able to change a diaper, plan an invasion, butcher a hog, conn a ship, design a building, write a sonnet, balance accounts, build a wall, set a bone, comfort the dying, take orders, give orders, cooperate, act alone, solve equations, analyze a new problem, pitch manure, program a computer, cook a tasty meal, fight efficiently, die gallantly."

"I HAVE ANOTHER TRICK FOR YOU. WANNA SEE ME MAKE ALL THE WHITE PEOPLE DISAPPEAR?"

—THE CARD TRICKSTER, *THE BROTHER FROM ANOTHER PLANET*

JOHN SAYLES'S 1984 FILM features an eponymous protagonist: a gawky, mute alien who coincidentally happens to resemble a black man. In very short order, it was embraced by non-white geeks as a cutting-edge classic, a perfect parable of race in geekdom. There's a central dilemma they deal with: because most geeks have, historically speaking, generally identified as outcasts on the margins of society, they often have trouble understanding that it's possible for some geeks to be marginalized even within geekdom due to other qualities of identity, such as gender, race, and class. The Brother of Sayles's movie struggles to find his place in the surreal and blighted landscape of 1980s New York—specifically, Harlem. He has almost nothing in common with his fellow Harlemites but the color of his skin. Yet in a society so powerfully impacted by race, skin color is more than enough to forge a common bond.

The titular Brother was portrayed by Joe Morton, who would later achieve further geek cred as Dr. Steven Hamilton on *Smallville* and the guy who destroyed the future in *Terminator 2*.

"MONSTERS, JOHN!
MONSTERS FROM THE ID!"

—LT. "DOC" OSTROW, *FORBIDDEN PLANET*

MORE THAN ANCIENT squid creatures from another dimension, atomic-powered giant insects, and chain-saw-wielding zombies with frickin' laser beams attached to their heads, we fear that which is in ourselves. Humanity's ties to our primitive past are not as distant as we'd like to believe, and in our hearts we know it. Our darkest thoughts, wants, desires—these things are a terror far greater than any monster we could conjure, not simply because they're so difficult to confront, but because they show that we're a mere half-step removed from the animals. Worse still, our minds are fragile things. Barely controllable. If we were to lose control? We fear we'd cease to be human, because more than any amount of spirituality, faith, or technical know-how, it is our conscience, self-awareness, and desire to rise above our primitive roots that is the soul of man. If we retreat to the id—our unconscious, instinctual mind—we abandon all that separates us from the apes. And that is the most frightening thing imaginable.

Freud introduced the concept of the id in his 1920 essay "Beyond the Pleasure Principle." *Forbidden Planet*, the greatest science-fiction film ever inspired by Shakespeare, explored the id more tangibly in 1956.

"ONLY SPARTAN WOMEN GIVE BIRTH TO REAL MEN."

—QUEEN GORGO, *300*

"THE ANALYTICAL ENGINE WEAVES ALGEBRAIC PATTERNS, JUST AS THE JACQUARD LOOM WEAVES FLOWERS AND LEAVES."

—ADA LOVELACE, ON CHARLES BABBAGE'S ANALYTICAL ENGINE

THE REAL QUEEN GORGO of Sparta was a political mover and shaker on par with the modern age's most respected power brokers. She was also a geek and early cryptanalyst, helping her fellow Spartans find the code hidden in a chiseled wooden board that warned of impending Persian attack. And, predictably, she may also have been one of the first targets of geek sexism, for she is lauded in many historians' accounts not for her own (substantial) accomplishments, but primarily for her relationship to the men around her—as the daughter, wife, and mother of kings. But while Gorgo's quote in Frank Miller's *300* is a fairly accurate rendering of her words as recorded by Plutarch, the true context was quite different. Per Plutarch, Gorgo didn't use the word *real*—and she was speaking to a woman from Attica who asked her how Spartan women had gained the power to rule Spartan men. Placed in this female-to-female context, Gorgo's declaration becomes less a statement on her value in the eyes of men and more subversive—perhaps an encouragement from one woman to another on methods of escaping oppression and gaining power of her own. Gorgo may also have been implying that men can be partners in this process, if they are willing . . . or pawns, shaped from birth by the power of maternal influence, if not.

Nineteenth-century writer Ada Lovelace may be one of the first women to triumph over the historical biases against Queen Gorgo. Though in her lifetime she was most known as the poet Byron's daughter, today she's remembered as the world's first computer programmer.

"OUT OF MY WAY. I'M GOING TO SEE MY MOTHER."

—SEPHIROTH, *FINAL FANTASY VII*

SEPHIROTH: BADASS. Super-soldier. Terrifying megalomaniacal mass-murdering sociopath . . . and mama's boy. An entire generation of geeks was transformed by *Final Fantasy VII*, for reasons that had little to do with the game's groundbreaking graphics or gameplay. Games with complex plots and three-dimensional characters had been popular in Japan for some time, but *Final Fantasy VII* was the first introduction for many American gamers to the concept of games as an art form—as truly interactive storytelling. What made it work was the way so many of the characters resonated as their facets were gradually revealed. True, none of us were stereotypical fantasy-story warriors able to wield gigantic swords or summon dragons, as the game's hero Cloud appeared at first glance. But all of us could understand the kind of crippling insecurity that lurked behind Cloud's stoic facade. Most of us had no great desire to dominate the earth, but we all knew what it was to struggle for the approval of a parent or authority figure. Even if that parent was an incomprehensible alien life form—or the real-world equivalent thereof.

Final Fantasy VII was released in 1997—a decade into the series' life. The saga continues today: *Final Fantasy XIV* debuted in 2010.

"WHAT IS YOUR DAMAGE, HEATHER?"

—HEATHERS

YOU KNOW WHAT'S THE WORST? High school. Every geek has seen the havoc high school can wreak, in a way few mainstreamers can understand. Somehow, most teen movies construct their stories so that their heroine ends up with the dream date at the school dance, their hero wins the big game, and everything ends up all right. But most of high school is not all right, and *Heathers* realized that. Head bitch Heather McNamara's signature catchphrase manages to be dismissive, aggressive, and superior at the same time—the soul-crushing gift of the high school cliquemaster—and literally haunts the counterculture girl Veronica long after Heather is dead. Everyone who's been bullied recognizes the power play at work in this putdown; an important geek rite of passage to adulthood is trying to move past the power your too-cool enemies had over you. If you can't quite get there, well, we can hardly blame you—some meanness is immortal. As long as you don't start playing strip croquet with strangers, you'll probably be fine.

By starring in the quick triple threat of *Beetlejuice* (1988), *Heathers* (1989), and *Edward Scissorhands* (1990), Winona Ryder became the face of girl geekdom for a generation; it would continue with *Dracula*, *Little Women* (Jo is a protogeek!), and *Alien Resurrection*, among others.

"RAY, IF SOMEONE ASKS YOU IF YOU ARE A GOD, YOU SAY YES!"

—WINSTON ZEDDIMORE, *GHOSTBUSTERS*

"TELL HIM ABOUT THE TWINKIE."

—WINSTON ZEDDIMORE, *GHOSTBUSTERS*

G HOSTBUSTERS WAS, in its way, a straight-ahead satire of New York City. We laughed as much at the unflappability of the typical New Yorker as we did at the ridiculousness of the Stay-Puft Marshmallow Man. It wouldn't surprise us that any New Yorker might be so irreverent and arrogant as to claim godhood; in fact, many of us were surprised when Dan Aykroyd as Dr. Ray Stantz tried to deny it. *Ghostbusters* also poked fun at the arrogance of geeks. Ray and Egon, the brains of the outfit, might not have had the business acumen of Venkman or the earnestness of Winston, but they had this: *they were right.* The Twinkie comparison, the disaster of biblical proportions, the unlicensed particle accelerators; the whole thing was cockamamie, and it's a miracle any of them survived. But they knew their stuff and refused to back down from the importance of their knowledge, despite a city full of jaded naysayers. Because of their dogged insistence, the city was—more or less—prepared for a major disaster. So, when you get right down to it, Winston was right, too: after all that, a little bragging would have been completely apropos.

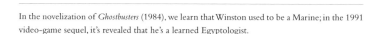

In the novelization of *Ghostbusters* (1984), we learn that Winston used to be a Marine; in the 1991 video-game sequel, it's revealed that he's a learned Egyptologist.

"WHY SO SERIOUS?"

—JOKER, *THE DARK KNIGHT*

BATMAN'S NEMESES over the years have rarely been superpowered; they were usually just a bit crueler and weirder than the norm. In earlier adaptations, the Joker was a Technicolor prankster who was more pun than prudence. After filmmaker Christopher Nolan's 2005 movie reboot, however, Batman's world was far darker, and it needed a Joker to match. The Joker of *The Dark Knight* as portrayed by Heath Ledger was a force of violent chaos, shocking even in the stakes-upping world of comic-movie sequels. Though superhero movies are nominally escapist fare, each iteration of Batman has reflected not just the Bat-world but the real world as well—which makes this Joker's rallying cry a bitter reminder that life today is just as messy as Gotham City, and that recent news headlines have featured quite

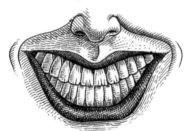

a few criminals who could give the Joker a run for his money. It might be a stretch to say that the Joker is giving us a direct call to arms—but sometimes there's nothing wrong with taking stuff a little more seriously.

The Dark Knight (2008) was Heath Ledger's final complete performance before his untimely death at the age of twenty-eight.

"TRANSFORM AND ROLL OUT!"

—OPTIMUS PRIME, *THE TRANSFORMERS*

MORE THAN JUST A KICK-ASS CATCHPHRASE, the call to arms of Autobot leader Optimus Prime en route to impending battle with the evil Decepticons represents a philosophy that, when you cut it to the quick, isn't altogether different from what Martin Luther King Jr. was alluding to when he said: "Change does not roll in on the wheels of inevitability, but comes through continuous struggle." There's an underlying truth to the idea that one must enact change on the microcosmic level before attempting change on a global scale. And if there's anyone who nobly represented the dichotomy of both continuous struggle and the wheeling in of change, it was the Transformers. While Optimus and his robotic cohorts are perhaps overly literal exemplars of King's thesis, we take our wisdom where we find it. For an entire generation of children who came of age in the 1980s, that wisdom came from an animated robot who had a very deep voice, and who spent half his time disguised as a Mack truck.

In addition to playing Optimus Prime and Eeyore from *Winnie the Pooh*, voice actor Peter Cullen is the ear-catching basso whose narration has for decades heralded the introduction of countless action-movie trailers.

"YOU'RE TRAVELING THROUGH ANOTHER DIMENSION, A DIMENSION NOT ONLY OF SIGHT AND SOUND, BUT OF MIND."

—ROD SERLING, *THE TWILIGHT ZONE*

"I WAS BOLD IN THE PURSUIT OF KNOWLEDGE, NEVER FEARING TO FOLLOW TRUTH AND REASON TO WHATEVER RESULTS THEY LED, AND BEARDING EVERY AUTHORITY WHICH STOOD IN THEIR WAY."

—THOMAS JEFFERSON

THE WORLD is most often changed by ideas rather than by guns, bombs, and fists. Albert Einstein. Karl Marx. Thomas Jefferson. Carl Sagan. Men like these have sparked revolutions and given us new ways to see and understand our world. This is no surprise; geeks throughout history have long known the power of the mind. It wasn't until the twentieth century, however, that we developed a robust subculture that embraced the kind of flights of fancy that have come to define us. Jefferson correctly saw a need to fuel the mind, a cultural desire for speculation that gave people insight into the human condition. What he probably couldn't have imagined is how modern geek artists such as *The Twilight Zone*'s creative mastermind Rod Serling would take that same need, that same appreciation for the power of the mind, and apply the metaphorical trappings of surely frivolous juvenilia—*talking dolls! space aliens!*—to achieve pure entertainment at the same time as profound enlightenment. In their own way, the storytelling tropes that emerged from Serling's influence have been as sweeping a cultural revolution as anything Jefferson could have imagined.

Sometimes, geekery is of such high quality that it takes over mainstream culture. The Hollywood trade journal *Variety* called *The Twilight Zone* (1959) "the best that has ever been accomplished in half-hour filmed television."

"TO DOUBT EVERYTHING OR TO BELIEVE EVERYTHING ARE TWO EQUALLY CONVENIENT SOLUTIONS; BOTH DISPENSE WITH THE NEED FOR THOUGHT."

—HENRI POINCARÉ, *SCIENCE AND HYPOTHESIS*

WHETHER WE'RE TALKING about religious institutions or the news media, there are times when it's crucially important to doubt the information we're given and other times when the need to believe in *something* can be the only thing that offers any respite. Our tendency, however, is to choose one side or the other of that split and stay there. As human beings, we're fundamentally lazy. We don't like doing any more work than we have to or thinking any harder than we need to. That's at least partially to blame for the age of extreme partisan polarization we find ourselves in: reason has been removed from the discussion, and it's become all about the ego we have invested in our point of view. What Poincaré points out, in addition to underscoring that inherent laziness, is how much more difficult it can be to navigate that razor's edge right down the middle. If we're ever to achieve true progress, it's concomitant to have both faith and doubt comforting us in equal measure.

French mathematician Poincaré (1854–1912) laid the groundwork for the modern fields of topology and chaos theory.

"ME FAIL ENGLISH? THAT'S UNPOSSIBLE!"
—RALPH WIGGUM, *THE SIMPSONS*

O N EVERY OTHER PAGE OF THIS BOOK, you will find us elaborating on the quotations above. On this page, you will not. Ralph's confused exclamation is like unto a Zen koan, and we suggest you meditate upon it. Then meditate upon it some more. We've been doing so for many years, and we still continue to find fresh nuances within.

We would like to humbly suggest that Ralph Wiggum, like Rose Nylund and Phoebe Buffay, is an avatar of Delirium of the Endless.

"MONKEYS' BRAINS, WHILE POPULAR IN CANTONESE CUISINE, ARE NOT OFTEN TO BE FOUND IN WASHINGTON, D.C."

—WADSWORTH, *CLUE*

THE WAY YOU SOLVE MYSTERIES is by identifying anomalies and tracking them to their source. In *Clue*, the ultimate parody of a murder mystery, everything was an anomaly; there was no baseline from which to deviate. That made the whole story an exercise in farce, but it also provided the opportunity for any number of complete-unto-themselves truisms. Here's one: you can't decipher a clue if you don't observe it. The above revelation was offered toward the end of the film by the Boddy mansion's butler, Wadsworth, as a key element in his chain of reasoning in solving the murder—but it's a total and deliberate cheat, as the very *fact* that monkeys' brains were the main course at dinner had never been mentioned. The line is emblematic of a narrative technique known formally in English masters' programs worldwide as "pulling something out of your ass." In a real mystery, that's against the rules; in a mystery parody, it's the source of humor; and in life, sometimes it's just what you gotta do. (Speaking of English classes. . . .)

Clue is a rarely cited credit of geek filmmaking icon John Landis (*The Blues Brothers, An American Werewolf in London*), who cowrote it with director Jonathan Lynn.

"YOU'RE A VAMPIRE. OH, I'M SORRY. WAS THAT AN OFFENSIVE TERM? SHOULD I SAY 'UNDEAD AMERICAN'?"

—BUFFY SUMMERS, *BUFFY THE VAMPIRE SLAYER*

BECAUSE SHE DOESN'T wear a skintight action suit, people sometimes miss the fact that Buffy Summers is, for all intents and purposes, a classic comic-book-style superhero. She exemplifies the life of every high-school girl—and, more than that, of every human being—writ on a larger, brighter canvas, the angst of her adolescent relationships exaggerated but not fundamentally changed by the fact that her daily routine puts her up against not just jerks and jocks but vampires and demons. This literalization of the metaphors of daily life stretches into the realm of identity politics when she sneers at her tormented vampire boyfriend, suggesting that perhaps his struggles will be less painful if the monstrous terminology of his existence is dressed up in politically correct language. Like Buffy, we've all caught ourselves on occasion saying snide, hurtful things to the ones we love—maybe even mocking or spurning something that matters profoundly to them. Yet beneath that moment of nastiness, Buffy can't forget that she found it in her heart to recognize and love Angel's damaged humanity in the first place. There's a lesson here for all of us: if you're going to breach the line of decorum, do it with someone you can trust to accept your apology later.

Writer Joss Whedon's snappy banter borrowed heavily from the flavor of Marvel Comics' trademark bickering on the battlefield, which is why fans cheered in 2004 to see him take up the pen to write Marvel's new Astonishing X-Men series.

IV.
KNOWING IS HALF
THE BATTLE

(WISDOM ABOUT CONFLICT)

"HEY, YOU—GET YOUR DAMN HANDS OFF HER."

—GEORGE MCFLY, *BACK TO THE FUTURE*

I F YOU EVER DOUBT that there can be a lot going on in one sentence, take a look at George McFly: his utterance of these eight words ties together mistaken identity, sexual assault, burgeoning heroism, protoincest, and the twisting of the space-time continuum—and that's all before Biff even turns around. We all have instances in our lives in which it seems as though our many problems and dreams coalesce into a single, terrifying moment, and we know that how we decide to act in those crucial moments will change who we are. Oddly, George's true pivotal moment was making the decision to act at all; that inertia spilled over into real actions and real change. In the movie, it's a triumphant climax. In real life, making a tough decision at a crucial juncture often means that different troubles lie ahead. Yet the tough decision is often the right one, and it's always worth fighting a good fight.

Crispin Glover's portrayal of George McFly in *Back to the Future* (1985) was so memorable, it's hard to conceive anyone else having done it. That didn't stop the producers of the sequel from replacing him with an actor who accepted a lower salary.

"I FIND YOUR LACK OF FAITH DISTURBING."

—DARTH VADER, *STAR WARS*

ADMIRAL MOTTI thought he knew what he was dealing with. His boss, imperial high honcho Grand Moff Tarkin, had this right-hand man, Darth Vader, who got to do *whatever* he wanted *whenever* he wanted and was just *way* impressed with himself. Meanwhile, Motti, a good, hardworking soldier, spent a whole freaking decade wrangling the logistical nightmare of constructing a battle station the size of a freaking moon, only to be dismissed with a hand wave by this heavy-breathing asswipe. It's not hard to see that, after who knows how many management staff meetings where Vader doubtlessly kept mouthing off about "the power of the Force" this and "the power of the Force" that, Motti had had about enough and was ready to put Vader in his place. Here's where Motti went wrong: he misjudged his rival's moxie. He thought he knew the sort of response to expect after calling his coworker a douchebag. It never occurred to him that being maybe choked to death right there on the spot was even within the realm of possibility. So gauge your opponents correctly. How far will they go?

We would like to take this footnote to suggest that, the next time George Lucas goes back to mess with his films for another digitally altered version, perhaps he should replace all footage of the unmasked Anakin Skywalker with newly filmed and de-aged shots of James Earl Jones.

"GOOD DAY, SIR! . . . I SAID, GOOD DAY!"

—WILLY WONKA, *WILLY WONKA AND THE CHOCOLATE FACTORY*

J ON STEWART has appropriated this huffy conversation-ending phrase in recent years, and though he always plays it for laughs, it really does epitomize in seven words the "extreme moderate" philosophy that fuels Stewart's appeal. See, when Willy Wonka hurls this dismissal at Charlie Bucket in response to Charlie's having broken the rules of the chocolate factory tour, he does so because he's angry—furious, in fact, that Charlie, for whom he had great hopes, has let him down. But he doesn't let his disappointed fury consume him. He doesn't call Charlie names. He simply expresses his anger . . . politely. His voice is loud and upset, but he keeps his words dignified. He quotes the contractual terms Charlie has violated, spells out the logical conclusion, and leaves it there. And by stopping short of the nuclear option, by being angry without becoming truly nasty, he thereby leaves an opening for Charlie to offer one more statement—which is exactly what it takes for the two to come back to the table and find a happy ending for their story. That distinction between forceful honesty and abuse is the line that Stewart—and the millions of Americans who love his show—wishes today's politicians would remember how to draw.

Chocolate Factory author Roald Dahl was a World War II flying ace who flew combat missions over Greece, was promoted to wing commander, and subsequently worked in British Intelligence alongside Ian Fleming.

"I HAVE COME HERE TO CHEW BUBBLEGUM AND KICK ASS, AND I'M ALL OUT OF BUBBLEGUM."

—*THEY LIVE*

ROWDY" RODDY PIPER'S LACK of bubblegum is not what prompted his alien ass-kicking spree. He had come to chew bubblegum *and* kick ass, after all. No "or" in the equation. If given the chance, he'd probably have been chewing that bubble gum *while* kicking alien ass, which is a lot more than most of us could hope to accomplish. Those goofy one-liners may be absurd, but they also say something about ourselves. It's like this: the wish fulfillment inherent in badass one-liners isn't merely about looking cool—it's about keeping your composure in situations that would make most of us curl up into the fetal position and cry. The ordinary-man-turned-hero is a mainstay of geek entertainment, yes, but we return to the witty tough guy for a reason. As much as we dream of overcoming great adversity and being a hero, what we really want is to do it without pissing our pants. So pass the bubblegum, please.

In 2010, acclaimed novelist Jonathan Lethem published a 208-page deconstruction of *They Live* (1988), which remains filmmaker John Carpenter's cult-favoritest work today.

"DON'T PANIC"

—DOUGLAS ADAMS, *THE HITCHHIKER'S GUIDE TO THE GALAXY*

WHEN *DUNE* AUTHOR Frank Herbert referred to fear as a mind killer, he composed an entire litany to emphasize that point. On the other hand, Douglas Adams was able to convey the same sentiment with two simple words in all caps. While *The Hitchhiker's Guide* had the above legend emblazoned on its cover to avoid discouraging those who might fear the titular device was too complicated, no less an authority than Arthur C. Clarke called it the best possible advice for humankind. It's not about whether life will throw a you curveball, because if you've spent any time at all as part of the human experience, you know the odds are already pretty well stacked in favor of that happening. But the true test is how you react once the inevitable occurs. Don't be overwhelmed. Don't be discouraged. Don't. Panic. In fact, once you step back and think things through, you may just find, as Adams said elsewhere in the guide, that the whole thing is "mostly harmless."

The phrase "Don't panic" was subsequently used by a young Neil Gaiman as the title of his nonfiction book—most recently rereleased in 2009—about Douglas Adams and *The Hitchhiker's Guide.*

"AT LEAST I HAVE CHICKEN."

—LEEROY JENKINS, *WORLD OF WARCRAFT*

SOCIAL ISOLATION is an unavoidable part of the geek maturation process. It's tough being different during childhood and adolescence, given the immense social pressure to conform imposed by family, society, and schoolmates. This is why, when geeks finally find one another and form their own groups, nothing short of nuclear assault will  sever those hard-won social bonds. Take, for instance, the Leeroy Jenkins incident: a now-infamous *World of Warcraft* video from 2005, documenting a game in which a whole players' guild was decimated thanks to the foolishly enthusiastic recklessness of one member who went wildly charging into battle, oblivious to the group's well-thought-out plan. Everyone from Conan O'Brien to the U.S. armed forces has cited this video as an example of crass stupidity and poor communications (on Leeroy's part) as well as taking things too seriously (that would be his fellow gamers, who grew very upset with him). But there's a more important message in the way Leeroy's guild reacted when he ignored their elaborate plan and ran straight into a deadly lions' den: *they all followed him.* They tried to save him, even though it meant that all their characters died in the process. Because, see, that's how geek friends roll.

The literal meaning of Leeroy's final comeback to his friends, "At least I have chicken," is harder to explain. Supposedly, the reason Leeroy's player Ben Schulz didn't understand the plan is because, while it was being made, he'd gone to the kitchen to get some dinner. Whether this is true is open for debate.

"THERE ARE FOUR LIGHTS!"

—JEAN-LUC PICARD, *STAR TREK: THE NEXT GENERATION*

TORTURE DOESN'T WORK . . . because torture does work. When you mess with people's minds, you can't be certain how their minds will respond. Sometimes they'll give you the truth you're looking for. Sometimes they'll be determined not to, and your efforts to force it out of them risk turning untruths into their new reality. Can you tell the difference? Maybe. Or maybe not. Torture isn't just when a Cardassian officer ties up Captain Picard in the dark and uses pain to seek military intelligence. Torture is when a school bully smacks a kid in the face every single day for three years. It's when a spouse abuses the intimacy of a marriage to turn a would-be partner into a frightened slave. It's not only a cruel game, it's a dangerous one—because if the powerless ones suddenly find themselves unexpectedly holding a weapon, heaven only knows where they may end up pointing it.

The 1992 episode "Chain of Command," whence this quote comes, was cowritten by Ronald D. Moore, who later explored torture in outer space at much greater lengths in *Battlestar Galactica*.

"I CAN KILL YOU WITH MY BRAIN."

—RIVER TAM, *FIREFLY*

GEEKDOM IS A CELEBRATION of the mind. There are lots of athletic or physically attractive geeks out there, but in the end geek identity is centered on the intellect and the willingness to be different. Unfortunately, these qualities are not much celebrated in wider society. So how cool is it that in so much of geek literature—science fiction and fantasy, in other words—there are people who can kick ass with brain- and willpower? The enduring popularity of the psychic or psionic in the geek zeitgeist is ultimately about the power of the mind and its relative worth in society. The heroes and heroines of these tales often fear their power or struggle to control it—but once they've mastered it, no force in the 'verse can stop them.

Firefly (2002) may not have lasted more than fourteen episodes, but a decade later its star, Nathan Fillion, could still be found dropping in-jokes on his new TV show *Castle*.

"YOU HAVE BEEN WEIGHED, YOU HAVE BEEN MEASURED, AND YOU HAVE BEEN FOUND WANTING."

—COUNT ADHEMAR, *A KNIGHT'S TALE*

WHAT A DELICIOUSLY *utter* prick Count Adhemar was, getting off on squashing the hopes and dreams of earnest young would-be knight Sir Ulrich von Lichtenstein, aka William Thatcher. Do you know a guy like this? A guy who's totally impressed with himself for having the great genius and talent to have gotten himself born the favored son of a wealthy family of society's ruling class? Who takes it for granted that he deserves to be handsome, deserves to win trophies, deserves to have the ladies fawn all over him? You'd kinda like to knock him off a horse, wouldn't you, with a big stick and a satisfying crashing sound? Well, we're gonna be honest: you probably won't get the chance to do that. But you can imagine it. And you can take quietly sadistic comfort in the fact that, eventually, whether or not you're there to see it, he's going to zig when he should have zagged, and the look on his face just before it abruptly smacks into the ground will be all you might have hoped.

A Knight's Tale (2001) included the character of a wayward young Geoffrey Chaucer, who hadn't yet written *The Canterbury Tales*. Anyone who enjoyed the fictionalized Chaucer performed by Paul Bettany would do well to explore the separate but equally entertaining online world of *Geoffrey Chaucer Hath a Blog*.

"TWO AND TWO MAKE FIVE."

—GEORGE ORWELL, *1984*

MATHEMATICAL EQUATIONS should be frightening only to elementary school children, but there is something chilling about the above equation: a reminder that no matter how strong we think we are, the mind is weak. We all think we're smart, perceptive, and, beyond all else, rational—geeks especially think highly of the machine that is their mind, and often for good reason—but fear, oppression, and hopelessness are weapons that can savage any mind. Goebbels and the Nazi propagandists whipped a country into a frenzy of genocidal hatred not because the German people were weak minded—to the contrary, the Germans have often been intellectual pioneers—but because a person's mind is softer than flesh. Take advantage of fear (rational or otherwise), of prejudice, of want and desire, and a mind can be broken easier than a bone. Otherwise good people can be brainwashed to look away while millions are sent to their deaths, to ignore the stench of decay and pretend that, yes, two plus two does indeed make five.

George Orwell's *1984* is one of a handful of dark-geek science-fiction novels that has long enjoyed the official sanction of the academic literary canon.

"I'VE GOT A BAD FEELING ABOUT THIS."

—HAN SOLO, *STAR WARS*

"I HAVE A BAD FEELING ABOUT THIS."

—PRINCESS LEIA, *THE EMPIRE STRIKES BACK*

"I HAVE A REALLY BAD FEELING ABOUT THIS."

—HAN SOLO, *RETURN OF THE JEDI*

WHEN THE CHARACTERS in *Star Wars* have a bad feeling about something—which they frequently do, since it's the longest running and most familiar gag of the entire saga—the humor comes at the metatextual level: that statement having been uttered, the viewer knows a twist in the narrative is imminent. Life isn't much different. Sometimes you *know* something just isn't right. Whether it's fate or instinct or the subconscious mind at work, we have a way of recognizing when the walls of life's trash compactor are about to start closing in. It's that tingle in your gut that says, "If I take one more step, I'm going to lose control of the situation." That feeling, alarming though it may be, is a healthy one. Experiencing it means you're experiencing life, which means that, although by definition you can't know what unexpectedly curving path you may one day find yourself diverted into, you can rest assured there's one coming eventually. Just as "I've got a bad feeling about this" is a playful wink to the audience, the real thing is life's wink at you. Keep an eye out for it.

Other characters who've said it: Obi-Wan Kenobi, Anakin Skywalker, Luke Skywalker, C-3PO.

"HE IS THE ONE."

—MORPHEUS, *THE MATRIX*

"I KNOW KUNG FU."

—NEO, *THE MATRIX*

MOST CRITICAL ANALYSES of the *Matrix* films are quick to point out its Christian religious allegory—despite Jesus never having done much in the way of flying around or looking cool, and his method of dealing with enemies was to love them, not beat them to a bloody pulp. Neo's un-Messianic behavior may stem from the fact that "turn the other cheek" is a tough sell to geeks, many of whom have endured bullying and other forms of societal injustice. Neo—like other superheroes, into whose ranks he neatly fits—makes a more palatable savior for some because he not only rejects injustice but *attacks* it, in a wholly visceral and satisfying way. But Neo isn't very Jesus-like in another, perhaps more chilling way. The *Matrix* franchise makes much of the fact that "blue-pills" are all potential enemies, working for the system and able to be essentially possessed by Agents at any given time. Yet they are still, in essence, innocent bystanders. And although Jesus made an effort to save such people, casting out demons and calming mobs, Neo mowed them down with machine guns and flying roundhouse kicks.

Neo, then, is not Jesus. He is a savior, but only of those who ask; a redeemer, but only for those (his fellow red-pills) who are as knowledgeable and savvy as he is. His miracles are the result of his programming knowledge and mastery of the operating system that is the Matrix; he wields knowledge itself as a weapon. In this he is merely human, and deeply flawed at that. But he is, at least, a true geek avatar.

Comic-book geeks continue to squabble with movie geeks about whether the name Morpheus, out of context, should be taken as a reference to Laurence Fishburne's character in *The Matrix* or to the protagonist of Neil Gaiman's *Sandman*.

"ALL YOUR BASE ARE BELONG TO US."

—*ZERO WING* VIDEO GAME

ZERO WING WAS A CLASSIC example of early video game imports, which were frequently plagued by semicomprehensible "Japlish"—an affectionate term for Japanese dialogue translated badly into English by companies too cheap or too broke to localize the game properly. Even by the rough standards of the day, however, *Zero Wing*'s translation was so awful that it achieved a kind of surreal artistic brilliance. "All your base are belong to us"—dear lord, there are tense problems, plurality problems, passive-voice problems, all in the span of seven words. But mangled or not, the quintessential sense of betrayal communicated by such *Zero Wing* phrases as "somebody set us up the bomb" was painfully clear, which may be why so many geeks used the phrase in response to any kind of double-cross or undeserved attack. There was something poetic about it all, even if unintentionally so. In 2003, teenagers in Sturgis, Michigan, posted "All your base . . . " signs all over town—purportedly as an April Fool's Day protest against the war in Iraq, lending these flubbed translations an even greater social-justice significance. Not bad for an otherwise mediocre game.

Zero Wing was originally an arcade game in Japan (1989) before being ported to Sega home systems and desktop PCs several years later.

"OH, BOY."

—DR. SAM BECKETT, *QUANTUM LEAP*

ONE OF THE MOST IMPORTANT things in life is maintaining the proper perspective—realizing that no matter how important or Earth-shattering our problems may seem at any given minute, someone else is dealing with something that, to them, is just as profound and/or just as devastating. This is something Sam Beckett became intimately familiar with, because if anything will force you to metaphorically look at the world through another person's eyes, it's literally looking at the world through another person's eyes. Sam spent five seasons exiled helplessly from his own existence, quantum-leaping into the lives (and bodies) of various unfortunates scattered across the timestream. And it tells you something that, after discovering each time that his latest leap wouldn't be the one to finally bring him home, Sam did not succumb to desperation or despondency. He just allowed himself a momentary respite, a succinct "Oh, boy." Then he got down to the business of setting right what once went wrong.

Here's some really obscure geek trivia: Allan Sherman, the 1960s song-parodist precursor to Weird Al Yankovic who wrote "Hello Muddah, Hello Faddah," also recorded a little ditty titled "Oh, Boy." Sadly, Sam Beckett never met him onscreen.

"NOBODY EXPECTS THE SPANISH INQUISITION!"

—MONTY PYTHON'S FLYING CIRCUS

"WHAT IS THE AIR-SPEED VELOCITY OF AN UNLADEN SWALLOW?"

—MONTY PYTHON AND THE HOLY GRAIL

WE SEEK SOLACE IN SILLINESS. This was the simple formula the madcap sketch-comedy geniuses of Monty Python stumbled upon as they shone their uniquely British (well, five Brits and a Yank) spotlight on all manner of absurdist tableaus—whether the aforementioned Spanish Inquisitors busting anachronistically into a scene far removed in time and space from their own, or a pet-shop owner insisting that a stiff and motionless parrot is most certainly not dead, or an armless and legless Black Knight defiantly proclaiming that it's "just a flesh wound." Indeed, so influential were these funnymen in reshaping the landscape of millennial humor that the very term *Pythonesque* has garnered inclusion in dictionaries as a signifier of the loopy, punch-drunk surrealism that their routines encourage each of us to free inside ourselves. You might not think it on those days when you're up at six, stuck in bumper-to-bumper traffic, and headed to a job you despise working for a boss you detest, but sometimes the only way to empower yourself and push back against the various vicissitudes life throws at you is to take a step back, see yourself as part of an awesomely ridiculous joke that's as big as the whole damn universe, and just let yourself laugh out loud at it, whether or not anyone else thinks it makes a lick of sense. It *doesn't*. That's why it's funny.

Monty Python's Flying Circus originally aired on the BBC from late 1969 through 1974. For geek context: that's the Jon Pertwee era of *Doctor Who*.

"I SAY WE TAKE OFF AND NUKE THE SITE FROM ORBIT."

—RIPLEY, *ALIENS*

MOVIE LOGIC FRUSTRATES most geeks. It just doesn't make sense for the people in a horror film to go one by one to investigate that strange noise in the dark—that didn't work out so well for the last five people, did it? It's *stupid* for the evil overlord to capture the intrepid hero and then leave him alone in a room full of convenient tools; any overlord with a brain would just kill the guy right off. All too often, Hollywood characters choose the more dramatic path through hardship rather than the smart one. This was why the *Alien* films were such a breath of fresh air. Ripley, faced with a planetary colony full to overflowing with unstoppably murderous alien beasts, actually understood what she was up against. Never mind trying to safely capture an alien—it *wasn't going to happen*. Ripley pushed instead for the Occam's Razor method of problem-solving: simple, overwhelming, effective. Thus "take off and nuke the site from orbit" has become geek shorthand for putting a decisive end to any dangerously messy problem. Overkill? Maybe. But sometimes you just have to be sure.

In our personal version of the *Alien* universe, Newt and Ripley and the cat are all off somewhere living happily ever after. They deserve it.

"IT'S DANGEROUS TO GO ALONE! TAKE THIS."

—CAPTION FROM *THE LEGEND OF ZELDA*, TURNED INTO A LOLCAT MEME

SMART PEOPLE ARE OFTEN self-sufficient and confident, particularly when it comes to our particular area(s) of expertise. The average geek is often the only person in the group who's capable of solving some arcane and specialized problem. Which presents a whole 'nother problem: even though geeky confidence and competence can sometimes lead to obnoxious and undeserved arrogance, the plain fact of the matter is that, frequently, when it comes to a particular topic, the geek really is the most knowledgeable person in the room. That doesn't stop other people from trying to help, though—often with contributions that seem absurd or useless. The foolish geek rolls his or her eyes at these offers of help, but the wise geek takes them as they're meant: a sincere desire to share in the geeky joy of problem-solving. And hey, you never know—that doofus might just have a point.

Please feel free to consider this book as a "this" that just might possibly be helpful.

"NOW WE KNOW. AND KNOWING IS HALF THE BATTLE!"

—*G.I. JOE* (CARTOON)

G.I. JOE, like many cartoons of the 1980s, taught us the meaning of irony. Every week, after watching a privately funded mercenary squad fire thousands of lasers, missiles, and BFGs at its enemies, we then endured a brief lecture on morality, including the need to resolve problems without violence. But we saw no real contradiction in this, since compartmentalization is a necessary and welcome part of the geek mindset. How else are we to keep separate our many realms—not just our fictional realms of fantasy and science fiction and role-playing games, but our real-world realms of entertainment, work, and social life? So ingrained is our ability to suspend disbelief at will, and to separate fantasy from reality, that we are often stunned when non-geeks *don't* do this, or don't believe us when we say we can. Could this be why we embrace the fantastic, while non-geeks frequently fear or disdain it?

One of the great triumphs in the field of Internet snark is the viral-hit G.I. Joe–themed pie chart in which we are informed that "The Battle" is made up of 50 percent knowing, 25 percent red lasers, and 25 percent blue lasers.

"FLY CASUAL!"

—HAN SOLO, *RETURN OF THE JEDI*

O R: "NEVER LET 'EM SEE YOU SWEAT." Or: "There is nothing to fear but fear itself." Attempting to sneak past an imperial blockade in which Darth Vader's cruiser is close enough to scratch the paint, smuggler-turned-rebel-general Han Solo uses humor and a little bit of swagger to assure his crew that all is well, even as most of us would quiver and crumble under similarly dire circumstances. That is why we love Han. Not because he doesn't feel the same panic we all do, but because he doesn't allow it to cripple him; instead he finds a way to power through it. Granted, the line between swagger and stupidity can be thin, and only the passage of time will determine which side we end up on. Regardless of the aphorism you wrap it in, the sentiment expressed by Solo—casual confidence in the face of insurmountable odds—is not only what we hope to see in our leaders, it's what we hope to find inside ourselves.

There are geeks who opine that *Return of the Jedi* (1983) was where the *Star Wars* saga began to stink. There are a handful of still geekier geeks itching to one-up them and claim *Empire* is where it went wrong. *Those* geeks? Even we want to give them wedgies.

"AS AN ONLINE DISCUSSION
GROWS LONGER,
THE PROBABILITY OF
A COMPARISON INVOLVING
NAZIS OR HITLER
APPROACHES 1."

—MIKE GODWIN, GODWIN'S LAW

GEEKS LOVE TO FIGHT, and those fights are often epic in their awesomeness. The advent of the Internet merely updated a longstanding geek tradition of launching interpersonal battles over minutiae—which, prior to the Internet, expressed itself in the form of months-long arguments in the "Letters to the Editor" columns of comic books, dueling Cthulhu Mythos tales in fanzines, and so on. But the Internet also made it clear that geek arguments follow a predictable pattern—and any  dispute that goes on long enough will always, inevitably, reach the "scorched earth" stage, past which any discussion becomes irrelevant. (Oh, so preferring Batman's black-armored movie costume to his classic grey tights is the opinion of, not just *another guy*, but a *jackbooted fascist*? Really, boywonder953? Really?) This has become such a truism that weary blog commenters, smelling a nasty fight in the making, will often preemptively mention Nazis just to cut things short. And it's alarming to see that the non-geek portions of the media have taken the same path; heck, the Jon Stewart/Stephen Colbert rally of 2010 was mostly an attempt to ask, "Can we please stop calling each other Hitler?" It would seem the answer is no.

At least some geeks are fighting to take back the Hitler epithet in the name of good-spirited silliness. Thousands of YouTube videos have mashed up a scene in the Hitler bio-film *Downfall* with topics ranging from Xbox to *Twilight*.

"I LOVE IT WHEN A PLAN COMES TOGETHER!"

—JOHN "HANNIBAL" SMITH, *THE A-TEAM*

HAN SOLO MAY HAVE SHOWN us the seat-of-your-pants thrill of improvising, but Hannibal Smith taught us there's something to be said for taking the long view. And one thing you can't accuse the jocular leader of the A-Team of is not taking the long view, with his daisy-chain schemas of elaborate disguises, car crashes, and lots of pyrotechnics making it all the sweeter when he deployed his trademark catchphrase as the payoff to a job well done. As Smith and his *Team*-mates showed week in and week out between 1983 and 1987 (and once in 2010), sometimes planning isn't about anticipating every exigency down to the last detail; it's about knowing how to react when the unexpected occurs. He may never have led an army across the Alps atop elephants like the Carthiginian general from whom he took his name, but Hannibal nonetheless exemplified the same lesson: the bigger the risk, the greater the need for planning—and the bigger the thrill when it falls into place.

Geek thrills that follow much the same principle: dominos, Rube Goldberg machines, and Odyssey of the Mind tournaments.

"DON'T CROSS THE STREAMS. IT WOULD BE BAD."

—EGON SPENGLER, *GHOSTBUSTERS*

EGON'S WARNING TO his fellow Ghostbusters was perhaps the most casually deadpan mention of possibly accidentally blowing oneself to bits ever committed to voice. It's typical, though. In the eyes of mainstream society, most geeks tend to get excited by all the "wrong" things. From raging battles over which is the best X–Man to the abject joy that ripples through nerddom whenever a new Hubble image is released, there's no doubt that geeks are passionate people. Yet, all this passion for offbeat, unique things sometimes leaves little room in our cerebral cortex for getting excited about relatively ordinary things . . . like, say, the possibility of a violent, horrific death. Death, after all, happens to everyone; there's nothing especially unique about it. But *a Goldilocks-zone exoplanet*? Now that's worth an exclamation point or two. Of course, this means that whenever a geek laconically suggests that taking a particular course of action "would be bad," those passionate about their own continued well-being should probably pay really, really close attention.

Hey, what's a Goldilocks–zone exoplanet, anyway? We're gonna let you look that one up. Consider it an exercise in geekiness.

**"JOIN THE ARMY,
MEET INTERESTING PEOPLE,
AND KILL THEM."**

—STEVEN WRIGHT

**"ITS FIVE-YEAR MISSION:
TO EXPLORE STRANGE
NEW WORLDS."**

—OPENING NARRATION, *STAR TREK*

THE MILITARY REPRESENTS a jumble of mixed feelings for young geeks, and Steven Wright's classic one-line gag pretty much sums it up. Growing up on a diet of epic adventure stories tends to cultivate a sense of romanticism, which means we get excited at the prospect of sharing a quest with a band of comrades, of taking part in a grand struggle that's greater than ourselves. Also, we love tech—and who has better gadgets than the military? On the other hand, our natural inclination to always question authority, to push back against dogma, means that we chafe against any sort of hierarchical command structure that might require us to take direction from anyone whose view of the universe is smaller and meaner than our own. It's no coincidence that Gene Roddenberry changed the broad face of science fiction by creating a tale that managed to have it both ways: starfleet is a military-structured organization whose first mission is peaceful exploration; the *Enterprise* carries a crew who are willing to buck the rules whenever they think it's necessary, and, miraculously, they almost always turn out to be right. There's no screaming drill sergeant threatening to rip out a trainee's eyes in *Star Trek*, and there's rarely an Abu Ghraib, either. (That's why the rougher, rawer *Battlestar Galactica*, not *Trek*, was the science-fiction success story of the 2000s.) Could there ever be a real Starfleet—a force using military organization to effectively promote individual accomplishment throughout its sphere of action? Countless disillusioned Peace Corps vets suggest no—and yet our geeky hearts still want to say yes.

Colonel Tigh, the drill-sergeant archetype in *Galactica*, was the one who got his eye gouged out. We're pretty sure that's irony.

"TO LEARN WHICH QUESTIONS ARE UNANSWERABLE, AND NOT ANSWER THEM: THIS SKILL IS MOST NEEDFUL IN TIMES OF STRESS AND DARKNESS."

—URSULA LE GUIN, *THE LEFT HAND OF DARKNESS*

SOMETIMES, SCI-FI CHARACTERS offering advice veer into the realm of the overcooked. But sometimes a piece of wisdom hits you right between the eyes. Geeks in particular have a tendency to overthink—to insist on making sense of everything from every angle so we might come at an answer from a place of omnipotence. As nice a situation as that might be, reality generally precludes it; we live in a quick-and-dirty world that functions largely on snap decision and compromise. That can often take some adjustment for geeks, who prefer their world-building logical and their decisions foolproof. And it's disheartening to realize that the world is also far more stress and darkness than sweetness and light. The good news is that if anyone can separate the components of a situation and solve only for the bug-free variables, it's geeks. The trick is to recognize the unsolvable when it appears; there, you're on your own.

A counterpart to Le Guin's point has been expressed in the realm of pure mathematics: Gödel's Incompleteness Theorem (1931) says that any mathematical system will include facts about the natural numbers that are true, yet cannot be proved.

"THIS IS MY BOOMSTICK."

—ASH, *ARMY OF DARKNESS*

WE LOVED ASH in *Evil Dead* and *Evil Dead 2*, but it was in *Army of Darkness*, when he played a modern-day Yankee in King—er, Lord—Arthur's court, that he really shone. And we loved it, because Ash was a geek *and* a badass. He knew more than everyone around him. He was unversed in the social graces of the era, but that was okay; he made his own rules. We also loved the subtle critique of geekiness that the film displayed. Ash's cockiness made him his own worst enemy, and his love life might have turned out a lot better if he hadn't been such an ass. But he didn't care about those things, either. In the end, it was his confidence, deserved or not, that made him powerful and admirable. Even if some of us never did forgive him for screwing up *klaatu barada nikto*. He lost some geek points for that one.

Geek Hall of Fame alert: Bruce Campbell's portrayal of Ash kicked off a career that spanned such cult classics as *Bubba Ho-tep*, *Escape from L.A.*, *Xena: Warrior Princess*, and *The Adventures of Brisco County Jr.*

"THE FIRST RULE OF FIGHT CLUB IS: YOU DO NOT TALK ABOUT FIGHT CLUB."

—TYLER DURDEN, *FIGHT CLUB*

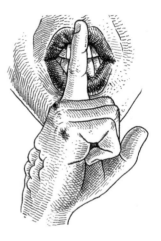

THERE'S SOMETHING to be said for exclusivity. After all, haven't you ever had a favorite band that you lived and breathed until it committed the cardinal sin of becoming too popular? Haven't you had a favorite movie you began to hate once everyone else started quoting it? Didn't Facebook lose some of its luster when you got that friend request from your great-aunt Polly? The "fight club" at the center of Chuck Palahniuk's book and David Fincher's film isn't so much a social movement as it is that hardcore indie band you just don't want to see sell out. But that's the inherent problem with anything that impacts society enough to bring about lasting change: its success carries within it the seeds of its eventual dissolution. If history teaches us anything, it's that the rebels of today are inevitably the establishmentarians of tomorrow—whether Fidel Castro, Kurt Cobain, or Mark Zuckerberg. And so, can you really blame Tyler Durden for wanting to keep a lid on his new favorite thing for just a little while longer?

The novel *Fight Club* (1996) established Chuck Palahniuk as a major author of disturbing fiction. His short story "Guts," about unfortunate masturbation accidents, established him as an author who could cause people to faint while listening to him read out loud.

"TO CRUSH YOUR ENEMIES, SEE THEM DRIVEN BEFORE YOU, AND TO HEAR THE LAMENTATION OF THEIR WOMEN."

—CONAN, *CONAN THE BARBARIAN*

T HE HEARTLESSNESS OF THE CONQUEROR is something most people are incapable of understanding. We are empathetic beings; the roots of our greatest civilizations, and thus our greatest accomplishments, lie in our inherently social nature. Even we geeks—solitary creatures of the modern world—feel the same pull. The great conquerors did not. For Alexander of Macedon, life was the campaign. For Genghis Khan, a day dawning without plumes of smoke rising from the cities behind him was not a day worth living. Napoleon Bonaparte's conquests were not an expansion of the French Revolution and the emperor's ideals, but a result of his irrepressible need to run roughshod over others. These were great men in their own way, men whose deeds help continue history's inexorable march toward the modern world. But they were also troubled in a way most of us cannot grasp. Considering the broken families and endless gravestones left in their wake, maybe we ought to be glad that such greatness is rare.

Conan's most famous quote from *Conan the Barbarian* (1982) comes not from the classic stories by author Robert E. Howard but is adapted from an anecdote related in the 1927 Genghis Khan biography *Emperor of All Men*.

"SOME DAYS, YOU JUST CAN'T GET RID OF A BOMB."

—BATMAN, *BATMAN* (1966)

TRUER WORDS have never been spoken, you know? Of course, you'd never expect Batman to have a problem disposing of a bomb—the man has a handmade tool belt that navigates a submarine, for crying out loud—but this is the Adam West version we're talking about. Of all the Batman incarnations, this deliberately cartoonish take on the savior of Gotham ruined Batman's street cred with the other superheroes for decades afterward. It's comforting in its own way to think that, even if we can't have sound-effect bubbles when we head out for capers, we can at least relate to Batman every time we have an explosive situation that can't be easily dismissed. (Figuratively . . . we hope.) It's understandable that sometimes a situation is more than you can clean up. The world is a tricky place, and, superhero or not, sometimes you just can't make a problem go away.

Legendary ham Adam West and legendary ham William Shatner appeared together in an early-1960s pilot for the would-be television adventures of Alexander the Great. Alas, it didn't happen, and we had to settle for Kirk and Batman.

"REPENT! THE END IS EXTREMELY F—KING NIGH!"

—28 DAYS LATER

THE AWKWARD THING about living in a postmodern world is the general expectation that everyone has a quip ready to go when the monsters attack. (If you don't have one ready, think of one now. We'll wait; this is important.) The darker side of general-monster-preparedness is the accompanying general expectation that we'll all be able to handle it with the aplomb of a balding franchise headliner, when really, if hideous hordes ever came at us snarling and clawing, it would be exactly as horrific as it sounds. In the Internet age, a lot of cultural cool-points are derived from seeming jaded enough to joke about genuinely terrible things; as we've noted, many an Internet meme has sprung up around natural and humanitarian disasters. While humor is a well-known coping strategy, there's also nothing wrong with getting upset for the right reasons—so go ahead and call bullshit when people dismiss problems that you know matter. And if you get shit for it, you have a quip ready to go! (Emergency preparedness: geeks have it.)

The zombie film *28 Days Later* (2002) gains extra geek points on top of its fundamental awesomeness for featuring Christopher Eccleston, who three years later would star in the triumphantly relaunched *Doctor Who*.

"THERE'S ONLY ONE RULE THAT I KNOW OF, BABIES—GOD DAMN IT, YOU'VE GOT TO BE KIND."

—KURT VONNEGUT

MAN SHOWS INHUMANITY TO MAN. It's axiomatic of our existence. It's the story of our past, it's the story of our present, and it will very likely be the story of our future. Indeed, it's a lesson that's reinforced every day, whether we're watching the evening news or the latest entry in the *Saw* series. However, our history is also littered with awe-inspiring examples of men and women showing incredible compassion in the face of unspeakable evil and insurmountable odds. Every story of tragedy has a story of heroism to go with it. For every Holocaust, there's a Schindler. Vonnegut's words, spoken so simply, are nonetheless laced with considerable profundity. The imperative to be kind to one another may seem obvious, but part of being human means that both the right thing and the wrong thing are forever at arm's reach. It doesn't hurt to be reminded every now and then which one we should choose.

Vonnegut's novel *God Bless You, Mr. Rosewater* (1965) is less overtly geeky than the likes of *Slaughterhouse-Five*, *Breakfast of Champions*, and *The Sirens of Titan*, but aside from being just as great, it does tie into the rest with several cameo appearances.

"SO SAY WE ALL."

—BILL ADAMA, *BATTLESTAR GALACTICA*

W E HOLD THESE TRUTHS TO BE SELF-EVI-DENT, that all men are created equal." These words, from the American Declaration of Independence, represent an admirable ideal that America took rather a long time to live up to. Fortunately, for most of us, these words eventually came to represent more than landowning white men. Bill Adama was *Battlestar Galactica*'s Thomas Jefferson, and *BSG* was, at its heart, the story of a nation's formation. Like Jefferson, Adama was a man of great contradiction: a supposed visionary who lied about the vision (the mythical existence of Earth); an authoritarian who turned out to be more democratic in principle than the democratically elected president he served; a confessed bigot who allied with, and even came to love, the objects of his hatred. The resolution of the story ultimately came down to the question of whether disparate groups—military and civilian, human and Cylon, even humanoid Cylon and robotic Centurion—could learn first to recognize one another as people, then to live together. Eventually, they did. Thus Adama's words, which first applied only to members of the military under his own command, came to embrace all of humankind, and humanity's children as well.

Bill Adama was actor Edward James Olmos's second chance to explore dangerous, artificially created humanoids; the first was *Blade Runner* (1982).

"MISTER MCGEE, DON'T MAKE ME ANGRY. YOU WOULDN'T LIKE ME WHEN I'M ANGRY."

—DAVID BRUCE BANNER, *THE INCREDIBLE HULK*

"PARDON ME FOR BREATHING, WHICH I NEVER DO ANYWAY SO I DON'T KNOW WHY I BOTHER TO SAY IT, OH GOD I'M SO DEPRESSED."

—MARVIN, *THE HITCHHIKER'S GUIDE TO THE GALAXY*

GEEKS notoriously have trouble expressing emotion. That's why Spock became our great iconic hero: he, too, dealt with the confusing struggle of his feelings by burying them beneath a near-fanatic devotion to intellectual calculations and philosophical ponderings. And the fact that he came from a whole race of people like that gave us hope that maybe we weren't as pathetic and alone in our fear of emotional vulnerability as we thought we were. Doctor Banner's famous line from the opening credits of *The Incredible Hulk* perfectly encapsulates this inner turmoil, saying what all repressed geeks want to say whenever people try to get under their skin: *i have made staying in control of myself a firm rule of life, and I fear that out-of-control me will be something terrible to behold, so why don't you just not make me go there*. The flip side of this phenomenon is the cynical geek who, rather than burying all emotion beneath reason, buries any explicit acknowledgment of idealism or romance beneath a protective shield of pessimism: because this geek "knows everything already," you see, there's nothing to get excited about. That, in a nutshell is Marvin, the super-genius robot in Douglas Adams's *Hitchhiker's Guide to the Galaxy*. He wants you to know just how depressing the whole world is, because it can't possibly present anything new or interesting to him. But it *could*, if he'd let it—just as Spock, Banner, and all the other nerds out there could figure out how to enjoy being a little bit out of control once in a while if they'd just stop envisioning their primitive impulses as a terrifying, rampaging monster.

"VIOLENCE IS THE LAST REFUGE OF THE INCOMPETENT."

—HARI SELDON, *FOUNDATION*

INTELLECTUALS BELIEVE in the power of the mind. If you have to resort to force, you've already failed. This is a noble and admirable belief, and muchly if not entirely true—but there's something more interesting at work here. We all tend to believe that our own best characteristic represents "true strength," just as we're all instinctively inclined to believe that a person who agrees with us a lot must be a very smart person indeed. Therefore, as intellectuals, we find physical force abhorrent in the extreme, in part because it just plain is, but also in part because our self-esteem *depends* on believing that mental power is more important. At the same time, it's worth noting that, in *Foundation*, überbrainiac author Isaac Asimov deliberately crafted a story where the careful application of nonviolent smarts was able to triumph over every single violent threat that his protagonist nation faced—which rather flies in the face of all human history. Sometimes, violent people make targets of the most peace-loving among us, and the choice to fight for survival doesn't necessarily mean we're incompetent; Asimov, a WWII–era Jew, never argued in real life that military force shouldn't be employed to stop the Nazis. The key to fully embracing this quote lies in the particular diction: not *tool*, but *refuge*. Violence may be sadly necessary at times, but anyone who finds solace in its application is a poor human, indeed.

"TRY NOT. DO. OR DO NOT. THERE IS NO TRY."

—YODA, *THE EMPIRE STRIKES BACK*

YODA OFFERED LUKE SKYWALKER THIS WISDOM in reference to extricating a crashed X-Wing Fighter from the swamp on Dagobah, but he might as well have been talking to Thomas Edison as the first inklings of incandescent light germinated in his mind. He might as well have been talking to Michael Jordan as he laced up before his first college game. He might as well have been talking to you before going in for that big promotion. Far too often, our fear of running headlong into our own limitations contents us with merely trying to accomplish our goals. That way the bar is adjusted downward to mean that, hey, even if we didn't succeed, we didn't really fail either. And though there are times, sure, when the effort we invest in a task can be its own reward, let's be honest with ourselves: there are other times when effort can be measured only against its completion. So don't look for reasons why a thing can't be done. Just go ahead and make it happen.

Nike is not as wise as Yoda but does make very effective commercials.

"RAYMOND SHAW IS THE KINDEST, BRAVEST, WARMEST, MOST WONDERFUL HUMAN BEING I'VE EVER KNOWN IN MY LIFE."

—BENNETT MARCO, *THE MANCHURIAN CANDIDATE*

"YOU TAKE THE BLUE PILL, AND THE STORY ENDS; YOU WAKE IN YOUR BED AND YOU BELIEVE WHATEVER YOU WANT TO BELIEVE. YOU TAKE THE RED PILL, AND YOU STAY IN WONDERLAND AND I SHOW YOU HOW DEEP THE RABBIT HOLE GOES."

—MORPHEUS, *THE MATRIX*

W E'RE BEING BRAINWASHED CONSTANTLY. Not necessarily by communists (like in 1962's *The Manchurian Candidate*) or a transnational corporation (like in the 2004 remake), but by talking points. After all, what is Ben Marco's rote description of his wartime compatriot, implanted in his mind by a sinister Sino-Russian cabal and repeated ad nauseam, but an expression of the talking points that saturate the mediasphere daily. They ensure that debate has already been framed and decided for us long in advance of our forming an actual opinion. They let us know what to think without having to do the hard work of getting there on our own. Whether we're talking about Raymond Shaw or WMD or death panels, the inherent danger of talking points is that they become so ingrained through sheer force of repetition that we're rendered incapable of seeing the reality that may be lurking just underneath. Luckily, Bennett Marco broke through his conditioning in time to give his story a semblance of a happy ending. So did Neo, who needed the symbolism of Morpheus's red pill more than he needed the pill itself. As Confucius said, the journey of a thousand miles begins with a single step. More precisely, it begins by choosing to *take* that step—even when the consequences of that choice are as yet unknown.

"I'M THE BEST THERE IS AT WHAT I DO. BUT WHAT I DO ISN'T VERY NICE."

—WOLVERINE

WRITER CHRIS CLAREMONT committed these two sentences to the page in 1982, and in doing so cemented Wolverine's place as a geek icon long before Hugh Jackman turned him into a movie idol. Although this epigraph refers to the character's lethal skill with his knuckle-knives, it could just as easily be applied to Han Solo shooting Greedo (first!), Dirty Harry roughing up Scorpio, or John Bender mouthing off to Principal Vernon. It's why we love our antiheroes: they do what we wish we could do and say what we wish we could say. In fiction, if not in life, antiheroes offer a release for the frustration we feel from the bonds of polite society, and we tacitly accept that though they may not conform to our notions of civil justice or (in the case of Bender) polite discourse, their personal codes are no less "pure." What Wolverine does is indeed not very nice—and yet there's an important addendum implicit in the above: "But it needs to be done."

Exercise in geekery: how many multisyllabic rhymes for "Wolverine" can you find? Extra credit for a complete sonnet.

"THERE CAN BE ONLY ONE."

—HIGHLANDER

I N THE DAYS WHEN VIDEO GAMES weren't much more than a bunch of squares shooting at other squares, *Highlander* vicariously offered us the ultimate concept in live-action roleplaying. The movie and TV series characters—most of them too shallow to be anything but archetypes or caricatures—satisfied a visceral urge in all of us, an unfulfilled yearning for the romanticized rugged individualism of earlier days. Thus these rampantly macho, stubbornly primitive warriors never sought to band together or forge their own society, nor did they impact society in any of the thousand ways that the presence of a separate subspecies of humanity *should have* affected the world, realistically speaking. No, they stuck to swords even into the age of Glocks and persisted in honoring their frankly nonsensical rules—e.g., no killing on holy ground—simply because to do otherwise would break character. In the end, it didn't have to make sense and wouldn't have been half as much fun if it had. Who *doesn't* secretly yearn to be able to swing a real sword, whether during a combat reenactment at the Society for Creative Anachronism or just during a bad day at work?

A friend of a friend of ours reportedly liked to utter another *Highlander* quote midcoitus: "What you feel is the quickening." This is geekery at its creepiest. Don't do it.

"TAKE YOUR STINKING PAWS OFF ME, YOU DAMN DIRTY APE."

—TAYLOR, *PLANET OF THE APES*

IMAGINE FOR A MOMENT that you're Colonel George Taylor. You've woken from the two-thousand-year nap of a one-way space trip—only to find that, of all the planets in the universe where you could possibly have landed, you *happen* to be on the one where talking, intelligent apes like to hunt human beings like you for sport. But it doesn't stop there. In rapid succession you're shot in the throat, caged, beaten, and burned. You're forced to mate in front of an audience like an animal and threatened with emasculation. You see your fellow astronaut stuffed and mounted in a museum; you're whipped, dragged by horses, and pelted with fruit. Now, in the final indignity, you're captured in a net and are being jeered and clawed at by a gathered crowd of simians. Let's face it. It's been a *bad* couple of weeks. After all that, what would *you* say? Yep. Standing up for yourself feels good, doesn't it?

"A STRANGE GAME. THE ONLY WINNING MOVE IS NOT TO PLAY."

—JOSHUA, *WAR GAMES*

THERE IS A WORD, a concept, in Zen Buddhism that doesn't quite translate perfectly into the English language: *mu*. Mu is the response given by a Zen monk to a question that cannot be meaningfully answered. It suggests that the question's premises are not real, that there is a state of emptiness that lies beyond yes and no, that the asker should unask the question—indeed, that anyone who would ask such a question in the first place might do well to question his entire perspective on life. Though the word was never uttered in 1984's seminal teen-computer hacker-political thriller *War Games*, the idea lies at the heart of the conflict that fuels the movie: a new Pentagon supercomputer that controls the nation's nuclear launch codes is caught up in a relentless war-game simulation trying to answer the question, "How can the United States win a nuclear war?" *We* all know it's a flawed question—the whole point of the Cold War arms-race theory of "mutual assured destruction" was that, in a world of opposing superpowers, the sheer volume of weaponry is meant to deter the use of any nukes at all. But back in 1984, when computer networks were new and exotic, it seemed entirely reasonable to worry that an artificial intelligence might start firing missiles based on the inhuman outcome of an algorithm. Of course, the computer finally found its Zen. What about you—can *you* tell when it's time to remove yourself from a defective game board?

The first several years of Matthew Broderick's career were all about nuclear paranoia: first *War Games*, then *Project X* (1987), wherein laboratory chimps suffered inhumane radiation testing.

V.
BILLIONS
AND BILLIONS

(WISDOM ABOUT THE UNIVERSE)

"ALL THESE WORLDS ARE YOURS, EXCEPT EUROPA. ATTEMPT NO LANDING THERE."

—ARTHUR C. CLARKE, *2010: ODYSSEY TWO*

"A STARSHIP CAPTAIN'S MOST SOLEMN OATH IS THAT HE WILL GIVE HIS LIFE, EVEN HIS ENTIRE CREW, RATHER THAN VIOLATE THE PRIME DIRECTIVE."

—JAMES T. KIRK, *STAR TREK*, "THE OMEGA GLORY"

THE EARTH WON'T ALWAYS BE the only place where humankind rests its collective head. Assuming we don't destroy ourselves first, we'll one day find that our grasp extends upward and outward, to places about which only the geek has daydreamed. Considering how well we've managed this blue orb in our 5,000 years or so of recorded history, Arthur C. Clarke's warning (delivered through the entities that control his mysterious monoliths) about not treading on places that may contain life appears well founded. See, Europa is a special place. No other body in our solar system has a better chance of containing life than that ice-covered moon of Jupiter. Through wit, intelligence, and innovation we've earned the right to tread on other celestial bodies . . . but have we earned the right to interfere with life not of this Earth? With life only just beginning its own journey down the evolutionary path? Given history, it's hard to answer in the affirmative. Gene Roddenberry took this same concept and extended

it far beyond Europa to cover the entire galaxy; the Prime Directive of *Star Trek* is that Starfleet officers must not interfere with the natural development of less technologically advanced alien species. And though Captain Kirk did somersaults around that directive as often as he followed it, his success at doing so seems to be the exception that proves the rule.

Europa is the sixth moon of Jupiter. Galileo discovered it (see next page). It has an oxygen atmosphere. And NASA and the European Space Agency hope to send a joint unmanned mission there circa 2020 to get a closer look.

"THE BOOK OF NATURE IS WRITTEN IN THE LANGUAGE OF MATHEMATICS."

—GALILEO, *THE ASSAYER*

NEVER MIND THAT THERE ARE geometric shapes in mineral crystals, fractals in vegetables, chaotic equations in weather patterns. We get all that. Galileo was onto something even deeper: the idea that nature itself could be read and encapsulated as a book or any other comprehensible source of information, rather than simply elided as beyond human understanding. This, of course, is what got him into trouble with the Catholic Church, which positioned itself as the defending champion in the age-old contest of the spirit versus reason—or, more precisely, politics versus facts. There is that indefinable something in the geek nature that rejects such distinctions as a false dichotomy, insisting that reason informs the spirit and politics should be rooted in facts. Sadly, society just isn't that rational, as Galileo discovered after his prosecution and lifelong house arrest by the Inquisition. Yet it was Galileo's geekish insistence that he was right, and his willingness to die to prove his rightness—and, mind you, the fact that he *was* right, which matters—that helped make the world a safer place for proper geekery. For this, as much as for his scientific accomplishments, he should be celebrated.

Galileo's scientific manifesto *The Assayer* (1623) was written primarily as a slam against Jesuit astronomer Orazio Grassi. In doing so, Galileo pissed off a number of Jesuit scholars who might otherwise have stood with him during his Church troubles. Trolling: risky since 1623.

"TO A NEW WORLD OF GODS AND MONSTERS!"

—DR. PRETORIUS, *BRIDE OF FRANKENSTEIN*

I N TOASTING HIS IMPENDING CREATION of a mate for Dr. Henry Frankenstein's misbegotten monster, Septimus Pretorius betrays a barely concealed glee at his impending traversal of the boundaries between the laws of man and the laws of god. In that glee, he anticipated the new world that would arrive just a few years hence, birthed in the crucible of science, where man's ability to harness the power of the atom would elevate him to godhood, and the subsequent unleashing of that power would debase him to monsterhood. The simple lesson of Pretorius, and Frankenstein before him, is the need for man to balance his unending thirst for knowledge—the "what" and the "how" and even the "why"—with the consequences of that knowledge—the "what next." Simple enough to make the enduring appeal of Mary Shelley's immortal story (and its most famous movie sequel) easy to understand but, unfortunately for us, not so simple that we've taken that lesson to heart.

Bride of Frankenstein (1939), for all its good points, might well have faded into obscurity as an unnecessary follow-up to a self-contained classic if not for the incredible power of the pure visual. The Bride's iconic two-tone tower of a hairdo ensured that she could never be forgotten.

"THE CLAW IS OUR MASTER.
THE CLAW DECIDES WHO WILL GO
AND WHO WILL STAY."

—VENDING MACHINE ALIEN DOLLS, *TOY STORY*

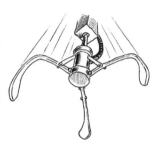

EVERY ONCE IN A WHILE, you meet someone who just doesn't seem to know what the deal is. They sit next to you in the movie theater and guess the plot loudly and incorrectly; they laugh at the joke three lines before the punch line. Usually the culprit is a fundamental glitch in perspective. The dolls stuck in *Toy Story*'s claw-grab machine don't understand the scope of the world, because they literally have no outside perspective. And yet, even as we smile at them, the alien dolls are a source of pity; their myopia is a result of circumstances beyond their control; they're victims of their own little plushie predestination. It can be tempting to dismiss those whose views differ fundamentally from ours in ways that make us socially uncomfortable. However, it's worth remembering that everyone is a victim of circumstance in one way or another, and that when one is under the regime of the Claw, it can be hard to get a good look at the larger universe.

The Claw is not to be confused with *Inspector Gadget*'s villainous Dr. Klaw, voiced by animation legend Frank Walker, who is also Megatron, Baby Kermit, and Fred from *Scooby-Doo*.

"NOW I AM BECOME DEATH, THE DESTROYER OF WORLDS."

—J. ROBERT OPPENHEIMER, QUOTING/TRANSLATING THE *BHAGAVAD GITA*

IMAGINE, IF YOU WILL, being central to the development of a power that could snuff out tens of thousands of lives in an instant. Not in the geeky world-domination-daydream kind of way, but in a real, tangible, fire-and-horror-and-corpses kind of way. When Oppenheimer watched the Trinity atomic bomb test on July 16, 1945, he knew he had helped usher in something so frightening as to be almost godlike in its power—hence his quoting Vishnu, supreme god of the Vaishnavism tradition of Hinduism. So, too, had America taken an enormous power upon its shoulders, a responsibility so vast it's unlikely many of us could truly grasp it. Science-fiction writers had been warning of atomic holocaust for some years already, but when their speculation was made reality, the world changed. We stood then on the third stone from the sun, animals still, but now animals with the ability to crack the very stone upon which we stood. Oppenheimer did not need Stan Lee to tell him what wielding such great power meant.

This has become one of the two most clichéd quotations in science fiction. The other is Percy Shelley's "Look upon my works, ye Mighty, and despair."

"THE COSMOS IS ALSO WITHIN US. WE'RE MADE OF STAR STUFF."

—CARL SAGAN

"WE ARE ALL CONNECTED: TO EACH OTHER, BIOLOGICALLY; TO THE EARTH, CHEMICALLY; TO THE REST OF THE UNIVERSE, ATOMICALLY."

—NEIL DEGRASSE TYSON

FAMOUSLY AGNOSTIC, Carl Sagan carried us with him on his search for God. That search extended to the edges of the universe, and on an episodic basis Sagan reported back to us with his results: that we were insignificant, yet magnificent. That human life, and Earth itself, formed a part of the cycle of stellar birth and death. In a way, Sagan almost single-handedly fought off the modern encroachment of creationism, intelligent design, and other religious efforts to downplay science, by offering a competing and equally powerful spiritualism—the conscious awareness of our place in the physical universe. He made us *feel* his excitement and humility at astronomical discoveries; using the latest technologies, he *showed* us the miracles taking place at any given moment, at the limit of our telescopic vision. For any number of geeks and non-geeks, Sagan was the only priest whose catechisms made sense, and his temple—the vault of the heavens itself—became the only church worthy of their worship.

Sagan's iconic catchphrase "billions and billions"—of stars, that is—is another one of those linguistic formulations that fans distilled from several almost-but-not-quite things their hero actually said. Sagan eventually picked up on it and made it so.

"IT'S A NOBLE GOAL THAT SCIENCE SHOULD BE APOLITICAL, ACULTURAL, AND ASOCIAL, BUT IT CAN'T BE, BECAUSE IT'S DONE BY PEOPLE WHO ARE ALL THOSE THINGS."

—MAE JEMISON

"HE WHO BREAKS A THING TO FIND OUT WHAT IT IS, HAS LEFT THE PATH OF WISDOM."

—GANDALF, *THE LORD OF THE RINGS*

THE EXISTENCE OF GEEKDOM is proof that science can never be just science. Geeks are science's *fans*. We love it, celebrate it, grok and cherish it, and are willing to defend it to the death—occasionally with a fervor bordering on zealotry. But this is necessary, as the fans of science have a collective nemesis: the anti-intellectualism so pervasive in much of American society. Given the influence that this anti-intellectualism exerts over education, religion, politics, the media, and more, it's a good thing so many of us are in science's corner. Science could use a friend or two.

At the same time, it's important to pay attention to who, exactly, is befriending it.

In the early 1940s, using victims from their concentration camps, the Nazis began a series of experiments on humans that even today chills the blood. Body parts such as bone and muscle were removed without anesthesia. In chronicling the effects of freezing on the human body, some victims were forced to endure agonizing hours inside tanks of ice water. Thousands of victims were poisoned, gassed, or burned using phosphorous material from incendiary bombs. Those who were not left mutilated and disabled—and many who were—were then murdered so that Nazi scientists could study the experiments' impact on their bodies postmortem. Few dispute the unspeakably barbaric, inhumane nature of these experiments, but as a fait accompli, they nonetheless presented humanity with a dilemma: whether it's ethical to use the data derived from them.

So consider Gandalf's distinction: there is knowledge and there is wisdom. They are in no way mutually exclusive; nor are they the same. Science brings us one; it can bring us the other. If we are attentive.

THERE ARE REASONS TO FEAR SCIENCE. For every valuable advance it gives us—extending and improving human life, providing sufficient food for billions of people, generating energy from wind and water—it has its ugly moments, too. The Tuskeegee syphilis experiments, replicated in Guatemala. Early nuclear weapons testing, which irradiated locations like Bikini Atoll and afflicted the inhabitants with death, miscarriages, and deformities. Early pseudosciences like phrenology and eugenics, which did more to advance bigotry than understanding. Science is a tool like any other, and it can be subverted to serve even the basest human aims. The Large Hadron Collider, however, was not one of these perversions. Much of the concern over its activation was the result of media sensationalism and wild speculation by amateurs: *could it create a black hole that will consume the entire planet???* Well . . . no. And though many knowledgeable geeks found it hilarious, the public's reaction was both predictable and preventable, given science's history of keeping horrors on the down-low. If scientists want to avoid future hysterias, they're going to need to find better ways of talking with the rest of us. Easier said than done, we know. But come on, scientists, you're supposed to be smart.

The awesome thing about this website is that it contains only one word. The even awesomer thing is that it would do its job just as well with no words at all.

"REALITY IS MERELY AN ILLUSION, ALBEIT A VERY PERSISTENT ONE."

—ALBERT EINSTEIN

T O THINK OUTSIDE THE BOX, one must first forget there *is* a box. Ours is a reality infinitely more complex and downright strange than we realize. Given how persistent such bothers can be, it's easy to forget that our world is not in fact made of 40-hour work weeks, bills to be paid, and lawns to be mowed—though, sure, those things are real—but rather is constructed of miraculously tiny neutrinos passing through our bodies by the billion, galactic clusters on a scale more immense than the human mind can fathom, particles that can exist in two places at once, and seemingly magical universal laws that dictate the movements of invisible atoms and distant stars. The stuff of our world, both on the large scale and the small, comes together to create a cosmos that looks mundane to our unimaginative eyes yet operates as a practically incomprehensibly complex interlocking system of functions. So is our experiential everyday reality the true one, or is the invisible reality of micro- and macroscopic models the true one? The answer, of course, is *yes*.

It's an urban legend that Einstein had a wardrobe filled with multiple copies of the same suit so he wouldn't have to waste mental energy figuring out what to wear. But it's a popular enough legend that Marvel Comics writers decided Bruce Banner was emulating Einstein, and used that as justification for why the Hulk was so frequently depicted wearing purple pants.

"THERE IS NO SPOON."

—THE MATRIX

O F ALL THE PEOPLE who tried desperately to make Neo understand a damn thing that was happening in *The Matrix*, it was the spoon-bending child who got closest, by pointing out that the world is malleable because the world isn't real. A little disheartening to a man invested in the realities of his known world, to be sure, but this little home truth came to Neo at a key moment. We've all been the recipient of one of these; at a time when we're confused and unsure, someone tells us some-

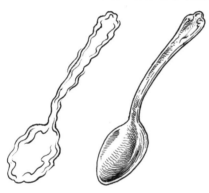

thing that seems not only contradictory to what we want to hear, but unhelpful to the point of non sequitur. On the other hand, just because we don't want to hear something doesn't mean it's not good advice. If even Neo was able to grasp that—*whoa*—surely we can, too.

Inexplicably bending spoons became a visual signifier of supposedly paranormal phenomena during the 1970s boom in ESP studies, thanks to self-declared psychokinetic performer Uri Geller.

"SPOON!"

—THE TICK, *THE TICK*

WELL. APPARENTLY, YOU CAN have it both ways. That, or this is just an example of one innocuous object being given two very different contexts. (Too bad—a Tick-on-Neo fight already feels like one of the most amazing missed opportunities in cinema history.) Strangely, this battle cry has more in common with the quasi-Zen aphorism than would seem immediately apparent: the world in which the Tick lives is mostly imaginary, too—an impenetrable, self-congratulatory headspace. In the real world, the Tick is less likely to be a costumed crime-fighter than he is to be your office's project manager, unable to understand what's really going on but enthusiastic about it nonetheless (and more than happy to take the credit for anything that goes well). Since there's little you can do to get rid of him, maybe seeing him as a "Spoon!"-shouting butt of the joke will at least keep you from boiling over and stapling his hand.

"WE DO NOT FOLLOW MAPS TO BURIED TREASURE, AND X NEVER, EVER MARKS THE SPOT."

—INDIANA JONES, *INDIANA JONES AND THE LAST CRUSADE*

AUTHOR ANDRÉ GIDE ONCE SAID: "Man cannot discover new oceans unless he has the courage to lose sight of the shore." Steven Spielberg may have had Indiana Jones offer the above refutation of archaeological stereotypes to the audience with a wink and a nudge, but it nonetheless conveys the truth that worthwhile discoveries can come about in unexpected ways. Sometimes it's just a matter of looking up from our maps long enough to see them. Certainly that is something the good Dr. Jones embodied in a lifetime of daring adventures that he rarely sought but that always managed to find him. Whether he was tracking down Moses's box, Jesus's cup, or a space alien's skull, it was always the journey itself that proved far more important than the artifact—both for Indy and for the audience. And that's usually the way it works. Setting out with specific goals and specific ends in mind is great—except when that single-minded focus keeps us from finding real treasure buried just a few degrees off center.

An exercise for the reader: who would win in a scavenger hunt, 20th-century archaeologist Indiana Jones or 51st-century archaeologist River Song?

"IT'S A COOKBOOK!"

—PAT, *THE TWILIGHT ZONE*, "TO SERVE MAN"

W E HAVE A RATHER WISHY-WASHY relationship with our imaginary alien races, don't we? For every serene, benevolent alien species appearing in our skies and offering us something we need—usually the wisdom to avoid nuclear war or environmental catastrophe, or the tools to fight off some other cosmic danger—there are two more that just show up and start shooting or, just as frequently, hide their sinister intentions behind smiles. The disguised reptilioids of *V*; the artificial intelligences of *The Matrix*; and, of course, the hungry Kanamits of "To Serve Man." There's no mystery behind the yin and yang of these fictional advanced races: they are us. Look back through Earth's history and we find that many are the "primitive" people who met an "advanced" society of fellow humans, greeted them in trust, and were betrayed with a shit-eating grin. One can almost hear Geronimo or Sitting Bull: "This is no land treaty. It's a cookbook!" So: a planet full of nonhumans smart enough to trap us and use us as they will? Simple projection of our own guilty anxiety.

Legendary science-fiction editor George Scithers, under the pseudonym "Karl Würf," got permission from *Twilight Zone* episode writer Damon Knight to write and publish a "cookbook for people," titled *To Serve Man*, in 1976.

"WHEN THERE'S NO MORE ROOM IN HELL, THE DEAD WILL WALK THE EARTH."

—PETER, *DAWN OF THE DEAD*

A CTOR KEN FOREE ISSUES this signature utterance in George Romero's 1974 *Dawn of the Dead* as well as the 2004 update by Zack Snyder, and both times it illuminates the fundamental truth that we seek divine rationalizations for those problems we can't understand. So it's not too surprising that this bromide offers the motley survivors of *Dawn* solace from the zombie plague in which they find themselves. Beyond merely explaining the unexplainable, the implication is that those stricken with the undead munchies are paying the price for lives of sin and transgression. After all, they had to be going to hell for a reason. At once, we're absolved of any blame and responsibility. If that sounds insensitive or even incomprehensible, tell it to those who said Hurricane Katrina was God's punishment for homosexuality, or that the Haitian people had it coming when the Earth swallowed up half their country. Blaming victims for their tragedies is the most predictable occurrence in the world; we can count on it with reliable regularity even when it's dead wrong.

It's fascinating that the evolution of zombie tales has followed the same path as the evolution of rational thinking: early myths present the shambling undead horrors as supernatural, whereas the most recent stories find scientific explanations for the reanimation of dead tissue.

"THE FORCE WILL BE WITH YOU. ALWAYS."

—OBI-WAN KENOBI, *STAR WARS*

W E'RE BORN ALONE, WE DIE ALONE, and we spend our entire lives trying not to be alone. However that need manifests, whether physical companionship or comfort from the divine, it's something Ben Kenobi spoke to when issuing his valediction to Luke Skywalker, and it's something George Lucas understood when creating *Star Wars* in 1977. With the Force, the mystical energy field that serves as the spiritual underpinning of his entire fictional universe—quoth Kenobi, "It surrounds us and penetrates us. It binds the galaxy together"— Lucas created a catch-all upon which audiences religious and irreligious could hang their respective beliefs without shouldering anyone out. Of course, that was before *The Phantom Menace* tried to tell us the Force was parasites in our bloodstream, making it the intergalactic equivalent of ringworm. We didn't take that bit of exposition very happily, did we? No—the Force withstands any such attempts to ground it explicitly in science, because it transcends reason and speaks to something more fundamental about human nature: our desire to hold onto something bigger than ourselves.

In the same breath that *The Phantom Menace* (1999) gave us a gimmick to scientify up the Force, Lucas revealed that these very "midi-chlorians" meant Darth Vader was a virgin birth, just like the story of Jesus. Has there ever been a ballsier attempt to have something both ways?

> **"COME ALGEBRA, ANATOMY, ASTRONOMY, BIOLOGY, CHEMISTRY, GEOLOGY, GEOMETRY, MATHEMATICS, METEOROLOGY, MINERALOGY, OCEANOGRAPHY, PALEONTOLOGY, PHYSICS, PSYCHOLOGY, SOCIOLOGY, TRIGONOMETRY, AND ZOOLOGY!"**
>
> —PETER DICKENSON, *THE FLIGHT OF DRAGONS*

NOTHING KILLS THE (LITERAL) MAGIC of childhood faster than watching an evil wizard ground into dust by the furious recitation of scientific disciplines. This diatribe, uttered by New Yorker inventor-hero Peter, is an act of last resort that both saves his magical allies and locks him out of their world forever. There's no denying it was a clever way to rid oneself of an insurmountable sorcerer, but it sent a clear message about the Pauli Exclusion Principle of fantasy: *science and magic can't occupy the same space at the same time*. Admittedly, the acceptance and understanding of a scientific universe is a critical part of growing up—try as you might, you ain't gonna summon that salt shaker to you with the Force—but many geeks never stop pining for the days when every broomstick was a lightsaber. Nor should they. Myth, too, holds power in the world. The trick is to remember the element that magic and science have in common: imagination. It's both a world-builder and a problem-solver and, when properly applied, can lead you to triumph over just about anything.

The beloved 1982 cult classic animated film *The Flight of Dragons* was based in part on a children's book of the same name by namesake author Peter Dickinson [sic] as well as on the even more classic adult fantasy novel *The Dragon and the George* by Gordon R. Dickson.

"WHAT POWER WOULD HELL HAVE IF THOSE IMPRISONED HERE WOULD NOT BE ABLE TO DREAM OF HEAVEN?"

—DREAM, AKA MORPHEUS, NEIL GAIMAN'S *SANDMAN*

OUR WOES HAVE LITTLE POWER over us without the knowledge of greener grass on the other side of the hill. The search for a perfect, trouble-free world is an inherent part of human nature—a holdover from our days in the African savanna, dreaming of an oasis over the next rise even as we dreaded the den of predators in the next grove. Heaven and Hell are merely those ideas taken to a logical extreme. Neil Gaiman's king of the dream realm knows this. He recognizes that the darkest things we can imagine are meaningless without something to contrast them against. One need not have faith in a higher power to see this in action: what misery does poverty offer without the knowledge of wealth? How repulsive is ugliness if it cannot be set next to beauty? In some respects, ignorance truly is bliss. Yet look again. If humankind cannot see the possibility of a better world, how can we ever strive to create a better world? Our figurative heavens give power to our hells, but so, too, do our hells inspire us to reach for our heavens.

Hell in *Sandman* is ruled by a Lucifer whose appearance is clearly modeled on David Bowie, thus once again proving our theory that *geeks love David Bowie*.

"KLAATU BARADA NIKTO!"
—HELEN BENSON, *THE DAY THE EARTH STOOD STILL*

"LIVE LONG AND PROSPER."
—SPOCK, *STAR TREK*

"HASTA LA VISTA, BABY."
—T-800, *TERMINATOR 2*

WE GEEKS LOVE OUR CATCHPHRASES. Whether brandishing split-fingered salutes and encouraging one another to "Live long and prosper" or saying see-ya-later in a mock Teutonic accent, there are certain sci-fi bromides imprinted on the geek collective to such a degree that we divine meanings from them both profound and profane. Of these, one of the most interesting is the collection of alien gibberish "Klaatu barada nikto"—deemed "the most famous phrase ever spoken by an extraterrestrial" by critic Frederick S. Clarke—used by the Christ-like alien Klaatu to stay the alloyed hand of his robotic emissary Gort from fulfilling its mission to end humanity. Think of it as the most important safety word of all time. The specificities of its meaning lie shrouded in mystery (and remained so even when Bruce Campbell dispatched the same phrase—to unfortunate results—in *Army of Darkness*), but its portent is easy to see. It serves as an uncomfortable reminder that our destinies are sometimes shaped, if not outright decided, by forces beyond our choice and even, sometimes, our comprehension. We want to know the answers—but sometimes, we don't get to.

"Klaatu" has also been the name of a minor alien in Star Wars, a minor alien in Marvel Comics, and a Canadian prog-rock band.

"HE CHOSE . . . POORLY."

WOULD-BE HOLY GRAIL HUNTER Walter Donovan thought he could identify the Last Supper cup of Jesus Christ by its glory. He was wrong, and the divine power of the Grail destroyed him. The immediate humor of the guardian Grail Knight's dry response comes from our delight in seeing Donovan get his comeuppance—he'd just shot Indy's father, and man, ain't karma a bitch. But the deeper appeal of the quotation is the truth we find in its sincerity. Anyone who thinks the glory of Christ can be equated to earthly riches, finery, luxury—in short, to any kind of expression of egotism—is engaging in utter folly. The whole point of God incarnating as man is humility, as is pointedly expressed in Matthew 25:45: "I tell you the truth," Jesus says, "whatever you did not do for one of the least among you, you did not do for me." In other words: god may be great, but that greatness is found in its very smallness and humanity.

The Holy Grail is one of very few supernatural artifacts of legend to impact modern pop culture twice over, in both a semiserious story (*Indiana Jones and the Last Crusade*, 1989) and an utterly frivolous one (*Monty Python and the Holy Grail*, 1975).

"THERE ARE MORE THINGS IN HEAVEN AND EARTH, HORATIO, THAN ARE DREAMT OF IN YOUR PHILOSOPHY."

—HAMLET

LIKE HAMLET AND HORATIO, many of us are conditioned to view existence in "real world" terms. We comfort ourselves with the idea that reaching the limits of worldly education will prepare us for everything that life will throw at us. In the geek canon, this immortal selection from Shakespeare's immortal play sits comfortably alongside Socrates' "All I know is that I know nothing" and (believe it not) "May the Force be with you" as acknowledgment that, no matter how much we think our education has prepared us, sometimes we simply reach the limits of understanding. It's a realization that the Bard's Danish prince arrived at rather suddenly—being spurred to vengeance by the spectral image of your dead father does tend to make you question things—but it's a realization that we'll all likely come to at some point in our lives, though probably not by exactly the same means.

Hamlet has been a nexus of geekery in the past decade—not just the London production starring *Doctor Who*'s David Tennant, but the many references found in the instant-classic comic book series *Y: The Last Man*.

WHAT SOME GEEKS CAN DREAM OF, some others will do. As Americans set their sights on the moon in the late 1960s, a boom in science fiction on the page and on the screen created a feedback loop of the thrill of space travel. The moon landing of 1969 was a scene straight out of *2001: A Space Odyssey*, made real by those who had caught the fever of imagination from generations of dreamers. Unfortunately, imagination and funding don't always go hand in hand, and eventually the plug was pulled on the Apollo program. This plaque is bolted to the stairs of the *Apollo 17* landing module, the last manned mission to another world, and is a bittersweet acknowledgment of the end of an era. It's all the more poignant in light of NASA's decision to shut down the space shuttle program. Having traveled no farther than we did in 1972, another era of human exploration is over, and this plaque might be the last ambassador from Earth any alien sphere will see for a while.

A question with no particular answer: what does it say about our cultural values that a hit movie has been made out of a moon-mission disaster (*Apollo 13*), but not out of any of the successful moon voyages?

"WE'RE ON A MISSION FROM GOD."

—ELWOOD BLUES, *THE BLUES BROTHERS*

CONVICTION. Without it, you got nuthin'. And we're not talking about the sort of conviction that Jake Blues had on his police record. When Jake got out of jail, he was a man adrift: what to do, what to *do*? He could easily have ended up wandering through his days alongside brother Elwood, feeling nothing but vague dissatisfaction until he ran afoul of the law again—but then he was inspired. Inspired through such an abrupt and unexpected epiphany that surely it must be *divine* inspiration: he would raise money to save his old Catholic orphanage by getting his old blues band back together and playing to a sold-out crowd. Okay, so it was an unlikely plan, but it gave Jake a reason to live—a reason larger than himself. That's what makes the difference between a life and an epic life: the ability to envision the big picture and commit to it, to resolve to leave a mark on the world that goes beyond the imprint of pure self-gratification. And that's true whether the god fueling your mission is Jake's God, a secular awareness of the larger cosmos, or something else entirely.

"THIS IS AN IMAGINARY STORY. BUT THEN, AREN'T THEY ALL?"

—ALAN MOORE,
SUPERMAN: WHATEVER HAPPENED TO THE MAN OF TOMORROW?

From the 1950s through the 1980s, DC Comics would occasionally publish Superman stories based on offbeat scenarios that weren't part of the ongoing continuity of the regular monthly serial. The editors distinguished these fun hypothetical tales (President Superman! Superman's bratty kid! Superman and Batman as adopted brothers!) by noting on the cover: "An Imaginary Story"—as opposed to the "real" continuing saga of the familiar Superman. Yet this terminology begs the obvious question, which DC finally allowed postmodern comics pioneer Alan Moore to pose in the introduction to *Superman* #423. Yes, indeed, they are *all* imaginary stories—a fact that can get lost sometimes by the devoted fan of any serial set in a long-running, carefully consistent fictional world. DC, its rival Marvel Comics, the *Star Trek* franchise: all these massive narrative constructs created fans who frequently loved cataloging and cross-referencing the details of the world as much as they loved the characters themselves. That's one big reason why geeks often get so upset at the news that their favorite fictional property is going to be "rebooted" for a new audience. But the thing is, that's precisely how a legend grows and endures—by being retold again and again. Would anyone remember Hercules today if the Greek storyteller who first spun his tale insisted on maintaining creative control? If the fifteenth-century balladeer who sang rhymes about Robin Hood had been able to force all those who came after him to refrain from spinning their own variations, would Maid Marian or Richard the Lionheart have ever shown up? As hard as it may be to look at a long-running quasi-epic and admit, "You know, this was awesome, but I'm bored—let's start over and do it differently," there's probably no better way to take a regular old good story and elevate it to the realm of timeless myth.

VI.
IN THE YEAR 2525

(WISDOM ABOUT THE FUTURE)

"END OF LINE."
—CYLON HYBRID, *BATTLESTAR GALACTICA*;
ALSO, MASTER CONTROL PROGRAM, *TRON*

"RESISTANCE IS FUTILE."
—THE BORG, *STAR TREK: THE NEXT GENERATION*

"UPGRADING IS COMPULSORY."
—THE CYBERMEN, *DOCTOR WHO*

T HERE'S SOMETHING EXISTENTIAL about modern culture's fear of "the Singularity," author Vernor Vinge's name for the moment when technology will have advanced so far that it transforms humanity, or perhaps transcends it, in a way we cannot yet anticipate. That hasn't stopped us from envisioning that posthuman future in stories, and usually we figure it'll be pretty terrible for those of us still confined to meat-sack bodies when the time comes. That's because the mechanized consciousness—which we imagine will approach the world with algorithmic fascism, uttering stark declaratives that allow no dissent—is always terrifying, whether it comes in the form of evil software like *Tron*'s Master Control and *Terminator*'s Skynet or flesh-and-blood entities like *Battlestar Galactica*'s Hybrid and *Star Trek*'s Borg, so cyberneticized as to be unrecognizable as human. But why are we so sure future evolution will produce souls lesser than the ones we have now? Humans are always afraid of anything they see as "the Other." But isn't it likely that new intelligences will look upon us "old" earthlings—so biased, change resistant, and irrational that we don't even need to wait for tomorrow's people to enthusiastically slaughter groups of our fellow humans today—and find us much scarier?

When the Borg debuted on *Star Trek* in 1989, *Doctor Who* fans immediately lamented that they were an improved rip-off of *Who*'s Cybermen, first introduced in 1966. Both spacefaring cyborg races would ultimately be pwned by the badassery of the reimagined *Battlestar Galactica*'s Cylons (2005).

"ANY SUFFICIENTLY ADVANCED TECHNOLOGY IS INDISTINGUISHABLE FROM MAGIC."

—CLARKE'S LAW

SOMEDAY, history will look back and name science-fiction author Arthur C. Clarke one of the twentieth century's most visionary thinkers. Never mind that he invented the concept of the modern satellite communication network back in 1945 (and not just in a work of fiction; he formally proposed it in a technical paper). Clarke's Law posits a truth that ought to remind atheists and believers alike to be humble about their philosophies. If you could go back in time and land a helicopter in front of a crowd of ancient Babylonians, they would think you must be a god or a wizard. This teaches us two things: first, the obvious conclusion that things appearing to be magic aren't truly supernatural but are merely based on knowledge unknown to the viewer. And, second, the too-often-neglected corollary that, at any given point in human history (including right now), a vast amount of knowledge *still is* unknown to us. Clarke's Law sums up the point of his classic *2001* in just eight words—for all the miracles science has uncovered and produced, we're still just infants in the perspective of the cosmos. And the idea that "the ultimate truth of existence" can even be *imagined* by the human mind is hilariously preposterous.

Clarke offered up three laws of futuristic prediction in the 1960s and '70s; it was the third that grabbed the popular imagination and was remembered as "Clarke's Law."

"THE SKY ABOVE THE PORT WAS THE COLOR OF TELEVISION, TUNED TO A DEAD CHANNEL."

—WILLIAM GIBSON, *NEUROMANCER*

TECHNOLOGY is not the warm, inviting thing we've been led to believe; so says William Gibson in the opening line of *Neuromancer*. Our world is blanketed in tech—so much so, we don't notice just how amazing it is. Yet despite these remarkable devices that hold us together, that feed us information, that wire us into something much larger than ourselves, the world can be as empty and ugly and barren of genuine humanity as it has ever been. It's a dead channel, flickering, gray, unclear. So Gibson asks: as we march inexorably forward into our world of circuits and wireless, when do we look back to consider what we're leaving behind? In the world of *Neuromancer*, we don't. It's as bleak

and hopeless as the Black Death or the Great Depression. In the end, technology in and of itself changes nothing. The poor are still poor. The streets are still dangerous. And human beings are still human beings. So we've got to ask the follow-up question: how do we make sure that doesn't happen to us?

William Gibson coined the word *cyberspace* and was a key figure in launching the science-fiction subgenre of cyberpunk. We should not, however, blame him for science fiction fans' corollary practice of adding the word "punk" as a suffix to anything else they've subsequently wanted to dub an exciting subgenre.

"ROADS? WHERE WE'RE GOING, WE DON'T NEED ROADS."

—DOC BROWN, *BACK TO THE FUTURE*

HEARING DOC BROWN'S FAMOUS oh-by-the-way line today, twenty-five years after *Back to the Future*'s release, with nary a flying car or floating skateboard in sight, one can be forgiven for thinking screenwriters Bob Zemeckis and Bob Gale may have missed the mark just slightly when positing their far-flung future world of 2015. However, as Doc shuffles Marty McFly into the newly airborne DeLorean time machine, the import of his words can be seen reverberating through the history of human innovation going as far back as the mind can wander, in our ability to consistently rethink reality and expand the boundaries of the possible. To enact the *paradigm shift*. That phrase, popularized by Thomas Kuhn in the 1960s before it morphed into a clichéd business buzzword, may have withered from extreme overuse in the '80s and '90s, but it remains a potent concept that's put into practice every time we venture off the beaten path for a great advancement that changes the world, whether you're talking about the invention of fire or the cellular phone network. Those flux-capacitor moments aren't as rare as they seem, but they're every bit as profound.

In a making-of documentary of *Back to the Future Part II* (1989), filmmaker Bob Zemeckis deadpanned the facetious "fact" that hoverboards were a real invention being kept from American streets by regulatory red tape. A remarkable number of people believed this.

"I'LL CONTROL-ALT-DELETE YOU!"

—WEIRD AL YANKOVIC

EVERY GEEK KNOWS WEIRD AL—usually more comprehensively than said geek's roommates would prefer. If Al's not turning gangsta rap into a computer-nerd anthem, he's recasting the roughest, toughest hits of balls-out hard rock as bouncy polka melodies. And if the universe is just, Al will live to enjoy the serious critical acclaim he deserves as a creative visionary. It's easy to write off songs like "Eat It" and "I Think I'm a Clone Now" as goofy, juvenile parodies. But when you get right down to it, Al was pioneering the musical trend that would eventually lead to DJ Danger Mouse's *Grey Album* and subsequently to the spinoff literary phenomenon of *Pride and Prejudice and Zombies*. By inserting elements of an unexpected genre into the chart-toppers of another, Al arguably became the first superstar of mash-up culture. To those who argue that such Frankensteined hybrids cheapen the original art, we'd point out that they usually serve to make the original sell *better*. And to those who argue that there's no true creative spirit at work in this kind of endeavor, we would invite them to take a serious stab at doing it themselves first, to find out just how wrong they are.

Why is Weird Al shaking a tambourine in the Hanson brothers' 2010 music video "Thinking 'Bout Somethin'"? We presume it's for the same reason that there was a watermelon in the laboratory in *The Adventures of Buckaroo Banzai across the 8th Dimension*.

"WITHIN A FEW YEARS, A SIMPLE AND INEXPENSIVE DEVICE, READILY CARRIED ABOUT, WILL ENABLE ONE TO RECEIVE ON LAND OR SEA THE PRINCIPAL NEWS, TO HEAR A SPEECH, A LECTURE, A SONG OR PLAY OF A MUSICAL INSTRUMENT, CONVEYED FROM ANY OTHER REGION OF THE GLOBE."

—NIKOLA TESLA

"WITH THE OPENING OF THE FIRST POWER PLANT, INCREDULITY WILL GIVE WAY TO WONDERMENT, AND THIS TO INGRATITUDE, AS EVER BEFORE."

—NIKOLA TESLA

THANKS TO (A) THE WORK of a certain '90s-era hair-metal band, and (b) the Internet's existence providing a forum for large masses of geeks to casually research history, popular culture has rediscovered the awesome genius of Nikola Tesla, the Austrian American who was Thomas Edison's more brilliant but less business-savvy rival. Tesla invented the process for alternating-current electricity, made a host of electromagnetic breakthroughs that made possible today's information age, and, oh yeah, by the way, envisioned the technological future more fully than just about anyone else then or ever—not just the scientific and engineering feats humanity would accomplish, but the social ramifications that would follow in short order. Geek culture has begun to idolize Tesla as the Smart Rebel Underdog Who Was Right in conjunction with demonizing Edison as the Ruthless Monopolist Who Crushed Dissent. And, you know, it's true, but it's also worth asking if our instinctive fetishizing of nerd martyrs isn't a bit counterproductive. When visionary geniuses get marginalized, get relegated to second-dog status beneath Machiavellian power players, we shouldn't *only* identify with their unappreciated minds. We should recognize where and how they failed to build the relationships that might have made things come out differently—and resolve to make that human factor a priority in our own endeavors.

In addition to lending his name to that metal band, Tesla has also appeared in Christopher Priest's novel *The Prestige* (adapted to film with a portrayal by David Bowie) and, more recently, been used as the namesake for a cutting-edge electric-car manufacturer.

"VIDEO GAMES ARE BAD FOR YOU? THAT'S WHAT THEY SAID ABOUT ROCK AND ROLL."

—SHIGERU MIYAMOTO, CREATOR OF MARIO AND *THE LEGEND OF ZELDA*

ROCK AND ROLL isn't always good for you. There's a reason it usually gets paired with sex and drugs. There's nothing wrong with the former if it's consensual and safe, or with the latter if it's legal, but we all know that isn't always the case. Video games have their unpleasant baggage, too, though nothing as cool as sex and drugs—more on the order of repetitive-strain injury and MMORPG-fueled poverty. Thing is, video games are for geekdom what rock and roll was to the post–World War II generation: a kind of coming into our own. We have created a unique entertainment form spawned from unexpected and disparate sources—computer science, film, tabletop gaming, art, fiction—whose appeal reaches far beyond the audience that created it. And like rock and roll, video games have their share of detractors who warn feverishly that they bring doom and destruction. We should hope so. Games are always more fun when stuff blows up.

"FANTASY IS THE IMPOSSIBLE MADE PROBABLE. SCIENCE FICTION IS THE IMPROBABLE MADE POSSIBLE."

—ROD SERLING

WE GEEKS SPEND AN INORDINATE amount of time defining and categorizing the ways in which we retreat to worlds that do not exist. Looked at closely, however, Serling's variation on the distinctions usually drawn between fantasy and science fiction serves to underscore not the differences between genres but, rather, the similarities. In doing so, it ties geek culture together as a community of daydreamers. *Intelligent* daydreamers. Ultimately, we all want to see and experience worlds that are not our own. Our motivations may differ: we want escape; we want to envision what the world could be; we want to explore dreams both possible and impossible. Yet our need to daydream remains the same. Whether it stems from dissatisfaction with our lives or from an impulse to see shades of fantastic in an otherwise mundane world, one thing is clear: we geeks all share an important trait. It's not just that we can imagine—everyone can—it's that we're *not afraid to.*

Serling's *Twilight Zone*, like the magazine *Weird Tales* that presaged it, inhabited a funky storytelling space where the tropes of science fiction, fantasy, and horror swirled around and through one another rather than maintaining rigidity. Over the past decade, geekdom has begun to break down those artificial boundaries once again.

"MY NAME IS TALKING TINA, AND I'M GOING TO KILL YOU."

—THE TWILIGHT ZONE, "LIVING DOLL"

I N 1970, ROBOTICIST MASAHIRO MORI coined the term *the Uncanny Valley*—at last putting a name to what generations of children have innately understood: dolls, masks, mirror images, and other not-quite-fully-human faces can be unbelievably creepy. Many theories surround this response, ranging from an evolutionarily reinforced fear of difference to a Freudian fear of death. So it's not entirely surprising that so many geeks see these fears and raise them by murder—or even scale up to genocide in the form of the android or zombie apocalypse. There is an added dimension to this fear for geeks, however: fear of obsolescence. We eagerly anticipate the posthuman Singularity—which science-fiction writer Ken MacLeod dubbed "the Rapture for nerds"—yet secretly fear that, when it comes, we will be left behind. We fantasize that magic or spiritual manifestations might bring our toys to life . . . and then, finding us useless or a hindrance, those new beings might make toys of us. It wasn't Talking Tina's appearance that most of us found terrifying—it was her superiority to her human master, whose death she orchestrated with implacable efficiency. After all, anything that so closely emulates humanity is likely to contain its own measure of the human urge to dominate and destroy.

Also: clowns. We must never forget to beware clowns.

"IT'S A MAGICAL WORLD, HOBBES, OL' BUDDY . . . LET'S GO EXPLORING!"

—THE FINAL *CALVIN AND HOBBES* STRIP

THE WORDS ARE SIMPLE and seemingly uplifting, but also heartbreaking. Bill Watterson's *Calvin and Hobbes* was more than a mere comic strip—it was a window into the sometimes carefree, sometimes cynical, and always absurd mind of a kid who was, if we're to be honest with ourselves, a little slice of you and me. Yet, for all its deliciously ironic sensibility, Watterson ended *Calvin and Hobbes* on a note of beauty and hope and vast possibility. That's because he realized childhood never has to end. Not really; not in any lasting way. We grow up and have families and pay bills, yes. But those of us blessed with the heart of a geek never really let go of the excitement of creation and discovery, do we? Watterson saw what even we geeks too often forget: it's a magical world. Let's see what happens next!

Calvin and Hobbes were named after two very old-school geeks: philosophers John Calvin and Thomas Hobbes.

"PEOPLE ASSUME THAT TIME IS A STRICT PROGRESSION OF CAUSE TO EFFECT—BUT, ACTUALLY, FROM A NONLINEAR, NONSUBJECTIVE VIEWPOINT, IT'S MORE LIKE A BIG BALL OF WIBBLY-WOBBLY, TIMEY-WIMEY . . . STUFF."

—THE DOCTOR, *DOCTOR WHO*

A S THE LAST of the Time Lords—an ancient alien race who watched over the proper flow of time across the cosmos—the Doctor has a unique relationship with the endless stream of instant to instant, day to day, year to year. He sees the odd quirks of chronological existence: for instance, that sometimes it's impossible to predict how a seed planted today will blossom and affect life four years hence, or four hundred. That sometimes you can't even be sure the rules of cause and effect *will* point reliably from past to future. That, basically, our perceptions of reality are fragile and open to debate. While the Doctor is a handy fantasy-myth device for exploring such ideas, once we're open to them it's hard not to see them at work in the real world. Was there a massive conspiracy to kill President Kennedy, or did we do such an intense job of speculating about one that we planted the idea in the mass consciousness and made such a thing more likely in the future even as we retroactively inserted it into the history books? Interestingly, *Doctor Who* first premiered the day after Kennedy's assassination. We're sure there's no connection.

Actually, you can still find the occasional used copy of the 1996 exposé *Doctor Who: Who Killed Kennedy*?

"MY GOD—IT'S FULL OF STARS!"

—DAVID BOWMAN, *2001: A SPACE ODYSSEY* (NOVEL)

ONE DAY—PERHAPS—the human race will progress past this mortal coil, transcending the terrestrial and leaping headlong into the unknown next stage. In fact, it already happened once ten years ago. It's right there in Arthur Clarke's history book *2001* (from which director Stanley Kubrick spun a very successful documentary, which you may have seen). In case you missed it on your local news, astronaut David Bowman discovered that a giant obsidian monolith in orbit of Saturn was in fact a gateway to the next stage of our evolution. At that moment, standing at the precipice of human understanding and overlooking the infinite, Bowman sent one final, garbled message back to Earth that attempted to ground what he was seeing in the spiritual and the scientific. But he found that both modes of thought were simply too small to encompass the totality of what he was experiencing. What would you say in that situation? What would any of us say? Maybe one day—if we're *very* lucky—we'll get to find out.

This quote, which plays such a large role in the sequel to *2001*, is—like the Saturn-vs.-Jupiter question (page 64)—an anomalous difference between the novel and film versions of the science-fiction classic. It appears only in the former.

INDEX

INDEX

INDEX

INDEX

INDEX

INDEX

If you have enjoyed this book
we would love to hear from you.

Please send your comments to:
Hallmark Book Feedback
P.O. Box 419034
Mail Drop 215
Kansas City, MO 64141

Or e-mail us at:
booknotes@hallmark.com

BOBBY DARIN

BOBBY DARIN

A Life

Michael Seth Starr

TAYLOR TRADE PUBLISHING
Dallas • Lanham • Boulder • New York • Toronto • Oxford

First Taylor Trade Publishing edition 2004.

This Taylor Trade Publishing hardcover edition of *Bobby Darin* is an original publication. It is published by arrangement with the author.

Published by Taylor Trade Publishing
An imprint of The Rowman & Littlefield Publishing Group, Inc.
4501 Forbes Boulevard, Suite 200
Lanham, MD 20706

Distributed by NATIONAL BOOK NETWORK

Library of Congress Cataloging-in-Publication Data

Starr, Michael Seth.
    Bobby Darin : a life / Michael Seth Starr.—1st Taylor Trade Pub. ed.
      p.   cm.
    Includes index.
    ISBN 1-58979-121-5 (cloth : alk. paper)
    1. Darin, Bobby.   2. Singers—United States—Biography.   I. Title.
ML420.D155S73   2004
782.42164'092—dc22   2004016594

∞ ™ The paper used in this publication meets the minimum
requirements of American National Standard for Information
Sciences—Permanence of Paper for Printed Library Materials, ANSI/
NISO Z39.48-1992.

Manufactured in the United States of America.

Contents

Acknowledgments

The author would like to thank the following people who agreed to be interviewed for this book:

Joyce Becker Sugarman
Steve Blauner
Pat Boone
John Bravo
Kathe Brenner
Al Caiola
Ernest Chambers
Tony Charmoli
Rudy Clark
Dick Clark
Quitman Dennis
Mike Douglas
Ahmet Ertegun
Geoff Edwards
Connie Francis
Mimi Greenberg
Don Gregory
Anthony Grosso
Jimmy Haskell
Saul Ilson
Shirley Jones
Lois (Brady) Kanter
Joel Kaswan
Roger Kellaway

Terry Kellman
Don Kirshner
Charles Koppelman
Steve Landesberg
Dick Lord
Brent Maher
Tom Mankiewicz
Roger McGuinn
Terry Melcher
Bill Mullikin
Laurie Newmark-Falken
Bob Newhart
Tony Orlando
Stefanie Powers
Walter Raim
Bob Rozario
Neil Sedaka
Stella Stevens
Nino Tempo
Sandra Dee Thomas
Gary Walden
Andy Williams
Bud Yorkin
Ronnie Zito

I would also like to cite several terrific resources I tapped into while researching this book. Jeff Bleiel's book, *That's All: Bobby Darin On Record, Stage & Screen*, which Steve Blauner gave to me, was an invaluable tool in helping me keep track of the chronology of Bobby's career. Jeff also interviewed some of Bobby's friends and co-workers for his own book, published in 1993, and I have cited those instances where I used quotes from Jeff's original interviews.

The official Bobby Darin website, www.bobbydarin.net, which can also be accessed at www.bobbydarin.com, is an incredibly organized repository of anything and everything related to Bobby Darin's life and career. Kudos to the site for a terrific online resource chock-full of interesting links and archival material. The site is an all-around informative and fun tribute to Bobby's life and legacy.

Sandra Dee Thomas, who worked as Bobby's assistant in the 1960s, was kind enough to contribute several valuable photographs, as was Jerry Wexler, who was instrumental in launching Bobby's career at Atco. A huge thank you to both. Ann Limongello at ABC was her usual efficient self, as was Kathy War at the University of Las Vagas Special Collections Library. And kudos to the folks at Bettman/Corbis, Globe Photo, and Getty Images.

I would also like to thank my agent, Tony Seidl, for making this happen, and Michael Emmerich at Taylor for his patience. Patricia McCarthy was a huge help in plowing through hours of interviews and accurately transcribing the information, saving me an enormous amount of time. Paul Ward at TV Land generously opened his bottomless Rolodex and came through in the clutch for me, several times.

And, of course, a huge thank you to Gail and Rachel for their love and support. I couldn't have done this without you.

1

In 1996, John Schriver lay dying in a Florida hospital, his weak heart no match for the diabetes and Parkinson's disease ravaging his body. Forty years earlier, the vigorous young man, an avowed Frank Sinatra fan, had shifted his musical allegiance to the brash newcomer, Bobby Darin. Bobby's "Mack the Knife" was sweeping the nation and it became John's favorite song.

It was also the last sound he would hear on earth.

Back in New Jersey, Gregg Schriver's phone rang. It was his mother, Juanita, calling from the hospital. John was dying and the doctors didn't expect him to survive the night. Gregg stayed on the phone with Juanita, wanting her to describe to him his father's final moments, hoping he was comfortable and wasn't in any pain.

"I brought dad's Walkman and put his earphones on and played his favorite tape," his mother told him. "He turned up the volume and I was able to hear what he was playing. 'Mack the Knife.' A smile came across his face, and his hand that I was holding was tapping to the rhythm of the song. Suddenly the tapping stopped and he was gone.

"But the smile remained."

The smile. The tapping. With Bobby Darin, they seemed to go hand-in-hand. Ahmet Ertegun remembered Bobby on a blustery fall day, thirty years and a lifetime removed from the singer's death. The legendary founder of Atlantic Records sat regally at his desk, impeccably dressed, the walls of his midtown Manhattan office plastered with photos of the greats from the worlds of rock, R&B, and jazz. Ertegun had, in one way or another, influenced them all. But it was Bobby he spoke passionately about, the years melting away as he tapped his big

oak desk—*dum, dum, dum, dum*—to the hypnotic, familiar beat of
"Mack the Knife," remembering the recording session that produced
Bobby's greatest hit.

> That record swings, of course [tap, tap]. Great arrangement [tap,
> tap]. And you know, before he even started singing, when I was writ-
> ing down the arrangement, I said this is a hit record, whatever Bobby
> does. I mean, the arrangement was fabulous. I think the first day it
> sounded like a smash. We did it again just to please everybody, so
> the band could play better. We had two or three takes, and some of
> the live performances that we have down at the Copacabana sound
> just as good.

Ah, yes. The Copa. Bobby opened there in 1960. He was all of
twenty-four, and the New York critics couldn't wait to stick it to the
brash kid who'd already made it a point—in *Life* magazine, no
less—to proclaim he wanted to "become a legend" by his twenty-fifth
birthday. *One more year to go kid*, they wrote sarcastically. Are you serious? This *pischer*, this Bobby Darin who swaggers like Sinatra but lip-
synchs "Splish Splash" on *American Bandstand*? On the biggest stage
in the biggest city facing the biggest challenge of his career? Sammy
Davis Jr. shattering records here is one thing. But Bobby Darin at The
Copa? *Fuggedaboutit!* It'll never work.

Earl Wilson, June 3, 1960: "The Copacabana was so crowded this
evening at Bobby Darin's opening that when Louis Prima attempted
to smooch his wife, Keely Smith, he missed and kissed composer Jule
Styne. Maybe that's an exaggeration, but only one more male could
have squeezed in: Eddie Arcaro."

Walter Winchell, June 7, 1960: "Darin, 24, opened a sensational
engagement at the famed nightclub last Thursday night and has been
playing to capacity throngs since. It was his first New York engagement after making show-business history on the West Coast."

It wasn't the first time, and it certainly wouldn't be the last, that
Bobby Darin would confound his critics. Confidence wasn't a problem. He knew he had the talent, and screw everyone else if they didn't
agree. He didn't care. All he needed was the stage.

"I like people who don't know me to dislike me," he said shortly

after his record-breaking Copa engagement. "It gives me great pleasure to get bum-rapped.

"I thrive on it."

IT WAS THAT SPUNKINESS that accompanied Walden Robert Cassotto
when he came kicking and screaming into the world on May 14, 1936.
The Cassottos lived in a South Bronx tenement, a mixed neighborhood
on East 135th Street comprised mostly of Italian and Irish immigrants
who hadn't quite cashed in on the American dream. Nonetheless, the
Cassottos were, by all accounts, a happy, loving lot who made do with
what little they had in their tiny railroad apartment, getting by on
government assistance and Polly Cassotto's odd jobs. Walden Robert
soon became known as Bobby—a blessing for a kid in a tough neighborhood. "There was a rough element," Bobby recalled. "Some of the
boys are doing time in local and federal penal institutions, but a small
percentage. Most were basically good, but victims of poverty."

Bobby, when he was old enough to understand such things, was
told that his father, Saverio "Sam" Cassotto, had died just months
before Bobby's birth. An Italian-immigrant cabinet maker, Sam was
also a part-time inventor who, according to family lore, had the brilliant idea of putting ice cream on a stick. Exactly what else he did in
his spare time has been the source of some speculation; according to
Darin archivist Jeff Bleiel, Sam was reportedly partners in a bar with
Frank Costello, one of the most notorious underworld figures in the
annals of New York City crime. One version of the story even had Sam
convicted of pickpocketing, sent up the river to Sing-Sing, and dying
there. Bobby himself repeated the Sing-Sing story to high school pal
Steve Karmen, who recounted an exchange in his memoir, *Me and
Bobby D.*

"He died in prison."

"No!"

"Yeah. Nina won't tell me the whole story; I think she's afraid. And
Momma breaks up when she starts to talk about him. He owed money
to somebody, and didn't pay up. Gambling, something, I don't know.
He thought he could tough 'em out, but somebody set him up and he
was arrested. Then, one day, Momma got the call. They made him an
example for the rest of the neighborhood."

But Bobby, for the most part, didn't ask questions about Sam, and no answers were offered—or forthcoming.

Bobby knew that his mother, Vivian Cassotto, who everyone called Polly, had been a vaudeville singer. She was born Vivian Fern Walden, the daughter of a millowner in Pascoag, Rhode Island, and grew up in the Chicago area. Her parents divorced shortly after Polly was born and her mother married a Chicago restaurant owner. Polly had actually attended college but dropped out, working the vaudeville circuit under the stage name of Paula Walden. While in Chicago she met Sam and, shortly thereafter, chucked her stage career and became a schoolteacher, settling down with Sam in New York City and having Bobby late in life. She was around forty-five when Bobby arrived, but no one ever really knew Polly's exact age. She was in show-business, after all, and shaved a few years off here and there.

Polly had also developed a drug habit after taking some medication for dental problems. "Not that she was high all the time but she needed just enough morphine to keep her sane," said her grandson, Gary. "She had gotten addicted to it for dental problems when she was in the business."

Now, with Sam dead and a new baby in the cramped quarters, Polly worked a string of menial jobs trying to support the family as best as she could, with the city of New York providing some assistance in the form of food coupons.

Bobby's sister Nina was seventeen years older than her baby brother. Nina, a heavyset woman, was forced to work at a young age in order to help with the family's expenses, including supporting Polly's morphine addiction. The age difference between Nina and Bobby made Nina more of Bobby's protector—roles that would be reversed in later years once Bobby became a star.

"My mother went to work and they found themselves on home relief, because what kind of job was she going to find without a high school diploma and no skills?" said Nina's son, Gary. "You're going to get factory work, whatever you can possibly get. And her mother still had a morphine addiction. Drugs had to be expensive; they're expensive now, imagine what they cost seventy years ago. They were never cheap."

Nonetheless, there was nothing about the Cassotto family that stood out in those early years. The tenement neighborhood was poor, and they were poor. Everyone worked if they could. That's just the way it was.

"In most ways we were like everyone else on our block," Bobby said. "Mom worked while my sister and I were in school. We worried a lot, and never stopped hoping that some day things would change.

"In the evenings we'd sit together and talk about our dreams—how Mom would have a piano again so she could sing to us like she used to, how we'd leave the city and have a house with trees and grass and flowers.

"We were as poor as you can be in a slum, but we were rich, too. Mother never forced anything on us. She told us anything we wanted to know. She gave me a free hand and trusted me enough to let me do whatever I wanted."

Young Bobby was extremely frail and sickly, but he was also inquisitive and bright. Polly, the former schoolteacher, thought he should be home-schooled, and didn't enroll Bobby in public school until he was seven-and-a-half. He went straight to first grade and quickly proved to be an excellent student, earning a reputation as the neighborhood "genius"—exactly the *wrong* reputation to have in such a rough-and-tumble environment. He offset the reputation with a sense of humor.

"I hung around with kids a couple of years older. They at least tolerated me," he said. "They used to think I was pretty funny and they liked to have me around to make them laugh. Kids on our block used to call me 'the walking dictionary' because I could spell the hard words like 'delicatessen' and 'restaurant.'"

He was a voracious reader, a habit not only encouraged by Polly, but one that he would pursue zealously throughout his life—spurred, perhaps, by the feelings of intellectual inadequacy he assumed was part-and-parcel of the Cassottos' proximity to the poverty line.

"Bobby was this intellectual sponge," remembered Hollywood friend Tom Mankiewicz. "He wanted to know everything about everything. I played a lot of tennis and Bobby said, 'I've got to play tennis, too.' So I got him an appointment with Alex Almedo, who was a terrific player at the time and the pro over at the Beverly Hills Hotel. And Bobby got all the equipment . . . the wristbands and all that. He wanted to be able to do everything right away.

"But in the meantime, he read every single thing about tennis there was to read. So all of the sudden I'd be talking to him and he would say, 'Did you know that Don Budge only won three sets at Wimbledon in 1939?' I mean, he *knew* the history of tennis. He bought fourteen books on tennis, had six rackets. The phrase I would always say about Bobby was that he always 'jumped into the deep end of the pool.' He never took steps."

It was a plunge the young boy, and later the man, always seemed willing to take. Grab life by the horns—NOW—because God only knew what was lurking around the corner. It was a lesson Bobby had learned early on. The illness that afflicted him as a child, beginning at the age of four and leaving him weak and bedridden a handful of times, was finally diagnosed as rheumatic heart disease, which eventually damaged the heart valves. Polly and Nina shielded eight-year-old Bobby from the truth, which was grim: It would be a miracle, the doctors told them, if Bobby made it past his teens. There was no cure.

"My earliest recollections were of being in bed, stiff, hurting," he would recall. "I used to read or do coloring books. I couldn't do what everybody else was doing."

What he *could* do, however, was sing. Even at an early age, and despite his frailty and poor health, Bobby proved to have an impressive set of pipes, and loved performing for the family. Often, with baton in hand, he would conduct the orchestras he heard on the radio. Polly, who played the piano, neither encouraged nor discouraged Bobby's musical dabbling—but it was apparent the kid had talent.

"Bobby started singing when he was two-and-a-half," Nina said. "I remember he came over to me one day and said, 'Nina, I sing for you, okay?' 'Okay,' I said. I thought I was going to hear something like 'Mary Had a Little Lamb.' So what does he do? He begins to sing 'McNamara's Band.' Honest to God, the whole thing, about twelve verses. Just from hearing it on the radio.

"And then he follows it with a song called 'Turkish Delight,' word for word. And then he picks up the harmonica, one of those dollar-and-a-half Woody Herman things we had laying around the house, and he starts to play 'The Sabre Dance' by Khachaturian!

"Well, I figured then, that day, that we had a real honest-to-goodness musician on our hands!"

Armed with his burgeoning musical skills, sharp intellect and a sense of humor shielding him from the neighborhood toughs, Bobby breezed through elementary school, completing the equivalent of six years in only four before continuing on to Elijah D. Clark, an all-boys junior high school over on 145th Street.

It was there that he met John Bravo, and the two boys found that they had a lot in common. They shared the same birthday—Bravo was a year older—they were both frail and slightly built and they shared an interest in show business.

"Bobby was always frail and he wasn't the most popular kid at that point. He couldn't do sports because of his heart," Bravo said. "We palled around and were buddies in that period. We'd go to the Bronx Opera House, which wasn't really an opera house, to see old Charlie Chaplin, Laurel and Hardy, Hope and Crosby, and Marx Brothers movies. There were two vaudeville theatres, the RKO Royal and the Loews National. The RKO Royal was vaudeville one night a week and the Loews National had a matinee.

"At 6 p.m. they kicked the kids out—we weren't allowed to be in the theater at night—but we would go up to the bathroom or up in the balcony and try to find someone in the orchestra who looked like they could be our parents, and we'd sit next to them and watch the show.

"I remember he was always poorer than my family and it always surprised me that he had a telephone," Bravo said. "We couldn't afford a telephone. He was on welfare and he loved his mother very, very much and was very close to her. But it's strange; as well as I knew Bobby and as friendly as we were, I was never invited up to his house. I don't know if that's because he was poor, or if he was ashamed."

Bravo also became the Bronx's own Duncan Yo-Yo champion and would travel around the borough teaching kids how to work the yo-yo. "Bobby was not good at all, he didn't have the knack, and he begged me to let him win—it was very important to him," he said. "He wanted to be a winner, to get one of those patches he could sew on his sweater. We always used to joke about that.

"Bobby had a way about him that, whenever he met somebody, he would always remember some obscure fact about your relationship with him that would surprise you," Bravo said. "He would always ask and would remember something about your mother, and that was always touching. It brought you close to him. He had this steel-trap mind; if you met him five years later he would remember some stupid thing you'd be shocked to hear about."

Bobby also showed an interest in the drums, and took some lessons from a school pal, Joel Kaswan. "He used to come to my house and I taught him how to play the drums," Kaswan said. "I remember when we met—he was a little kid, comparatively slight, and was a very sick child. We met in glee club in junior high school. He used to come over to my house after school and I tried to teach him on my drums, which were two cheap little drums and cymbals, not a big fancy set. He really took to it and enjoyed it."

Bobby eventually ordered his own cheap drum kit from a catalogue. He would spend hours in the basement of the apartment building, thrashing around and driving the neighbors crazy with the racket. He also taught himself piano, skipping lunch in school to spend an hour hammering away on the beat-up old piano in the cafeteria ("gradually I learned to put two hands together"). Bobby also enjoyed playing the harmonica "and he played it very well," Bravo said.

"He was probably the most musical person I ever knew," he said. "He could listen to a record and if someone hit a flat note, he'd hear it. If someone went off the rhythm, he'd hear it. He could pick up virtually any instrument and play it by ear."

Another neighborhood friend, Anthony Grosso, was, like Bobby, a sickly kid. They found they had a lot in common.

"He used to cut up 145th Street and he'd be in my neighborhood, which was mostly Irish," Grosso recalled. "You see another Italian face and you become pals. We'd walk up to school together and talk about casual bullshit, the stuff thirteen-year-old kids talk about.

"As a kid I was an asthmatic and wasn't allowed to participate in physical activities at school. And Bobby, with his rheumatic heart, he'd sit on the side with me so he was a familiar face. We talked a lot—he was a little smug sometimes, as thirteen-year-old kids will be, but he always had plenty of energy coming off him."

Junior high wasn't much more challenging to Bobby than grade school had been. He pulled an A average, continued to play the drums and read prodigiously. Polly liked to remind Bobby that he had an IQ of 137, and all the hard work paid off. Bobby skipped a few grades and, at the age of fourteen, earned a berth at the prestigious Bronx High School of Science.

"We both had very high IQs and we had discussed going to the High School of Performing Arts because we were both interested in show business," said pal John Bravo. "On the ill advice of a guidance counselor it was recommended we go to the Bronx High School of Science or to Stuyvesant, the two top schools in the city. We decided on the Bronx High School of Science because of our proximity to the school and we went there together, as partners in a sense."

Established in 1938, the school was already a highly respected institution that required its applicants to pass a rigorous exam to qualify for admission. School officials like to boast that ninety-eight percent of Bronx High School of Science graduates entered some type of professional field.

"That's where I learned that I was nowhere near being a genius," Bobby said. "I met guys whose IQs began at 180. They pulled grades in the high nineties and mine were in the eighties." In its short life, the school had counted E. L. Doctorow, Mark Rydell, Harold Bloom and William Safire among its graduates. Each man would eventually make his mark as author, Hollywood director, professor, and columnist. Soon, Bobby would be added to that distinguished list.

The transition from Clark Junior High to Bronx High School of Science was a tough one for Bobby and John Bravo. "We were kind of thrown into it and it was a culture shock for us, these two poor kids from the Bronx," Bravo said. "There were a lot of middle- and upper-class Jewish kids who came from a totally different income strata, lifestyle and religious background.

"And it was also a financial shock," he said. "Bobby and I were kind of misplaced there. At one point, after about a year there, they took the two of us and put us in a room by ourselves and gave us an aptitude and personality test. They never gave us the results of those tests, or never even told us why they were giving us those tests, but they picked Bobby and I to do that.

"We were really way out of our league in that school."

LIFE IN THE CASSOTTO HOUSEHOLD took on a different dynamic as Bobby entered his teenage years. Nina had married and moved out of the house. Her new husband, Charlie Maffia, was an uneducated, good-natured, charming mechanic and truck driver who struggled to find work. He shared his passion for Big Band music with Bobby, taking an immediate shine to his young nephew. "Charlie looked like Clark Gable—he was a very good-looking man," a family friend remembered. "And he had a very good sense of humor and no education. So he would say things in places where you wouldn't expect him to say them."

Soon Nina was pregnant, giving birth to Vivian, or Vee Vee as they called her, and then to Vana four years later. Bobby, who had never been very close to Nina, mostly because of their age difference, relished his new extended family, delighting in his two nieces and enjoying Charlie's company and his brother-in-law's occasional malapropisms. Before long, Nina, Charlie and the girls moved back in with Polly and Bobby to help with the expenses.

Bobby, meanwhile, entered high school with some trepidation. "These were future professional people—lawyers, doctors, scientists . . . suddenly I was with people not pressured financially, people uninvolved with food, rent and clothing," he said.

"I had gone, overnight, from the non-thinkers to the thinkers. It was as shattering as it was abrupt. Then I got up off my knees, decided to park my dungarees, and *do* something."

That "something" turned out to be music, the one area in which Bobby always felt the most comfortable. He became passable enough on the drums to join a band fronted by schoolmate Eddie Ocasio, who played the piano and recruited sax player Steve Karmen, trumpeter Richard Behrke and guitarist Walter Raim to round out the fivesome.

"Karmen was much better looking and was taller than Bobby, but he never had Bobby's charisma," John Bravo said.

Within a few weeks the band had worked up a repertoire. In his memoirs, Karmen recalled the band being particularly strong on Irving Berlin's "You're Just In Love," from the Broadway musical *Call Me Madam*. Drummer Bobby had fashioned a microphone stand in woodshop, to which he attached to his drum set. He was the featured singer on "The Lion Sleeps Tonight" and "You Call Everybody Darling."

The band knocked around a bit, playing the odd gig—sometimes paid in sticks of chewing gum—and got their first big break through Laurie Newmark, a friend of Bobby's from the Bronx whose mother booked local bands for summer gigs in the Catskills.

"The whole band came to our apartment to audition," Newmark recalled. "That's what my mother did. She used to book bands in the mountains. To get us away for the summertime, she would book the bands and I would be a counselor so that I could meet young men. Waiters and busboys. And one of those bands she booked was Bobby Darin, Steve Karmen, Dick Behrke, Walter Raim and Eddie Ocasio. She collected maybe 10 percent of what they made.

"Bobby and I liked each other after that audition," she said. "He was really great."

Newmark's mother spent her summers as the camp director at the Hotel Sunnyland, located about 90 minutes north of the city in Parksville, N.Y. She booked Bobby Cassotto and the boys to play there for the season. Laurie, of course, would be a counselor, with her main goal—or at least her mother's main goal—to meet a nice Jewish boy.

The Hotel Sunnyland was owned by Russian immigrants who expected the band members to contribute elsewhere during the day—as waiters, counselors, sports instructors and all-around *tummlers*, entertaining the guests and catering to their every whim. This was customary for the hotels, largely populated by a Jewish clientele, dotting the "Borscht Belt" circuit during that era, and for Bobby and the guys it was no different.

"Bobby worked in the concessions and as a children's waiter and at night he was in the band so he had a full summer," Newmark recalled. "He had one pair of jeans, so he used to jump in the swimming pool with the jeans on to clean them. At night he was the drummer. There was one big cottage with a wall dividing the area in which the band slept and where we slept. We used to try to peek in on them."

As if his day wasn't busy enough, Bobby was also going to summer school—he'd failed a course that spring—and would rise early, hitchhike into town about a half-hour away to attend his class, then hitchhike back to the hotel to start his work day. "I don't know how he slept," Newmark said. "He went to bed at 2 in the morning and had to be at summer school at 8 a.m."

The band, meanwhile, having attained a level of modest musicianship, began performing nighttime shows at other hotels in the area like The Flagler and The Morningside. "That's when he got bitten with the bug," Newmark said. "We used to go from hotel to hotel and put on these little shows and everyone worked very hard for very little money."

Bobby was also establishing a reputation as a handsome Romeo of some note. Richard Loeb, who would later morph into Bobby's close friend Dick Lord, was working at the Melody Country Club in nearby Liberty that summer. Like Bobby, he was a drummer. Unlike Bobby, he wasn't having much luck with the ladies.

"This girl liked me and we were sitting on a swing and she reached for my fly. I got scared and she said, 'That's okay, I'll go see the drummer at Sunnyland.' So that got me curious," Lord said. "So I told the other guys in the band, let's go see the band at Sunnyland. They were getting 15 dollars a week and we became friendly. And Bobby was going to summer school. I think it was in Liberty. I was very impressed by that."

Bobby and Laurie Newmark had also fallen in love—or at least what passed for love for two teens still in high school. "We went steady that summer and he gave me his ID bracelet. You know, that was really serious stuff," she said. "He was just adorable and he was really cute but my mother never liked it because Bobby wasn't Jewish. But he was really respectable and nice."

Karmen, in his memoirs, remembered a different Bobby that summer, catting around with a girlfriend named Sue Ellen Berger and instructing his bandmates—crudely and explicitly—on the fine art of lovemaking.

Newmark remembered it differently.

"He wasn't too 'fast,' as we called it in those days," she said. "Steve Karmen, in his book, had him as a womanizer at a young age, but he really wasn't. He was a very sweet Bronx boy, very nice.

"But he really wasn't planning on going into show business until that summer. He really wanted to be like Donald O'Connor," she said. "He was a really good dancer; he tapped, he could do all kinds of impressions, Fred Astaire, those kinds of things. He wanted to do everything."

And quickly. Bobby knew that time was definitely not on his side. The rheumatic heart that should have killed him by now was still tick-ing. Bobby Cassotto was sixteen and not even sure he'd make it to his seventeenth birthday. Time was of the essence.

IN JUNE 1953 Bobby graduated from high school and enrolled at Hunter College, where he planned to major in drama and speech. His experiences with the band, and at Sunnyland, convinced him he had a future as an entertainer; exactly *how* he was going to achieve that goal remained a mystery.

His living conditions, now that he was a freshman in college, weren't any better than they'd been in the South Bronx tenement. Polly, Nina, Charlie and the girls had moved to a slightly larger apartment on Houston Street, while Bobby moved in with Dick Behrke, who'd enrolled in the Manhattan School of Music after graduation. Behrke had a small apartment over on 71st Street, and invited Bobby to move in.

"Dick Behrke's parents were divorced; his father had a new wife and he didn't want to live with them," recalled Dick Lord, who was going to Brooklyn College at the time. "Bobby lived for a while in the Bronx with his family and he really didn't love spending that much time there. So Dick and Bobby had this studio apartment on West 71st Street, and I would visit. The first day I visited, and I'll never forget this, I said to Dick, 'Where's Bobby?' He was on the ledge of the building, outside of this window, tap-dancing. I said, 'This guy's nuts!'

"Bobby was starving then, so what we used to do since there were a lot of luncheonettes on Broadway, we would steal bagels," Lord said. "The first night they lived there, they cooked dinner; they had a little sink and all the dishes were in the sink. The dishes were in that sink for a year, same pile of dishes, and every time I'd walk by they'd say, 'Yeah, we know.'

"And one night we all went out to this place, Club 78, there was a little band and a singer and we would hang out there. And one night we came home and nobody said anything. Behrke got a pillowcase, I took the dishes and put them in the pillowcase, and Bobby opened the window and dropped them into a garbage pail below. And nobody said anything. We just kept talking."

One trait Bobby always possessed, from his youngest days, was a sense of humor, which helped him cope with his poor upbringing and would come in handy throughout his life. Dick Lord was no slouch in the humor department himself—he'd later become a stand-up comic—and witnessed Bobby's sense of humor first-hand, with some potentially dire consequences.

"It's 1955 and Bobby and Dick Behrke are living with Behrke's sister and brother-in-law, who's an artist, in Brooklyn, in a big apartment in a kind of mixed neighborhood," Lord recalled.

"The Brooklyn Dodgers had won the World Series and it's pandemonium, it's like 2 o'clock in the afternoon, it's like New Year's Eve. Bottles are flying out of windows. Cars are triple-parked. People are running around in the streets.

"So we're passing a bar, and it says, 'Jam Session Tonight' in the window, and Bobby says, 'Yeah, we'll go back tonight and we'll play.' Behrke says, 'That's a great idea.' And I'm looking around and I'm saying, 'We're the only white people here. I don't think it's such a good idea,' and they're both shocked. So, you know, we laugh a little and I'm praying they're going to forget about it.

"But they didn't forget," Lord said. "It's time to go in and Bobby says, 'Here, you hold the drumsticks,' and we go back to the bar and the jukebox is playing and there's a room in the back with a band. I'm telling you, we walked in and everything stopped. I couldn't believe it.

"Bobby says, 'Can we sit in?' and the bartender didn't even answer him and Bobby says to me, 'You hold the drumsticks' and he and Behrke go to the back and ask if we can sit in. I don't know what to do with myself. I order a beer. I look over and there's a circle of guys around me. And this big guy says, 'Who did you bet on?' and I said, 'Well, I didn't bet.' And he says, 'Well, if you *did* bet, who would you bet on?' I said, 'the Dodgers,' and he said, 'That's too bad.'

"He takes a Yankees pennant and he unzips his fly, and puts the pennant in his fly and says, 'Kiss the flag.' Now, my back is to the bar and I'm thinking, 'pain hurts,' and suddenly Bobby comes out of the back room and sees what's happening. He jumps on the bar and tells me to give him the drumsticks, and he starts playing on the bottles and he takes a napkin and opens his fly, puts the napkin in his fly, and does an impression of that guy.

"Now, they're all laughing, and I look at him and I'm laughing, and the three of us run out. I never forgot that my whole life."

That flair for the dramatic was something Bobby wanted to explore, and with his rat-tat-tat speech and natural gift of gab, he decided to give acting a shot that first semester at Hunter. He managed to win roles in student productions of *Hedda Gabler, The Valiant* and *The Curious Savage*, but he was frustrated with college life and desperate to break into the business—*NOW.* He couldn't wait. His heart condition continued to dog him, and even walking up a flight of steps was risky. Dick Lord remembered Charlie Maffia driving to Hanson's drug store to pick Bobby up so he wouldn't exert himself on the walk home. And who knew how much longer he had? So he decided to drop out of Hunter.

"I still kind of figured that maybe there was something I could get from professors or college students. I was wrong," Bobby said. "And I was tired of wearing dungarees and the same shirt. In the back of my mind, it seemed to me that I was always trying to decide whether I was meant for show business. After my first year at Hunter, I went to Mom and told her I wasn't going back to school and that I wanted to leave home . . . She was hurt, but she didn't stop me."

Bobby and John Bravo, who had gone on to City College of New York, occasionally worked small-time shows together to earn a few bucks, "like the USO Canteen on a much lower level," Bravo said.

"I did comedy magic and Bobby did impressions and played the harmonica. He didn't sing," he said. "He didn't do very well in that period and I think that's what discouraged him from being a comedian. He wanted to be an impressionist; he was doing Jimmy Cagney, James Stewart, Clark Gable, Jimmy Durante—which he did very well with a fake nose he brought on Broadway.

"But it just didn't work out for him," Bravo said. "One of his biggest idols in that period was Donald O'Connor, but Bobby couldn't dance because of his heart. He even developed O'Connor's mannerisms and that little smile. Bobby was very chameleon-like; whatever the trend was, he could fall into that and do it very well or superbly."

With his college career kaput, Bobby pounded the pavement, landing a job with The Salome Gaynor Theater for Children, a touring theatre troupe, where he played an Indian chief in a production of *Kit*

Carson on a 45-day tour up and down the Eastern seaboard. He fell in love for the first time with an older woman (she was thirty-one), an exotic dancer whose name he would never divulge. The romance was short-lived and Bobby returned home, perhaps a little wiser in the love department. It was later rumored that the dancer committed suicide several years later—dressed in a nun's habit.

"They gave me forty a week, and out of that I had to pay all of my expenses except transportation," Bobby said of his professional theatrical career. "But I felt good. I came out of that experience feeling, 'This is where I belong.' I had the world by the chops—and then I got back to the city and discovered there were only forty thousand other actors in this vast metropolis.

"I don't know whether you know how it is, when you're seventeen and you find you don't belong anywhere. But I was in a depression. I turned to songwriting, where I could lay all my gripes on the line."

2

If Bobby Cassotto was a modest 5'9" and weighed 159 pounds—soaking wet—then Donny Kirshner was his funhouse-mirror image. Kirshner, the Jewish son of a Bronx tailor, was 6'2" and a solid 180 pounds by the time he graduated from George Washington High School in 1952. Where Bobby's brains had gotten him into Bronx High School of Science, Kirshner was a self-professed jock who spent his years at George Washington dreaming of playing professional baseball or basketball, preferably for his beloved New York Knicks.

Kirshner arrived at his career in the music business, and on Bobby's doorstep, through a circuitous route. Working as a bellhop and busboy at the Atlantic Beach Hotel and Surf Club in Atlantic Beach, New Jersey, and at the Lido Beach Club, Kirshner had brushed up against show-biz types, waiting on Dean Martin and Jerry Lewis—then at the height of their fame—and chasing Sid Caesar's golf balls.

Swimming in the Surf Club pool one day, Kirshner heard a sixteen-year-old Long Island kid named Morty Berkowitz playing the piano. Swimming over to the pianist, he suggested Morty put some words to his lovely melody. Donny, whose best subject had always been English, composed a song he called "In All of My Dreams."

"The title meant absolutely nothing," he said. "But at the hotel is Frankie Laine. As a kid I used to groove to his 'Cry of the Wild Goose' and 'Lucky Old Son' and 'Mule Train' and I couldn't believe I was carrying his bags. I took him to his room and I said, 'Mr. Laine, I wrote a song, can Morty and I play the song?' And he said, 'Let me hear what you got, kid.' So we played the song and he said, 'Well, it's not for me, but make a demonstration record.'"

Not having the slightest idea exactly what a demonstration record actually *was*, Kirshner took Laine's advice and, together with Morty Berkowitz, scraped together fifty bucks and recorded "In All of My Dreams" at a Manhattan recording studio—recruiting a local bartender to croon the tune. It was Don Kirshner's entrée into the music business.

"So I make the piano lower and I have the kid sing it and I came back to my neighborhood as captain of the basketball team and I publish the song—which means absolutely nothing unless you get a record. I can't get to first base," he said.

"I'm at Kirtzman's Candy Store in New York—I had moved from the Bronx because I had a croup condition as a kid and my dad wanted a higher location, which was Washington Heights. And I'm in there ordering an egg cream and a girl by the name of Natalie Twersky comes up to me because I was a big shot, I had just published a song.

"And she said, 'I've got this friend of mine, he's a really talented guy, he's a songwriter, an artist, he's this and that . . . would you meet him?' And I was a little cocky and I said, 'Let me see what he's got.' He walks over to me. He's a brash, confident kid. I remember it was a cold day and he had a scarf which had spots on it.

"Natalie had a piano in her place on the fourth floor in Washington Heights, across the street from me. In those days, I couldn't afford a piano.

"She said, 'Can you come up to my place?' I was excited to listen to someone else's songs. So he plays me five or six songs. And you know you have the chemistry, you know it's going to be a friend; it's an instinct you just feel. I don't remember the tunes he played at the time, but I stopped him at the fourth or fifth song and said, 'Let's team up, we'll be the biggest thing in the entertainment business.' You have to understand, at the time I couldn't get arrested. I didn't know anybody, I had never really been to a publisher's office.

"But Bobby had such a raw, vital talent and spark—he was writing melodies mostly at the time—and teaming with me was a good alternative to cleaning latrines because my mom and dad would take him in and give him chicken soup," Kirshner said. "He would sleep over and then he would go back to the dorm with me at school."

Kirshner had transferred from Seton Hall University to Upsala College in East Orange, New Jersey, just outside of Newark. Bobby would often join him there at night and on weekends, the two new partners trying to hash out a plan to break into the music business. "I was trying to find a way to make us both songwriting stars and Bobby a singing star," Kirshner said.

"And Bobby was really the talent. I would write the lyrics . . . but there was no doubt Bobby was the talent. I was starting to shine with vicarious thrills through Bobby's talent. I was really becoming important through Bobby. He had the showmanship."

Kirshner, at least, had one published song under his belt; Bobby, while writing furiously, had yet to publish anything. He spent his days working at a variety of jobs—building garage doors, cleaning parts in a gun factory—and his nights writing and writing.

Bobby and his new partner needed a plan, and Kirshner had an idea. "I was getting a little desperate. Bobby had no money. I had no money. We had to find a way to get money.

"The big publishers in those days were Hill & Range, Freddy Bienstock, Lou Levy, Goldie Goldmark . . . and we couldn't even get into their offices," he said. "Finally, one day we got into Lou Levy's office at Leeds Music. I didn't even know what the back side of a record was. And for some reason, Bobby and I wrote a song called 'Wear My Ring,' which was corny. There was a guy called Gene Vincent who was big in those days and had done a thing called 'Be Bop a Lula'. His second record was 'Lotta Lovin',' which went to the Top Ten, and Lou was able to get us the back side of that record."

That was all well and good, and was certainly a huge break for Bobby and Don. But there was one problem: money. They just didn't have any. Their royalties from 'Wear My Ring' wouldn't come in for another eight months, Kirshner said. "I was really getting desperate because Bobby was getting crazed. I had a meeting set with Atlantic, they cancelled, and I had a meeting set with Mercury—five calls to them and no one is picking up the calls. And I knew either our relationship would break up or we would have to take a serious job."

But if necessity is the mother of invention, their next move proved to be the ice-breaker.

"Bobby and I are sitting at home, you know, you could starve until the royalties came in," Kirshner said. "We didn't know what to do with ourselves. But I was listening to a radio station in New Jersey called WNJR, which was, I think, primarily a black station and they had the worst, most annoying commercials." Kirshner had an idea. Why not pool their talents and write some jingles for the local stores?

"I said, 'Bobby, I got an idea. We'll take a tape recorder—I'll carry it,' because I was always conscious of Bobby's rheumatic heart—'and we'll schlepp from store to store. We'll go to the Orange Furniture Store, Bushberg Brothers, we'll pitch them, and if they like it, we'll go back to Upsala and we'll write the ad in the school cafeteria and put it on the air'—never dreaming they'd ever take it.

"So we go for two weeks in the heat and Bobby is getting tired and we're taking buses . . . and we went to the Orange Furniture Store in Orange, New Jersey. The owner was Herman Sokoloff, and I think to get rid of us, said, 'Okay, I'll give you $500, write a jingle.' So I wrote the lyrics, Bobby wrote a melody: *For values you can't beat/Start talking to your feet/Hop a bus and come with us to 205 Main Street/We'll go to Orange Furniture Store.* They put it on the air on WNJR and people are starting to love it. And $500 in those days was good money."

One of Bobby's more endearing qualities, at least in the early days, was his loyalty both to friends and family. In the months after dropping out of Hunter College, the old band had broken up, with Dick Behrke moving on with another group of musicians, Walter Raim pursuing his college education and Eddie Ocasio, the band's leader, dropping music altogether to focus on becoming a doctor.

Bobby was still friendly with all of them and saw Steve Karmen frequently. They hung out together, frequenting Vinnie's, an Italian restaurant in the Bronx. (Karmen, in his memoirs, recalls Bobby playing piano and singing to Karmen's guitar accompaniment).

"I met Bobby's friend, Steve Karmen," Kirshner said. "I was a fan of Harry Belafonte and Stevie used to sound like Belafonte, so Bobby and I wrote a thing for Build Right: *You're gonna buy right at Build Right/You can buy it in the morning and have it in the night.* Karmen puts it out, Bobby sings it and it's a hit."

"I didn't have any expectations," Bobby said of his jingle-writing days with Kirshner. "Don said that we could write and sell radio commercials. I thought he was nuts. But, within four months we made about twelve hundred dollars. We knocked out some songs. A couple got on records, but I don't think we made twelve dollars for the year out of those."

But Bobby was being modest. The jingles he and Kirshner wrote were good, and their talents were starting to pay off as they received more and more exposure on WNJR. "All of the sudden, we're becoming the king of the jingles," Kirshner said. The jobs came pouring in: Bushberg Brothers, Wilco, Rogers Furniture Store. "It's $500 then $1,000 and we were always copying people like Tito Puente," Kirshner said.

For Rogers Furniture Store, they wrote "The Rogers Cha Cha," a takeoff on Puente's Latin beat. Eight months later, their first royalty check for Orange Furniture Store came in: $5,000, which they split down the middle. Things were starting to look up.

Don knew Connie Franconero, a local singer from Belleville who sang under her stage name, Connie Francis, and was under contract to MGM Records. As a favor, Connie and her manager, George Scheck, agreed to meet with Don and Bobby. Don wanted her to record a song he and Bobby had written called "My First Real Love," and they added Scheck's name as a co-writer (he was listed as George M. Shaw) as an incentive.

Connie knew Kirshner well and knew what to expect. But she was less-than-taken with the hard-charging Bobby Cassotto, always looking to get ahead and not afraid to speak his mind.

Francis described the scene, in detail, in her memoir, *Who's Sorry Now?*

Donny was complimenting me on my lackluster record that it was so profuse that it became almost embarrassing, especially in the presence of his partner, Bobby Darin, who obviously couldn't care less.

Suddenly, Bobby interrupted Donny. "Okay, enough with the garbage, Kirsh. Look, lady, do you want to listen or not?" "I'm dying for a hit," I explained enthusiastically. "Join the club," he responded. "I dig." "You do? For what company? Is this lady a gas, Kirsh, or what?"

"On the first day, I just thought he was a truly offensive person," Francis told the author. "It was only when we got together and started talking about music and working on the song that I grew to respect him. As far as I was concerned at first, he was just another teenage songwriter . . . but I learned to respect him very quickly."

The interaction with Francis also opened another door for Bobby and Don. George Scheck took an interest in the songwriting pair, and signed on to be their manager. "He gave us a card and wanted to manage us," Kirshner said. "He saw a lot of raw talent there."

Connie Francis' recording of "My First Real Love" didn't set the world on fire (Bobby liked to call it "My First Real Flop"), but it was another important stepping stone in Bobby's career. And with George Scheck now on the scene, Bobby's luck was about to change.

Bobby Cassotto the showman knew that he couldn't succeed in show-business with his given surname. Cassotto wasn't exactly a marquee-grabber, and besides, everyone in show business changed their names. It went along with the territory. A behind-the-scenes guy like Don Kirshner, who had no aspirations to perform, was one thing; but Bobby wanted to be a star. Bobby Cassotto just wouldn't fly.

Bobby had experimented with different names dating back to his summers at Sunnyland: Robert Walden, Walden Roberts, Bobby Walden and, according to Karmen, even Bobby Titan. The name he eventually settled on was Bobby Darin, and there's some debate among Darin scholars as to how he chose the moniker. Bobby himself told several variations through the years. One story has Bobby walking past a Chinese restaurant advertising its Mandarin cuisine, the first three neon letters having burned out leaving only "darin." Another tale has Bobby borrowing the first name of actor Darren McGavin and changing the spelling. The third, more plausible theory, has Bobby picking the name "Darin" out of the phone book. That's the story he repeated in an interview with David Frost years later.

"I went to the letter 'D,' don't ask me why. . . . I'm not a numerologist or letterologist. . . . In any event, the letter 'D' has always attracted me, and I just went to the phone book and I just ran it down until I found one that was spelled slightly differently . . . and I just changed it a little bit . . ."

So, in 1956, Bobby Casssotto became Bobby Darin—and it was Bobby Darin who was about to get his first national exposure. Early that year George Scheck, with Don Kirshner's help, had wangled Bobby a contract on Decca Records. Don and Bobby had written "Talk To Me," featuring Bobby's vocals, and Don brought the platter to Milt Gabler, the head of Decca Records.

"Donny Kirshner had [a demonstration record] taken to Decca," Bobby said. "They signed me on as an artist and I recorded four songs." In March, Bobby recorded "Rock Island Line," already a skiffle hit for England's Lonnie Donegan, "Timber," "Silly Willy" and "Blue-Eyed Mermaid." Decca informed him that, in four days, he would make his national television debut to sing the songs, and would open his road tour in Detroit (at the Gay Haven) four days after that. Bobby brought Steve Karmen along to play guitar on his television debut.

Jackie Gleason, already an established television star, was in the midst of filming what turned out to be the so-called Classic 39 episodes of *The Honeymooners*. Gleason's company also produced *The Honeymooners'* lead-in, *Stage Show*, an important musical-variety showcase hosted by Tommy and Jimmy Dorsey. A young Elvis Presley, in the first flashes of fame, had appeared on *Stage Show* six times leading up to Bobby's performance. This was the big time, and Bobby knew it.

"To plug the first one they got me on *Stage Show*, the old Dorsey Brothers series. I'd never sung professionally before," he said. "I went on 'cold,' scared to death, and sang 'Rock Island Line.' It bombed. So did the other three tunes."

With only four days to learn all the words to his songs, Bobby hadn't been sure he would pull it off on national television, and, as a precaution, had written the words to "Rock Island Line" on his left hand. In the black-and-white kinescope of the show, Bobby can be seen looking down at his hand while singing the tune. It was an inauspicious debut.

"It was the greatest thing that ever happened to me," Bobby said later with typical self-assessment and not a bit of panache. "I was hit with the hard taste of success. Everyone was patting me on the back and giving me the business, 'How does it feel to be a star?' And I was buying it. Then I went on the road to play clubs, and found nobody knew me. Sure, I had been on television. So what—so had a lot of other guys.

"I had a record. Well, [Lonnie] Donegan's recording was a lot bigger than mine," he said. "I began to understand for the first time what a star really is. A star is really Sinatra or Peggy Lee or Cary Grant. It's not someone who happens to have one or four hit records. A star is someone who comes to understand his audience through years of doing. I learned that you don't get it by watching or reading or being told. You learn only by doing."

Personally, things were looking up. Bobby was in love. Although Connie Francis didn't have much luck with "My First Real Love," she and Bobby took the song's title to heart and embarked on a hot-and-heavy romance. They had to keep it a secret, though, because of Connie's jealous, over-protective father, George Franconero, who famously micro-managed Connie's career and ruled his daughter's life with an iron will. George didn't want anything or anyone—especially a fast-talking, brash young man—to impede Connie's rise to the top. In reality, George simply didn't want anyone coming between him and his daughter.

"They were always hiding and playing around because of her father," Don Kirshner said. "Her father wanted her career, he wanted to handle it and he didn't want to fool around. He was a strict disciplinarian."

George's hold over Connie would, eventually, take its emotional toll on a frail psyche. But, fifty years later, Connie still gushed like a schoolgirl when talking about her relationship with Bobby.

"We would meet every day at Hanson's Drug Store and talk about the business. Everybody would just be sitting there, wrapped in awe listening to Bobby," she said. "We dated a year and a half, much to my father's distress. Bobby would take me to the Apollo [Theatre] with his friends and we would see acts like I had never seen before, like James Brown and Ray Charles and all the blues singers.

"He was so far ahead of his time, he was so brilliant. He could talk

about politics, he could talk about any subject at all. He was so intelligent and bright."

Bobby confided in his pals that he was head-over-heels for Connie,
but that her old man was making it a pain in the ass for them to be
together. One night, Bobby and Connie decided to make their relationship permanent.

"We eloped one night," Connie recalled. "My father had had my
luggage outside the house when I came home because I had another
date with Bobby. So Bobby said, 'We're going to get married.' I said,
'Bobby, my father will kill me.' So we started to drive and we stopped
at a park and began to talk. And he said, 'Some day we'll be the Italian
Nelson Eddy and Jeannette McDonald or we'll just be two happy people, that's all.' I said, 'Bobby, you've got to take me home now, you've
got to take me home. My father will kill us.'

"And he said, 'If you go home now, he will continue to be the
world's number-one tyrant.' So he took me home and after that he
didn't see me for a couple of weeks because he was angry—but then
he called and we resumed our relationship."

If George Franconero feared that Bobby was besmirching his
daughter he was wrong. Connie insists she and Bobby never consum-
mated their relationship.

"Bobby wanted people to do their thing and to be themselves, but
he was a womanizer, I mean, even when we were seeing each other,"
she said. "He would write to me from New Orleans, 'This place is
better than I thought it was going to be.' He said he was with a woman
the night before 'but couldn't concentrate on what I was doing
because you were always in my mind's eye.'

"I mean, he would tell me because I certainly wasn't going to have
relations and he didn't want to get pimples," she said. "My father
thought we would have sexual relations, which we never did."

Bobby managed to coordinate his sneaking around with Connie
with his touring schedule and his commitment to Decca, which didn't
seem long for the world. After the *Stage Show* debacle he recorded four
more songs, "Hear Them Bells," "The Greatest Builder," "Dealer In
Dreams" (written by Bobby and Don Kirshner) and "Help Me," none
of which did anything on the charts. Kirshner took a stab at managing
Bobby, getting him gigs on the road to pay the bills, but IT, the huge

break, wasn't happening. Nowheresville was beckoning just around the corner.

"Bobby was one of the greatest talents I ever saw, and in those days, by ear, he was playing ten-to-twelve instruments," Kirshner said. "The problem we were having was that Bobby didn't have his own identity. When he sang, he would imitate Little Richard, Fats Domino, Chuck Berry, Pat Boone. And why he was struggling was because instead of creating his own identity, he was copying everybody."

While Bobby struggled on the road and in the studio, trying to record something that would click, the family back home welcomed another addition. Nina had given birth to her third child, a boy she and Charlie named Gary. Bobby delighted in his new nephew, visiting the family whenever he had some time off from the grueling road schedule.

George Franconero, meanwhile, had been keeping a close eye on his daughter, and—in his mind, at least—her illicit romance with Bobby. "It would have been any boy, but especially Bobby," Connie said. "He saw Bobby as a threat. He just hated him. He saw a guy in my dressing room in 1970 who looked like Bobby and he beat him up. He said, 'You look like someone I hate.'"

Still, they continued to see each other, stealing away when they could, often with Don covering for them. "It was a pretty hot-and-heated love affair," Kirshner said. "You know, 'Stay here, let us know if George [Franconero] comes back.' It was craziness.

"It was just one of those things that her parents objected to," he said. "It was like Romeo and Juliet; it wasn't any fun, but they were really crazy about each other. They respected each other's mutual talents. He was a writer and she was a singer. She would sing a song that he could harmonize in a minute."

Joyce Becker, who was Connie's secretary at the time, witnessed the fury that George Franconero directed at Bobby over his relationship with Connie.

"Connie and Bobby were both booked onto Dick Clark's Saturday night show which he used to do in New York on West 44th Street and Broadway," she said. "We went to do the show and Connie didn't tell Bobby she was going to be there. My father drove us in and dropped us at the theatre. Connie had all her luggage because we were then going to call her father to pick us up after the show.

"And we walked in and there's Bobby. She started to shake and he started to shake and off they went privately . . . I turn around and there is Connie's father in the doorway. 'Okay, where are they?! Where's my daughter, where's Connie?!' And he's banging on doors, and the door opens and he sees Bobby. 'Get the hell outta here! What-the-hell are you doing alone with my daughter?!' I was embarrassed because he's screaming at his daughter, who is now a very big star, and he's screaming at Bobby, who's wondering if George is going to pull out a gun and blow his head off.

"The whole ride back home George is screaming at Connie, 'If I ever, ever find out that you are near him, I'll kill you both!' He just totally wanted Bobby out of her life," Becker said. "I think he was afraid that Bobby was a strong-willed guy who would take Connie away from him, who would be her leader and have total control. But sadly, what George Franconero didn't know is that not only would Bobby not have done that, but that [George] could have controlled Bobby's career, too. Because Bobby needed a family. And I think anybody who showed Bobby a bit of kindness, that would have been it."

The Bobby-Connie situation came to a head before Connie's appearance on *The Jackie Gleason Show*. Bobby was visiting Connie in her dressing room when George stormed in with a gun—intending to either shoot Bobby, intimidate him or both. Connie re-created the scene in her memoirs.

My father created this sound . . . I thought World War III had begun when he came in and George Scheck, [Bobby's] manager and my manager, said "Run, Bobby! Run!" On the telephone to Bobby from the theater that night, I was in torrents of tears and I knew that if Bobby had said just one wrong word to me, I would make a fool of myself.

"Did you see it?" I asked tentatively in a little girl's lost voice. "Take it easy, baby, it's okay," he said soothingly. "Listen to me, honey, tonight was just one little step backwards. Tomorrow it will be twenty-one steps forward . . . Years from now when you are a big star and no one could ever touch you or hurt you again, you'll laugh about everything that happened today. Some day when we're both very, very old, we'll laugh about it together, you'll see." And he never called me again.

Connie never got over her love for Bobby. Years later and a lifetime removed from their affair, she still sounded a melancholy, whimsical note about their relationship ending so abruptly.

"I did regret it. My whole life, you know, if Bobby had been a part of my life, no one that ever came along would have even stood a chance with me. I still love him," she said. "I loved him until the day he died and beyond that."

Unlucky in love, Bobby wasn't having any better luck in his recording career. Decca finally dropped him near the end of 1956, and he decided to do what Bobby Darin always did best in times of crisis: follow his instinct.

3

Bobby was freed from his commitment to Decca, but that meant, once again, the uncertainty of what lay ahead. For the time being, he and Don were able to support themselves through Bobby's club bookings and through songwriting royalties. LaVern Baker and Bobby Short had followed Gene Vincent's lead and recorded several Darin-Kirshner compositions with modest success—Baker cutting "Love Me Right" and Short recording "Delia."

"I would be lying if I said that I didn't have lots of moments when I thought my songs must be lousy," Bobby said. "I kept writing them, and some of them were big sellers for other recording artists. But not for me."

Don Kirshner was content to continue in the songwriting mode in the background, managing Bobby's career and churning out the tunes. But Bobby had bigger aspirations. Having tasted the big time with Decca and *Stage Show* he wanted more. Forget about trying to imitate the singer-of-the-moment. He'd been there, done that, with shitty results. It was time to be Bobby Darin.

In May 1957, while on tour in Birmingham, Alabama—and headlining at Mike's South Pacific Club—Bobby made the move. He borrowed money from some local DJs and musicians, booked a studio, and recorded four tracks he hoped to shop to the labels when he returned to New York: "Wear My Ring," "Talk To Me Something," "Just in Case You Change Your Mind" and "I Found a Million Dollar Baby (in a Five and Ten Cent Store)."

Atco, a subsidiary of Atlantic Records, was the only label to show an interest in the demos. Founded by Turkish-born Ahmet Ertegun and Herb Abramson, who brought aboard Jerry Wexler and Ertegun's brother, Nesuhi, Atco was looking to make a name for itself and saw some potential in Bobby.

"One of the first things Jerry did was to buy some masters that a couple of entrepreneurs had made," Ertegun recalled. "I remember one of the songs was 'I Found a Million Dollar Baby (in a Five and Ten Cent Store).' Anyway, Jerry brought the masters, which were very straight pop records without much of a change. However, after we had bought these records and were preparing to release them, Bobby Darin would come up to the office to see what was going to happen with the promotions, publicity and all of that.

"Bobby would come up to the office and Herb [Abramson] would very often make him wait," Ertegun said. "So Bobby would be in the waiting room, which was next to my office. And in the waiting room there was an upright piano. So while Bobby was waiting, I would hear him through the wall playing the piano and singing different songs. He had all these Ray Charles songs that he would play in his own way. He was a real good writer and singer who could accompany himself on the piano.

"He sounded terrific to me."

What didn't sound terrific to Herb Abramson, however, were the paltry sales reports on Bobby's Atco releases. Bobby's first Atco release, "I Found a Million Dollar Baby," backed by "Talk to Me Something," bombed. And two more singles released in August 1957, the Darin-Kirshner-penned "Don't Call My Name" and "Pretty Betty," also went nowhere.

But Atco showed tremendous faith in its twenty-one-year-old Decca reject, and booked Bobby on Alan Freed's television show, *The Big Beat,* where he appeared alongside Chuck Berry, Frankie Lymon and Andy Williams. Next up was a spot on Freed's rock 'n' roll revue at the Apollo Theatre in Harlem, and Bobby's first spot with Dick Clark on *American Bandstand* in December.

But it still wasn't enough.

"Herb came into my office one day and announced that he was releasing Bobby Darin from his contract," Ertegun said. "I said 'Please don't. I want just one session with him myself.' And I stopped Herb from giving Bobby his release."

With Ertegun in his corner, Bobby had one more shot with Atco to either put up or shut up. And he reached into his deep bag of tricks for his next surprise.

Throughout his travels on the road, and when he was back in New York, Bobby's show-biz radar always honed in on schmoozing the right people who could help him get ahead. In the music business of the late 1950s, that meant, primarily, the all-powerful disc jockeys, people like Alan Freed or "Murray the K" Kaufman, who had a popular show on WINS in New York. Guys like Kaufman, who hosted stage shows and local television shows, could hype a new act and make or break a career. In his heyday, Kaufman was *the* deejay in New York, and a mention from him was akin to a mention in Walter Winchell's column. It meant that much.

Bobby had struck up a friendship with Kaufman, whose mother fancied herself a songwriter and was always ready with a catchy title (but often no tune to go with it). One night, Bobby was over at Kaufman's eating dinner, when Murray's mother called. She had a catchy title, "Splish Splash, Take a Bath"—could Murray or Bobby do something with it? Kaufman laughed and hopped in the shower, preparing for his show that night. By the time he emerged from the bathroom, Bobby had written "Splish Splash." It had taken him all of ten minutes. The song itself was inane, yet Bobby had written a catchy, hook-laden melody to go along with the mindless words.

Armed with "Splish Splash" and several other original tunes, Bobby went back to Atco and Ahmet Ertegun in April 1958. Ertegun was still trying to keep Herb Abramson from terminating Bobby's contract. Bobby had one more chance to get it right.

"We went in and on that first date we recorded three hits, including 'Splish Splash' and 'Queen of the Hop,'" Ertegun said. "And we had a great time because I got along very well with Bobby."

"I felt confidence like I'd never known before," Bobby said of the recording session. "Somehow, I knew ['Splish Splash'] would move. It felt so right when I sang it."

"He was very secure, very confident, very gifted," recalled Neil Sedaka, a young piano player who knew Bobby casually through Don Kirshner. "He knew he was going to be a star. He played me 'Splish

Splash' before it came out, in Donny's office, and I said, 'Oh my God, that is sensational.' It reminded me of a black artist."

"Splish Splash" was an immediate smash. It received huge play, of course, from Murray the K (his mother, Jean Murray, received a songwriting credit) and was soon blanketing the radio. It also propelled the largely unknown Bobby back onto television where, that summer, he sang "Splish Splash" on Dick Clark's *Beechnut Show* and on *The Bob Crosby Show*, where he caught the eye of actor Jackie Cooper, who was starring in the television series *Hennessey*.

The song also pushed Bobby into the spotlight alongside teen idols Pat Boone, Frankie Avalon, Fabian and Elvis Presley (or, as *Newsweek* dubbed them, "those vacuous young idols of the rock 'n' roll set"). It wasn't exactly the sort of company Bobby had in mind. He had bigger fish to fry.

Within three weeks, "Splish Splash" had sold 100,000 copies, a number that surpassed one million by year's end, carrying "Judy Don't Be Moody" (co-written by Don Kirshner) on its coattails. In July, Atco released its first Bobby Darin album, simply titled *Bobby Darin*, and by August, "Splish Splash" had reached #3 on the charts.

Yet even with his sudden success, Bobby still worried that Atco would drop him. Convinced of that inevitability, he went back into the studio to record "Early in the Morning," a song he'd written with his new musical partner, Woody Harris. Bobby had every intention of selling "Early in the Morning" to his new label once Atco cut him loose. He recorded the song under the *nom de plume* of 'The Ding-Dongs' to sidestep his contractual agreement with Atco.

Bobby's concerns were unfounded; "Early in the Morning" was yet another hit in his growing pop portfolio, and Buddy Holly rushed into the studio to get *his* version of the song out (with only moderate success). Bobby's haste to record "Early in the Morning" under an assumed name almost came back to haunt him once the song became a hit. Darin archivist Jeff Bleiel recounts how Bobby appeared on Dick Clark's Saturday night show, where he was presented with his gold record for "Splish Splash"—and was then asked to sing his new hit, "Early in the Morning."

Atco generously turned the other cheek and rejiggered the credit for "Early in the Morning" to read "Bobby Darin and the Rinky Dinks."

But Bobby wasn't satisfied. He didn't want to be a teen idol. "Now I am in the worst situation I've ever been in. I have a rock and roll hit. This makes me one of a thousand guys," he told *Life* magazine's Shana Alexander. "Now I got to prove I can sing. I had to get beyond rock 'n' roll."

Bobby considered "Splish Splash" a trifle, a piece of schlock he could use as a stepping-stone to bigger and better things. Bobby had always idolized the balladeers, the crooners like Sinatra, Crosby and Bennett. *That's* what he was striving for. "Splish Splash," "Plain Jane," "Queen of the Hop" and "Early in the Morning" had made him famous.

Now he wanted to become a legend.

THE TRAPPINGS OF SUDDEN FAME brought a new dimension to Bobby's life. The success of "Splish Splash" meant he was no longer the poor kid from the Bronx, waiting for the next royalty check he'd have to split with Don Kirshner. "Kirsh," as Bobby liked to call his old writing partner, had given up managing Bobby to start his own publishing company with a new partner, Al Nevins. Kirsh remained close to Bobby and even published some of his hits that year, including "Splish Splash" and "Queen of the Hop."

Bobby and Woody Harris started their own company, Darwood, to look after their publishing endeavors, and Bobby used his newfound financial windfall to outfit himself in the best suits money could buy. At 5'9" and 155 pounds, he remained a wiry ball of energy but was troubled by an inescapable fact: He was beginning to lose his hair.

If Bobby needed any validation of his newfound fame he only had to look as far as the FBI which, in 1958, opened its secret file on "Bobby Darin a.k.a. Walden Robert Cassotto."

FBI chief J. Edgar Hoover had a thing for celebrities; information, in Hoover's mind, was power, and he kept secret dossiers on most major stars. It was potentially embarrassing information Hoover could easily dredge up if he needed a favor—or if he simply wanted to destroy the career of someone he deemed "un-American."

Hoover got around to Bobby in July, when Bobby's draft board in The Bronx, Local 18, notified the FBI that Bobby had failed to report for induction into the military. The FBI, in turn, tried calling Nina, without success. According to Bobby's FBI report, "Mrs. Paula Cassotto" called the New York field office on September 3, informing them Bobby was "working as a singer," had been on the road for a few weeks and would be returning home September 8.

The FBI's report was dated September 11, 1958.

On September 9, 1958, Walden Robert Cassotto was interviewed at the New York office commencing at 8:53 a.m. He was advised of his rights. He stated as follows:

He was born May 14, 1936. At the present time, he is working as an entertainer and singer and works on the road continually. He uses his mother's residence as his home. He resided at 629 East 135th Street, Bronx, until approximately three years ago, and moved to 60 Baruch Drive, New York City. He lived at 60 Baruch Drive until approximately a month ago when his family moved to [blacked out]. He reported his change of address . . . to the Local Board sometime after he moved. He had no intention of avoiding military service and his delinquency was not wilful (*sic*). He suffers from a rheumatic heart as a result of being afflicted with rheumatic fever four times in his childhood.

Bobby told the FBI agent he was "willing to be inducted" and was, in fact, given a physical the very next day for purposes of entering the military. Not surprisingly (and Bobby surely knew this would happen), he failed his physical—and was rejected for military service because of obvious medical reasons.

With the fame of "Splish Splash" came the requisite teen-magazine articles in publications like *Teen Digest* and *Teen Magazine* recounting the familiar story: Bobby's rise from the fatherless, destitute, sickly South Bronx kid with the loving mother and much-older sister to the young up-and-comer wise beyond his years.

Joyce Becker was writing a story on Bobby for her newspaper at Walton High School in the Bronx. Like Bobby, she was a Bronx kid, and she wanted to profile the hometown "Splish Splash Boy" who'd become a teen sensation and was the talk of her classmates.

"My father took me to pick Bobby up at the post office and there stands this short, thin, cute guy on the steps of the post office. I can visualize it like it was yesterday," she said. "He was wearing a gray coat that was so thin, and he was shivering and had a scarf he had wrapped around his hands in front of him.

"So he gets in the back of the car, leans over the front and gives me a kiss on the cheek and says to my father, 'Hello, Mr. Becker, I'm Bobby Darin.' And my father kind of shot him a look. We went back to our apartment and he must have spent twelve hours there. I mean, it was like he didn't want to leave. My mother invited him to stay for dinner and we talked and he let me hear this new record that had just come out and it was 'Splish Splash.' My sister and I danced around the living room like two teenagers and Bobby just became family from that minute on.

"When he left my house my father and I gave him a pair of gloves, which he took with glee, but he was wearing a thin cotton shirt. My father said, 'You don't have an undershirt on?' and ran in his bedroom and took a shirt out of a package and handed him the shirt, and then he took the rest of the package of shirts and gave them to Bobby, which he took."

Bobby was desperate to break out of his teen-idol mold, but was savvy enough to realize that his young audience would grow older with him—and, if he played his cards right, would still buy his records as he moved his singing career in a different direction.

"Everyone wants to grow up and be an adult and so do I, and I want to have an adult audience, but I know that the teenagers of today will be adults tomorrow," he said. "So long as they like me, I'll continue to sing for them.

"Maybe when they get older and turn to Sinatra, as everyone seems to do eventually, then they'll like me, too," he said. "I've never been a snob about anything and I'm not about to start now. I'd be less than honest if I were to say that I didn't enjoy and find pride in my success with the teenage audience."

Still, he hungered for a more "adult" sound and wanted his follow-up to the *Bobby Darin* album to reflect his maturation as a recording artist. But Ahmet Ertegun, Herb Abramson and the other Atco executives had different ideas. Why not milk the teen-idol cash cow for all it was worth? There was time to go in a different direction. Bobby, after all, was only twenty-two. What was the big rush?

Bobby wasn't having any of it.

"I've heard a few people say I'm being premature about going for adult audiences, but I have to be the one to decide that," he said. "I made up my mind to be a star by the age of twenty-one or I'd blow my brains out. Well, I was a year late, but when I was twenty-one I knew it was just a matter of time. One year to be exact.

"I didn't fit with teenage audiences. Kids like to identify with kids their own age," he said. "And even as a young singer, I've always been more of a grownup in my attitude. There's never been a moment in my life when I didn't know that I was going to be a star. Everything I've done has been dedicated toward that goal, and I don't let anything get in my way or slow me down."

Bobby certainly wasn't going to let Atco slow him down, and if they weren't interested in helping him evolve, then so be it. Using the money he'd earned from "Splish Splash," Bobby informed Atco he would finance the next album himself.

In mid-December, Bobby entered the studio with Ahmet Ertegun and a lineup of solid studio musicians including drummer Don Lamond, bassist Milt Hinton and trumpet player Carl "Doc" Severinsen, who would later find fame and fortune as part of Johnny Carson's *Tonight Show*. On the agenda were a slew of tracks Bobby wanted to record, including a rendition of "Mack the Knife" from Kurt Weill's "Threepenny Opera"—which Bobby had been performing in his nightclub act for about a year—and "Beyond the Sea," a French love ballad.

" 'Mack the Knife' was something we cooked up together," Ertegun said. "I was great friends with Lotte Lenya, who was Kurt Weill's widow. Oddly enough, I had had lunch with her a few months before that session. And she said, 'Why don't you record any of my late husband's work?' I said, 'Listen, we're not in that kind of business.' I was trying to explain to her, which was almost impossible for her to understand, that we were making a totally different kind of music.

"However, I called her and said I think we're going to do 'Mack the Knife' because Louis Armstrong had made a record of 'Mack the Knife,' and that was really the inspiration for Bobby's record. Every singer in the world owes Louis Armstrong because he taught everybody how to sing with swing.

"And Bobby got that lesson better than anybody."

Bobby and Ertegun entered the Atco studios on December 14, 1958, to begin the sessions for the next album. Ertegun remembers Bobby completing "Mack the Knife" in about three takes. "I think the first take it sounded like a smash. We did it again just to please everybody, so the band could play better and so on," he said. "That record swings, of course. Great arrangement."

The arrangement for "Mack the Knife" and the other songs cut during those mid-December sessions was the brainchild of Richard Wess, a young composer who had worked with Connie Francis. Harriet Wasser, a close friend of Bobby's for several years, had ties to the record industry. Harriet, or "Hesh" as her friends called her, knew Wess and introduced him to Bobby, helping to create a powerhouse combination. Among the Darin faithful, Hesh is an unheralded hero.

After "Mack the Knife" became a huge hit for him, Bobby always waffled on whether he actually heard Louie Armstrong's version of the song, which Satchmo recorded for Columbia Records in 1955. It's hard to believe he didn't hear Armstrong's version, considering its popularity and the close attention Bobby paid to the music business. Nonetheless, it was still a drastic step for Bobby and Wess to take the dirge-like ballad and transform it into a swingin', up-tempo number with a bouncy bass line complemented by Don Lamond's sharp drumming.

"Mack the Knife," known in its original German version as "Moritat von Mackie Messer," was first performed in Bertold Brecht and Kurt Weill's "The Threepenny Opera," which opened in Berlin in 1928. Brecht and Weill, in turn, were inspired by "The Beggar's Opera," a parody of Italian opera written in 1728 by John Gay that incorporated topical figures into its storyline. Marc Blitzstein had translated the German version into English, which was the version Armstrong recorded.

Macheath, better known by his nickname of "Mack the Knife," is a murderous thief who prowls the streets of London in 1837, working for master beggar Peachum while juggling mistresses Jenny Diver (Low-Dive Jenny), Suky Tawdry and Lucy Brown.

The song, in its original vocal version, was dour and depressing, describing how Mack the Knife sneaks up on his victims and stabs them in the back. In Bobby's hands, however, "Mack the Knife" was transformed into a bubbly, effervescent, orchestral splash—music to murder by with a lush, Big Band sound and Bobby's playful vocals. Never had poor Louie Miller's murder been celebrated in such an upbeat, joyous manner.

The song also marked the introduction of Bobby's hep-cat, Sinatra-type phrasing (*Oh the shark, babe/Has such teeth, dear*) and his scat-like approach to interpreting the lyrics. He even threw in a thank-you of sorts to Kurt Weill's widow (*Look out to Miss Lotte Lenya*).

In addition to "Mack the Knife," Bobby used the December sessions to record "Beyond the Sea," "Through A Long And Sleepless Night," "It Ain't Necessarily So," "Some of These Days," "That's All" and several other songs—all in the brassy, Big Band style he hoped would set him apart from the Pat Boones and Frankie Avalons of the world.

BOBBY ALSO LAVISHED some of his "Splish Splash" money on his family, buying a small house in rural Lake Hiawatha, New Jersey, about an hour outside of Manhattan. Polly, thrilled to be out of the city, moved there in 1958, and was joined by Nina, Charlie, Vee, Vana and Gary, now turning two. Bobby also used the Lake Hiawatha cottage as his home when he wasn't on the road, which wasn't very often. Still, the cottage was a place where he could unwind, shoot the shit with Charlie and lavish attention on Gary, who was showing some musical talent of his own. Bobby was always extremely fond of Gary, and kept a picture of his nephew in his wallet.

"Every time Gary sees a jukebox, he asks for my record and, if it's not there, he tries to beat up the box," he told a reporter proudly. "I want him to be in show business. He's a beautiful kid, and already I can see he has a bundle of rhythm. I want him to have music lessons. I want him to have a piano. I want to cry when I think of my wasted years.

"Gary fills a strange void in my life," he said. "I love my sister's other two children, too, but there's something special about little Gary. I've known it since he was a year old. I was watching him one day, and for heaven's sake, there he was, coming on strong, with a big beat.

"I mean that in terms of personality, of course," he said. "There's something so very, very wonderful about him. It isn't the intelligence and talent I suspect are there. It isn't hearing about his frantically pounding on the TV set trying to communicate with me when I'm on

Clark and the others. It isn't the terrific welcome I receive when I come in off the road.

"He's the fulfillment of a need," Bobby said. "Gary and I have some sort of, as yet unspoken, pact. He's for me. I'm for him. It's a simple as that."

The extended Cassotto family didn't freeload off their famous relative. Bobby put Nina and Charlie on the payroll, Nina as a secretary of sorts, going through his fan mail and organizing his schedule, Charlie traveling on the road with Bobby as his Man-Friday and all-around *schlepper*.

"The fact is that my mother and father worked for Bobby. It wasn't like, well, here's $50,000 or here's a house," Gary said. "They were working. My mother did all his fan-club work and my father was road manager and gopher and valet and anything else. I think as soon as Frankie Avalon made it, he built his mother a beautiful house, furnished with two new cars, the whole deal.

"That never happened with us," he said. "That wasn't Bobby. He did that with other people, but as far as his own family was concerned, they had to work for what they got."

Bobby's relationship with Charlie was also very close. It was Charlie who carried young Bobby around when he was too weak to walk, or who picked Bobby up at Hanson's drug store so he wouldn't stress his bad heart walking home.

"Charlie was a funny guy, but he was sometimes inappropriate," Dick Lord recalled. "Bobby called me one day and said, 'You're not going to believe it. I took Charlie to the Coliseum [in Rome] and you won't believe what he said. He said, 'Jesus, it's like the fucking South Bronx.' But that's the kind of guy he was. He loved Bobby."

Bobby's relationship with Nina, however, was tenuous at best. He constantly needled her about her weight, and her mere presence often seemed to annoy him.

"What he complained to me about [Nina] was that it was never enough," Lord said. "Nina and all of them grew to dislike anyone who was close to Bobby, jealousy, whatever. Dick Behrke, myself, all of us. In the beginning we used to go to the house in Lake Hiawatha. Nina was a great cook and we would go there and she would make all kinds of food. Slowly, it went the other way.

"One day Bobby asked me to keep his car for him when he was on the road," Lord said. "It was a pain in the ass because I lived in Brooklyn, I didn't have my own house, and it was alternate-side-of-the-street parking. Every morning I would have to get up and move his car. And finally when I returned it—I think Charlie came to pick it up—Nina called me. She said, 'One of the tires is damaged and you owe me eighty dollars.'"

The relationship cut both ways. Steve Blauner, who would become Bobby's agent, remembers Nina resenting Bobby.

"Nina was always embarrassed by him and you know, she was his sister and it's like, 'I don't particularly like my brother, but he's my brother. I don't reach out for him because he never reached out for me. I guess he's kind of jealous because I had this rapport with my parents and I told him, after they were both dead, I figured you were entitled to it. I *work* at it.'"

The family put aside whatever tensions were building, at least for the time being, when Polly died in early 1959. She was sixty-eight, give or take a few years, and had been sick for a long time. Bobby was on the road in Los Angeles with Steve Blauner when Nina called to break the news.

"I took Bobby to see Jerry Lewis at the Moulin Rouge and at the time nobody knew who Bobby was, even though he had two hit records," Blauner said. "And Jerry, this is after [the split with] Dean Martin, as part of his act, used to come into the audience with a microphone and let people say and do stuff. And so I took Bobby backstage to meet Jerry before the show, so he came over during show and did this skit with Bobby.

"Afterward, Bobby and I went to a Chinese restaurant and I said to Bobby, 'You know, somebody came up to me and said there was a phone call for you and I thought it was bullshit because no one knew you were going to be here.' So he said, 'Well, I'm going to call home.' So he went to the pay phone and called. His mother had died. He went back home the next morning; I put him on a plane and he went back for the funeral and buried her."

Bobby was heartbroken over Polly's death. "My mother was sick for a long time. Matter of fact, from the time I was born," he told a magazine writer. "She wasn't supposed to have a baby and I guess I've always had a lot of guilty feelings about bringing on her initial sickness. But, as you grow older, a lot of other things take shape.

"I'll tell you, this is the first time I ever truly missed anyone. I miss her every day. I picture things about her. It might be only for five seconds. I can see where she'll be with me for the rest of my life. I know, if I do something good, I look up and wonder if she's watching. And, if I do something I'm not particularly proud of, I'll say, 'Gee, Mom, don't get made at me.' It's just like a quick thought."

Bobby had been through four managers before Steve Blauner arrived on the scene. A big, burly, prematurely balding go-getter, Blauner had graduated from New York University in 1955, spending two years in the Air Force before getting a job as a gofer at General Artists Corporation, or GAC, then the country's third-largest talent agency behind MCA and William Morris.

"I was one step out of the mail room," Blauner said. "I had an office with no window that I shared with another agent. Those were the years in television where anybody who could sing had a television show. We had Nat King Cole with a show, Guy Mitchell with a show, Patti Page with a show, Pat Boone with a show, Perry Como with a show. So my job was to find an availability of guests from the agencies around town to feed these shows."

Blauner had become friends with Sammy Davis Jr. while they were both in the service, and it was through this association that Blauner began building his name and his reputation. Harriet Wasser, who had introduced Bobby to Richard Wess for the "Mack the Knife" sessions, approached Blauner about Bobby. "I told Harriet to get Bobby Darin up to my office and I borrowed somebody else's outside office, with a window, and Bobby came up and I gave him a whole song-and-dance," Blauner said. "And I tell him, 'We're going to get you on the Bob Crosby summer show,' and I signed him. And then I say to myself, what have I done? I felt so bad because we had nothing for him to do.

"So the first date we get him is a charity show in Bridgeport, Connecticut. There were three acts that opened the show, which was hosted by Dick Clark, and Bobby was the first one on—that's how low on the totem pole he was," Blauner said. "It was Bobby, the Kalin Twins, another act I don't remember, intermission and then Steve [Lawrence] and Eydie [Gorme], who were going to replace Steve Allen for the summer.

"So I just felt awful and I got somebody to drive me there because the least I could do was go see him. Out comes Bobby doing rock 'n' roll. I was stunned. There was something about him on that stage that just knocked me for a loop. And I went, 'Wow.' I said to Steve and Eydie's manager, 'You know, you ought to book Bobby for the summer show.' He said, 'What are you talking about? We got Jackie Cooper—at least he can play the drums.' "

Blauner, blown away by Bobby's stage performance, returned to his GAC office in Manhattan the next day. "I went up and down the aisles saying that Bobby Darin could be one of the biggest stars of all time. And everyone laughed at me. They said, 'Kid, get outta here,' with the exception of a woman agent named Roz Ross, who understood and believed."

Shortly thereafter Blauner was transferred out to the West Coast, working in GAC's Los Angeles office, when he encountered Bobby, who was doing a high school record hop, earning about $500. "He wasn't making a lot of money. I had rented a house off Sunset Strip with another guy and Bobby would come and sleep there," Blauner said. "And I remember one day we were driving down Sunset Boulevard when Bobby asked me to manage him. I said, 'What, are you out of your mind? Number one, it wouldn't be right because I'm your agent, it would be unethical. Number two, I'm in the business less than a year and a half. I don't know enough.' I was scared to death."

Polly's death had shaken Bobby, but hadn't dampened his obsessive quest for more success. In March, he went back into the studio to record some Atco singles, including a sweet number he'd written called "Dream Lover," which would become a huge hit and cement Bobby's unwanted status as a teen-idol. The song featured a young Neil Sedaka on piano.

"Bobby and I became good friends and he used me on several tracks, to play piano on 'Dream Lover' and, on the B side, 'Bullmoose,' which was a song about a piano player," Sedaka said. "Ahmet Ertegun was the producer for a couple of those songs, and I remember vividly going into Atlantic Records. Bobby was recording 'Dream Lover' and was asking for suggestions.

"So I told him to put the guitar riff up an octave on 'Dream Lover,' which he loved, and then there was one take of 'Dream Lover' where I sang a double voice for the whole track with Bobby, but that version wasn't used.

"The session was a little hectic. Bobby was scared," Sedaka said. "He knew there was something in it, but the record started off very shaky, and the arrangement was not great. The tempo was wrong. The chorus parts were wrong; the guitar was wrong. I remember Ahmet saying, 'Neil, you've got to come in and help us.' And Bobby said, 'What would you do?' And I put the guitar up. I knew, when we left, that it was a smash."

Pat Boone, driving in to Manhattan from his home in Teaneck, New Jersey, to rehearse his ABC television show, heard the song on the radio.

"I heard what I thought was me singing a song that I didn't recognize at all, because I had done a couple of songs that were big hits, 'Almost Lost My Mind' and 'Chains of Love,' that both called for me to do an octave jump. And not many people could do that," he said.

"And I'm hearing this song and I don't recognize the song and it has an octave jump. It doesn't sound like a black guy but I thought it was me—I thought, when did I do that? And then when it ended, the deejay said 'That's Bobby Darin's new record.' He was a chameleon. He could take any style, practically, and do it well."

That same month, Atco released Bobby's second album, *That's All*, compiled from the December 1958 "Mack the Knife" sessions which also included the album's title song. Atco lined up an April appearance for Bobby on *The Perry Como Show* to promote the album. Ertegun, Abramson, Wexler and the other Atco executives were worried, and rightly so; *That's All* represented an extreme departure for the teen-idol "Splish Splash" crooner who had yet another burgeoning teen-heartthrob hit with "Dream Lover."

Now Bobby, all of twenty-two, suddenly expected his audience to buy him as a sophisticated balladeer crooning slower, more melodic songs wrapped in lush arrangements. If there was any indication of things to come, perhaps it was in the form of a telegram Bobby received from Sammy Davis Jr.: "Just heard the dubs for your new album. What can I say? They're so good I hate you!" Sammy began mentioning Bobby's name at his nightclub engagements, telling people they had to hear this talented young kid.

The effect *That's All* would eventually have on Bobby's career wasn't immediately apparent, even once it was released. "Mack the Knife," the album's signature tune, was hyped by Atco and began to get some airplay early on, but it was "Dream Lover" that carried Bobby for the time being, reaching #2 on the Billboard charts by July.

Steve Blauner, meanwhile, working behind the scenes, heard that George Burns was planning his first-ever nightclub act. Burns would open in Lake Tahoe and then move on to the Sahara Hotel in Las Vegas. Blauner had a masterstroke idea: Why not see if Burns would be interested in having Bobby share the bill? The publicity would be huge. It was the first time that Burns was working solo. His beloved wife, Gracie Allen, had retired once the couple's television show, *The Burns and Allen Show*, ended its long run the previous year. All the stars would be in Vegas to see George and to cheer him on, helping him kick off his new act. Unspoken, of course, was the curiosity factor: Could George pull it off as a solo act?

"I was told that George Burns is going to Las Vegas. He'd played vaudeville, of course, but it was the first time he ever played a nightclub," Blauner said. "More importantly, it was the first time he's going to work without Gracie.

"So I got somebody to get me in to see George. I never played him 'Mack the Knife.' The first song I played him was 'Some of These Days' because I figured he could relate to it. So I played him a ballad and then the last thing I played him was 'That's All.' And he buys Bobby Darin. Two weeks in Tahoe, I think Bobby got $1,500 a week, and then four weeks in Vegas. George became a father figure. Bobby just loved him."

"I heard a record of this fellow and I was very impressed by the vitality and drive of his singing and the positive way of his phrasing," Burns told *The Saturday Evening Post*. "I treated him like a twenty-two-year-old boy. That's all he was, you know. He's a darling little boy. Gracie and I love him."

Bobby was thrilled. With "Dream Lover" on its way to earning

Bobby his third gold record, and "Mack the Knife" beginning to get noticed, everything was jelling. Even a potential glaring problem worked itself out, no small thanks to Bobby.

Blauner had worked wonders getting Bobby booked with George Burns, but Steve was still only Bobby's agent. Bobby's managers, Joe Csida and Ed Burton, had already arranged for Bobby to tour England—at the same time he would be appearing with Burns in Lake Tahoe and Vegas. It didn't bode well, particularly since Bobby, who had signed with Csida and Burton the year before, was growing disenchanted with their management of his career. "Bobby not only wanted his managers to get results, he wanted them to leave a trail of blood," said one friend. "He wanted the manager to smack the desk and leave the booking agent bleeding on the floor."

That wasn't Burton or Csida's style, and Burton later admitted they had underestimated Bobby.

"He did a couple of his songs for us, jumped on the piano, stuck a cigar in his mouth and ran around the room imitating Groucho," Burton recalled. "Our reaction was: This kid is nutty, but he's right. We figured him for a real big rock-and-roller. To be honest, though, we never saw the ultimate in him. He saw it in himself all along."

Especially now. The booking with Burns was big, and Bobby knew it. He wasn't about to let another rock 'n' roll tour get in the way. "Get out of it," Bobby snapped at Burton. "We can't get out of it. We're committed," Burton told him. Bobby's response? "Get uncommitted." They did.

Bobby's brashness and cock-sure attitude would have been off-putting in a much older man; it was downright disarming for a twenty-two-year-old singer who hadn't yet proven himself outside the recording business. "He was brash, and he was an easy guy not to like if you didn't know him well," said Dick Clark, who was very close to Bobby in the early days. "On the other hand, if you knew him, he was kind and generous and loyal, always by your side, everything you would hope for. But he was always full of stress or seemed to have a gun to his head. I guess he knew that his time was short."

Bobby's attitude wasn't winning him many fans in the business, most of whom weren't aware of his rheumatic heart and the long shadow it cast over his life. Booked on *The Perry Como Show* in April,

Bobby astounded the laid-back Como, and his crew, by barking orders as soon as he showed up on the set to rehearse a duet with The Sweatered One.

"All right, babe, how will it be? Do you want to take the harmony or the melody?" Bobby said to Como. After the run-through, Como walked off. "My, the boy comes on pretty strong, doesn't he?" he said to a stagehand.

Ahmet Ertegun recalled another "Bobby story" from the *Como Show* appearance. "The producer of the show comes over to Bobby and says, 'Try to be a little more down key with Mr. Como. You know, Fabian was here last week, he was very respectful and Perry treated him very well and it went off very well.

"So Bobby says, 'Fabian? He can't sing. I'm Bobby Darin, man, what are you talking about?' But you know, so what? It was true. Bobby had that American feel. He was a star. And he felt like a star even before he was a star. I thought he was a star before he was a star. I don't expect somebody to behave like a wimp. Bobby had humility, but he also had pride."

The cocky attitude carried over into Bobby's first appearance with Burns in Lake Tahoe. "Bobby walked out on stage on opening night like he thought he was Jolson, or, better still, Sinatra," Burns said. "They'd look at him, and you could see them thinking, 'This little boy can't be that good.' They resented him in the first number and they resented him even more in the second.

"But a funny thing happens," Burns said. "By the third number he gets older. They forget they don't like him because they're too busy watching him."

The act with Burns was a success. Bobby would sing "Splish Splash," "Some of These Days" and "Mack the Knife," then reappear on stage a little later to engage in some soft-shoe banter with the old master. "This boy works hard easy," was how one columnist described the performance.

And if the armchair psychologist was looking for a textbook case of the young man looking for the father he didn't have, well, Bobby admitted as much. "Mr. Burns is a father symbol to me," he said. "And you can omit the word 'symbol.'

"I've been fatherless of course, since birth," Bobby said. "I call him for advice wherever I am—not just show-business advice but advice on personal problems—yes, including love."

The relationship hit a snag, however, once George and Bobby reached Las Vegas. Bobby had been gambling, and lost over $1,500 at the craps tables. The news got back to Burns, who didn't take kindly to the news—and promptly slapped Bobby in the face backstage.

When it came time for them to perform on stage that night, Burns introduced Bobby but refused to shake his hand. Bobby ran after Burns in the wings, telling him he wouldn't be able to go on unless George came back out and shook his hand in front of the audience. Burns, ever-the-showman, turned it into a routine. He told the audience about Bobby's gambling losses, and then turned to Bobby. "Bobby, if I forgive you, will you promise you won't ever do it again?" Bobby had learned his lesson.

"I stopped him from gambling in Vegas," Blauner said. "Because in Vegas, even if you weren't a gambler, you were a gambler because what else is there to do? The windows are covered; you can't get to your room without going through a casino. So I cut him off. I wrote every hotel on the strip that if they extended Bobby any credit it was their own problem—they would not get the money back."

Bobby turned twenty-three in May 1959, and "Mack the Knife" was starting to pick up steam. Atco still hadn't released it as a single, even though *That's All* had been out for several months. One night, Bobby called Dick Clark from the road.

"When we were tight, in the early days, we were talking a little more frequently than we did later in life," Clark said. "Bobby called me from God-knows-where. He said, 'They're playing my latest release. I'll play it for you on the phone.' And he played 'Mack the Knife.' I said, 'Are you crazy? You're a rock 'n' roll star, you're not a saloon singer or a balladeer. Are you out of your fucking mind? This is a bad mistake.'"

Steve Blauner, meanwhile, had quit his job at GAC and had gone to work for B-movie king Sam Katzman, who was paying Blauner seventy-five dollars a week, mostly to accompany him to the racetrack.

"So I'm going to the racetrack and I'm saying to myself, I didn't come here to go to the racetrack," Blauner said. "So I call Bobby, he was playing a nightclub in Boston, and I said, 'Look, if you still want me to manage you, okay, but it's got to be now. I can't stay here.' "

Bobby agreed, but there was the little problem of wriggling out of his contract with Burton and Csida. So Bobby made a swift decision, one that Blauner thought showed just how much Bobby wanted Steve to manage him.

"They said, okay, we'll let you out of the contract, but under the following basis: That they would publish everything that he wrote and recorded until they hit the $100,000 mark, and then Bobby would be free. They would continue to own those copyrights forever, so that $100,000, who knows, by now it would be millions. And Bobby accepted that.

"I never thought I would be a manager. The only reason I became an agent was I figured I wanted to be in show business and this would send me off in some direction," Blauner said. "So I said to Bobby, look, you're going to be up on that stage and do whatever you want— I'm going to be all over you, do this and do that, and the final answer will be yours. And you'll do what I need you to do. I don't want to come to you and say, 'Will you?' I want to come to you and say, 'You *will.*'

"We never had a contract, only a handshake," Blauner said. "I was getting fifteen percent, and he lived by that. He gave me his life."

Burton had always told Bobby that, 'You're not living in a bowling alley. You just can't go around knocking people over like tenpins." After leaving Burton and Csida, Bobby sent Burton a watch, with an inscription on the back:

"Ed, To Time the Bowling Match. Bobby."

STEVE BLAUNER WAS CONCERNED that Atco still hadn't released "Mack the Knife" as a single, and worried that Bobby would lose whatever momentum he had if that particular situation wasn't quickly remedied. Bobby had sung "Mack the Knife" on *The Ed Sullivan Show* in May, the finger-snapping that would become his trademark already in place. Now it was July, and the *That's All* album had been out since March. Bobby needed a single from the album to propel the next step of his career. "Mack the Knife" was the logical choice.

"When we were out at a nightclub, he's doing two shows a night, so we'd get to bed in the wee hours of the morning and you'd sleep to the afternoon," Blauner said. "So I would get up and did what I had to do, and I went to the record stores. And I would take Bobby's albums to the stores, that kind of stuff. And I'm in this record store, and this happened two or three times, and somebody would come in and say, 'You know, there's a record I want to buy called Mackie, Mack, The Knife,' and they wouldn't know the title.

"So now I get Bobby and Ahmet Ertetgun and I say, you've got to release it. I mean, it was no coincidence for me to be in two record stores in two different towns and have people come in just when I'm there, asking for the song," Blauner said. "And Bobby and Ahmet thought I was insane because it was only rock 'n' roll on the charts at that point in the Top 10."

Bobby was scheduled to open in mid-August at The Cloisters in Los Angeles, on the site of the storied El Mocambo nightclub. It would be nice, Blauner thought, if "Mack the Knife" could be released as quickly as possible to capitalize on the song's growing popularity.

"I remember the exact date—it was July 31 because Bobby was rehearsing to open at The Cloisters," Blauner said. "It was a big engagement for him because it was Hollywood and I was trying to make him a star out here so that I could get him a picture deal.

"The Cloisters was a small club and it had a bar. And there was a phone call, and the bartender said it was for me and Bobby from Ahmet Ertegun. So I get Bobby offstage and we go and sit at the bar with the phone between us. Ahmet's saying we've got to put 'Mack the Knife' out as a single and now I'm concerned that it's too late, we blew it. I said, 'Jesus Christ, Ahmet, by the time you get it out, this thing is going to be over!' He said, 'I'll have it out in two weeks.' I said, 'You've never had anything out in two weeks.'"

In the meantime, Bobby took The Cloisters by storm, opening to a packed house and rave reviews.

"I was there opening night and he was unbelievable," recalled actress Shirley Jones. "He was like the 'New Elvis' at that time, the new person on stage, the new look. He was a remake of Sammy Davis Jr. yet he wasn't quite that. He could do everything—he could dance and he moved great. You saw that total star quality immediately."

Atco rushed out "Mack the Knife" at the end of August, and by

September the song was taking the country by storm. Bobby sang "Mack the Knife," along with "Dream Lover," on *The Dick Clark Beechnut Show*, then followed that appearance with another television appearance two weeks later on *The Ed Sullivan Show* (no "Mack the Knife" this time, however). Bobby's heart condition acted up after the Sullivan appearance, but he ignored it. He was simply too busy, and had too many things to do, to worry about his health. The end of September found him as the star attraction on Jimmy Durante's television special, where (yet again) Bobby sang "Mack the Knife" and clowned around with Old Schnozzola.

By now, "Mack the Knife" was getting blanket airplay around the country and was climbing steadily up the charts. By October, it reached #1, where it would stay for nine weeks. It eventually sold over two million copies.

"Everybody was surprised. I mean, it was uncalled-for. If you look at the charts from that time you'll see what I'm talking about," Blauner said. "There was nothing like 'Mack the Knife.' It was all rock 'n' roll [on the charts]. And the other thing that was different was that . . . you never took a single out of an album in those days. When you went in to do sessions, you did four songs a session, a twelve-song album. If you went in to do the single session, you could also do four songs and hopefully you'd get a single out of it. This was one of the first times that something had been taken out of an album and made into a single."

Everything was happening very quickly now. With "Mack the Knife" going through the roof, the movie offers began rolling in. Bobby, whose real ambition was to act, had always believed that a hit record would translate into a movie career.

William Michaeljohn, the head of Paramount Pictures, heard "Mack the Knife" and, at Blauner's urging, instructed one of his directors, Norman Taurog, to go and see Bobby perform. Taurog was impressed, and brought Bobby back to Paramount for a screen test. Bobby did two screen tests, the first a scene from *The Gilded Lace*, which had starred Fred MacMurray. The second screen test was one of James Dean's scenes from *East of Eden*.

"Bobby did very well. He didn't try to imitate Fred MacMurray, and he didn't try to imitate Jimmy," Taurog said later. "The minute they saw the test they said it was a huge success and Jack Karp immediately signed him to a long-term contract. My prediction is that this boy's gonna go far in the motion-picture business."

Blauner worked out a seven-picture deal with Paramount reportedly worth $1 million. Bobby's first movie would be *Cry For Happy* starring Glenn Ford, which was scheduled to go into production in early 1960.

In October, Bobby also made his first episodic television appearance when he guest-starred in an episode of Jackie Cooper's CBS sitcom, *Hennesey*. Bobby played Honeyboy Jones, a musician who's drafted into the Navy but wants out to pursue his career and make money.

"Mack the Knife" was also causing a bit of controversy in New York. The song, in its basic form, was a narrative about murder— which was easy to forget, with Bobby singing joyously about "a body, oozing life," "scarlet billows" starting to spread, and Macheath wearing gloves "so there's never, never a trace of red." WCBS-AM in New York was caught up in the brouhaha over the television quiz-show scandals plaguing the industry at that time. The station, extremely sensitive to offending its listeners, deemed "Mack the Knife" too risqué to play on the air.

In September, one of the WCBS deejays thought it would be a good idea to play "Mack the Knife" immediately after reading a news report of a teen who'd been stabbed. That was the final straw for WCBS management, and the station pulled the song off the air. The ban, however, didn't last too long; with "Mack the Knife" roaring up the charts, it would be folly to ignore it.

With the success of "Mack the Knife," money concerns were a thing of the past. Bobby was commanding $10,000 for every television appearance, *That's All* was well on its way to selling nearly half-a-million copies and Bobby's nightclub fees were skyrocketing. His estimated income was expected to pass $300,000 by the end of the year (over $1 million in today's market).

"To tell you what kind of a person Bobby was, it was my birthday, we were in New York and we went to see my parents," Blauner said. "And Bobby came over to the apartment, took me aside and he said, 'I didn't know what to get you for your birthday and I didn't want to get you a piece of jewelry.'

"He said, 'This has nothing to do with money, because hopefully we will never have to worry about a nickel, but this is the only way I can show my appreciation—to give you five percent more.'"

The appearances were now coming fast and furious. In October, twenty-three-year-old Bobby became the youngest entertainer to ever headline in Las Vegas when he opened at the Sands in the Copa Room—which would become home to the Rat Pack's famous "Summit Shows" three months later during the filming of *Ocean's Eleven*.

Bobby's Vegas opening was a big deal for the kid who'd been singing "Splish Splash" a year earlier, and *Newsweek* marked the event with a full-page articled entitled "Splish Becomes Splash."

"I said to myself I had to be a star at 21 or I'd blow my brains out. Well, I'm a year later but I guess that's all right." An Italian-American boy from the Bronx with the unlikely name of Walden Robert Cassotto had finally made it. He is presently the hottest young rhythm singer in the business in the same billing league with Frank Sinatra, Dean Martin and Sammy Davis Jr. His future looks as rosy and heady as pink champagne.

Cassotto's professional name is Bobby Darin and last week was the most exciting and successful of his young life. He was a headliner for the first time at the Sands Hotel in Las Vegas, his Atco disk "Mack the Knife" was the biggest selling pop record in the U.S. and his gross income for the year will exceed $250,000.

"There hasn't been an organized teenage movement for a singer since Eddie Fisher caught on," Darin shrewdly noted. "It's tough these days—the kids are fickle. They do more flipping over the songs than they do over any one singer." Bobby also felt that he came on a little too old for the teenagers. "I didn't fit," he observed. "Some people would say it's premature for me to be booked into the Sands. But I know I can handle it and the Chez Paree and the Copa afterward. I've always had a drive to do everything the best."

The Sands gig went well and Bobby earned solid reviews—despite some jitters that lasted a little longer than he would have liked.

"On opening night I'm afraid to say word one. Three nights later I still know I'm doing bad shows. I'm still frightened," he said. On the fourth night, Bobby had an epiphany—or so it seemed when he described the scene to journalist Sidney Fields in his popular syndicated newspaper column, "Only Human".

The fourth night, before the show, sitting alone in his dressing room, he saw in his mind's eye the stage and the faces of the waiting audience and he saw some of the others who had been on that stage: Frank Sinatra, Jerry Lewis, Jimmy Durante, and his memory told him: "They don't fight the audience; they enjoy them."

"So for the first time I went out to enjoy the audience," Bobby said. "I wasn't abrupt anymore. My confidence wasn't forced. And for once I had a good time and I think they did."

In the fall, Bobby reunited with George Burns as a guest on Burns' television special, *The Big Time*, and prepared for the Grammy Awards, which were being televised for the first time in their three-year history.

If Bobby needed any more validation that he was now a huge star, it came in the form of Ed Sullivan. The prickly Sullivan was famous for picking well-publicized fights with everyone from Walter Winchell and Jack Paar to comedian Joey Bishop. Now, as the Grammys approached, Sullivan zeroed in on Bobby.

The preceding May, Sullivan had signed Bobby to appear exclusively on *The Ed Sullivan Show* four times before the end of the year at $1,000-an-appearance. At the time the deal was signed, Bobby's big hit was "Dream Lover." "Mack the Knife" wasn't yet the phenomenon it would become over the summer.

By the time September rolled around, however, "Mack the Knife" was huge. But Bobby couldn't sing the song on *The Ed Sullivan Show* because CBS was still uneasy over the quiz-show-scandal uproar (and, as previously noted, had banned the song from WCBS AM).

Now, with NBC airing the Grammys directly opposite *The Ed Sullivan Show*—and with Bobby scheduled to sing "Mack the Knife" during the Grammy telecast—Sullivan was seething. He demanded that Bobby not sing on the Grammys.

"Jimmy Durante wanted him for a special. Timex wanted him for another, George Burns for another and Revlon for another," Sullivan told *New York Post* TV columnist Bob Williams. "I said yes, every time. Bobby's fee went up to $7,500 and then $10,000—and there I'd signed him for $1,000-a-show last spring.

"I was delighted over his success, of course, but I did feel that somebody should at least have shown the courtesy to have asked me," he said about the Grammys. "And I told them I wouldn't approve the appearance. But Eddie Elkort of General Artists Corp. and I talked it over and, of course, I agreed."

Bobby's version of the story, which he related in his Damon Runyon-like way of speaking, was slightly different.

"I went to see Sullivan myself, as one man of character speaking to another man of character, and I told him I had a chance to better myself. That's all there was to it," he said. "Mr. Sullivan is a gentleman."

The 1959 Grammy Awards were being televised for the first time, and whatever bad karma Sullivan sent Bobby's way didn't make a difference. Bobby not only sang "Mack the Knife," but he went on to win Grammys for Best New Artist of the Year—the first-ever winner in that category—and for Record of the Year ("Mack the Knife").

Bobby was thrilled and flush with his success. Never one to mince words, he was honest—and not a little cocky—when he was cornered by UPI Hollywood correspondent Vernon Scott after the ceremonies during a cocktail party at the Beverly Hilton Hotel. The story, which went out over the wires the next day, made headlines around the country and marked one of the most infamous moments in Bobby's career. When he died fourteen years later Bobby's words to Scott were *still* being quoted as indicative of the Bronx kid's cockiness and arrogance.

The contretemps erupted when Scott asked Bobby about the inevitable comparisons to his idol Frank Sinatra, who Bobby had praised time and again in interview after interview.

"I hope to pass Frank in everything he's done," Bobby was quoted as saying. The words set off an uproar. Sinatra himself was said to be livid, and even Sammy Davis Jr., one of Bobby's biggest cheerleaders, had some choice words for his pal: "Let me know when you stop being a legend, so we can start being friends again."

Bobby claimed he'd been misquoted, that his words were taken out of context. Blauner was thrilled: The publicity was enormous. Just make sure you spell the kid's name right and we're in business.

"We're in the lobby and Vernon Scott stops us," Blauner said. "And he says to Bobby, 'Do you want to be bigger than Sinatra?' And Bobby says, 'Why would you do that to me? We're from a different era. I want to be the best and biggest Bobby Darin that I can be.' Scott says, 'Well, you want to do everything Frank's done?' and Bobby said, again, 'Why would you do that to me?' End of interview.

"The next day, the *Journal-American*, *The World Telegram*, *The New York Post*, *The New York Times*, it made headlines and I loved it. My attitude was, 'I don't care what you write, as long as you spell the name right,'" Blauner said. "The headlines said, 'Darin Wants to Be Bigger Than Sinatra!' I never talked to Vernon Scott again. It doesn't mean that I didn't like the story. I loved it."

It didn't seem to bother Bobby much, either, despite his wan protestations that he'd been misquoted. "There is a difference between conceit and egotism," he said. "Conceit is thinking you're great; egotism is knowing it. If you have no talent, you have to be a nice guy, so you walk out humble.

"I don't think Al Jolson was a humble man, performance-wise or otherwise—or Crosby or Sinatra. I've seen some of these Mr. Nice Guys off-camera, and all you hear out of them is 'I, I, I.'

"Humility? Humbleness? The biggest thing between you and God is death. The biggest success in the world walks around with the knowledge that he is going to die like everyone else. That's the only source of my humility—the *only* source. As for my talent, it has been given to me to use while I can.

"I will use it the way I think best and I will never apologize for it."

BOBBY'S POP-CULTURE STATUS was cemented, Eisenhower-Era style, when he was ambushed just days after the Grammy Awards by genial Ralph Edwards for an episode of *This Is Your Life*. The popular NBC show, which had been a staple on radio before crossing over into television, was a corny, kitschy exercise in quickie biography (which was brilliantly lampooned by Sid Caesar and crew).

A celebrity would be lured to Edwards's studio under some pretense and, once there, would be surprised by family, friends and long-lost childhood companions. The surprise guests would introduce themselves by saying a few words off-stage and would then be brought out by Edwards, who would earnestly narrate the celebrity's life story. There were always plenty of tears; through the years, *This Is*

Your Life had surprised the likes of Stan Laurel and Oliver Hardy and George Burns and Gracie Allen.

Now it was Bobby's turn. As the *This Is Your Life* cameras rolled, Edwards spoke to a national television audience outside a Hollywood sound stage.

"Now listen to the voice inside this rehearsal studio," Edwards whispered, the unmistakable sound of "Mack the Knife" emanating through the door. "Yes, it's perhaps the most electrifying young entertainer in America today."

Cut to Bobby, nattily attired in suit and tie, fingers snapping, hips swaying while he lip-synchs "Mack the Knife," ostensibly for a public-service announcement for the March of Dimes. Edwards walks in and surprises Bobby in mid-song; Bobby at first looks angry, but quickly flashes a smile when he realizes what's going on.

"I think he's pretty sneaky, that's what I think!" Bobby says. "I don't know what to say and I usually have a lot to say!"

Edwards introduces Steve Blauner. "The first time I ever saw Bobby I believed in him," Blauner says. "And he's just starting to fulfill his promise."

"You sneak!" Bobby jokes to Blauner.

Edwards introduces Nina and Charlie (mispronouncing their last name as "Maffie"). Charlie tells a story about buying Bobby his first new suit, which was ruined when a neighborhood dog tore through the seat of Bobby's pants. Nina remembers Bobby riding on the handlebars of his bicycle and waving a baton around while listening to 78s ("Benny Goodman and Tommy Dorsey," Bobby says).

Edwards then introduces Dick Behrke, Dick Lord, Don Kirshner, "Murray the K" Kaufman, Sammy Davis Jr. ("A guy has to be pretty good for me to steal from," Sammy says of Bobby) and, finally, George Burns.

"He's been like a father to you, Bobby," Edwards says.

"He's been a lot more than a father," Bobby replies.

"I love Bobby. I'd like to adopt Bobby . . . I'd make a fortune," Burns says to a big round of laughter. "The reason I love Bobby is that the first time I saw him work" (turns to Bobby), "you were so good. I knew you couldn't be that good if you didn't love show-business."

Burns then tells a story of how he and Bobby, in their act, did "a little sand dance, and we'd put sand in our pockets before we made our entrance. But one day Bobby had no sand and I got very angry at Bobby," he says. "I thought he was getting careless and I went into his dressing room and bawled him out."

With Dick Behrke at the piano, Bobby and George then re-enact their "sand dance," a little soft-shoe shuffle in which Bobby kneels down and sweeps the sand off the floor. "That's enough—Sammy Davis will steal it!" Burns exclaims.

Edwards then brings out Norman Taurog, who had given Bobby his first screen test, and presents Bobby with a special plaque, "The Bobby Darin Music Award," which will be awarded each year to a talented senior at Bobby's alma mater, the Bronx High School of Science.

The show ends with Vee, Vana and three-year-old Gary being driven onto the stage in a Cushman golf cart. Bobby lifts Gary up and gives him a big hug. "Do you love me?" Bobby asks Gary. "Say it. 'I love you.'"

"I love you," says Gary, who appears a bit tired and dazed by the bright lights.

Bobby told Dick Lord afterward that he really wasn't surprised by Edwards—that he knew all along about the show but played along, not wanting to spoil the "surprise."

"I said, tell me the truth, did you know?" Lord said. "And he said, yes, that when Ralph Edwards Productions called the house, he and Steve Blauner were in separate rooms and picked up the phone at the same time."

Joel Kaswan's mother, watching Bobby on *This Is Your Life*, called her son to tell him the news: Bobby had mentioned Joel, by name, on the show when telling Edwards about his roots as a drummer. Joel, who attended Stuyvesant High School after Clark Junior High, hadn't seen Bobby again once they went their separate ways.

"I had no idea who he was when it aired," Kaswan said. "Who is this guy? We couldn't find anything until somebody found his name in a fan magazine—and once I heard his *real* name, I knew who he was, of course.

"We tried to call him and we were successful. Bobby and I talked for a while, and I'll never forget this line for as long as I live. I said, 'How-the-hell did you remember me?' And he said, 'I never forget the people who were good to me.'"

4

Just days after his appearance on *This Is Your Life*, Bobby was back in New York. This time it wasn't fun and games. New York District Attorney Frank Hogan was investigating the widening payola scandal, in which record companies and some recording artists were accused of paying off deejays to get their songs played on the air. Bobby and singer Eileen Rogers were subpoenaed, and were brought in to Hogan's office to answer questions. Hogan wanted to know about their appearances on Alan Freed's television show, on which Bobby had appeared several times, and the "circumstances" under which Bobby was booked on the show.

Bobby told reporters afterward that he "discussed questions pertinent to the record business," while Rogers said she "paid no money to Alan Freed." Yes, she was asked, but do you think payola exists? "Maybe it does exist and maybe it doesn't," she answered. "I have my own thoughts about that, but I can't discuss them at this time." Les Paul and his wife, Mary Ford, followed Bobby and Rogers into Hogan's office later that day.

Bobby emerged from the payola scandal unscathed with his reputation intact and no further aspersions cast on him. Freed, however, wasn't so lucky; he was scarred by the scandal and never recovered. He was fired from WABC radio, blackballed in the industry and drank himself to death six years later.

Bobby's quick rise to fame, however, did make him prime fodder for the fan magazines, which now began focusing on his love life. Up until now, only Bobby's relationship with Connie Francis had been publicized in the fan magazines as his "one great true love." Every now and then a magazine article would mention the mysterious "older singer" who had broken Bobby's heart five years before. Bobby, for his part, insisted he wasn't ready to marry and hadn't yet found "the right girl." But, when he did, by golly, he'd know it, and he'd be ready to start a family. Right now wasn't the time, though.

"I have to keep looking, at least for a while yet," he told *Starlife* magazine at the end of 1959 in a feature entitled, what else?, "Bobby Darin: I Have to Keep Looking."

"Since my mother died last February, I have really nothing to go home for, and no one to tell things to," Bobby said. "Maybe I can make a home for myself here in Hollywood. There's a girl I know that I'm quite seriously interested in, but I haven't thought about marriage and I won't until I'm really secure.

"For at least a year I can't be sure where this is leading me," he said. "It isn't bad for a single guy, and I'm enjoying every minute of it, but I can't think of settling down until I know the answer for myself, inside."

Bobby repeated the mantra to another reporter. "I don't want to marry until my career has settled down and I don't have to move so much. Perhaps when I get my own TV show, or become established in Hollywood . . . then maybe I can marry and raise lots of children. For me, marriage is sacred and beautiful, and when I marry I want it to be once and for all.

"I want to give my kids something I never had: A father they know."

That was for public consumption. There's no doubt Bobby meant what he said about not wanting to settle down and get married. Behind the scenes, however, Bobby was indulging in the fruits of his fame and gaining quite the reputation as a Romeo—who wasn't always discriminating in his appetites.

"There were always groupies," Steve Blauner recalled. "There were always girls and I was always concerned. I'd be sitting around and I'd see this girl come on to Bobby before the show and he would be with her after the show and then she would leave. And then I'd see her talking to some sleazeball that she hooked up with and I'd go back to Bobby and I'd say, 'You're not going out with this girl after the show. Something's going on.'

"It's like Sammy Davis," Blauner said of his good friend. "If you saw him on the street you'd cross over to the other side. This little gnome with a big head and the pushed-in nose, he'd get on that fucking stage and he was King Kong. Every white woman in the joint wanted to fuck him. And he became the most beautiful guy in the world out of sheer talent. Well, I never thought Bobby was too handsome, but women just thought he was great-looking. They thought he had 'doe eyes.' He got more women than anyone I ever saw."

Bobby never thought of himself as a sex symbol, and seemed genuinely surprised that women would find him appealing. Although he was still thin and kept himself in decent shape, he thought his nose was too big and his face too puffy. It didn't help that he was losing his hair, and had begun wearing two small hairpieces—which he nicknamed "Oscar"—to camouflage his receding hairline.

"In the beginning he wore what looked like big eyelashes," Blauner said. "I remember one night at The Cloisters, he was doing a show and all of the sudden I see this one [eyelash] start to fall off. And he's singing. And I'm hysterical. And it's a tiny room. I'm laughing and he hears me and he runs off stage. He almost lost it."

Although he was acutely aware of his own physical shortcomings—at least in his mind—Bobby often went out of his way to make others feel better about themselves. He didn't practice what he preached, but it made others feel much better.

"One day I had a personal problem and Bobby said to me, 'Listen, Steve, when I get up in the morning and I look in the mirror, you know what I see? A short, balding, Italian with a double-chin, a big nose and a pot belly,'" Blauner said. "'But when I walk out the door, I'm fucking Rock Hudson.' That tells you a lot about the man, just that one thing. He was trying to help me at his expense."

The one girlfriend Bobby *would* talk about publicly was Jo-Ann Campbell, a young blonde singer he'd met several years before during a television appearance. Their romance heated up during a 1958 tour of Australia, which also featured Chuck Berry. Teen fan magazines being what they were—and still are today—Bobby's comments regarding Jo-Ann have to be sifted through the filter of embellished prose. Bubblegum bibles like *Teen* magazine were, after all, written for young girls with romance on their minds—and a young prince like Bobby Darin ready to whisk some young starlet away to paradise.

Still, Bobby seemed to have genuinely fallen for Jo-Ann. Born in Jacksonville, Florida, she was two years younger than Bobby and had experienced some modest success, first with a 1957 single called "Come On Baby" and then with an appearance in the movie *Go Johnny Go*, in which she sang two songs.

"I've fallen in love and that's for good," Bobby said about his new love. "For the first time in my life, I know I'm really in love with somebody. I never felt this way before. Now, when I do something, I feel that I'm doing it for two people, not just myself.

"Once before, I thought I was in love and it was a bomb, so I think I'm pretty lucky to get another opportunity to regain what I'd lost," he said, alluding to the mysterious exotic dancer. "We're not formally engaged and we expect to wait at least a couple of years before we marry. We've learned a lot about each other and we've got more to learn.

"Anyway, neither of us can afford to get married at the moment because of the status of our careers, but there's such a beautiful rapport that I know it has to work."

It didn't bode well that both Bobby and Jo-Ann were focused with laser-like intensity on their careers, leaving little time for each other. "She was sort of a rock 'n' roll girlfriend," Blauner said. "I liked Jo-Ann, she was nice—but she wanted her own career."

THIS IS DARIN, Bobby's third Atco album, was released in January 1960. The album was cut the previous May in New York, with Ahmet Ertegun once again calling the shots and Richard Wess providing the lush arrangements. Much like *That's All*, *This Is Darin* is a swingin' affair, providing Bobby a platter of meaty, upbeat tunes and several ballads around which he wrapped his unique phrasing.

"Any doubts that Mr. Darin can stand up on his own are dissipated in *This Is Darin*, an excellently programmed set on which Mr. Darin's musical personality comes across in electrifying fashion," raved *The New York Times*. "The flip, casual, finger-snapping brashness which gave his 'Mack the Knife' much of its vitality is present once again in the out-and-out rhythm numbers, but this time without obvious bor-rowings."

The album opened with "Clementine," a cousin to "Mack the Knife" with its bouncy bass line and Bobby's enthusiastic, hep-cat interpretation. Like "Mack the Knife," "Clementine" was concerned with death; not murder, in this case, but the accidental drowning of "chubby Clementine," whose hefty girth—"Whoops!"—dumped her "into the foamy brine." In Bobby's hands, the song became a light-hearted ballad. As for poor Clementine, well, them's the breaks. Bobby closes the song with an exuberant "Bye!"

"He has obviously learned a lot from Mr. Sinatra but the thing that distinguishes him from others who have gone to the same school is the magnetic musical personality he has built on this solid founda-tion," the *Times* concluded. "This is a disk that belongs with the best work of such masters of the genre as Bing Crosby and Mr. Sinatra."

The album also included Bobby's rendition of "Guys and Dolls"—a nod to Sinatra, perhaps, who seemed to be on Bobby's mind a lot these days. The two singers were constantly being compared, not just for their singing styles but for their similar tastes in clothes and show-biz parlance. Bobby's post-Grammy comments to Vernon Scott—"I want to pass Frank in everything he's done"—still rankled many in the business who thought of him as a boastful, immature lout.

"He was never really accepted by the Sinatra mob," said Ahmet Ertegun. "Sinatra didn't like him. I guess he saw too much competi-tion there. Sinatra was not an especially nice fella. I mean, he was very engaging, a great singer and could be a great friend, but he could turn on you at any point.

"But Bobby wouldn't fit into the Rat Pack. He would have liked to have been a part of that group, I think."

Now Bobby was spouting off again, this time in an interview with Shana Alexander in a *Life* magazine article published in January 1960, just as *This Is Darin* was hitting the stores.

"I Want To Be A Legend By 25," blared the headline. "Hit Singer Bobby Darin Has Big Ambitions, Prospects to Match."

"I want to make it faster than anyone has ever made it before," Bobby told Alexander. "I'd like to be the biggest thing in show business by the time I'm 25 years old. With 'Mack' I have knocked down my biggest door. The public knows me.

"I want to be in the upper echelon of show business to such an extent it's ridiculous."

The article continued:

Darin yearns for the respect of the successes like Sinatra and George Burns. "These people should say: 'Yeah, you belong in the center of the circle, kid.'" To this end, he has begun to work harder toward achieving a stage personality all his own. Darin's forte on stage, he believes, is to be "a singer who moves well, a singer who moves like a dancer. That's my billing, and I intend to sell the hell out of it."

Darin's dilemma was neatly summed up recently by his friend Jerry Lewis, who should know. Drawing Bobby aside in the corner of a TV studio, Lewis warned him: "Right now, your head is full of a million ideas. Just keep them all sloshing round and round in your brain. Listen to everything, watch everybody.

"Do you realize you're alone in your generation? Sammy, Dean and I are all ten years ahead of you. Unless you destroy yourself, no one else can touch you. If you louse it up, it's only going to be your fault. Because you have the talent, kid. You're alone. You're alone."

In a sense, Bobby *was* alone. His romance with Jo-Ann Campbell was waning, and he was on the road most of the time in places like Syracuse, Pittsburgh, Detroit and Buffalo. His only traveling companions were Steve Blauner, road manager and brother-in-law Charlie Maffia, and Dick Behrke, who Bobby hired as his conductor. There were women on the road, lots of them, but they were nothing more than one-night stands, casual sex that was forgotten the next day.

"We would be like kids on the road," Blauner said. "One day Bobby gets me to play chess and I knew he can beat me. I haven't played chess since college. So I stand up and say, 'I gotta go to the bathroom,' and I knock the table over and the pieces go flying. And he goes crazy. I never played him again.

"The road is tough—you're out there from one hotel to another," Blauner said. "I remember we played one place in Syracuse; they had built a diner on the property and they had a little motel that we lived in to make it easy, instead of going all the way into Syracuse. And so, at night, we would go into the diner and we'd start a pie fight. We'd throw pies. And I would pay everybody a lot of money to clean it up. We would do these silly things.

"There was a time when we were playing in Washington where we had a little one-bedroom suite for Bobby, Dick Behrke and I to stay in to save money," Blauner said. "Bobby brought a girl home and arranged it so that she would screw all three of us. Dick went in first and now Bobby has a glass up against the wall. I never understood that. What the hell was going on? Bobby was really a freak that way. I had a maid once, who was like seventy, and he chased her around the house. A lot of it was fun. But he would fuck anything."

With Charlie in the small entourage, Bobby had a touch of home on the road. But while he obviously loved his brother-in-law, Bobby, the perfectionist, sometimes had problems with Charlie's less-than-minute attention to detail in getting Bobby from one gig to the next.

"Charlie was not the brightest guy in the world and he would frustrate Bobby because it was a big job organizing the bookings, the planes, the hotels," said Dick Lord. "And Charlie would sometimes screw up. If it had been anybody but his brother-in-law, he would have been gone. He was never gone. And Bobby would say, 'Why can't he remember the soap, why can't he remember the fucking soap?'"

It was in Syracuse, while Bobby was playing the Three Rivers Inn, that a fourth member joined his traveling road show in the form of drummer Ronnie Zito.

"I was in the [house] band. I was actually there for about a year; I was pretty young and I was playing for different people," Zito said. "And then Bobby came in with just a piano player, Dick Behrke. He came in for about a week. There wasn't a lot of business, I remember, but, you know, Bobby was great. He put on a great show and everybody in the band, we were talking, like 'Wow! This guy's good!'

"Then, at the end of the engagement, he asked me if I would go to Washington with him. I said, well, I'll have to ask the conductor and he said, go, we'll get someone, and when you're done, if you want to come back, come back.

"But then I went to Washington with Bobby and he packed the place and he asked me, at the end of the engagement, if I would stay," Zito recalled. "He wanted me to stay with him. We really hit it off

likes Bobby Darin. The next week I meet a man who loves Bobby
Darin AND horses. I can wait to marry. In this business you don't stay
married to someone you don't love—no economic reason to."

In March, Bobby began a tour through England with Duane Eddy
and Clyde McPhatter. The English crowds expecting Bobby to come
on and sing "Splish Splash" and "Queen of the Hop" were disappointed when he opened with "My Funny Valentine," drawing boos
from the crowd. The tour, at least as far as Bobby was concerned,
wasn't a big success, and the disappointment on both sides of the
Atlantic was exacerbated by negative comments Bobby made to *Melody Maker* magazine upon his return home: "I'll never tour Britain
again in a rock 'n' roll package tour."

Bobby opened at The Cloisters on the Sunset Strip in May, smashing
box-office records there for twenty-one consecutive nights and tuning
up for his big opening at the Copa. During the three-week gig, a
young man named Frankie Edward Cooper took the opportunity to
break into Bobby's dressing room in an attempt to steal some personal
items from the famous singer. Cooper was caught at around 2 a.m. by
Mike London, a part-time actor and parking-lot attendant at the club
who happened to step into the dressing room. Police said Cooper was
caught with "several expensive tailor-made tuxedoes and a solid-gold
money clip with $28 in it."

Bobby's run at The Cloisters also won him a new fan: Columnist
Walter Winchell, whose career was in decline. Winchell, at that point,
was no longer the most powerful, feared columnist in the country, and
his popular radio show was a thing of the past. He was, however,
experiencing a mini-revival of sorts, thanks to his staccato voiceover
narration on the CBS television series *The Untouchables*, which docu-
mented the (mostly fictional) exploits of Federal Agent Eliot Ness in
Prohibition-era Chicago.

Winchell was so impressed with Bobby that he followed him on to
Washington, D.C., where Bobby spent a week at the Casino Royal.
Winchell would also be at the Copa for Bobby's big opening there.
"It's personality that attracts you to anybody," Winchell said of his
new pal. "And by definition, personality is indefinable. The best I can
do is to say that he has a zing to him, both on the stage and off."

Bobby's romance with Jo-Ann Campbell, meanwhile, had ended.

For the moment, there were no serious women in Bobby's life, although he kept up a seemingly endless string of dates with wannabe starlets including Dore Orlando, Bonnie Carroll, Judi Meredith, Asa Gaynor, June Blair and Penny Petersen. Bobby was even rumored to be dating singer Keely Smith, whose marriage to bandleader Louis Prima was nearing its end. But none of these were serious romances and most of them were, at best, only a date or two—despite the best efforts of the fan magazines to turn them into something bigger with articles blaring the headlines "Bobby Darin Caught Making Love!" or "The Girl Bobby Darin Will Marry!" or "The Truth About Bobby Darin."

THE TRUTH ABOUT Bobby Darin was that he was focused on his opening at the Copa. Atco was anticipating something special, and made plans to record the first two nights for a possible album. It would also be a huge test for Bobby before the tough New York critics, guys like Leonard Lyons and Earl Wilson. The critics and columnists were nothing, however, compared to club owner Jules "Julie" Podell, a notoriously gruff SOB who was said to have ties to the Mob (the *real* owners of the Copa, it was whispered).

"Everybody was frightened of him," Dick Lord said of Podell. "Waiters that worked there for twenty years would literally shake. If he had a couple of drinks, he could fucking kill you. He would bang his ring and when he banged his ring, I'm telling you, people would shake. I remember the first time I was there, I was there with Bobby. And Bobby said to me, 'Don't talk to him. Just don't talk to him.'

"I have a friend who was working as a comedian at the Copa and he went over to Jules Podell and he said, 'Mr. Podell, my girlfriend is one of the dancers here, and all my life I wanted to work here and I'm finally appearing at the Copacabana, the best nightclub in the world, and I'm so proud.'

"And Podell just said, 'Who gives a shit?'"

Bobby opened at the Copa on June 2. *Darin at the Copa*, Atco's recording of the June 15 and 16 dates, gives a sample of what those shows were like. Bobby doesn't sing his first big hit, "Splish Splash," but does perform "Mack the Knife," "Dream Lover" and "Clementine." Bobby sings a series of medleys throughout ("Swing Low, Sweet

Chariot"/"The Lonesome Road" and "By Myself"/"When Your Lover Has Gone"), croons a Cole Porter tune ("Love for Sale") and throws in some Ray Charles ("I Got a Woman") for good measure.

In between, Bobby jokes with the crowd, shows off his talents on the vibraphone ("Red Norvo, watch out!") and sounds at ease with his show-biz, hep-cat parlance. "That vamp you hear in the background of course is to the popular Bolivian folk song," he jokes to the familiar opening bars of "Mack the Knife." When a young girl shouts out "'Splish Splash!,'" Bobby responds, in his best W.C. Fields voice, "You're going back further than I care to remember . . . little tired of living on my laurels," then shoots a remark to Keely Smith: "About time you woke up, Miss Smith!"

At the end of the night, Bobby introduces the Paul Shelley Orchestra, singling out his drummer, Ronnie Zito, and "My conductor, my pianist, the best friend I have in the entire world, Mr. Richard Behrke."

The critics and columnists were awash with praise for Bobby after his triumphant opening night.

Louis Sobol, *The New York Journal-American*: "Bobby Darin made it look like old times at the Copa—with tables jammed in almost to the orchestra podium. He deserves all the praise showered on him by the advance notices—and the loudest whistler and cheerer was our neighbor who has appointed himself his personal unpaid drum-beater: Walter Winchell."

Earl Wilson, *The New York Post*: "Bobby Darin, a hippie from N.Y.C., Tonsil No. 1 in the 'New York Noise' sweeping America, completely conquered all the New York hippies. He gave the gals the jiggles—not the giggles—the jiggles. They jiggled in their chairs. At least one sitting back to back with me did. A picture of perfect poise, Darin did his celebrated 'Mack the Knife' early. He got a standing ovation—with the dames leaping up first. A memorable debut."

Dorothy Kilgallen, *The New York Journal-American*: "Bobby Darin's debut at the Copacabana last night was a triumph—he has a good voice, fine arrangements, an almost completely tasteful selection of songs, and the nerve of a bank robber. The Copa isn't apt to have any empty tables showing during his engagements."

Walter Winchell, *The New York Mirror*: "Bobby Darin's premiere at the Copa went down in the Copacabana history books as one of the

Standouts. Darin received so many wires of congrats that Western Union told him, 'You hold the record for telegrams in one night.'"

The accolades continued and, by the time his Copa run ended, Bobby had shattered the nightclub's old attendance record held by Frank Sinatra. The only blip was on June 6. Bobby was finishing his first show of the night when he suddenly felt ill with what was reported as "severe abdominal pains."

"The new singing idol, a product of the Bronx, was rushed to his dressing room, where a team of doctors started examining him," Winchell reported. "He was too ill to appear at his second show of the evening and this reporter helped round up a group of entertainers to go on for the stricken star."

Winchell emceed the second show, with Keely Smith and Louis Prima, Jean Carroll, Dick Roman and the Bell Tones providing the entertainment. Earl Wilson reported that Bobby's sudden illness was the result of an infection and a resulting temperature caused by a pimple. It was, more likely, his heart. But that went unreported.

So, too, did a strange occurrence on opening night, when Bobby and Steve Blauner were approached backstage after the show.

"Afterward, there was a spread in the lounge and there was a big table with lox and bagels and cream cheese," Blauner said. "This particular night we're sitting there and a guy comes over, a short guy. He introduces himself and says to Bobby, 'I used to know your father, and I was a friend of your father's. And Bobby says, 'Where were you when I need you?' and I get a kick under the table.

"So the guy says, 'Well, if you ever need anything, let me know.' That ended and then everybody left. I remember we walked out of the Copa, the sun was already rising, it was like 6 in the morning. And Jules Podell said the following, which always fascinated me. He said, 'Look Bobby, I knew your father too. He was a butcher up in the Bronx. And if you want to know more about your father, let me know, we'll put you in a room in midtown Manhattan and we'll give you a folder on him that you can read and then you'll give it back.'

"I've always said to myself, where is *this* coming from? Why does the Mafia, or whatever they wanted to be called at the time, have files on people?," Blauner said. "So we're walking back to where Bobby was staying and I said, 'Look, Bobby, leave it alone. Thank your father for putting you on the straight and narrow—that you are who you are and you don't want to cross that line because that's probably how he ended up. Just leave it alone.'

"I don't know if he ever did the paperwork," Blauner said. "I know that if I had been him, I would have."

Bobby must also have wondered about that kid, Tony Orlando, who was always in the lobby of the Copa after the show, hoping to shake Bobby's hand and bend his ear.

"My uncle was Carmine Fava, who was the maitre d' of the Copacabana," Orlando said. "So whenever I wanted to see Bobby, all I had to do was go, and my uncle would sneak me behind the sound console and I would watch Bobby Darin.

"Now, understand, I was underage. They could have lost their license," Orlando said. "But I would sneak in behind Doug Harry, who was the sound and light man at the Copa, and I would watch every move Bobby made. So my relationship with Bobby was always the kind of relationship thereafter, me coming to the backstage area, hoping he would see me and give me his twenty minutes and that was it.

"It wasn't a friendship that developed, it was always Tony the fan who loved Bobby, and Bobby had to tolerate me," Orlando said. "He must have been saying to himself, 'He's out in the lobby again? Don't tell me.' I was never a pain in the ass, but whenever I got a chance to be there, I made sure I just got a chance to shake his hand."

Bobby's success at the Copa didn't mitigate the negativity, sometimes even downright hostility, he engendered in the press. If anything, it made it worse, now that the twenty-four-year-old singer had put his money where his mouth was, lived up to the advance hype—and was even better than expected. Bobby didn't help his image of the affected performer; he now smoked a pipe during many of his interviews (claiming it stopped him from becoming a chain smoker).

Still, he made no apologies for what was deemed, time and again, cockiness and brashness unbecoming to such a young performer. "It served my purpose as well as theirs," he told the *Saturday Evening Post*, which entitled its article, "Little Singer with a Big Ego."

"If I showed the arrogant, cocky side of myself, it must be because I want it shown. All publicity has helped me. Ask me anything you want. Make it rough, I'll applaud. If it's a smart question, you'll get a smart answer. If it's an honest question, you'll get an honest answer. But if it's a smart-aleck question, I've *got* to give you a smart-aleck answer. I've *got* to bury you. That's my defense mechanism."

Yes, Bobby, the magazine writer wondered, but where does the attitude come from?

"All the arrogance you read about stems from those days in high school," he said. "It all stems from a desire to be nobody's fool ever again. All the kids were smarter than me—scientifically, academically and semantically. They were better versed in Schopenhauer and Chopin, Bach and Berlioz. They'd throw lines at me and poke fun, and I'd take it because I felt unequipped to answer back.

"And then one day, I realized that creatively—in sensitivity, *in my soul*—I buried them all. I looked at myself as into a mirror and I knew what I had. Now, it's conceivable that thirty million people will read your article, and I have to let them know I'm something. And when a little girl from a high-school paper comes to interview me, I have to let her know I'm something too."

The Copa gig put Bobby in the A-league of performers, and he tried, once and for all, to distance himself from comparisons to Sinatra—the man whose attendance records he'd shattered in the most famous nightclub in the biggest city in the world. What else was there to prove?

"I've been accused of comparing myself to Sinatra, in terms of career climbing," Bobby told *Down Beat* writer Gene Lees. "Certain people have said I want to beat him out. First, I never said this, the press said it. Second, to me, Frank Sinatra is the greatest living lyric interpreter, and that ends the admiration.

"My idol is the step beyond the great image of today. In other words, it's an indefinite goal."

Steve Blauner also tried to put the nagging Sinatra controversy to bed. "I arranged the meeting that they had so that it could be straightened out," he said. "Frank once said to Dick Bakalyan, the actor, that there was no one else like Bobby. 'He's got it all to himself,' Frank told him. "'He's the best because it's a whole new generation.'"

"I got to be an idiot not to know Frank's a genius," Bobby said in yet another *mea culpa*, this time to columnist Earl Wilson. "We even got together and he gave me some pointers. But I never saw him work but once and I don't have a pop record in my collection. Everything I got is classical . . . it's music that I don't understand."

The Sinatra controversy notwithstanding—and now, hopefully, put to rest for good—the year was shaping up nicely. Bobby expected to gross over $1 million by the end of 1960, and with five gold records behind him, and "Mack the Knife" still going strong, he would soon fly to Portofino, Italy, to begin filming *Come September*.

Already in the can was a guest-starring role in the premiere episode of a new NBC series, *Dan Raven*, airing in September. It was Bobby's second episodic television appearance. Blauner had negotiated a three-year, Las Vegas and Miami nightclub contract paying Bobby $20,000 per week. He also worked out another movie contract, this time with Universal, that would pay Bobby $1 million.

BOBBY SOMEHOW FOUND TIME during his Copa run to guest-star on George Burns' NBC special along with Jack Benny, Betty Grable and Polly Bergen. He sang "My Funny Valentine," which was becoming a standard part of his act. "Mr. Darin is a popular and well-paid young vocalist," sniffed *The New York Times*. "But his distortion of this number was a painful thing. Mr. Rodgers and the estate of Mr. Hart are entitled to substantial damages."

In late June, Bobby joined a group of other young stars—Frankie Avalon, Annette Funicello, Paul Anka, Ed "Kookie" Byrnes, Bob Denver and Anita Bryant—on *Coke Time*, an ABC television special hosted by Pat Boone.

"I was about twenty-four and all the others were younger. I was the grand old man, the Bing Crosby hosting the new singers," Boone said. "Coke laid out ample cash and it was each of us doing hits of our own and combining to do some things and it was fun and bouncy.

"From time to time we sat around on breaks while they were setting up and we'd gather into a group and laugh and share stories and kid each other and so on," Boone said. "Although I was the host of the show, Bobby somehow wound up taking center stage.

"He had little jibes and we kidded him and he poked fun at us and it was all good-natured," Boone said. "However, Paul Anka was the youngest, and Bobby seemed to take a little special delight in poking fun at Paul. I don't remember if it was the piled-up hair, how young he was, baby cheeks or whatever, and the girls all tittered and laughed.

"So Paul took me aside at one point and said, 'Bobby keeps making all these wisecracks and jokes and I can't think of anything to say back to him. Can you help me?' And I said, 'Yeah, I've got something for you.' At the time, it was already clear that Bobby's idol was Frank Sinatra. Mine was Bing. There was a guy in Palm Springs named Duke Hayslett who was making a living out of being Frank Sinatra in little clubs—he'd come out with a trench coat over his shoulder and a snap-brim hat and collar undone and his tie a little loose and he'd come on snapping his fingers and singing all of Frank's songs.

"Well, I told Paul who Duke was and I said, 'The next time Bobby is kidding you, wait until you can be heard so that people don't miss what you're saying, and say, "Bobby, you know, ever since we've been working together, I've been trying to think who it is you remind me of," Boone said. "So when that happened and Bobby said, 'Oh yeah, who?' Paul said, 'Duke Hayslett.' And all the singers and some of the dancers, and especially the background singers, howled with laughter.

"Bobby's face got red and, well, it was the worst thing I could have done for Paul, because from then on, Bobby came in with fresh barbs every day and just skewered Paul."

Atco rushed out *Darin at the Copa* in July—produced by Ahmet and Nesuhi Ertegun—and followed that in quick succession with *For Teenagers Only*, the bulk of which Bobby had recorded two years earlier. Bobby wasn't thrilled with the album's title; he'd worked hard to move in a more "mature" direction since *That's All* the previous year, and hoped his teen audience would grow along with him. Still, he never criticized Atco publicly, and stuck to his mantra of not abandoning the audience that launched him into superstardom.

"The big mistake of a lot of people in this business is overestimating the teenagers. Now there's no question that teenagers are the big record buyers, and they can make you famous," he said. "But teenagers are terribly fickle. They really don't know what they like. They're led like sheep to what they're told is good. Once in a while they manage to like something good, but not enough to gamble on them.

"And once the teenagers drop you, what's left if you're not prepared? I already figure maybe I'm getting a little too old for teenagers," he said. "I bet my career on the idea that ballads are coming back—that rock 'n' roll is on the wane—and it paid off. My ballad albums are big sellers, and incidentally, teenagers are buying them too.

"I have nothing against rock 'n' roll. I think the kids who really like it will graduate to better things. It's a great training ground for jazz. But the way the music business has gone berserk, rock 'n' roll has ruined a lot of people's lives."

Everything was moving in the right direction now, but there *was* one that got away from Bobby that year. Robert Rossen, who had just written the screenplay for *The Hustler*, had seen Bobby on *The Mike Wallace Interview*, a half-hour ABC interview show hosted by Wallace. Rossen thought Bobby would be perfect for the lead role of brash-yet-tragic pool shark "Fast Eddie" Felson.

"Robert Rossen was finishing up his screenplay; he didn't know what a Bobby Darin *was*," Blauner said. "He turned off the TV and turned to his wife and said, 'I just found my hustler.'"

Rossen returned to California and his agent sent the script over to Fox. "They wanted to pay Bobby $75,000 for the movie and I said, 'You've got a deal,'" Blauner said. "I said, 'You're going to want options,' so we concocted a deal, an option for two pictures and we would have to pick up an option for another four pictures after that.

"So we made the deal," Blauner said. "Bobby is going to be 'The Hustler.' This is going to be his entry into the really big time in the movies."

In quick succession, Fox then cast Jackie Gleason as pool-hall hustler Minnesota Fats and Piper Laurie as Fast Eddie's alcoholic girlfriend, Sarah Packard.

"Okay, so now we're at the racetrack on a Saturday, in between races, they're doing a charity race and Bobby is in it to raise money," Blauner said. "And someone turns to me and says, 'Gee, it's too bad about 'The Hustler.' He was shocked that I didn't know." What Blauner and Bobby didn't know is that Paul Newman, who was in France making *Paris Blues* with Sidney Poitier, Joanne Woodward and Louie Armstrong, had suddenly become available. Now Fox wanted him for Fast Eddie in *The Hustler*—a fact no one had relayed to Bobby, Blauner or Bobby's agent, Martin Baum.

"I'm at the racetrack and once the races are on, the pay phones are locked up," Blauner said. "So I had to leave the track, find a phone outside the track someplace and call Marty Baum. He didn't know anything about it, and I said, 'We blew it.' And Marty said, 'We'll sue them.' And I said, 'What good is that? I didn't do this for the money to begin with.' I would have paid them $100,000, $500,000 if I had it to get this part for Bobby. This role would have made his career. And so we lost the picture. That was a heartbreaker. Of course Paul Newman was a better actor and I understand that. But it was tough to take at the time."

Martin Baum had a slightly different take on the movie role that never was.

"I submitted Bobby for the part of the hustler and the head of production at Fox came to me and we made a deal on the telephone," Baum said. "He said, 'Go down to my office and sign with the head of casting. Make the deal. You've got it.' I went down the hall, and by the time I got from the head of production to the casting office, Paul Newman had the part.

"Newman's agent had turned it down, he didn't think it was important enough," Baum said. "Newman read the script and said, 'I like this. I want do to this' and Fox said, 'You've got a deal.' He had the part."

The trades also reported that Bobby would co-star with Jack Benny in an Allied Artists movie, *Rip Van Winkle in the Twenty-First Century*. That project never came to fruition.

5

In September 1960, Bobby flew to Italy for his role in *Come September*, which would be filmed in and around the picturesque town of Porto-fino on the Italian coast. The movie boasted an all-star cast headed by Rock Hudson, who was producing the movie and coming off his *Pillow Talk* series with Doris Day. Italian sexpot Gina Lollobrigida would play Hudson's love interest, while veteran character actor Walter Slezak provided the comic relief.

Sandra Dee, all of eighteen, was cast in a supporting role. Dee, though, was no slouch in terms of burgeoning Hollywood royalty. The perky blonde, born Alexandra Zuck in Bayonne, New Jersey, in April 1942, already had an interesting history. Her parents, John and Mary Zuck, divorced when she was a toddler, with Mary raising Alexandra herself until 1950, when she married New York real estate developer Eugene Douvan.

Alexandra's beauty won her a modeling contract and, by her teens, she was raking in $72,000 a year. Shortly thereafter she was "discovered" by Hollywood producer Ross Hunter and was signed to a seven-year contract with Universal, adopting the stage name Sandra Douvan. When Eugene died several years later, Mary and Sandra moved to Hollywood to pursue Sandra's acting career. Years later Sandra revealed that her stepfather had sexually abused her. That only added more emotional anguish to the anorexia Sandra developed during her modeling days in a bid to retain her girlish figure and stay thin. The anorexia, of course, went undiagnosed at a time when little was known about eating disorders and their psychological origins.

Sandra Douvan morphed into Sandra Dee and, in 1959, at the age of seventeen, she landed her first big role in the beach-blanket comedy *Gidget*—following that with *Imitation of Life*, *A Summer Place*, and *Portrait in Black*. By the time she left to film *Come September*, Sandra had already earned the girl-next-door, "America's Sweetheart" label that would cement her status as a pop-culture icon.

Still, Sandra was only eighteen, and Mary Douvan, already known as an overprotective "stage mother," wasn't about to let her daughter out of her sight, especially with the womanizing Bobby Darin hanging around. Mary joined Sandra on the trip to Italy.

The plot of *Come September* wasn't going to tax anyone's imagination. Hudson was cast as Robert Talbot, a wealthy American industrialist and confirmed bachelor who owns a beautiful villa where, every September, he romances his Italian mistress, Lisa Fellini (Lollobrigida). Lisa loves Talbot but, tired of waiting for his elusive marriage proposal, has decided to marry stuffy Englishman Spencer (Ronald Howard).

What Talbot doesn't know is that, for the eleven months of the year when he's away, his butler, Maurice (Slezak), transforms the villa into a bustling, five-star hotel, turning a handsome profit that he plows back into the villa's upkeep. When Talbot decides to visit Italy in July, two months earlier than expected, he discovers Maurice's ruse and blows his stack, kicking everyone out of the hotel.

But there's a gaggle of American schoolgirls staying at the hotel and they have nowhere else to go. Robert, goaded by Lisa, decides to let them stay a few extra days. One of the comely young lasses, Sandy Stevens (Sandra), catches the eye of Tony (Bobby), a wisecracking premed student who's leading college buddies Beagle (Joel Grey), Larry (Chris Seitz) and Ron (Michael Eden) on a summer-vacation jaunt through Italy when they chance upon the villa—and the girls.

The movie plays itself out as a generational comedy, with the "older" Talbot trying to teach horny Tony and his college pals a thing or two about being gentlemen—unaware that his non-committal attitude toward Lisa is just as sophomoric. Bobby spends his screen time chasing after Sandy and sparring with Talbot—taking time out to (inexplicably) sing the movie's theme song, "Multiplication," at a local nightclub in a silly scene thrown in to showcase Bobby's singing (he also wrote the song).

On location, Bobby was no less brash and cocky than he was back home, holding court on the Via Veneto in Rome for *New York Herald Tribune* columnist Joe Hyams.

"Modesty doesn't exist for me," Bobby told Hyams. "When a man pays another man to come in and fix his sink he expects a good job. If one plumber can't fix it he gets another. I have the security of an A-1 plumber.

"Now I'm working as an actor and I am entering a new battleground. Rounds one, two, three and four are over and it's a fifteen-round bout. If I don't fight me, I grab my money and run. Look at it this way. Anybody can be a member of the luck party in the beginning of a career, but it's not until you meet up with two or three opportunities—for me it was singing—that you get someplace.

"I play a roguish type of college boy in this movie," he said. "I'm a personality rather than a singer. I sing only one song and that's not for exploitation. I took my time choosing my first picture because I didn't want to do a film exploiting me. I am not significant in this picture. The other co-personnel carry it."

What Bobby failed to mention to Hyams was that one of his "co-personnel" had rocked his world. Bobby and Sandra Dee had fallen in love.

Steve Blauner flew to Italy during the filming of *Come September* to check on Bobby, meeting Sandra Dee for the first time.

"The first time I met Sandy was in Portofino," Blauner said. "It was one of those old hotels with the big hallways, magnificent. And I was walking down the hallway and a door opened and out came Sandra Dee and she was in a dress—sort of overdressed for Italy. It was off-season so nobody was there, it was practically empty. I heard her mother, 'Sandy, come back here! You have to put a belt on!' She said, 'Mom, I'm just going for a walk' and her mother said, 'I don't care.' I said, uh-oh, look at this. I already felt sorry for her. And Bobby, well, she had never met anyone like Bobby before.

"The story was that Bobby was standing on a dock and she was in a boat or something like that and she saw this guy; he was wearing a yellow suit or some garish-looking thing and he said to her, 'I'm going to marry you someday.' Well, it turns out that Bobby was going out with Sandy's mother," Blauner said. "Sandy would have nothing to do with him. She was scared to death of him, wouldn't even come out of her room. And finally her mother said, 'Oh, he's such a sweet boy.'

"It was similar to what must have been going on with Sammy and Kim Novak," Blauner said. "Here's Sammy, who felt he was an ugly-looking black person who wanted to be tall and white and he was now going to marry the American goddess that everyone wanted.

"Here's Bobby from the wrong side of the tracks and he's going to be married not to America's sexpot, but to the wholesome American girl," Blauner said. "They were certainly on different wavelengths. Everything about them was totally opposite. Sandy was used to being with her mother and few other people—and now she's with Bobby."

The romance blossomed during the two months Bobby and Sandra spent on location, and they decided to get married. They returned, separately, to the States in late November, Bobby arriving in New York first, followed by Sandra a few days later. She was sporting a large emerald-cut diamond engagement ring as they announced their engagement to the press, indicating that the wedding wouldn't be any time soon.

"He called me in the middle of the night and said, 'I'm getting married,'" recalled Dick Lord. "I'm in Brooklyn. I said, 'Is this a joke?' And when they got off the plane in New York, before he did anything, he came to my apartment. People were going nuts. Sandra Dee is in the laundry room. There's a limo outside. 'That's Bobby Darin!' They're going crazy."

Sandra's manager, Ross Hunter, insisted that she told him the marriage wouldn't take place until she finished her next picture, *Tammy Tell Me True*, which was scheduled to begin shooting two days after Christmas. Sandra said she would keep on working after the marriage "because Bobby is so proud of me."

Bobby, for his part, needed to focus on *Bobby Darin and Friends*, his NBC special airing in January. At twenty-four, Bobby would be the youngest performer to ever headline a network television show. He wanted to make sure he backed that up with a terrific show.

The engagement to Sandra seemed to soften Bobby up—but just a bit. "I have a strange desire to reform," he said after the big announcement, puffing on his pipe. "Suddenly your values change. I have now met a human being more important than I am.

"I definitely think she's responsible for me wanting to change," he said of Sandra. "I don't think I made too many friends when I worked at the Copacabana. People came to my door to say hello and I didn't say hello."

But the couple's desire to become husband and wife trumped their plan of waiting much longer. On November 29, Bobby and Sandra went to the town clerk's office in Parsippany-Troy Hills, New Jersey, to apply for a marriage license, Sandra's "blonde hair covered by an orange kerchief and her curves concealed by a billowing camel's hair overcoat," according to one newspaper account.

Sandra gave her name as Sandra Douvan, age eighteen, residing in Beverly Hills, California. Bobby signed the application as Walden Robert Cassotto, age twenty-four, listing the cottage in Lake Hiawatha (53 Dacotah Avenue) as his legal residence. Nina and Charlie—"Carmella and Carmine Maffia"—acted as witnesses. Bobby and Sandra signed a few autographs outside the courthouse before speeding off in a limousine.

Their original plan was to get married at noon the next day at the cottage in Lake Hiawatha. Afterward, they would throw a reception for about forty people.

Bobby was intent on keeping the actual marriage ceremony a secret until it was a done deal. But the press was already sniffing around, so he changed the original plan in order to throw them off the scent. He decided that the marriage would take place at Don and Sheila Kirshner's apartment in Elizabeth, New Jersey.

"I remember I was shopping somewhere and Bobby tracked me down," Kirshner said. "I think I was buying a suit for an affair, and he called me up and said, 'Kirsh, get a rabbi, get a priest, get someone. Sandy and I are getting married at your home tonight.' I said, 'Get serious, would you?' And he said, 'No, she's in town and we've got to do it because we have to fly to the coast.'

"But he used to be a little crazy, so a lot of times I tried to calm him down. I said, 'Bobby, if I go around and get everything arranged, are you going to embarrass me? I don't want to drive people crazy.'" But Bobby kept his word, showing up with Sandra at the Kirshners' apartment later that night.

"Bobby and Sandy had their blood test in my kitchen, which was small, two seats and a sink," Kirshner said. "That was the first time I met Sandy. Bobby walks in with Sandy and she's wearing the most gorgeous purple coat. And she came into our bedroom and sat there. She looked like a Kewpie doll. And I was so happy for Bobby, like, wow, he's marrying a movie star. And Bobby's telling me, 'Make sure there's no press.' I say, 'Bobby, not only don't I know anybody, but if you tell me you want no press, then there will be no press.'"

Bobby and Sandra were married at around 3 a.m. in the Kirshners' apartment. Newark magistrate Samuel Lohman conducted the ten-minute ceremony. "They kind of looked at each other and that was it," said Nina, who was the maid of honor. Dick Behrke acted as Bobby's best man. Charlie was there, of course, as were Vee, Vana and Gary, who was about to turn four. The group was rounded out by Behrke's wife; Lohman's wife; Charles Flicker, an aide to Newark Mayor Carlin; and Dick Lord's wife, Ellen.

Mary Douvan was conspicuous by her absence.

"Sandy's mother didn't go to the wedding—she was so against the marriage," said Steve Blauner. "I was going back on a plane for the wedding and Bobby called me and said, 'No, we just went and got a Justice of the Peace.' The photographers were driving them crazy. It was nothing compared to what goes on today, but it was bad. I mean, Bobby was big news, and so was she. This was America's sweetheart, Gidget."

Bobby and Sandra left the Kirshners' apartment and headed straight for Idlewild Airport in New York. "We'll have a five-day honeymoon before the work starts again," Bobby told reporters. "Sandra has a picture to do and I'll be back in Camden for two weeks. We'll stay in my house that I rented in Hollywood."

Sandra, carrying a Yorkshire terrier tucked under her arm, was asked about the rushed ceremony. "We wanted to get it over with," she said.

"The time doesn't make any difference," Bobby snapped before they boarded the United Airlines jet bound for Los Angeles—and their new life together.

THE HOUSE THEY RENTED in Bel-Air was either too small or too big, depending on whether it was Sandra or Bobby answering the question. "Relatively small," was how Sandra described it; Bobby thought it was "relatively large" but not nearly big enough for his new bride. "It amuses me to hear people talking about this big house we're going to live in," he said. "Actually, nothing is good enough for [Sandra]. Someday I hope to give her a house twice as big.

"But our marriage is going to be strictly private," he said, laying down the ground rules. "It has nothing to do with her career or my career."

Bobby, smart as a whip and already exposed to the hype surrounding celebrities, couldn't possibly have believed that statement. There was absolutely no way their marriage could stay "strictly private." He was one of the country's most popular singers, was earning over $1 million a year, was selling out in Vegas and had just wrapped his first feature film opposite Rock Hudson—*and* he was married now to "America's Sweetheart," one of Hollywood's most beautiful starlets. As a bachelor, Bobby had been tabloid fodder for years, his every romance breathlessly documented in the teen magazines. Now, his marriage simply upped the stakes for the twenty-four-year-old "cocky" crooner held in veiled contempt by most of the show-biz press. He might as well have drawn a bullseye on his back.

Still, time and again, Bobby drew the line at discussing his private life in these early days of his marriage. "I absolutely refuse to discuss my wife or family," he informed a reporter interviewing Bobby on the eve of his NBC special. "I'm sure our marriage will work," he said, grudgingly. To Hollywood columnist Sheila Graham, he was even more specific in his own Damon Runyan-esque way.

"Let me say this, in capsule, why I won't discuss it," he told Graham. "You've seen so much in Hollywood. So has every newspaper person. Well, speaking for myself, this boy-girl relationship will not be subjected to any cynical beratings or sideline platitudes either photographically or semantically. Reporters and photographers are free to pick up any bits of information through their normal sources. But not from me.

"I'll tell you this. When I was fifteen I read an article by a famous movie star. He said, 'I will never forget my allegiance to my fans.' A week later he got married. It was a terrible disappointment to his fans. So I will never say I will do this or that.

"My press agent is paid to create, to embellish, to flower," Bobby said. "But I'm with a very honest firm. All I know is that I resent any misinformation about me and that includes words of mine twisted and taken out of context—by my office, my studio or whoever.

"Most of the fan magazines today are as raggy as the scandal sheets were at one time," he said. "But they were for an adult public. Now they are writing for an average age of thirteen, naturally insulting the intelligence of my thirteen-year-old niece. So my contention is, if you're going to write about me, don't write down. The next thing you know the stories will not be fit for the average reader of fifty. Even though Hollywood is the biggest source of nonsense, they believe everything they read."

The battle had begun.

Bob Hope "would go to the opening of an envelope," or so the joke went, but it was a coup for Bobby to snare Old Ski Nose for *Bobby Darin and Friends*. Hope actually owed Bobby the appearance, since Bobby had done Hope's NBC special the previous October, appearing with Patti Page and Joan Crawford and dueting with Hope on a medley of "Thanks for the Memory," "Mack the Knife" and "Two Sleepy People."

"I went to Bob Hope's people, who wanted Bobby to do the Hope show," Blauner said. "And I said, 'We'll give you a trade. We'll do yours, you do ours.' They said no, so I said, 'Okay, Bobby will give you two shots and Bob will do one with us.' They still said no, so I said, 'Do me a favor. Go to Bob; he's always talking about up-and-coming performers and we need this and I don't want to be disrespectful to him—we'll do two shows.' So they came back and said yes. Now I have to sell the show. So I went and sold Bobby to NBC, with Bob Hope and Joannie Sommers as the only other guests."

Joannie Sommers, a young singer, would be making her network television debut. Getting her to do the special was no problem. Finding the right producer was another story. Blauner had his eye on Norman Lear and Bud Yorkin, who had produced several Fred Astaire specials. Yorkin also worked with Jack Benny and Tennessee Ernie Ford. According to Blauner, Lear and Yorkin weren't interested in producing any more television specials because they wanted to break into feature films.

"GAC had an office out here and they had a kitchen and dining room and I said, 'Just get them into the room with me for lunch,'" Blauner said. "So they got them into the room . . . and for an hour I paced and talked. And by the time I got through, they went down to their car, looked at each other and said, 'What have we done?'"

Of the two producers, it would be Yorkin working with Bobby on the special. That posed a minor problem, since Yorkin was not familiar with Bobby or his music.

"I was not a big Darin fan before the show and the guy that really talked me into it was Steve Blauner," Yorkin said. "He said, 'Why don't you come in, it's Bobby's first big show, he hasn't done one and you can do whatever you want.' I said, 'Well, let me hear some of his records.'

"But when I met Bobby I really became enamored with him and he became what I considered to be a close friend of mine for many, many years after that because he was so gifted in many, many ways.

"He was at that stage of his life, hot in many areas . . . I thought he could be a major motion picture star. In a strange way, he had that sort of Bogart quality," Yorkin said. "He could be rough, tough and ugly and yet he could turn around and there was a very simple, sweet side to Bobby, on the screen as well as in person.

"So I always thought he had way-too-big of a career to do a television show at that time. Most of the time, you're either just coming up and you need that break or you've passed it and you do your show, or you're going to be a television star. He was kind of an all-around; his career, at that time, looked to be huge in all areas.

"I went to see him play a club date but, you know, he was so gifted that I was looking forward to just doing the show and, in a way, to showing off how gifted he was," Yorkin said. "Normally I wouldn't say you had to open with a dance number, but with Bobby Darin, I wanted to show he could move. He was capable of doing everything."

There was a disturbing reminder, during rehearsals, that Bobby's heart problem could rear its head at any time. "Somebody told me at the time, 'You know, he has a rheumatic heart," Yorkin said. "And, in those days, it was pretty common. Nobody said you had to die from it. I hadn't even the slightest notion of that. As a matter of fact, I noticed that when he did his first number—that was a pretty big dance number that we did for him—I remember when he rehearsed he would stop and would be out of breath and would need rest. But I never even put that together that it was his heart."

With Yorkin on board, the special moved ahead smoothly. But it turned out that signing Bob Hope for *Bobby Darin and Friends* was one thing; getting him to actually show up turned out to be a headache for everyone involved.

"We were renting out space from Paramount and Bobby was dancing and rehearsing and I get a phone call—Bob Hope can't make it, he's sick, whatever," Blauner said. "So I'm on the phone calling, we're in trouble, we need help. And people were volunteering—Danny Thomas, Jackie Cooper—and Bobby is out there rehearsing, just hoping that Hope would get better.

"And our unit manager was Hope's unit manager and so he came out to Paramount, looked through the door and he said, 'Well, we just left Bob.' 'Yeah, where?' 'Well, he just did a reading for his new special.' And I said, 'That dirty son-of-a-bitch!' and I picked up the phone and called him. And I said, 'I'm gonna sue you! How dare you! Bobby Darin is in there dancing and hoping you would get well and you're pulling a thing like this?' And Hope said, 'Well, there was a dinner in Washington for Stuart Symington'—I swear, those were his exact words, 'and I thought it would help me with my taxes.' This man wrapped the first dollar he ever made. He owned either side of the 101 Freeway all the way to the ocean."

Hope did, finally, agree to come onto the show. "But he fucked the show up because it was written so that it wasn't like the normal variety show," Blauner said. "But now that he was coming in after the fact, we had to change it and he went down front and did his monologue just like any variety show."

That was only part of the show. Hope did, in fact, do a few sketches with Bobby and danced a little bit. The show opened with an elaborate dance number, choreographed by Tony Charmoli.

"I remember Bobby really adapted to the dance movements very well and enjoyed the rehearsals with me," Charmoli said. "He liked moving. It wasn't, 'Do I have to do this?' because he thought dance was essential to singing. He was rather physical, anyway.

"What I remember fondly about Bobby was that, when the special was over, he gave me a gift," Charmoli said. "In those days, when we worked we had to time everything. We didn't want to run overtime because it would cost much more money. I would time all the musical segments . . . and I always wore a stopwatch on a cord around my neck.

"Bobby was aware of this, and he gave me a wristwatch, it was comparable to a Swiss Army watch that had a stopwatch built into it, and on the back he had inscribed: 'Tony, thanks for putting my feet with the beat.' "

Bobby Darin and Friends aired January 31 on NBC. The reviews the next day were mixed.

"Performers who wear the rose of youth upon them are increasingly present in the television ranks, but we can't recall when their presence was as strongly felt as it was last night," enthused television columnist Marie Torre. "If there were any doubts about the quality of his talent . . . Darin proved last night that he earned the right to break through to the big-time. . . . As he begins to sing, the feet twitch, the head bobs, the fingers snap, and the figure seems to grow taller. Rhythm throbs through the TV screen with such infectiousness that it's a challenge to the home audience not to react."

Kay Gardella, writing in the *New York Daily News*, wasn't as charitable.

"Bobby (Mack the Knife) Darin may be an overnight success as a recording star and nightclub performer, but he'll have to make friends with his television audience before he hits the big league on the home screens.

"Holding sway last night as star of his first NBC special, the rock 'n' roll idol is a smooth, relaxed, easy-to-take performer who has cleverly incorporated mannerisms of such successful predecessors as Frank Sinatra, Dean Martin and, believe it or not, Donald O'Connor. But he forgot one thing. There's an audience out there beyond the TV cameras; he plays right over their heads."

"Bobby Darin headed the cast of his own variety show last night. In several songs, at a fast tempo, he demonstrated that he is an accomplished finger-snapper," wrote *New York Times* critic John Shanley.

"As a singer, he is considerably less accomplished—particularly when he attempts a tender ballad, such as 'I Have Dreamed.'"

Viewers, though, were interested in seeing how Bobby fared, and *Bobby Darin and Friends* scored solid ratings. The show's sponsor, Revlon, approached Bobby and Blauner with an offer. "They wanted to make a deal for six more specials, and so here I was in town and Bobby was someplace in the middle of the country, at the Hambletonian, I think, and I was telling him we've got this deal for six specials," Blauner said.

"He said to me, 'Do you think we should do that? You don't think we should just wait and see what happens?' So I hung up the phone and I thought about it and I decided to take his advice and I said no, we don't want to make the deal. And we never did another special."

Bobby Darin and Friends did make one enemy, however: Actress Sylvia Sidney. Sidney, fifty-one, was offended by a sketch in the show, in which a man asks Bobby, "Are you Bobby Darin?"

"Yes," Bobby replies.

"Are you the Bobby Darin that has Sylvia Sidney and her all-mother harmonica band on Tuesday in color?"

Sidney failed to appreciate the mention of her name and filed a $350,000 lawsuit against NBC in Los Angeles Superior Court. Sidney claimed that the line defamed her, invaded her privacy, impaired her reputation as "a dramatic actress who regularly appears on Broadway, in movies and television" and "misappropriated her name for commercial purposes."

"We wrote NBC and asked to see a kinescope of the trailer," said her Beverly Hills lawyer, Paul Caruso. "We saw it and in my mind it was libelous per se. Understand, Miss Sidney never gave her consent to the use of her name. She had no knowledge they were going to use it. She had never been engaged to appear on the show. We asked NBC for a retraction and they refused."

But that was just a small hiccup. Life in Hollywood was agreeing with Bobby and Sandra and Bobby, especially, took to his glamorous surroundings—maybe a little too much for some of his friends, like Dick Clark, who knew him from the old days back in New York.

"He wrapped himself in his fame," Clark said. "He got a big house, he had a blonde wife, he became an actor. He was really 'Hollywood' at one point in his life. He was totally Hollywood. But he was always there for me. I went though a bad period in my life where I was going through a divorce and he was very helpful, very consoling.

"I did a pilot once at my house in Philadelphia because I wanted to break out of the mold of just doing *Bandstand* and I wanted to do a morning talk show with all of the elements you see on talk shows these days—one of which was a live performance by Bobby, who came and sat in our family room, played the piano and sang a bit."

Ahmet Ertegun, who was still producing Bobby's albums, including a pairing with Johnny Mercer that was just being released, also noticed a change once Bobby moved to the West Coast.

"After Bobby went to Hollywood, the people around him, they tried to keep him away from me because I think they saw me, probably, as somebody . . . I had no particular interest in making money from him. I don't think their main interest was to make money from him, either," Ertegun said. "They really loved him. But apparently they thought of me as being somebody who could be taking some of his love away from them."

That didn't mean Bobby had forgotten old friends and acquaintances. Don Kirshner wasn't very involved in Bobby's business affairs anymore, but they remained friendly. One of Kirshner's new "finds" was a kid songwriter, all of fifteen, named Tony Orlando—the same Tony Orlando who snuck into the Copa and waited for Bobby in the lobby after the show.

"Donny says,'Come with me tomorrow over to the St. Moritz Hotel, you're going to meet Bobby. He's there with Sandra Dee,'" Orlando said. "They were newlyweds then. And I go up to their room and I bring my guitar and I walk into the room and there's Bobby, and he's sitting on the floor. He's inventing a game. It was a board game, based on the music business. He was into creating this game and I was watching his other creative side going. You know, he was a bit of an intellectual.

"That had an impact on me, how intelligent he was and at the same time, how caring he with this young kid. And I played him a song that I wrote and, when I think back to what I wrote and what I played for him, it amazes me that I even had the courage to play it. I played him a song called 'Old Napoli,' which I wrote, and it was like a bad Dean Martin song.

"Bobby says, 'Yeah, Donny, there's a lot of raw talent here.' And then Sandra Dee walked in and she says, 'I'm going to make some spaghetti.' She comes in with a full load of groceries into the hotel suite. It was my first time in a place you would call 'for the rich.' It was literally overlooking Central Park. It was humongous. And I'm about to be fed by Sandra Dee.

"So I got nervous and I said, 'Donny, I don't know if I belong here, I could walk home.' I just felt it was time to leave, and I did. So on the way out the door, Bobby said to me, 'Well, if you're not going to have dinner with us now, when you have your hit record you make sure when you get to Los Angeles you call me.'

"So sure enough out comes 'Halfway to Paradise' and it's a humongous record in two of the major cities, L.A. and New York," Orlando said. "I go and call Donny, I said 'I'm going on my first trip to Hollywood and I'm staying at the Beverly Hills Hotel and Bobby Darin told me to call. Should I call him?' So Donny said, 'Of course, here's his home number.' So I call Bobby and he invites me over to the house. Now I'm going to Sandra Dee and Bobby Darin's house.

"Now I have a record in the top 20 and on the major charts. So I'm walking in with a hit record. I take a cab up to Bobby's house in Bel-Air. I sit down and Sandra Dee makes mashed potatoes, pork chops with gravy and string beans. And I take the knife and fork and I go to make the cut and all of a sudden, my knife slips across my plate and the pork chop slides off my plate onto Sandra Dee's dress.

"I'm going to myself, holy shit!, only my luck to go to my idol's house and destroy it," Orlando said. "I'm so embarrassed I'm almost in tears. Now Bobby does half an hour of jokes on my klutziness. Now he has Sandra laughing to the point where we can't stop laughing because now the gravy is literally on all of us—it's on Bobby's hands and he puts it on my shirt and it's absolutely the most hysterical moment.

"That was the first time in the presence of my hero."

Bobby's album with Johnny Mercer, *Two of a Kind*, was recorded the previous August, before Bobby left for Italy to begin filming *Come September*. Mercer, the legendary tunesmith, showman and co-founder of

Capitol Records, was impressed with Bobby's talent and was a big fan. His teaming with Bobby was serendipitous now—or maybe it wasn't the coincidence it appeared to be.

Bobby was getting restless at Atco, and friends and colleagues were whispering in his ear that he deserved a bigger record company with the cachet Atco couldn't provide. And how convenient that Bobby was now working with Mercer in Los Angeles—home of Capitol's famously round landmark tower.

"Eventually, when he went to Hollywood, he was suddenly surrounded by a lot of young agents and would-be managers," Ahmet Ertegun said. "Everybody is talking to him, including Steve Blauner and the others, saying, 'Everything is great, except you're not with a major record company.' Now not many young singers were breaking out on any major labels.

"But after having made all those successes, I felt this was a cooperative effort," Ertegun said. "And we were getting along fine, everything was great. I mean, Bobby wasn't looking for another producer. We were making it. And we were making it because we understood each other and we understood how to make records that had soul, funk and also had rhythm and a general appeal.

"But, you know, we were up against some tremendous competition from people like Elvis Presley on one side and Frank Sinatra on the other and all the R&B singers," he said. "And we had to keep coming through. And they were in front of me saying to Bobby, 'Well, isn't it a shame that you are stuck on Atlantic.' They were all very impressed with that round building in Los Angeles."

According to Blauner, he came up with the idea to pair Bobby with Johnny Mercer. Both performers were scheduled to appear on a television show in New York called *The Big Party* hosted, ironically, by Bobby's *Come September* co-star, Rock Hudson. The short-lived, ninety-minute variety show was spun off from the old Tallulah Bankhead radio series, *The Big Show* (Bankhead appeared regularly on the television version) and was shot out in Brooklyn, where studios could accommodate the big, heavy equipment needed to broadcast in color.

"I went over to Bobby at one point and I said, 'How about you do an album with Johnny Mercer?' And he said he'd love to," Blauner said. "So I go over to introduce myself to Johnny Mercer and he said, 'I'd love to do it.'"

Blauner thought the album should be comprised of Mercer's tunes, an idea vetoed by both Bobby and Mercer, who decided to pick a mélange of songs together. "Johnny would come and sit in Bobby's trailer and they would start on an envelope the lyrics to a song which became 'Two of a Kind,'" Blauner said. "Bobby would throw a line here and there, and when the song was finished, Johnny gave Bobby co-writer's rights. Bobby said, 'I don't deserve this.'

"So we go to do the sessions, three sessions, four songs an hour, until we finished the album," Blauner said. "They both come to me and say we've got to do another session. I said, 'What are you talking about? We've got the twelfth song, we've got the album.' No, no, they said, we're having such a great time."

The enjoyment Bobby and Johnny Mercer took in working with each other is evident on the album entitled *Two of a Kind*. They mixed their choices of old show-biz tunes ("Ace in the Hole," "Lonesome Polecat") with off-the-cuff lines and good-natured, back-and-forth ribbing. The album's overall tone, set by Billy May's brassy, Big-Band arrangements and Ronnie Zito's steady drumming, is relaxed and upbeat—almost as if we're sitting in on two old friends fooling around in the recording studio. Bobby and Mercer even switch off singing the lyrics of *Two of a Kind*.

"I went to Ahmet and I said, 'There are parts where Bobby and Jimmy break up—don't take that stuff out, that's the charm of this album,'" Blauner said. "They took some of it out, but left some of it in. They were having such a good time. When Bobby was happy and singing, he would sing with his hands over his head. I mean, they had the greatest fucking time.

"Now the fourth session is done. Johnny Mercer comes up to me and says, 'Steve, I just want you to know that when you asked me about doing this originally, I thought you were blowing smoke. I didn't think anybody ever wanted to sing with me again.'"

Blauner claims that there were three or four songs from those sessions that were never released. "Atlantic was going to send them over to a warehouse in New Jersey to save money" but the warehouse caught fire and the songs were lost forever, he said.

Two of a Kind was released in February 1961. In March, Bobby returned to the Copa for the first time since his triumphant opening the previous June, squeezing in an appearance on *The Jackie Gleason Show* during his three-week run under Jules Podell's watchful eye.

Sandra had finished shooting *Tammy Tell Me True* and joined Bobby in his suite at the St. Moritz. She and Bobby hadn't yet announced their big news to the press: Sandra was pregnant.

The father-to-be bowled them over in his second go-round at the Copa, sharing the bill with impressionist Frank Gorshin, a regular on *The Ed Sullivan Show*.

"In the nine months since his last Copa appearance Bobby has acquired a vast amount of poise and stage presence," wrote *New York Post* critic Martin Burden. "Darin calls it confidence; his detractors call it smug cockiness. Whatever it is—and we say it's confidence—it enables the young man to grab the audience's attention and hold it tight. He may improvise extraneous chitchat—and he does, too often—but he keeps his customers with him every step of the way. And that's the real test of a big leaguer."

Bobby sang "Come Rain, Come Shine," "Up a Lazy River," "Don't Worry 'Bout Me," "Clementine," "That's All" and other standards. He included "Mack the Knife" in the set, of course, and even dragged out the "oldies"—"Splish Splash" and "Queen of the Hop." "*These* were the good old days!" he joked. As usual, Bobby showcased his versatility, playing the piano, banging around on Ronnie Zito's drum kit and wheeling out the vibraphone for a number.

"He had a good time [as a drummer] and he had a lot of nerve," Zito said. "He didn't care. He was just having a good time for himself."

Bobby's energy seemed to juice up the band. "It's hard to describe it as a drummer," Zito said. "When you're playing that instrument and there is something happening in front of you like that, you're listening and it's very inspiring to play.

"And we were friends and it was like we were all on each other's side, kind of supportive," he said. "Bobby would acknowledge you right on stage if something felt good to him. You know, he would turn back and smile, singing and dancing at the same time. I never saw anyone do what he did, outside of people like James Brown. You don't see that. It was amazing."

"The qualities that have made Mr. Darin an object of adulation are not immediately apparent when he walks into the spotlight," wrote *New York Times* critic Arthur Gelb after seeing Bobby's opening night at the Copa. "He is brash. He has a double chin, puffy eyes, a baby face. He singing voice is indifferent.

"While putting over rhythm songs by hurling his whole body into them, his attempts at romantic ballads such as 'My Funny Valentine' are often unsuccessful. He hasn't the smoothness, the grace or casual charm of a Crosby. He lacks the gaunt pathos (not to mention the persuasive voice) of a Sinatra. He does not try to woo his audience as an Eddie Fisher does.

"Mr. Darin defies his audience not to accept him and this, strangely enough, appears to be one of the major ingredients of his popularity," Gelb wrote. "His faith in himself is so great it would seem almost lesemajeste not to applaud him . . . In the course of a number such as 'Won't You Come Home, Bill Bailey?' he kicks, does bumps and grinds, doubles over, yanks at imaginary ceiling fixtures, drops the microphone from hand to hand, spins on his heel and shakes his head from side to side until it threatens to snap off. Throughout these contortions he wears a look of boyish glee."

The three-week Copa gig ran through the end of March, when Bobby was scheduled to return to Los Angeles to begin filming *Too Late Blues*, where he would play a jazz pianist in the John Cassavetes movie. His busy schedule meant less and less time spent with Sandra, which Bobby tried to reconcile by sending her fresh flowers every day the couple was separated while he toured. It was becoming an all-too-common occurrence, with Bobby out on the road or making a movie and Sandra at home with Clementine, her Yorkshire terrier. Now, with a baby on the way, it was something Bobby and Sandra would have to adjust to.

Bobby still refused to speak publicly about Sandra, but she agreed to be interviewed for the May issue of *Photoplay* magazine. "At Last— Sandra Breaks the Silence!" screamed the headline, but there really wasn't much "there there," although Sandra did open a very small window into the couple's private world. The young girl whose life had been so dominated by her mother seemed to enjoy her new role as a wife.

"When I met Bobby and fell in love, I changed. Life changed. My whole world changed. For the first time I have responsibilities," she said. "When I lived at home, my mother did everything for me, took care of everything, and that was just fine with me. I never planned anything, never took part or contributed to the way things were run.

"But I'm running my own home now, and even though we do have Nellie, the housekeeper, I feel things are and should be my responsibility. I plan things, I oversee what's to be done, I make those decisions a woman should make. It's really crazy, too, because it has all come to me so naturally!"

If Bobby wasn't willing to open up about his marriage, he felt no compunction about showing off his latest purchase: a custom-made car valued at $150,000 ("Well, actually it only cost $97,000 for parts. Bobby's been offered $150,000 for it," his press agent boasted).

The car was designed by Andy Didia, a clothing designer Bobby met on tour in Detroit. Didia worked with Bobby on customizing the maroon-colored car, which was completely aluminum and boasted an eight-cylinder engine and huge tail fins. The car also had dual gas tanks in the rear fenders, a mostly glass top, foot-thick doors, electric windows and swing-down headlights. Didia claimed the car was finished in thirty coats of "pure pearl oil of essence with added crushed diamond" to make it sparkle.

Didia said four men labored over the car for seven years, pre-dating his friendship with Bobby. Bobby, for his part, said he'd told Didia, back in 1957, that he'd buy the car "if I hit it big." The time had arrived.

And Bobby's assessment of the $150,000 car?

"It's a gas."

6

Shooting on Bobby's next movie, *Too Late Blues*, began in early April. The movie was a much-anticipated event. John Cassavetes, an actor by trade, had worked in live television in the 1950s and appeared in several movies including *Taxi* and *Crime in the Streets*. He was more interested, however, in *making* movies, carving out a niche for himself as an "auteur" of sorts with his 1960 movie *Shadows*, shot in 16mm and revolving around an interracial relationship—quite daring for a country just now stirring from its Eisenhower-era slumber.

Cassavetes was directing *Too Late Blues* and sharing screenwriting credit with Richard Carr. The movie figured to be a 360-degree departure from Bobby's lightweight role in *Come September* and, unlike that film, would be shot in a grittier black-and-white format.

Bobby's starring role of John "Ghost" Wakefield was originally intended for Montgomery Clift. The handsome actor, battling a host of inner demons including alcoholism and his closeted homosexuality, agreed to take the role—then had to drop out when his drinking became debilitating. Paramount then offered the role to Bobby.

Steve Blauner cautioned Bobby against taking the role. Bobby, however, insisted the dramatic part would be a radical departure from *Come September* and could only help his movie career by proving his versatility.

"I didn't want him to do *Too Late Blues*. I thought it was a piece of shit," Blauner said. "And it was. In fact, I quit over it. He wanted to do it so badly but I said, 'This is bullshit. Nobody is going to see this movie.' And when I quit, I went to the head of the studio and said, 'Take good care of him,' that I wasn't going to be with Bobby anymore." Blauner eventually relented. The estrangement from Bobby didn't last long.

Bobby's co-star and love interest in the movie was bombshell Stella Stevens, just coming off a co-starring role in *Girls, Girls, Girls* opposite Elvis Presley.

"I was forced to do the film I did with Elvis Presley by the studio bribing me that the next picture I would do would be with Montgomery Clift," Stevens said. "Montgomery Clift by that time was not well; he was pouring a lot of liquor down his body. He was like an icon to me; I adored him so much I was just wishing to work with him. So then I got another [icon], Bobby Darin. And I thought, 'This guy is a really good actor.'"

The plot of *Too Late Blues* revolves around idealistic jazz pianist Ghost Wakefield, who meets busty Jess Polanski (Stevens) at a party. Jess, an unsure singer lacking in self-confidence, catches Ghost's fancy and they fall in love. Ghost builds up Jess' self-esteem and abandons his on-the-fringes jazz combo to help Jess build her career. Ghost's band hits it big after he leaves, and his life takes a downward turn when he abandons Jess and becomes a kept man for a wealthy Countess. Jess, meanwhile, has turned to prostitution, but is rescued from her suicide attempt by Ghost. All is redeemed when Ghost reunites with his band, realizing his destiny lies with them and not with Jess.

"Bobby was gentle and sweet and looked directly into my eyes and he was sincere and kind and a perfect gentleman," Steven said of her co-star. "But he let you know he was also very sexy underneath that sweet, childish, boyish face. So that was good, too."

In Stevens' estimation, Bobby's mind was very sexually preoccupied. Although he never came on to her, and their relationship was strictly professional, she sensed a lusty underpinning to some of Bobby's comments to her during the filming.

"In the dance sequences of *Too Late Blues* we danced together and the camera is on my butt a lot," she said. "I started out in my career as a fashion model . . . and always wore a girdle. But Bobby looked at me as I was walking away and he said, 'Stella, lose the girdle.' So from that day on I never wore a girdle again. This shows you that Bobby's mind was always on sex—behind his boyish charm and his sweetness and politeness, there was always that thought in his head.

"One day on the set, he had this kiss with me and had to sort of push me up against the wall and kiss me," she said. "He was a really good kisser. And when the kiss stopped he stood back and he had the ultimate salute. And the guys up in the catwalk were looking down at us and they busted out laughing. He simply walked it off, came back and kissed me again."

The movie work was nice and the paychecks even nicer. Bobby was already planning for his next picture, the musical *State Fair*, which he would quickly follow up with the World War II drama *Hell Is For Heroes*. But he was smart enough to realize that America wasn't ready yet to accept him as "Bobby Darin, Movie Star." For all they knew, he wasn't much of a movie actor. After all, *Come September* hadn't opened yet and *Too Late Blues*, his big dramatic role, wouldn't hit the screens for another year. "My life ambition is to be a great actor," he said. "But I won't give up singing. How can you give up something you want to do? But acting is for me."

Bobby continued to speak his mind in interviews, rankling some, amusing others and stirring conflicting emotions in a public that didn't quite know if he was putting them on—or if he really *was* unbelievably cocky and obnoxious.

He was reminded by one journalist around this time of his impending twenty-fifth birthday—and his proclamation of becoming a legend by the time he reached that milestone.

"I won't make it," Bobby said. "How can anyone be a legend when he has been exposed to the public only two-and-a-half years? More people in the world don't know who I am than know who I am. That doesn't make me a legend."

Yes, Bobby was asked, but will you "eventually" become a legend?

"Absolutely," he said. "And I might add to my statement: I would like to be a legend by twenty-five, and an institution by thirty." He went on to proclaim that "I am my own idol" and said that the public's perception of him as being brash had been colored by journalists taking his quotes of out context.

"Perhaps, but that is because writers make omissions. Writers take part of what I say, but they omit certain things, or they don't convey the tone in which I said things.

"If the public conception of me isn't all good, perhaps that is part of a new wave of publicity," he said. "I don't try to hide anything; I'd say 97 percent of my publicity is true. Perhaps we are entering a new phase in which the public conception of a star doesn't have to be that he is completely nice."

Back on the music front, Bobby's next Atco album, *Love Swings*, was released in July. The album, produced by Ahmet Ertegun and recorded in March during Bobby's three-week Copa engagement, didn't produce any breakout hits with tracks such as "Long Ago and Far Away," "It Had To Be You," "Just Friends" and "Spring Is Here." Bobby was working for the first time with arranger Torrie Zito—the brother of Bobby's drummer, Ronnie Zito.

"I told Bobby about him and I said, 'Man, why don't you call my brother? He's a beautiful writer' and Bobby said, 'Send me a tape.' I called my brother and told him to send a tape," Ronnie Zito said. "We were in Vegas at the time. Bobby heard the tape and said, 'I want to use your brother on my next album.' Just like that."

Bobby gave the newspapers something to write about in the languid days of July when he rekindled his feud with Ed Sullivan, which stretched back to their clash just before the 1959 Grammy Awards. Darin-Sullivan "part deux" had been brewing for a while now, ever since Sullivan announced he would air some of Bobby's *Ed Sullivan Show* appearances from 1959 and 1960. Bobby felt the performances weren't up to snuff with his image as it stood now—or "my present capabilities as a showman," as he put it—and sent Sullivan a wire: Ed would have to cough up $15,000 if he wanted to run those shows. Bobby would then donate the money to charity.

"I don't even know which of the four appearances I did for you will be used," Bobby wired Sullivan, "but, in any case, it would be well over a year-and-a-half old and therefore a year-and-a-half detrimental to me.

"However, I will be only too happy to waive all rights to said film clips provided that your show, in lieu of personal payment to me, will donate $15,000 to the American Heart Fund."

Sullivan fired back, insisting that the contract Bobby signed with him in 1959—four appearances at $1,000 apiece—included a provision to replay those shows. Bobby didn't address that particular point, but sniped that Sullivan claimed "inaccurately" to have given Bobby his first "break" in television when, in fact, that honor belonged to Perry Como.

Sandra was four months pregnant now, and it was around this time that she and Bobby decided to make the information public. It simply couldn't be hidden anymore; Sandra had started to show and had begun wearing maternity clothes in public at the beginning of the summer. But if the strains of Bobby's constant touring schedule and his busy movie career were beginning to cause some cracks in the marriage, these were shunted aside, for now, in anticipation of the baby's arrival.

There was also a movie to promote. *Come September* opened on August 9, 1961, and Bobby's detractors in the show-business community waiting and/or hoping for the Boy Wonder to fail were sorely disappointed. The movie wasn't praised to the heavens but it wasn't panned, either, and it opened to big numbers at the box office.

Archer Winsten, writing in *The New York Post*, summed up the movie's general effect on the critics.

"Rock Hudson, tall and black-haired as he is, is not Cary Grant. Gina Lollobrigida, pretty and built, is not a major comedienne. Sandra Dee is little more than a blond geewhiz girl. Bobby Darin, small-mounted, blob-nosed, puff-eyed and more self-satisfied than Napoleon at Marengo, baffles appreciation until he sings. Then he's all or nothing—nothing to your correspondent but at least understandable.

"The two peaks of the picture, clearly visible no matter what your previous prejudices—this department had never gazed on Darin plain before—are the height of Rock and the ego of Bobby," Winsten huffed. "Obviously they're both going a long way, but not because Bobby is beautiful or has an ingratiating personality, and not because Rock is a magical performer with light comedy."

Variety was a little more charitable in its assessment of the movie: "Darin does a workmanlike job, and gives evidence he'll have more to show when the parts provide him with wider opportunity."

New York Times movie critic Bosley Crowther also weighed in. "As the principal youngsters at the villa, Sandra Dee and Bobby Darin are attractively droll and impish, though Mr. Darin does act at times as though he has seized, with a little too much fervor, the torch that Donald O'Connor has flung."

Although Bobby sang only one song in the movie, "Multiplication," it became a moderate chart success once *Come September* was released. The catchy song was laced with double-entendres, such as pointing out that "two hares with no cares" can soon lead to "a room full of rabbits." It reached #30 in the States and did even better in England, shooting to #5.

"Irresistible You," which was the A-side to "Multiplication," reached #15 in the States. Both saxophone-driven songs had catchy licks courtesy of Plas Johnson and a young horn player named Nino Tempo, who would appear on several of Bobby's albums.

"I was called by Jimmy Haskell to play and Plas Johnson was the other saxophone player," Tempo said. "Bobby was recording 'Irresistible You' and those two saxophones in harmony behind him were Plas and myself. I was so enthusiastic about coming up with that lick. It was a great song and Bobby delivered it beautifully.

"Ahmet Ertegun came over to Plas and me and said, 'Hey, if you guys think of something to play in those holes between where Bobby sings his lines' and I said, 'How about this?' and I played that lick. Ahmet loved it. And I loved doing it because I thought it was kind of an important little section for the record.

"It was a great song and Bobby delivered it beautifully," Tempo said. "We did that one and then we came in maybe a month later and also recorded 'You Must Have Been a Beautiful Baby' and 'Multiplication.'"

Tempo, a veteran session player, had never seen anyone record in quite the same way as Bobby did in the studio.

"He hired the final band to come in, have a session, three hours, cut two or three songs, and then he would call another session in a week or so and he would come back in and do the same song with the same band," he said. "I never heard of anybody doing that.

"He would go home and listen to the recording and any changes that he thought should be made, he would make notations or give Jimmy Haskell the notations, and then he would come back in and do it for real. When you are recording the song at the time, you have all the elements against you—you have time constraints, musician problems. This guy's got an option.

"I learned a lot from watching Bobby," Tempo said. "First of all, he was an extremely brilliant guy and had a wonderful, big talent. I had the greatest respect for him. But Bobby had kind of like an inherent sense of how much *not* to put into a song, vocally. He would leave spaces. He'd do those little things, but he wouldn't overdo it, because when you overdo it, it goes over the top. He knew where to put it in and where to leave it out. The space between the lyrics sometimes is as important as the vocal itself."

Tempo remembered Bobby having total control over the recording sessions. Steve Blauner was there "in a subordinate way," he said, while Ahmet Ertegun, who had the final say, paid close attention to Bobby's suggestions "because he realized Bobby was so filled with enthusiasm and talent." And, if one of the studio musicians had a suggestion, Bobby was open to new ideas.

"If the guys would say, 'Hey, Bobby, how about if we do this?' and he would listen and say, 'Yeah, do that' or 'No, I think it clashes.' He was not unapproachable, not untouchable, but he absolutely knew what he wanted. He was kind to all the guys in the band. He was never overbearing with us."

Bobby's schedule that summer and fall proved to be one of the busiest of his career. In quick succession, and with only a short time off between assignments, he filmed his roles in *State Fair* and *Hell Is for Heroes*, recorded an album of Ray Charles tunes and became a father.

Bobby had a short hiatus before traveling up north to Cottonwood, California, to begin filming Don Siegel's *Hell Is for Heroes*, which would pair him with another prickly performer, Steve McQueen. The cast also included square-jawed Fess Parker, Harry Guardino, James Coburn, Nick Adams, Bill Mullikin and young comedian Bob Newhart, making his big-screen debut after finding fame with his popular *Button-Down Mind* comedy albums.

It was extremely hot up in Cottonwood with temperatures regularly reaching 115 degrees morning, noon and night. That was bad enough, but the heat also created a combustible atmosphere between Bobby and McQueen. Before long, rumors were flying from the set that they were at each other's throats. Both Bobby and McQueen denied there was any friction between them.

"I've never hid my feelings before," McQueen said. "If Bobby and I were on the outs, don't you think I'd come right out with it?"

"I heard the rumors," Bobby said. "The fact is, we all led the quietest kind of life. If we hadn't, we'd have passed out. Sandy was with me and Steve's wife Neile had us over for dinner and taught Sandy how to cook some Spanish dishes, and she gave us lots of tips that will come in handy for our baby.

"But for seven weeks we were living in something like war," he said. "Even getting up at four in the morning didn't help us with the heat. We began shooting at six and, by noon, we could have used another night's sleep. By the end of the day, we were so exhausted, we couldn't have argued with each other if we wanted. We were just too tired.

"I'm not saying nobody ever blew his stack," Bobby said. "But, under the circumstances, we were a pretty tame lot. I'm personally not feuding with anybody."

Newhart agreed to do the movie a year before, and now found that the script had changed when it came time to shoot.

"Steve McQueen had been added," he said. "When I agreed to do it, it was Bobby, Fess Parker, maybe Harry Guardino. And now McQueen had been added and I'm not sure that Bobby was aware of that, or was crazy about that. I think he was originally set to be the star of the movie.

"The movie took on a Steve McQueen quality, the rebel against the establishment . . . and there were a couple of days when Bobby and Steve played the game of 'The last one out of the trailer is the star,'" Newhart said. "And we're in winter uniforms and we're waiting there and sweating and I finally said to Bobby, 'What the hell is going on? We're all standing out here hotter than hell and you and Steve are playing these games.'

"I got the feeling that Bobby felt he was supposed to be the star and then Paramount decided to make it a Steve McQueen movie," Newhart said. "They weren't crazy about each other."

Whether that was true or not was never clarified, although the newspaper gossip columnists continued to cluck that Bobby and McQueen weren't getting along. Maybe McQueen was just staying in character as his *Hell Is for Heroes* character, John Reese, a malcontent who shuns authority—and just about everyone else—but is an excellent soldier when the chips are down.

After trying to run down a colonel with his jeep, the surly Reese is busted down to Private and transferred to a ragtag platoon stationed in France near the Siegfried Line. The platoon is led by no-nonsense Sgt. Bill Pike (Parker) and his second-in-command, Sgt. Larkin (Guardino). Bobby plays wisecracking Pvt. Dave Corby, the supply chief with a knack for getting anything that's needed (for a price, of course). Homer (Nick Adams) is a displaced Pole rescued by the platoon who only wants to help crush the hated Germans. Henshaw (James Coburn) is the platoon mechanic who can fix anything and Cumberly (Bill Mullikin) is the good-natured daydreamer.

The platoon thinks they're about to finally be sent home, but the night Reese arrives they learn they won't be shipping out. Instead, they're ordered to hold the line and stave off a vastly superior German Army within sight distance. The platoon is divided into two groups, with Pike taking most of his men a few miles north—leaving only six weary soldiers under Larkin's command to determine their destiny.

The undermanned platoon gets a much-needed warm body with the entrance of Pfc. James Driscoll (Newhart), a bumbling supply clerk who gets lost while transporting a bunch of typewriters. Henshaw tinkers with Driscoll's jeep, making it backfire continuously to fool the Germans into thinking the Americans have an army of rumbling tanks. This buys the platoon some time to figure out a plan of attack before they're overrun by the enemy.

Director Don Siegel wasn't known for his character development—he relied on action and violence—but the rest of *Hell Is for Heroes* gives the actors a chance to stretch just a bit outside of the stereotypical war dramatics.

McQueen's Reese has his own agenda and clashes with Larkin, remaining the iconoclastic outsider who, in the end, proves selflessly heroic. Corby (Bobby) tries to remain calm and philosophical as the voice of reason among the last men standing, and proves to be brave in his own right. Homer (Adams) finally gets his wish to fight the Nazis. And Newhart provides the comic relief, reenacting his famous phone routine when Driscoll provides fake (and very funny) radio transmissions from inside a bugged pillbox in order to confuse the Germans.

"What impressed me was Bobby's dedication to becoming an actor which, when he put his mind to it, he could do," said Mullikin, who shared several scenes with Bobby, including a death scene. "I had that sort of Stanislavsky approach and was a studio actor and he wanted to be comfortable in that area.

"The script had my death scene and I spoke to him of my thoughts, where Cumberly passes along how wonderful life is. It was a very touching scene," Mullikin said. "When it came time to do it Bobby said everything Cumberly had said to him beforehand, 'Cumberly always said this, he always said that,' and I got an extra day's work because of that."

Mullikin said that "Mackie" was the original name of Bobby's character, "but they had to give him another name because of 'Mack the Knife,' just so he could get away from that."

Bobby had a short hiatus after *Hell Is for Heroes* wrapped, and then it was on to Dallas for the shoot of *State Fair*, a remake of the 1945 Rodgers and Hammerstein musical that starred Jeanne Crain, Dana Andrews, Dick Haymes and Vivian Blaine. Sandra, now roughly six months pregnant, accompanied Bobby to Dallas.

In this version of *State Fair*, directed by Jose Ferrer, Bobby played smooth-talking TV personality Jerry Dundee, who falls for country girl Margy Frake (Pamela Tiffin), while Margy's brother, Wayne (Pat Boone), falls hard for Emily Porter (Ann-Margret). Bobby sang two songs in the movie, "This Isn't Heaven" and "It's a Grand Night for Singing."

"Bobby played the hip, cocky guy in the movie. It was perfect," Boone said. "He was sweeping my film sister off her feet while I was getting swept off mine by Ann-Margret. But, again, it was sort of a continuation on the movie set of Bobby being a young Frank Sinatra and me not trying to copy Bing and taking an easy, natural approach. Bobby knew that I understood what he was about—that he was not only a talent and survivor but was very creative. He could always come up with ways to reinvent himself.

"We spent a good deal of time just schmoozing and talking," Boone said. "I had just bought one of the first Jaguar convertibles to hit the country . . . so I had it delivered to Dallas and drove it up to Oklahoma City. We were filming at the Dallas State Fair and the Oklahoma State Fair. So I drove Ann-Margret and Bobby and others around in that convertible a bit. We were just two young bucks, Bobby and I, but we didn't develop a close, lasting friendship because Bobby's lifestyle was so different from mine. And he was busy doing his stuff and I was busy doing mine. But there was I think—I know on my side—a real admiration. And I think it was mutual."

Bobby somehow found the time, in mid-November, to spend four days in the studio recording what would be his next release, *Bobby Darin Sings Ray Charles*. Bobby had long admired Charles, often citing him as one of his biggest influences, and usually included at least one Ray Charles song in his live act. With Ahmet Ertegun once again in the control booth, and Jimmy Haskell providing the arrangements, Bobby cut twelve Charles songs, including "Leave My Woman Alone," "Tell All the World About You," "What'd I Say" and "That's Enough."

Sax player Nino Tempo was asked to work on the album. "You know, Bobby did a great job on that album, but it's real hard for any white person to emulate a master R&B artist like Ray Charles," Tempo said. "I mean, Ray Charles is just so distinctive, no one can even touch him. It probably was a mistake on Bobby's part. Maybe Ahmet talked him into it—it's hard to say. But Bobby was very much in control. He absolutely knew what he wanted. There was nothing wishy-washy about him. He was very strong."

"Bobby was a very quick, bright guy who knew what he wanted in the studio," said arranger Jimmie Haskell. "He was pleasant to people who were listening to what he said and giving him what he asked for. It's that simple. To the musician, 'Play it louder in that section,' the musician plays it louder in that section next time.

"Bobby was pleasant to work with but he did not suffer fools," Haskell said. "So if somebody was hanging around him or trying to get his attention . . . Bobby would get a little nasty. But most of the time he didn't have to get nasty because people did want to listen to him. I mean, intelligent people recognize another intelligent person and a very talented guy."

WITH BOBBY WRAPPING *Hell Is For Heroes* and the Ray Charles sessions, Atco released *Twist with Bobby Darin*, a blatant attempt to reach Bobby's weakening younger fan base. The album was a mishmash of new recordings and older tunes that had been issued as singles ("Early in the Morning," "Queen of the Hop," "Bullmoose") and some new tunes, including "You Must Have Been a Beautiful Baby." "Baby" was a big hit for Bobby, who gave the song (lyrics courtesy of his pal Johnny Mercer) a hard-driving rock beat propelled by a twanging electric guitar.

"You Must Have Been a Beautiful Baby" was also a good omen: Sandra gave birth to Dodd Mitchell Darin on December 16, 1961, in Cedars of Lebanon Hospital in Hollywood. The baby weighed 6 pounds, 8 ounces and arrived at 2:19 a.m., or "Early in the Morning," as Bobby might have said. To anyone who asked, Bobby and Sandra said they chose "Dodd" because they liked the way it flowed with "Darin." The baby's middle name was in honor of Betty Mitchell, Sandra's press agent. Some further icing on the cake came in the form of the charts when "You Must Have Been a Beautiful Baby" shot up to #5.

Bobby and Sandra were ecstatic over their new son, so much so that the usually combative Bobby took it in stride a few days later when the Hollywood Women's Press Club named him runner-up to Marlon Brando as "The Year's Most Uncooperative Actor" and bestowed its "Sour Apple" on him. Bobby sent a telegram to the club's president: "Will attend your Christmas party to pick up the trophy; feel the Sour Apple awards are rotten to the core."

7

Bobby had a lot to look forward to in the coming year, in all facets of his career. On the movie front, *Too Late Blues*, his first dramatic role, would premiere in February, followed by the premieres of *State Fair* and *Hell Is for Heroes*. He and Sandra would make their second movie together, a fluffy romantic comedy called *If a Man Answers*. Bobby was signed to star opposite Sidney Poitier in the dark psychodrama *Pressure Point*, and Steve Blauner lined up television appearances with Burt Lancaster, Ed Sullivan, Merv Griffin and Bob Hope. Bobby was booked into the Copa later that spring, and that would be followed by a three-week tour with the Count Basie Orchestra.

Musically, though, the waters were murkier. With Bobby's five-year Atco contract nearing its end, he owed one more album to Ahmet Ertegun and Jerry Wexler before deciding what to do next. The whispers in his ear about Capitol, which started during the *Two of a Kind* sessions with Johnny Mercer, were growing louder and more persistent.

In February 1962, Bobby received a double-whammy of disappointing news. Atco's release of *Bobby Darin Sings Ray Charles* met with a resounding yawn and was largely ignored by Bobby's record-buying public. The album charted at #96 and even Bobby, who didn't easily admit defeat, conceded that it might have been a mistake. "It wasn't the greatest LP I ever made, but I had to get it off my chest," he told *Melody Maker* magazine. "It seems to be the fashion now to admire Charles. I'm proud to have been admiring him for a long time." Still, the album wasn't a total loss; Bobby's version of "What'd I Say" received a Grammy nomination for "Best R&B Recording." Darin archivist Jeff Bleiel points out that it was Ray Charles, ironically, who won the Grammy in that category for "I Can't Stop Loving You."

The news on the movie front was just a little better regarding *Too Late Blues*, the movie over which Steve Blauner temporarily quit the year before. Now, with tepid reviews coming in, maybe Blauner hadn't been too far off the mark.

Archer Winsten, *The New York Post*: "*Too Late Blues* is a picture which had more and better publicity than it deserves. Taking it as a representative of the avant-garde, improvisational filmmaker John 'Shadows' Cassavetes, we see the creator reducing his plot to mere comprehensibility, raising his casting sights to the awesome heights of pop singer Bobby Darin and pert, breasty Stella Stevens, and staying in there with camera closeups worthy of the finest facial gymnastics.

"Darin, despite enough self-confidence to enable the Queen Mary to take off like a Boeing 707, lacks those qualities of personal charm that make a hero or a star. Stella Stevens, on the other hand, could make it purely on what she's got in the face and on the figure."

"This is a commonplace film to which we wouldn't give a second thought but since it was directed by John Cassavetes it cannot be dismissed that quickly," wrote *New York Daily News* film critic Wanda Hale. "Cassavetes' artistry on his directorial touches and in the photography are too studied in this ordinary story and therefore ineffectual . . .

"I liked Bobby Darin in *Come September*. But the role in *Too Late Blues* is against him. It's heavy and he plays it heavily, failing to inspire any feeling for the character; neither does Stella Stevens for the loose girl she represents. The jazz music may appeal to the younger generation, but Darin fans will miss his singing."

The New York Times was brutal in its assessment of the movie itself— "All that *Too Late Blues* needs to make it one of the best movies ever about jazz musicians is substance"—and wasn't much better in assessing Bobby's performance, noting he looked like "a cocky squirrel."

"The real weakness is an arrogant punk of a hero, played to perfection by Mr. Darin, who seems more dedicated to himself than to music and whose belated humility doesn't quite jell."

While *Too Late Blues* tanked at the box office, it did little to damage

Left: A young Bobby, here with a younger playmate, was already flashing the smile that would melt young girls' hearts. (Globe Photos)
Right: Bobby in an early publicity shot, full of hope and optimism.

Bobby shakes hands with Herb Abramson after signing his Atco deal. Jerry Wexler (left) and Steve Blauner are all smiles. (Courtesy of Jerry Wexler)

A 1960 *Coke Time* special featured America's top young male performers (from left): Paul Anka, Frankie Avalon, Pat Boone, and Bobby. (ABC Photo Archives)

Steve Blauner (left), Bobby, and Jerry Wexler talk over business behind the scenes at Atco around 1960. (Courtesy of Jerry Wexler)

Bobby with his mentor, George Burns, and Ralph Edwards on *This Is Your Life* in December 1959 at the height of "Mack the Knife" mania. Edwards surprised Bobby in a Los Angeles TV studio. (Ralph Edwards Productions)

It's a gas! Bobby poses proudly with his $150,000 custom-made, all-aluminum car, which boasted dual gas tanks, foot-thick doors and swing-down headlights.

Left: Bobby and his drummer, Ronnie Zito, backstage at the Three Rivers Inn in Syracuse, N.Y., 1961.

Right: Young lovers: Bobby and Connie Francis had a passionate love affair that was broken up by Connie's overprotective father. Years later, Francis still spoke of Bobby as her one true love. (Getty Images)

Elvis Presley was a huge Bobby Darin fan, and often came to see Bobby perform in Las Vegas. This shot was taken in Vegas in August 1960, while Bobby was headlining at the Sahara Hotel. (Bettman/Corbis)

Bobby was twenty-four and Sandra Dee only eighteen when they met and fell in love in Italy on the set of *Come September* in 1960. Bobby romanced Sandra's mother, Mary Douvan, before moving on to her daughter. (Bettman/Corbis)

Bobby and Steve Blauner before one of Bobby's appearances on *The Ed Sullivan Show* in the early 1960s. Blauner became the big brother Bobby never had, protecting Bobby with a fierce devotion.

Bobby in happier times at Atco in the early 1960s with (from left) Jerry Wexler; Nesuhi Ertegun; and his longtime producer, Ahmet Ertegun. Bobby eventually left the label for a huge contract at Capitol, only to return to the fold several years later. (Courtesy of Jerry Wexler)

December 1, 1960: Bobby and Sandra arrive in Los Angeles just hours after their marriage in Don Kirshner's New Jersey apartment. (Getty Images)

Oh, to be young: Bobby and Annette Funicello on *American Bandstand* circa 1960. (ABC Photo Archives)

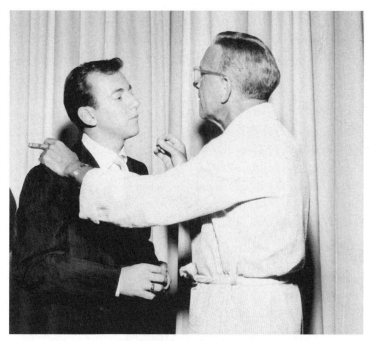

George Burns gives his young charge some pointers before their engagement in Las Vegas. Bobby considered Burns a father figure and was an honorary pallbearer at Gracie Allen's funeral. (Globe Photos)

Buss stop: Bobby and Dodd, whom he affectionately called "Moose," share a smooch. Bobby was wild about his son and spent as much time with him as he could. (Globe Photos)

Sandra and Dodd. (Courtesy of Sandra Dee Thomas)

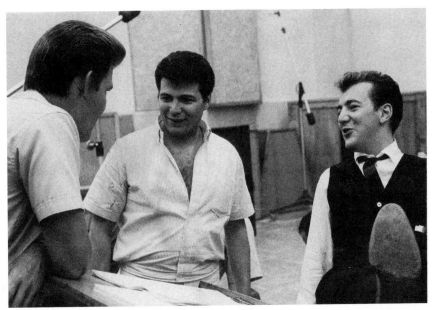

Bobby shares a laugh with producer Nick Venet (center) and young guitarist Glen Campbell at Capitol during the recording of the *You're the Reason I'm Living* album.

Bobby, who loved Westerns, made many episodic TV appearances during his career—including this 1964 episode of *Wagon Train*. (ABC Photo Archives)

Bobby and the Supremes on the ABC special *Stage 67: Rogers & Hart Today* (1967). (ABC Photo Archives)

Getting political: Bobby idolized Robert F. Kennedy, and campaigned hard for RFK's 1968 presidential campaign, including this April stop in Gary, Indiana—two months after he learned his family's shocking secret. (Getty Images)

Nearing the end: A wan, frail Bobby poses with Dodd. (Globe Photos)

BOBBY IN THE MOVIES (from below to end)

A soused Tony (Bobby) learns a valuable life lesson from Talbot (Rock Hudson) in *Come September*.

Bobby wrote the catchy, finger-snappin' "Multiplication," the title song of *Come September,* which he sang in the movie's nightclub scene.

Bobby in his first big-screen role, as the resourceful Pvt. Corby in Don Siegel's *Hell Is for Heroes,* co-starring Steve McQueen, Harry Guardino (shown here), Fess Parker, and Bob Newhart. Bobby and McQueen reportedly clashed on the set.

Bobby and Stella Stevens in *Too Late Blues*, his first big-screen dramatic role.

Bobby, Dick Bakalyan, and Mary Munday in a scene from *Pressure Point*, in which Bobby played a racist provocateur battling a prison psychiatrist (Sidney Poitier).

Bobby and Sandra in a publicity still for *If a Man Answers*.

Bobby earned an Oscar nomination for his riveting work in *Captain Newman, M.D.*, in which he played a haunted World War II casualty brought out of his shell by a sympathetic Army psychiatrist (Gregory Peck).

Tom Milford (Bobby) romances Joan Howell (Sandra) in *That Funny Feeling*, the couple's final movie together.

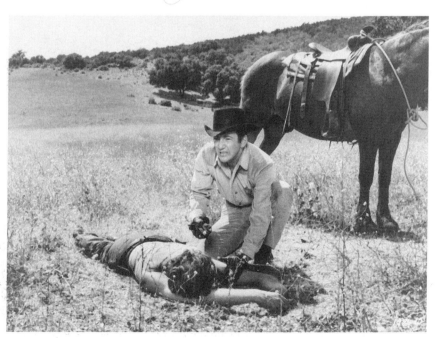

Gunfight in Abilene was Bobby's only big-screen Western. Bobby wrote the movie's score.

Bobby played an Italian gigolo in *The Happy Ending* and fell in love with Jean Simmons, the wife of the movie's director, Richard Brooks. Bobby was billed in the movie as "Robert Darin," and the experience inspired him to make his own movie, *The Vendors*, which was never released.

Bobby menaces a young Ron Howard in *Happy Mother's Day, Love George*. The thriller, directed by Darren McGavin, was Bobby's final movie role and was released in 1973 shortly before Bobby's death.

Bobby's popularity. Dodd's birth and his status as a new dad shielded him from his harsher critics. For now, they kept their sniping to a minimum.

BY THIS TIME Nina, Charlie, Vee, Vana and Gary had moved from the cottage in Lake Hiawatha to the working-class town of Ridgefield Park, New Jersey. While they reveled in Bobby's success, it was, sometimes, a hindrance—especially for six-year-old Gary and his older sister.

"What it was, unfortunately—and this turned out to be a real issue—was the fact that who our uncle was was put on our permanent file," Gary said. "Vee had stopped going to school because she went to acting school, and my sister Vana graduated in 1965, but it was on her permanent record that her uncle was Bobby Darin.

"So whether you're going to a new school, you carry that with you," he said. "So people have a false sense of where you're coming from because, 'Oh, you're Bobby Darin's nephew or niece, you must have money. You must be living in the lap of luxury.' And that was never the case. It became a burden because people thought of you differently. Vanna was a very quiet individual, as I was, in school. You know, we did our work, did what we were supposed to do."

Gary had seen his Uncle Bobby perform at the Copa and on television. He even vaguely remembered Bobby holding him in his arms on the *This Is Your Life* broadcast a few years earlier. But now that he was six, and more cognizant of his surroundings, he got an up-close-and-personal taste of the adulation surrounding Bobby.

"I got my first education that he was something other than my uncle when he came to visit us after he had done *State Fair* in 1962," Gary said. "He hadn't seen it and it was playing at our local theater. He was over and he said, 'Why don't we go and see it? I haven't seen myself on the big screen, we'll go.' So he wore a hat and sunglasses and we went to see the movie. And before the movie was over, there were girls in there that recognized him. We went through the exit and had the car parked right next to the theater.

"And before we could get Bobby into the car, it was mobbed. People were dressed to the nines and these were teenagers and they were going bonkers. Bobby Darin right here in Ridgefield Park! That was the first time I realized that, yes, he's that guy on the screen but these girls are also dying to get a piece of his clothing. That was the first time I realized that when you're a recording star or whatever, *this* is what it gets you."

Bobby might have received adulation from his fans, but his critics panned *State Fair* when it opened in early April.

"Twentieth Century Fox's remake of minor bucolic tribulations . . . is a basically obvious and, for the most part, dull fare," A.H. Weiler wrote in *The New York Times*. "This *Fair* is, at best, only fair." Weiler went on to name the movie's songs, including "Fair," "It Might as Well Be Spring" and "That's For Me."

"As interpreters of these tunes, a clutch of professionals—Pat Boone, Ann-Margret, Bobby Darin and Alice Faye—are not wanting in their efforts. They croon or belt them out, as the occasion requires, with understanding and feeling," he wrote. "But they are almost by rote, it would appear."

Weiler described Pamela Tiffin as "merely bland and vacuous in the role, as is Bobby Darin, who, while permitted to be as flip as a true hipster as her lover is, nevertheless, rather awkward as an actor."

The New York Post gave Bobby's performance a backhanded compliment.

"The other moot point, the personal appearance of Bobby Darin, is probably good for one more treatment. His continuing capture of good, fat movie roles despite a face somewhat less than beautiful is no mystery. He has real talent as a rhythm singer, and he projects a strong personality when his voice comes over alone.

"The projection was offensive when he could also be seen in all his odious self-confidence in his first pictures. Now he has toned it down. He's comparatively modest, and he does behave himself as a good little star should. It gives you pause as you realize that he may even, by sheer intelligence and will, win over such reluctant audiences as our correspondent . . . still, let's face the dreary fact that Bobby hasn't arrived yet in *State Fair*."

If Bobby's movie roles weren't setting the world on fire, he was still considered a top-drawer recording star with five gold records under his belt. Two of his songs from *Come September*, "Irresistible You" and its B-side, "Multiplication," charted strongly at #15 and #30, respectively. While *Bobby Darin Sings Ray Charles* hadn't sold well, Bobby's version of "What'd I Say" climbed to #24 on the charts, which was all the more impressive considering the album's sub-par performance.

Back at the Copa in May, Bobby was stricken with a sore throat, causing him to postpone an appearance on *The Ed Sullivan Show* and cancel two nightclub performances. Steve Lawrence and Jackie Wilson subbed for him at the Copa while Bobby visited vocal coach Carlo Menotti and rested with Sandra in his suite at the Essex House.

"This always happens when you take off a lot of time to do pictures," he said. "It happens to the best of them. You lay off singing and your throat gets out of practice. No excuses. I blew it, that's all. I blew it." Bobby recovered and finished out the Copa dates, which were all sellouts. Still, some columnists couldn't resist taking a shot at him. "Bobby Darin—never be humble! Always be yourself—arrogant," one wag wrote. "You started out meekly last night at the Copacabana, but I liked you better when you got a little heelish. So did Milton Berle, Joey Bishop, Jan Murray, Hal March and Sugar Ray—also Zsa Zsa."

Bobby's voice was in fine form May 19 when he joined Jack Benny, Henry Fonda, Maria Callas, Jimmy Durante, Danny Kaye, Peggy Lee and Peter Lawford as part of the "New York Birthday Salute to President Kennedy" at Madison Square Garden. It was the first $1 million political event in New York history. It was also among the first of many political events that would count Bobby as a participant.

In the meantime, he and Sandra began work on their first movie together as husband-and-wife. *If a Man Answers* was a piece of comedy fluff directed by Henry Levin from a Richard Morris-Winifred Wolfe screenplay. Sandra played rich socialite Chantal Stacy, who meets photographer Eugene Wright (Bobby) and tries to train him as the perfect husband under the tutelage of her mother, Germaine (Micheline Presle). The movie derived its title from Germaine's suggestion to Chantal to invent a mythical lover who hangs up whenever Eugene answers the phone ("It's the click that gets them," she tells Chantal).

Bobby wrote and sang the movie's catchy title song, "If a Man Answers," which was his first release for Capitol. It charted at a disappointing #32. As for the demands the movie placed on the couple's acting skills, well, it wasn't exactly Shakespeare. Bobby knew that and put a self-deprecating spin on his movie alter-ego.

"Have you ever noticed that all the astronauts are handsome? This is the age of the good-looking American. That lets me out," he said in discussing the movie.

"Now, in this picture, the movie audience is asked to believe that a beautiful girl like Sandra Dee would fall for someone who looks like me. They should have cast somebody like Warren Beatty or George Peppard. Their battle is half-won as soon as they show themselves on the screen. For me, it's an uphill fight all the way. I just walked down Madison Avenue and not one person recognized me. I tell you, I have a nothing face. Can you imagine that happening to Rock Hudson?"

Bobby knew his role in *If a Man Answers* was lightweight, and that was fine. America wanted to see he and Sandra in that particular light, and besides, it might mute some of the whispers about trouble in their marriage. There was talk that Bobby's temper and possessive nature were causing a rift between him and Sandra, still only nineteen and still very attached to her mother. Some of the gossips even talked of Bobby being jealous of Sandra's bigger role in their movie.

"Isn't that crazy? Can I look as good on the screen as she does?" Bobby said. "Can she get up and do an hour-and-a-half on a nightclub floor? That's what makes her a star and what makes me whatever I am.

"Sandra's got sixteen or seventeen pictures to her credit and I've got six," he said. "What kind of competition am I? And as for my terrible temper, it'd be different if I'd punched Sandy in the mouth on 52nd Street!"

Bobby was up for the fight with the press and gave as good as he got—he was better, in fact, when being challenged. Sandra, on the other hand, sounded all of her nineteen years in discussing the marriage—while at the same time sounding a note of caution that belied her youth.

"I knew that I was going to be very happy with him, which I am. It's funny, we've never had an argument about something that's happened, or about something immediate," she told a writer from *Modern Screen* magazine.

"I will argue with him about careers. By that I mean that I'll ask, 'Do you have to go to New York? Why can't you stay here? This is something I can't understand, and I forget that he's the man of the family, and that his job is the most important . . . I forget that he's the man of the family and that I have to follow him, because he can't follow me.

"Otherwise there's no marriage," she said. "If you don't look up to your husband as a man then there's—there's not too much left.

"It's pretty hard to take two people who've lived apart and suddenly put them together in the same house," she said. "There'll be a lot of disagreements like 'I don't like the way you do this . . . Why do you leave the cap off the toothpaste . . . So when you start having a family and discussing how to bring children up, it's really hard.

"So you can't work at it. You can't do it all according to some plan. You have to take it as it comes, because that's what life is."

There were hints, at least behind-the-scenes, that not everything in the marriage was as rosy as it seemed. Bobby's high school bandmate, Walter Raim, experienced this first-hand. Raim had made a name for himself as an arranger, working with Harry Belafonte among others, and Bobby hired him in the summer of 1962 to arrange an album called *Earthy!* Raim came out to Los Angeles to begin working on the album.

"When I got to L.A. I was met by some flunky of Bobby's who said, 'I'm taking you to your hotel and you are to wear a jacket and a tie. We're having dinner at Mr. Darin's house,'" Raim said. "And they picked me up and drove me to this place in the Hollywood Hills. All I remember of the house was a red lacquer front door, which was pretty bizarre, and a big white rug in the entranceway. In the dining room, there was a table about 40 feet long with Bobby on one end and Sandra on the other and me in the middle. And they were fighting. He was calling her various names. She was calling him various names. It felt like a tennis match."

BOBBY'S NEXT MOVIE ROLE was a complete about-face from *If a Man Answers*. In Hubert Cornfield's *Pressure Point*, starkly filmed in black-and-white, Bobby played a psychotic white supremacist thrown into prison for sedition during the early days of World War II. Bobby's character, known only as "The Patient," is introduced via flashback by the gray-haired Doctor (Sidney Poitier), who's trying to help a frustrated young psychiatrist (Peter Falk) understand why he can't make a breakthrough with his black patient.

Flash back to 1942. The Patient, a card-carrying member of the Bund, finds it hysterically funny that his prison psychiatrist, The Doctor, is a black man. But The Patient's taunts and race-baiting don't faze The Doctor, who's convinced that he can help The Patient by exploring his psyche to uncover the roots of his hatred and psychoses.

As The Patient and The Doctor spar, they slowly develop a working relationship of sorts. The Patient begins recounting his childhood memories of his sadistic, philandering father and ineffectual, incestuous mother. This in turn, leads him to a life of petty crime and an unrequited romance (with a Jewish woman he meets while selling apples on the street). A picture of The Patient begins to emerge as a man confused, scared and alienated—the perfect candidate to espouse the hatred of the American Nazi Party. In the end, The Doctor recommends keeping The Patient behind bars, feeling that he's made some progress but still hasn't learned to control his anger. He's overruled however, by the hospital board.

Bobby was excited at the prospect of playing The Patient, and wrote a first-person essay in *Ebony* magazine to explain why he chose to do the role—and perhaps to allay any criticism he might engender for portraying such a horrible character.

"I know the risk I am running in playing this kind of despicable bigot. There will be many Jews and Negroes who will walk out of the theater believing that I am really that kind of character," he wrote. "But motion pictures like this must be made and somebody must portray the dangerous people in our society so that the public will recognize them and their causes for what they really are. This picture is certainly going to shatter a couple of falsehoods—or at least establish them as just that."

Bobby didn't waste the opportunity in his *Ebony* piece to roil the waters a bit, noting that several other actors had turned down the role. "I don't say that the picture doesn't say what they don't believe. I do say that they didn't have enough courage to do anything any more intrepid than 'Let's run down the road and pick up daisies, fellows!' "

He also admitted to having used racial epithets growing up on 135th Street in the Bronx. "We did this with Negroes, Puerto Ricans, Italians, everybody. I never thought anything about it," he wrote.

"Then when I was about sixteen and playing mountain resorts around New York with Dick Behrke, who is my conductor and arranger today, and Walter Raim, who has worked with Harry Belafonte, a curious thing happened. I was telling them a joke one night and I used a racial epithet just as a matter of course. They called me down about it."

Bobby went on to explain how he learned a valuable lesson—"It was a period of enlightenment for me"—and related how, when he played a hotel in St. Louis several years later, he learned that a group of black disk jockeys hadn't been invited to the opening because of their skin color.

"I reminded the hotel that the only reason I was playing there was because people were hearing my records and wanted to see me and that among the people who were playing my records for the public to hear were those same disk jockeys who weren't invited. I haven't played their hotel since."

Bobby's next single, "Things," was released in early summer in conjunction with the album from whence it came, *Things and Other Things*. By that time, Bobby had made an important decision: He was leaving Atco.

There wasn't much doubt where he would land next.

Frank Sinatra's announcement in 1960 that he was leaving Capitol to start his own record company stood the industry on its collective ear. Frank put the icing on the cake when he announced he was bringing his former Capitol stablemate Dean Martin with him to his new label, Reprise—while Sammy Davis Jr. was leaving Decca to join his Rat Pack pals. Capitol, without its top draw, was still looking for someone remotely close to Sinatra's star power to replace Old Blue Eyes.

"I got a call from Frank's secretary. Frank was making *Sergeant's Three* at the Goldwyn lot," said Steve Blauner. "So I go down to the lot and Frank takes me to his dressing room and introduces me to a man I never heard of at the time, Mo Ostin, and says that he and Dean were leaving Capitol and he was forming Reprise and he wanted

Bobby [on the new label]. That shows you there was no feud. So I said, 'Look, I'll call Mr. Ostin tomorrow, let me sleep on it.'

"So I went right from Goldwyn to the [Capitol] tower and I got in to see Alan Livingston, who was running the company, and I made a deal for Bobby, who was going to be their white Nat Cole," Blauner said. "Bobby was suffocating [at Atco]. He'd have no competition from Frank at Capitol. Where was Bobby going to be with Frank's label?

"Frank had left Capitol, I think he was getting 5 percent," Blauner said. "He wanted 1 percent more and they wouldn't give it to him. He said 'Fuck you,' as only Frank could, 'I'm forming my own label.' In those days, if you were big, like Bobby was at the time, you probably could have gotten maybe a $1 million guarantee over ten years, maybe $100,000 a year, guaranteed, whether you made it or not.

"When I went to Alan Livingston—I was always a gambler, right or wrong—I took a shot, I said, 'Look, I don't want a guarantee if you can't pay us 5 percent.' And so I think that was the first contract that broke that barrier, where Bobby got 8.5 percent for singles and 8 percent for albums."

The deal made Bobby the highest-paid recording artist in history. Livingston looked like a genius when "Things" charted at #3 in August and sold over 1 million copies. It was an Atco release, but it boded well for Bobby's future at Capitol.

Hell Is for Heroes opened that summer to generally brisk business and solid reviews, both for the movie itself and for Bobby. "Bobby Darin has a colorful role of a battlefield boarder which he portrays with relish," *Variety* noted, while *The New York Times* thought that "Bobby Darin overplays a comedy role."

Pressure Point and *If a Man Answers* opened that fall, the fourth and fifth Bobby Darin movies to premiere in 1962. They provided a snapshot of Bobby's big-screen image as the gritty dramatic actor who could, in the blink of an eye, romp in a romantic farce.

"*If a Man Answers* was obviously calculated to please the junior miss, as something on the order of a manual on the care and feeding of husbands," opined *The New York Herald-Tribune*. "Bobby Darin is the husband, Sandra Dee his keeper. The plot is scanty and the title refers to her mother's idea of inventing a mythical lover who hangs up whenever Darin picks up the phone . . . Actually this basic situation doesn't appear until the latter half of the film by which time you may be too choked with the whipped cream to care."

Time magazine was markedly more snarky in its assessment of the movie. "Actor Darin and Actress Dee, who are Mr. and Mrs. in real life, just sort of stand there like Tweedle Dumb and Twiddle Dee. And the production is in the cheapest kind of expensive bad taste."

A.H. Weiler, writing in *The New York Times*, thought Sandra was "chic" and "pretty," while "Mr. Darin chomps a pipe, is cool in his repartee and casual in the extreme, without adding anything noticeable to the art of acting."

The age-old maxim that reviews don't really matter, at least for the general public, applied in this case; "Tweedle Dumb and Twiddle Dee" were an appealing on-screen team, and *If a Man Answers* sold a lot of tickets.

Bobby had better critical success with *Pressure Point*, which earned him some of the biggest accolades of his acting career. Most critics praised the movie's dramatic import, its message, and the performances of both Bobby and Sidney Poitier.

"*Pressure Point* is a picture about a homemade American storm trooper, analyzed with such ruthlessness, such fervor of cinematic energy, that it can leave no doubt that in Hubert Cornfield, who directed it, we are witnessing one step in the development of an American director of talent," enthused the *New York Herald-Tribune*.

"The directorial energy is the most noticeable fact about the film, but another surprise is Bobby Darin in the starring role. That this usually light romantic young man undertook such a vicious portrayal is evidence of his seriousness, that he brings it off with such ghastly sureness of touch underlines his talent with unexpected incisiveness."

Archer Winsten in *The New York Post* wrote that "Darin, naturally endowed with a personal brashness that translates with wonderful ease into an insulting attitude, fits into his role as if he'd been made for it." The movie's dark subject matter, however, gave it only limited appeal at the box office.

October also saw the release of Bobby's first Capitol album, marking the first time in four years that he'd been produced by anyone other than Ahmet Ertegun. Tom Morgan handled production duties on the aptly titled *Oh! Look At Me Now!*, which featured Billy May's arrangements and Bobby in a whimsical mood, swinging on tunes like "There's A Rainbow 'Round My Shoulder," "All By Myself" and "A Nightingale Sang in Berkeley Square."

But if Capitol was expecting a blockbuster, or at least an album that would draw some attention, they were sorely disappointed. *Oh! Look At Me Now!* sold poorly, and Alan Livingston was getting nervous. *This* was Capitol's new Sinatra?

8

Bobby was twenty-six now. He'd failed at his goal to become a legend by his twenty-fifth birthday—even he admitted that—but there was still time to catch up before he turned thirty. And who wouldn't want to be in his shoes? He was rich and famous, was married to a beautiful woman and was the father of an adorable little boy. To the average Joe, it was the ideal situation. What red-blooded American male *wouldn't* want to be Bobby Darin?

But there was trouble behind the façade. The tension between Bobby and Sandra, alluded to and whispered about in the gossip columns, was very real. There were unconfirmed rumors of a separation, yet Bobby stuck to his edict of sharing no information about their personal lives with the public. Sandra, too, had lived up to her end of the bargain. She gave the occasional interview to a fan magazine, but never revealed anything of substance regarding her marriage—which was beginning to unravel.

"As far as I was concerned their relationship was good. I mean, I would go over to the house every day and there were two things," Blauner said. "Whenever I went over we talked business and Sandra would space out, and I finally said to Bobby, look, when I come over from now on, if Sandy's here we can't talk business, it's not right. I know whenever Bobby and I were together we would have something to talk about that would be of no interest to anybody but Bobby and I, so I was always trying to be aware of the fact that his wife was a third party.

"I think Sandy married Bobby because she wanted to get away from her mother," he said. "Sandy's mother was this very attractive woman. She would sit on the set and bask in the reflection of Sandra and people would come up to her and say, 'Oh, you can't be her mother, you must be her sister,' because she looked younger."

Part of the problem, or so it was whispered, was Mary Douvan, who'd moved in with Bobby and Sandra. That put an additional strain on their marriage, as if their busy careers, frequent time spent apart and the demands of being first-time parents wasn't enough. It was obvious that Sandra, just turning twenty, was still very attached to her mother. She spoke of Mary in an almost childish way that belied the control Mary still exerted over her daughter—with Bobby pulling in the other direction.

"When I dream how things are going to be, I never picture anything but the best. When I think of my little baby growing up, to me he's going to be the best, the most well-behaved, and the happiest person in the world," Sandra said.

"The baby will do things that will hurt me very badly, because I've hurt my mother very badly from the time I was old enough to know what I was doing, five or six, going to school. I've been a disappointment many, many times to my mother. . . . I mean, even though I've done many things that have hurt my mother, things that every young girl does, that doesn't mean she's ever stopped loving me, or that she wouldn't want me for a daughter anymore."

Steve Blauner put it more bluntly. "Sandy was nice and sweet, but before Bobby she was with her mother, her hairdresser, her makeup person. Period. Never had a friend. She had no life as a kid. She had no friends—except these adults."

In January 1963 Bobby entered the studio to record his second Capitol album, *You're the Reason I'm Living*, released in February. The album's title song charted at #3 and Bobby began preparing for his next big-screen role. It would be another dramatic part, casting Bobby as yet another patient, this time opposite Gregory Peck's Army psychiatrist in *Captain Newman, M.D.* It was a Universal picture, which was beneficial to Bobby since he and Blauner had offices there. Blauner envisioned Bobby in the role of wisecracking Cpl. Jackson Laibowitz—a part that gobbled up more screen time—but Tony Curtis was hired for the role.

"I couldn't quibble with that," Blauner said. "Tony Curtis is ten times what Bobby Darin is worth. So I picked up the phone and called the head of the studio. I remembered one chapter in the book about this kid called Little Jim. I said, is Little Jim in the picture, like in the book? I want Bobby to play it. He said, 'We can't afford Bobby for the part.' I said, 'What's in the budget for the part?' He said '$25,000.' I said, 'You've got a deal.'

"But I said, 'You can't bill Bobby above the title.' They never heard that from a manager before. I said, 'Look, you've got Gregory Peck, you've got Tony Curtis, you've got Angie Dickinson. Bobby's only in the picture fifteen minutes, it wouldn't be fair to his fans, we'll figure out billing below the title.' The reason for that was, in those days, the Academy had the following role: If you were billed above the title you could only qualify for Best Actor; below the title, Supporting Actor.

"So I now send the script to Bobby. He's at the Sands hotel, and I'm just waiting. And sure enough I get the phone call: 'Why am I doing this movie?' And said, 'Bobby, because these are the parts you get nominated by the Academy for, if you're one-tenth the actor I think you are you will get a nomination.'"

Gregory Peck starred in *Captain Newman, M.D.* as the kind-hearted Capt. Josiah "Joe" Newman, tending to shell-shocked soldiers at an Army hospital in the Arizona desert in 1944 along with his devoted nurse (Dickinson) and smart-aleck orderly (Curtis). Among Capt. Newman's patients are a schizophrenic colonel (Eddie Albert), a lost-soul (played by a very young Robert Duvall), and Col. Jim "Little Jim" Tompkins (Bobby), a swaggering Southern flyboy who carried an acoustic guitar—and an attitude.

It's clear to Capt. Newman that Little Jim is covering up some deep-seated guilt, which he camouflages with booze and the need to keep busy (by strumming his guitar). Little Jim implores Capt. Newman to inject him with sodium pentathol (or "flack juice," as the soldiers call it) so he can unburden himself while under the spell of the "truth drug." Newman agrees to the treatment, puts Jim under and listens as he relives the horror of being shot down by Nazi aircraft, seeing his co-pilot get decapitated and blaming himself for not rescue his pal, "Big Jim," who's blown to bits when the plane explodes.

The "flack juice" does its trick. In his follow-up sessions with Capt.

Newman, Little Jim confronts his guilt, comes to terms with his grief and is sent home a happier soldier.

Bobby's fictional happiness, unfortunately, didn't translate over into his very real personal life. By March, he and Sandra couldn't hide their problems any longer, and newspapers across the country carried a UPI wire story reporting their separation. "Darin, Sandra Dee Break Up the Act," screamed a headline on March 27, with the accompanying story noting that "Rumors have been circulating for several months that the couple—both with highly successful individual careers—were on the verge of separation. But the rumors were denied."

There was no denying it now. A Universal-International Pictures spokesman confirmed the separation, emphasizing that the couple had no plans "at this time" to divorce. There was no statement from Bobby, who was performing in Lake Tahoe, or Sandra, who was in Honolulu. "We were never really separated, for one thing, and we had never gotten divorced, so we felt it would be kind of redundant to make an announcement," Sandra said later.

Bobby and Sandra were in touch, hoping to work it out, and for now business went on as usual. Sandra began working on her next movie, *Tammy and the Doctor*, which she followed up with *Take Her, She's Mine*.

Bobby, who continued touring and recording, now had something else that demanded his attention: The publishing company he'd recently purchased.

Bobby had always been somewhat envious of Don Kirshner's success in the music-publishing business. By the early 1960s, Kirshner's business acumen and publishing know-how had made him a very wealthy man. Bobby, always competitive—and with an eye toward the future—figured he could also get into the publishing game. In early 1963, he bought Trinity Music from his old managers, Joe Csida and Ed Burton, changed the company's name to TM Music and set up shop in the Brill Building on Broadway.

Bobby also began incorporating more folk music and blues into his stage act. He had recorded a bunch of folk and blues numbers for Capitol the previous summer and *Earthy*, the result of those sessions, was released in July 1963. For his new sound, Bobby added another member to his band, a banjo/guitar player named Jim McGuinn who would become famous a few years later when he changed his first name to Roger and founded The Byrds.

"I was playing with the Chad Mitchell Trio at the Crescendo Club in Hollywood, warming up for Lenny Bruce, when Bobby came in to see Lenny," McGuinn said. "The Chad Mitchell Trio was three guys who didn't play any instruments. I played banjo and guitar behind them, but I didn't sing with them.

"It was kind of boring for me, so I made faces and I started to mug and the audience started laughing because they thought I was doing it for them," McGuinn said. "Bobby caught this and liked what I was doing up there and said, 'Do you want to come and work for me? What are these guys paying you—I'll double it.'

"I went over to his house the next morning at some ungodly hour," McGuinn said. "He wanted to see if I could do it and he talked to me about what he wanted me to do. I was thrilled that Bobby wanted to do pure folk music, or what we called 'ethnic folk music.' He wanted to start a folk segment in his act and the next thing I knew I was at the Flamingo in Vegas. I'd come out and stand next to him and he'd sing lead and I'd sing harmony with him. It was a great gig for me. I was nineteen and I'd been in the business only a few years."

Bobby would open his live show, backed by Dick Behrke on piano and drummer Ronnie Zito. They would run through their usual repertoire, which might or might not include "Mack the Knife" (depending on how Bobby was feeling about the song that particular night). McGuinn would join them on stage about halfway through the act.

"Bobby would take off his jacket and tie like Harry Belafonte and he and I would do three or four folk songs and that was the end of my gig," McGuinn said. "We'd do songs like 'Makes a Long Time Man Feel Bad,' 'Alberta Let Your Hair Hang Low,' 'Bring Me a Little Water, Sylvie' and maybe a Leadbelly song. Then he would go into his Sinatra stuff and his impressions of people like Lionel Hampton."

Back at the Brill Building, Bobby began assembling a staff of TM songwriters who could churn out tunes to sell to other artists, or even songs for Bobby himself to perform. Rudy Clark was one of the first writers hired by Bobby and worked with him often when he was in town.

"I was working for another company and Bobby heard one of my songs and was impressed by that song, so he came to the company to find out if he could make a deal with them to hire me as a song-writer," Clark said. "A deal was struck and that made one writer, me, and then he hired Artie Resnick and Kenny Young, and then he got hold of Van McCoy and he was ready to roll. He took us on as a writing team."

Clark initially found Bobby a little off-putting but wasn't bothered by the attitude. "He was cocky and rude and everybody seemed to have had the same impression," Clark said. "It didn't get under my skin. I kind of liked it because I was ambitious myself. I was in a hurry, sort of like he was but for different reasons. I understood it. But I never understood the source until later on."

Don Kirshner also had an office in the Brill Building, which became a mecca of sorts for young songwriters like Carol King, Gerry Goffen and Neil Sedaka, Bobby's piano player on "Dream Lover."

"It was a very exciting time. We were teenagers writing for the teen-age market, the New York City sound, and at one point we controlled a couple of songs in the Top 10," Sedaka said. "Harry Greenfield and I were the first of the team to be signed by Donny and Al Nevins. I then brought in Carol King, who I was dating at the time. Then, later, there came Barry Mann and Cynthia Weil and Jeff Barry.

"I remember I had just had my first hit with 'The Diary,' which was like a doo wop ballad and I had come out with a song called 'I Go Ape,' which was like a Jerry Lee Lewis-pounding-piano sort of thing," Sedaka said. "And I vividly remember Bobby saying, 'Neil, I wouldn't put that out.' And he was so right. It nearly wrecked my career."

The time Bobby actually spent in the TM offices was limited, since he was touring, making movies and trying to reconcile with Sandra. But when he was there, his presence was felt. Strongly.

"My writing improved when I started writing with Bobby. We never had a top 10 record, but we always made the charts somewhere around 90," said Rudy Clark. "We had dozens of back sides, album cuts or whatever. Both of us did lyrics and music. But I had to get an idea for a song and music and he would add some lyrics, or vice versa, or he would come in with a lyric or title and I'd search around on the piano because he was busy and he expected me to get it started in a few days. I would have at least a melody line or something like this, and it was a very good relationship. He was very driving. Unbelievably driving.

"They used to call me 'The Slave Driver' but I couldn't keep up with Bobby. He was more driven than I could imagine," Clark said. "I really couldn't understand it all because I remember a few times, we'd finish up around 9 o'clock at night and he'd have a Copa date. So that means he had to go home, get ready and go to the Copa, or he had his clothes over at the Copa, which means he's going to leave about 3 or 4 o'clock in the morning, and he would set a time for us to sit down around 10 that morning. So at 10 o'clock when I got there, he already had the recorder set up. I'd never beat him there—he was always there before me."

"Under the Boardwalk," written by Artie Resnick and Kenny Young and recorded by the Drifters, was TM's first big success under Bobby's watch. Shortly thereafter, he opened a Los Angeles branch of the company in the Capitol Tower. One of his first moves was to recruit musician/songwriter Terry Melcher, the son of actress Doris Day. Melcher played off and on with a surf group called the Rip Chords who had a minor hit with "Hey Little Cobra." Melcher was working as the youngest-ever staff producer at Columbia Records when he got the call from Bobby.

"Bobby had just signed his deal at Capitol and moved permanently to L.A. with Sandra Dee," Melcher said. "They had a house that Sinatra used to live in on Toluca Lake; they had a house on the lake and a couple of little boats to putter around in. Bobby had offices in the Capitol tower and I was working at Columbia Records, which was close by, when he called me.

"All the record companies and publishing companies were in the same area in Hollywood in those days," Melcher said. "He said, 'Would you meet me for lunch?' I said sure, because I had always loved his records, like everyone else. He said he had a new deal at Capitol and he could use a publishing firm and was going to be producing this and that and that he'd like me to come over and produce some stuff for his company and work along with the publishing entity as well.

"I had just had my first really big hit at Columbia, a million-plus seller, a record called 'Hey Little Cobra,' which was something that I picked up the publishing on," Melcher said. "Bobby was aware of that, of course. He said, 'Look, I've got plenty of office space, it's great and you know where it is. Just to make it easy, rather than play around with your compensation, whatever it is that Columbia Records is paying you, I'll double it.'

"I said, 'Well, I like that. Good plan.' So I worked something out with Columbia and I kept the group, the Rip Chords, which was actually just me and Bruce Johnston, who's been in the Beach Boys. I used the Rip Chords name for the 'Hey Little Cobra' record, so Columbia let me keep that and go over to Bobby at Capitol. It was really interesting.

"When we first started we shook hands and I said, 'Okay, I'll start right after I get back from Hawaii,'" Melcher said. "Bruce and I were booked to do a little tour with the Beach Boys and Jan and Dean. It was my first and only rock 'n' roll tour. But it was great fun and we all had girlfriends along so I kind of stretched the time out a little. And pretty soon Bobby was calling me over there and he was saying, 'Melcher, get your ass back here! We've got stuff to do!' He used to prod me a bit, but in a good-natured, funny way.

"I spent a lot of time at his house. Every Sunday he liked to hang around on the lake. Either he would barbecue something or we'd go out and pick up a lot of food and bring it back. And he would have a few people like [his publicist] David Gershenson. I never really knew Sandra Dee."

Bobby was a tough boss who demanded a lot from his writers and expected them to work as hard as he did. When he was in New York, working in the Brill Building offices, it wasn't unusual for him to work until 9 or 10 at night, overseeing his writers, co-writing songs and laying down tracks. Clark, Resnick and the other writers rarely left before the boss, although they usually didn't drift into the TM offices until noon.

For Bobby, who was cutting back on his touring schedule, it was a different way of working. "This is a five-day-a-week situation for me and I do have my two days at home with my wife and the baby. Which makes it better for me than when I was just doing nightclubs seven days a week and in fifty different towns in one year," Bobby said at the time.

"In addition to screening songs from writers and would-be writers, I screen artists, in terms of their vocal sound. I listen to all tapes and demos that are submitted to TM Music. It takes an awful lot of time out of the day," he said. "In addition to that, of course, I have to find time during the same workday in order to read scripts that are submitted to me for acting roles, ideas for television series which are submitted to me, promotional ideas, details in terms of merchandising, advertising . . . there's an awful lot that goes into a full workday for me."

When Bobby was in L.A., the work at TM was no-less-intense and the staff, according to Melcher, never knew just *which* Bobby they might be getting on any particular day.

"The interesting thing about Bobby as a boss is that he had several different personalities when he was in the office," Melcher said. "I never noticed any of this out of the office. But in the office, I never knew who I was going to be encountering. I never knew what facet. But nothing scary. It took a couple of years to pass before I even realized it.

"One day I'd come in, he would be in a dark suit and tie with a briefcase and he'd say, 'Melcher, come on, I want to talk to you about budgets.' Yeah, sure. He would be very much the businessman," Melcher said. "He's looking at budget cuts and income and stuff like that. He would be crunching numbers. He'd pretty much stay in that mode for the day. I was just there for whatever kind of mood he was in.

"And the next day, I'd walk in and he might be in that same mode," Melcher said, "but then he had another kind of thing he'd like to do, a blue blazer and an open shirt and an ascot. Kind of Bing Crosby in *High Society*, everything but the sailor cap. I used to think of that as his kind of Crosby/Sinatra guise. And he might do that for a day or two and the next day he'd be there in Levi's and T-shirt at the piano doing 'Queen of the Hop' and 'Splish Splash' and he wanted to write some rock 'n' roll with me. Those were the three personas that I knew.

"I think Bobby was really fascinated by Donny Kirshner's success as a publisher and small label owner," Melcher said. "I think that's what the dark suit and tie were about. He felt competitive with Kirshner on those days. And the other days he felt competitive with Frank Sinatra. You know, when he wore the ascot and the blazer. And then the other days when he was in Levi's and very casual stuff and banging on the piano, I'm not sure he was competing at that point. He was a rock 'n' roller again in those moments. It was interesting."

Having the TM offices in the Capitol tower also made it that much easier for Bobby to fulfill his Capitol Records obligations. He recorded his next album, *18 Yellow Roses*, in the winter/spring of 1963. The album was produced by Nick Venet and featured several arrangers, including Walter Raim. Bobby sang a few standards, including "On Broadway," "Can't Get Used to Losing You" and "Our Day Will Come," but it was the album's title track that became its biggest seller.

Saxophone player Steve Douglas, who played on the *18 Yellow Roses* album, recalled that the sessions didn't always go smoothly, and that Bobby wasn't a particularly happy camper during that time.

"I remember we did one of the longest sessions in the history of the union at the time," Douglas told Darin archivist Jeff Bleiel. "We started a session at two in the afternoon. At 4 a.m., I'm on the phone, calling musicians, because guys are falling out. I think that session went until ten in the morning, non-stop. A few of us got rich in one night.

"Bobby didn't give a damn," Douglas said. "He kind of ran roughshod over everybody. He ruffled a lot of feathers over there. Of course, Bobby was only a mild taste of what was to come with the rock bands."

Bobby's ongoing separation from Sandra contributed to his crankiness during the *18 Yellow Roses* sessions, and the bad karma continued into the spring.

In late May, Bobby was playing the Concord Hotel in the Catskills and was in a particularly foul mood. Phil Greenwald, the resort's entertainment manager, asked him to introduce old-time nightclub performer Harry Richman, who was sitting in the audience at one of the shows. The audience introduction was a time-honored show business custom that Bobby, a keen student of those mores, should have graciously accepted. Instead, he balked, refusing to introduce Richman even after Greenwald asked him several times to do so. A furious

Greenwald vowed Bobby would never return to the resort. "Bobby's got a lot of talent—if only it wouldn't go to his head," Greenwald said.

Bobby's surliness continued when he butted heads, for the third time now, with Ed Sullivan. This time, the fight erupted when Bobby didn't show up for a taping of an *Ed Sullivan Show* appearance. When Bobby finally did arrive in the studio, several months later, he refused to do more than one take, although he was contractually obligated to do so if asked by Sullivan and his producer, Bob Precht.

"What Bobby doesn't realize is that the BIG stars are always very nice people, grateful people," Sullivan said angrily. Bobby's appearance was never used, and Sullivan didn't pay him for the wasted time.

While Bobby's dark moods were often aimed at outsiders like Sullivan, to those in his inner circle his generosity and good humor couldn't be matched.

"In 1963, I was working for Harry Belafonte in New York and I was also working on an album with Judy Collins, *Golden Apples of the Sun*," said Walter Raim, Bobby's high school bandmate. "Needless to say, Judy and I got pretty close.

"I was talking to Bobby one day, complaining that I hadn't seen Judy because she was in the hospital with a bad case of TB, and I had not seen her in months. So Bobby created a fictitious business meeting. He flew me from New York to L.A. to Las Vegas, and then back to New York, because he supposedly wanted to discuss some project. But that was baloney—there was no project. He was trying to get me out there to see Judy. He was matchmaking."

THE TOURING that summer continued. In July, Capitol released *18 Yellow Roses* followed by *Earthy!*, the folk album Bobby recorded in 1962. Neither disk sold particularly well. Bobby was losing his audience.

"Decked out with chorus and orchestra, the works—gospel, blues and other traditional songs—Mr. Darin offers are far from earthy in feeling," *The New York Times* wrote in its review of *Earthy!* "But he is a facile singer and an expert showman, and does not altogether miss the mark. There is still a lot more to penetrating to the heart of a folk song, even in a pop approach, than he has achieved here."

Bobby's sales woes weren't limited to Capitol. His old label, Atco, released a compilation album of previously unreleased tracks called *It's You or No One*, which was recorded three-and-a-half years earlier after Bobby's triumph at the Grammys. That album also tanked.

But Bobby's live shows were still packing 'em in, and in late July a big crowd turned out to see him on his home turf at Freedomland, an amusement park in The Bronx. It was an extremely hot day, and Bobby collapsed backstage during the show. He needed oxygen and was taken by ambulance to Mount Sinai Hospital, where he spent two days undergoing a battery of tests. His doctors advised Bobby to rest for six to eight weeks and to curtail any type of strenuous activity. Publicly, Bobby's collapse was attributed to exhaustion. Privately, it was believed he'd suffered a heart attack, although an official diagnosis was never released.

The Freedomland show also strained Bobby's relationship with his old friend and conductor Dick Behrke who, according to Dick Lord, came backstage while Bobby was inhaling oxygen and waiting for the ambulance to take him to the hospital. "Bobby is lying there and Behrke comes in and says the band is supposed to get 26 cents a mile for traveling," Lord said. "And Bobby calls me later and says, 'What's wrong with him? I'm fucking dying and he's telling me about 26 cents a mile for the bass player?' And Behrke is saying, 'Yeah, I'm doing my job, that's what I'm supposed to do.'" Their relationship was never the same, and Behrke left the band shortly thereafter.

Bobby was discharged from Mount Sinai Hospital and took a train back to Hollywood. From there, it was on to the house in Palm Springs, accompanied by Sandra. They hadn't officially announced they were back together again, "but the facts sort of speak for themselves," Bobby's publicist told the press. Sandra was later asked if Bobby's collapse at Freedomland brought them back together.

"No truth to that at all," she said. "Bobby and I are back together because we have always loved each other and because we never should have broken up in the first place."

Sandra's denials notwithstanding, the Freedomland incident sparked a renewed effort on the couple's part to make the marriage work. They obviously loved each other deeply but they obviously were polar opposites—making their love more volatile and unpredictable.

Even before his Freedomland collapse, however, Bobby was talking about taking his career in a different direction. "He said, 'You guys better start looking around, I'm not going to do this anymore,'" said drummer Ronnie Zito. "You know, he started cooling off and The Beatles were happening and all that and he decided to break up the group.

"By this time there was a bass player, too," Zito said. "Bobby decided to go to New York and do publishing. And he stopped performing for a while. So I went on the road with Paul Anka for about a year, and I was with Peggy Lee for a while."

Dodd was almost two now, and with their renewed commitment to each other Bobby and Sandra began to think about having another child. Bobby, of course, would never think of discussing this publicly, but Sandra—the family's unofficial publicist—had no problem divulging their plans.

"I told Bobby the other day we'll have to have another baby soon—preferably right away!—so that Doddie won't be more spoiled than he is," Sandra said in a *Screen Stories* feature ("Sandra Dee: She Lived Alone—But Didn't Like It!").

"Although he's so strong—Doddie is, I mean—sometimes I think if I do have another baby he'll kill it!" she said. "I'm kidding. But I'm not kidding when I say we're going to have at least one more baby, after I make about two more pictures."

Sandra would be shooting *The Richest Girl in the World* at Universal in late fall/early winter, while Bobby, still resting after the Freedomland heart attack, planned to focus on TM Music. He was paying particularly close attention to Wayne Newton, the chubby kid he'd just signed to the label.

Bobby had first seen Newton on *The Jackie Gleason Show* about a year earlier and was intrigued by the kid's high-pitched voice and his presentation. Some time later Bobby was at the Copa when, coincidentally, Newton was performing there with his older brother, Jerry. That's when Bobby called Steve Blauner.

"We're in New York, Bobby calls me at my parents' house and says, 'Listen, meet me at the Copa at midnight.' Okay. So I meet him," Blauner said. "We're sitting in a booth in the lounge, with Jules Podell, and we're having a conversation that's boring me, and I don't know why I'm here. They had a little stage in the corner and there is a trio up on the stage and I'm watching them. Out of the corner of my eye, I see Bobby staring at me. I said uh-oh, this is why I'm here. And we went downstairs and signed them to a record contract immediately."

"So two pieces of coincidence, like that, led me to go up and introduce myself and then I asked him if he was recording and I was sure I was going to get a 'yes' answer," Bobby said of Newton. "He said, 'No, I'm not.' I said, 'Well, if you can be at my hotel room tomorrow morning 11:30 or 12 maybe we can discuss something.' That was on a Sunday, and by Monday he had gotten about five or six offers from majors who had seen him the same Saturday night, waited until Monday.

"I do business on Sunday and the next thing you know he was loyal enough and nice enough to hear what I had to offer and weigh it against the other things and I guess, and as he says, because I was the first to approach him with it, he decided to go with me."

Producer Hal Fine had given Bobby the exclusive rights to record an English adaptation of "Danke Schoen," a German instrumental composed by Bert Kaempfert. Bobby didn't think it was right for him, but thought it was perfect for Newton's soprano range (some people hearing Newton sing "Danke Schoen" for the first time thought he was a woman).

"Wayne Newton was a fat kid with a high voice and Bobby told me he was going to record him, that he had an unusual sound," said Dick Lord. "And I remember being in the studio when he recorded an album with Wayne. I don't think it was ever released. Bobby wasn't that pleased with it.

"Then, another day, he said, 'Come to my office.' And he plays 'Danke Schoen.' It's just the two of us at 2 o'clock in the morning. He said, 'I'm giving it to Wayne Newton. He had the demo right there."

Newton's first single for TM, a Barry Mann/Cynthia Weil song called "Heart," charted modestly at #82. Bobby felt "Danke Schoen" could do much better for Newton and produced the song himself, bringing in Jimmy Haskell as the arranger.

"In those days, there were only so many tunes an artist was allowed to record within a certain period of time," Haskell said. "Bobby called me up and said, 'Jimmy, I have the greatest hit song that has come to me in recent years. I already filled my quota at Capitol or I would have recorded it myself.' He told me to come to Las Vegas. He said, 'I want you to meet a kid there and we're probably going to record him on this song.' Bobby recognized that Wayne was a great talent and he gave him what he considered to be his latest, greatest song.

"So I flew with Bobby to Las Vegas and we met Wayne Newton," Haskell said. "He looked like a baby. I paid attention to him because he was so amazing. And this voice he had. We were in the recording studio live. Leon Russell played piano on 'Danke Schoen.' Bobby and I discussed the intro, which was kind of based on the original recording made in Germany. So I wrote it out for Leon and I said, 'Leon, on the intro and on the first verse, you have to play these notes and nothing else.'"

"Danke Schoen" was a huge hit for Newton, charting at #13 on the pop charts and at #3 on the Easy Listening charts. More importantly, it launched Newton's career and became his signature song. Bobby had "Mack the Knife"; Newton had "Danke Schoen."

"'Danke Schoen' was 'Mack the Knife' backwards," Blauner said. "The publisher [Hal Fine] was outraged, until the royalties started coming in." Bobby did, eventually, record "Danke Schoen" in 1966. His version was never released.

The Osmond Brothers were another TM success story. The brothers, a big hit on *The Andy Williams Show*, had a deal with MGM Records.

"Paul Petersen, who was on *The Donna Reed Show*, had a big hit at the time called 'My Dad.' It was a big Father's Day hit," said Terry Melcher. "So all of the sudden, Bobby says, 'Melcher!'—he never called me Terry, ever—'Look, I've got a deal with MGM Records and they've got this group. You're going to produce The Osmonds.' I said okay. Bobby and I wrote a song called 'My Mom.' We said, this will be a great Top 40 for Mother's Day. I don't know what happened with it."

Roger McGuinn had gone to work at TM in New York, putting in nine-hour days in the Brill Building writing songs and sometimes recording with Bobby. McGuinn and fellow TM songwriter Frank Gehry wrote a song called "Beach Ball," which they brought to Bobby. "We took it down to Bobby and he liked it enough to book the studio that day," McGuinn said. "He came down and played drums and we all sang harmonies." The song was credited to the City Surfers and has become something of a cult hit.

"Bobby was not humble. He was well in charge of everything, had all his faculties about him and was sincere," McGuinn said. "He was well-meaning and had a big heart, but he wasn't humble. He was a take-charge kind of guy.

"He was a little like a mob boss; you get this kind of picture of a Don telling people what to do—there was some of that going on," McGuinn said. "He liked me and would kid around. I'd ask him how to make it in the music business and he'd say, 'You have to see everything that's going on around you all the time. You have to have 360-degree vision. One of the main things is to get up on stage in front of people, get the adrenaline and work under fire.'

"So I started taking his advice and going to the Village and working stage stuff," McGuinn said. "Bobby steered me from folk to rock. I was also interested in how he got into the movies and he said, 'Rock 'n' roll—if you can get into that, you can do anything else you want.' That's one of the things that got me interested in The Byrds."

McGuinn soon tired of the long hours at TM and left the company. "It was a 9-to-5 job, going into a cubicle and working all day, and I wasn't interested in doing that," he said. "I was interested in performing. It was good schooling for songwriting, but I didn't like it as a day job. It only paid thirty-five bucks a week. Bobby was into the romanticism of it, like a 1940s film where you made money on your songs."

Back in Los Angeles, Terry Melcher was also getting tired of the routine and he, too, decided to leave TM to produce Paul Revere and the Raiders—and, ironically, Roger McGuinn and The Byrds.

"I think Bobby was a little annoyed," Melcher said. "His two guys, you know, Melcher and McGuinn, were leaving. McGuinn was starting a whole new thing with folk-rock and it was a really big deal when [The Byrds] hit. Bobby was probably a little annoyed that he wasn't involved in that. If McGuinn had come to Bobby at Capitol, I would have ended up producing The Byrds records anyway, and they would have been on Capitol through Bobby."

Bobby's interest in folk music, and its emphasis on social injustice, reawakened his passion for "making a difference." In May 1963 Bobby again entertained at a birthday bash for President Kennedy. This time it was staged by the President's Club of New York, where he joined Eddie Fisher, Henry Fonda, Robert Preston, Van Johnson, Peter Lawford, Mel Ferrer, Tony Randall and Donald O'Connor in singing "Together."

In August, he joined Dr. Martin Luther King's March on Washington. "I'm here as a singer, and I'm proud and kind of choked up," Bobby told the huge crowd, which moved from the Washington Monument to the Lincoln Memorial to hear Dr. King deliver his "I Have a Dream" speech.

Bobby also decided to scale back on his touring schedule and focus more of his energies on TM Music. He made it clear that he wasn't retiring, but that he also wouldn't be accepting as many gigs now.

"I don't want to make it as a blanket statement as I'm gonna give it up because it's been much too good to me, to just suddenly turn around and say, well, 'bye bye birdie,' so to speak," he said about his decision to step back from performing.

"Actually what I'm gonna do is curtail the activities on the personal appearances slate for quite a while due to the fact that that requires an awful lot of traveling," he said. "And I don't think it's right to subject my son, or my wife for that matter, to the kind of routine and so forth. So what I'm gonna do is just kind of, as the expression goes, 'cool it' for a while."

The Freedomland heart attack scared Bobby. At least for now, he wouldn't tempt fate by subjecting his damaged heart to the rigors of live performing.

"I have come to the point where working on the stage . . . becomes such a grind and is so taxing on me physically as well as mentally that I just don't feel that I have much longer to contribute to it in a positive sense," he told Dick Clark during a television appearance. "It will cut my income by more than half in terms of hard-dollar income."

Golden Folk Hits, Bobby's fifth Capitol album, was released in November and, as the title suggested, was unabashedly folky, including Bobby's renditions of "Where Have All the Flowers Gone," "If I Had a Hammer," "Michael Row the Boat Ashore" and Bob Dylan's "Blowin' in the Wind." Bobby was rehearsing for a Judy Garland television special when the news broke that President Kennedy was assassinated in Dallas.

CAPTAIN NEWMAN, M.D. opened in late 1963 to positive reviews, with Bobby receiving generally excellent notices. That, in turn, spurred Universal to award Bobby a new two-picture, non-exclusive deal.

"Believe it or not, Bobby Darin plays the kid touchingly," wrote *New York Times* critic Bosley Crowther, while his compadre over at *The New York Herald-Tribune* felt a bit differently: "Bobby Darin is a gem of miscasting. . . . His contortions under sodium pentathol are at best embarrassing." *Variety* thought Bobby's scenery chewing might catch the attention of the Motion Picture Academy when the Oscar nominations rolled around.

Variety was right on the money. On February 24, Bobby received an Oscar nomination for Best Supporting Actor along with his *Hell Is for Heroes* co-star Nick Adams (*Twilight of Honor*), Melvyn Douglas (*Hud*), Hugh Griffith (*Tom Jones*) and John Huston (*The Cardinal*). *Tom Jones*, a British art-house movie, was the big surprise that year with ten nominations, edging past the Elizabeth Taylor/Richard Burton extravaganza *Cleopatra*, which snared nine nominations.

"It was probably two years from the point Bobby agreed to do the movie until the nominations," Steve Blauner said. "I went out to his house to congratulate him and he grabbed me and hugged me. That was worth more to me than a year's salary."

But it wasn't to be. In April, Melvyn Douglas walked off with the Oscar for Best Supporting Actor. Bobby was disappointed, but stoic. "The fact that I didn't win was totally unimportant," he said afterward. Blauner, convinced the Oscar nomination meant bigger and better movies for his client, decided Bobby needed to switch talent agencies.

"Steve Blauner came to me after Bobby got the Oscar nomination and said, 'You're not big enough to handle Bobby Darin, I'm going to take him to William Morris,'" Martin Baum recalled nearly forty years later with obvious bitterness. "I said, 'But I built his career, everything he's done.' And Blauner said, 'You're just not that important of an agent to do it.'"

There were other things to worry about, including the state of Bobby's recording career. His output at Capitol had been spotty at best—a few Top 40s, a couple of Top 10s—and neither side was completely thrilled with the other. The arrival of The Beatles in February, and their groundbreaking appearance on *The Ed Sullivan Show*, didn't bode well for Bobby's younger fans swept up in the hysteria of the so-called British Invasion.

Bobby wasn't alone, of course; Frank Sinatra, Tony Bennett, Eddie

Fisher, Dean Martin, Sammy Davis Jr. and others were feeling the pinch. The recording industry seemed to change almost overnight into a business dominated by loud British rock bands with long hair. Unlike the others, though, Bobby had youth on his side. At twenty-seven, he could still reposition himself with the younger record buyers *if* he was willing to do that.

In July, Atco dusted off some tunes Bobby recorded back in 1960 and released the jazz-flavored *Winners* album. Bobby recorded his next Capitol disk, a Big Band, brassy, show-tuney album called *From Hello Dolly to Goodbye Charlie*. The album included Richard Wess's lush arrangements of "Hello, Dolly!," "Call Me Irresponsible," "Charade" and "Once in a Lifetime." It was, in essence, Bobby's big "Fuck You" to critics who thought he should tailor his style for teenagers. But it was also Bobby's only Capitol album released that year.

Bobby also continued his rants against the tabloid magazines, which had had a field day after he and Sandra separated. And now that he and Sandra had reunited, there was even more grist for the gossip mill.

"They're not innocuous . . . when they fall under the realm of describing an industry that I happen to be a part of—body and soul—in such a manner and light as to make it a mocking point of the reader," Bobby told Dick Clark in a candid interview.

"I think they print about 1 percent truth and 99 percent nonsense and hearsay and . . I've proven it by suing . . . and having them print the fact that what they had written was hearsay," he said. "What I was going after was for them to print the fact that 99 percent of what they said was hearsay—that they wouldn't consent to. When you talk about fan magazines you're talking about a medium that is geared to a young impressionable mind."

Bobby's records weren't exactly exciting those "young, impressionable minds," but he wasn't about to fade into the background, either. He and Sandra were about to star in their third movie together, another lighthearted romp called *That Funny Feeling*, and he made a slew of television appearances that year, guesting on *The Jack Benny Show* in January and hauling *Mack the Knife* out of storage in February for an appearance on *The Edie Adams Show* just three days before The Beatles appeared on *The Ed Sullivan Show*.

Bobby also returned for his first episodic television role in over four years on ABC's *Wagon Train* and followed that five days later by co-starring with Janet Leigh in an episode of *Bob Hope Chrysler Theatre* ("Murder in the First").

In August, Gracie Allen died at the age of fifty-eight. She had suffered a series of heart attacks in the preceding years but her death was still a shock. George Burns was devastated, and Bobby rushed to be at the side of his old friend and mentor.

"When Gracie died, Bobby went to the house and wouldn't leave until he thought George could be alone," Steve Blauner said. "He'd sleep in the next bed. And George was saying he couldn't sleep, so Bobby turned to him and said, 'You know what? Why don't you sleep in Gracie's bed tonight?' He was there when George's son wasn't even there. I mean, that's how he felt about George Burns."

Bobby was an honorary pallbearer at Gracie's funeral along with Kirk Douglas, Cesar Romero, Gene Kelly, Danny Kaye, Danny Thomas, Jack Warner and Dean Martin.

Bobby and Sandra began shooting *That Funny Feeling* in Hollywood in October. Like *If a Man Answers*, *That Funny Feeling* wasn't going to tax anyone's brainpower. In the movie, Sandra plays Joan Howell, an aspiring actress who shares an apartment with Audrey (Nita Talbot).

Joan and Audrey work as maids while waiting for their big break, which comes in handy when Joan begins dating New York businessman Tom Milford (Bobby) after they've run into each other several times. Joan, embarrassed to take Tom back to her tiny apartment, takes him instead to a plush pad whose owner is away on a business trip.

It just so happens that it's Tom's apartment, and he plays along and pretends he's never been in the place. But now Tom has nowhere else to stay, so he's forced to move in with his business associate, Harvey (Donald O'Connor). This sets up the movie's farcical center, as Joan doesn't realize it's Tom's apartment, and Tom (initially) doesn't realize Joan is his maid.

"When the film was finished, the studio gave the cast and crew the usual farewell party," Sandra said. "Bobby and I thought we would drop in and leave early but we had so much fun with Donald [O'Connor] and Bobby entertaining, we stayed until the end, 2 a.m."

9

Lyndon Johnson was elected president in November 1964. Bobby, who'd performed twice for President Kennedy, was asked to do the same for LBJ—this time at his inaugural gala in January. The show, emceed by Alfred Hitchcock, featured Johnny Carson, Barbra Streisand, Carol Burnett, Harry Belafonte, Woody Allen, and Mike Nichols and Elaine May among its galaxy of stars.

Bobby's political activities didn't end there. He'd been impressed with Dr. Martin Luther King's "I Have a Dream" speech the previous August and was a vocal proponent of the Civil Rights movement, which was now gaining steam under President Johnson's "New Society."

In March, a large group dubbing themselves the "Freedom Marchers"—an outgrowth of the trailblazing 1961 "Freedom Riders"—marched the fifty miles from Selma, Alabama, to Montgomery to present a petition to Governor George Wallace concerning voting rights for blacks in Alabama's "Black Belt" counties.

Bobby was among the entertainers who performed in Montgomery on March 24 on the eve of the Freedom Marchers' entrance into the city. Dick Gregory, Alan King, George Kirby, Ruby Dee, Godfrey Cambridge, Nipsy Russell and Ella Fitzgerald were some of the stars who turned out to entertain and support the Freedom Marchers. Bobby's participation did not go unnoticed by the FBI, which noted in its report that:

"At 2:55 p.m., March 24, 1965, the Selma-Montgomery marchers commenced entering the campsite located in the rear of St. Jude Church, Montgomery, Alabama. The march terminated at 3:14 p.m.

143

March 24, 1965. Plans for the night included speeches by Martin Luther King, singing and entertainment by Bobby Darin, Dick Gregory, Harry Belafonte, Peter, Paul and Mary, and others. As of 4:00 p.m., no incidents had occurred."

Bobby also composed a song, "It's What's Happening, Baby," for President Johnson's "War on Poverty" campaign.

In May, Capitol released *Venice Blue*, Bobby's final album for the label, ending a mutually disappointing relationship. Capitol, for its part, invested millions in Bobby and didn't quite get what it expected; Bobby, try as he might, never became the dominant recording personality Capitol hoped would supplant Frank Sinatra as the symbol of its prominence.

Bobby, hoping lightning would strike twice, decided to return to Atco. Ahmet Ertegun, who would once again be producing Bobby—this time under the more prestigious Atlantic Records banner—now noticed a change in Bobby.

"He had become different in other ways. He had become more political," Ertegun said. "He was thinking about becoming more serious . . . probably thinking he was more like Bob Dylan. But at the same time, he also wanted the fame. It was hard to find both that way."

The fame, though, was starting to diminish little by little. Bobby's finger-snapping, shoulder shrugging styling was considered "square" now, and was no match for the kids buying Beatles albums. His immersion into the folk scene was greeted with scorn by music critics who viewed him as an opportunist, grasping on to whatever was popular at the moment. That didn't even seem to matter, since Bobby's folk-flavored albums weren't selling anyway. Even the television variety shows on which Bobby thrived were beginning to die out. The times were indeed a-changin'.

It sometimes seemed that Bobby just didn't "get it"—or maybe that he "got it" but didn't give a shit what anyone else thought.

"We had one odd thing happen, long before I signed up the Rolling Stones," said Ahmet Ertegun. "I gave a press party for Bobby at the Dorchester Hotel in London. And Bobby said he would love to meet Mick Jagger, would I ask him to come? I knew Mick as a friend, but had never worked with him. So I invited him to come to the party, and he came with, at that time, his sidekick and unofficial manager,

Andrew Oldham. They dressed in a very loose, revolutionary rock 'n' roll fashion.

"And Bobby somehow thought that this was a cocktail party, that he would wear black-tie," Ertegun said. "So he wore a black tie with a red-velvet dinner jacket. It was not what people were wearing. He dressed like what you thought a Hollywood star would dress like at that time—it was his whole idea of being slick or chic.

"Anyway, when Mick and Andrew came in, I introduced him to Mick and Mick just looked at him and started laughing. I said, 'Oh, God,' and just kind of broke that up. It was like Mick was saying, 'We're doing Muddy Waters and he's doing Frank Sinatra.' Neither was true, I mean, Bobby was doing Muddy Waters much more than they were."

That Funny Feeling opened in August to mediocre business and luke-warm reviews. Bobby's luck wasn't much better when he sang the title song for the Disney movie *That Darn Cat*, starring Hayley Mills and Dean Jones. "The color is good and Bobby Darin warbles a song at the start that may be amusing to humans but would probably fill Felix [the cat] with disgust," Bosley Crowther sniffed in *The New York Times*.

THERE WERE CHANGES in Bobby's personal life as well. Now that he was devoting himself to TM Music, and cutting back on his personal appearances, Steve Blauner found himself with little to do. Bobby offered him the chance to join the TM Music enterprise but he declined, and opted to quit the personal-management business and go to work for Screen Gems.

"I think it was just time to go," Blauner said. "In other words, Bobby got nominated for an Academy Award, what more could I do? On the other hand, knowing Bobby and the flame he carried, I probably wouldn't have left if he was still working.

"He wanted me to be part of the publishing company, originally, but I didn't feel I had a right to," Blauner said. "I had nothing to do with it; I didn't write, I didn't know anything about publishing. I wouldn't handle anybody else. At one point, Bobby came to me and said, 'Listen, I got Peggy Lee. I want you to be her manager.' I said, 'Bobby, you've got 20 percent of the action.' He said, 'Why? I haven't done anything. I don't want the money.' I said, 'Of course you have

20 percent—if it wasn't for you, I wouldn't have Peggy Lee—if it wasn't for you, she wouldn't want me.'"

There was also change in the extended Cassotto family. Charlie Maffia, the devoted brother-in-law who waited on Bobby hand and foot, divorced Nina and married his girlfriend, Josie, three months later. Charlie had been cheating on Nina with Josie, who was already expecting their second child. Bobby's nine-year-old nephew, Gary, was the one most visibly affected by Nina and Charlie's divorce.

"Charlie had this whole new family and basically didn't want any part of me," Gary said. "He would occasionally come over. He never paid child support. I went and spent one weekend over at his new house, but basically he didn't want to be bothered. He had another two sons.

"There was this other guy, Gene, who would come over to our house," Gary said. "He was a cop and he would come over on his days off. I didn't know what was going on, but it was an ongoing affair. And now that Nina was free, Gene didn't want to marry her. It was the cow giving the milk."

Bobby distanced himself from the family's problems—he had enough to deal with on his own plate—but he lavished attention on Gary whenever he could.

"He would call the house in Ridgefield Park and I would answer the phone. And Bobby would say, 'I haven't seen you for a while, sing something for me.' And I sang whatever song, and he said, 'You have a better voice then me.' And coming from him, of course, this is the biggest compliment in the world," Gary said. "I saw him a month or so later. We hadn't seen him in a while and of course I'm growing, I'm taller than he is. And he says to me, it's just the two of us, he said, 'I'm going to tell you something. You're better-looking than I am, you've got a better singing voice. But I've got something you'll never have. I've got the drive.'"

Gary also had fond memories of Sandra. "Sandy was, I can truthfully say, the most beautiful woman I ever saw," he said. "And this is at 8 o'clock in the morning or 2 o'clock in the morning. No makeup. She just radiated beauty. Just the most unbelievable, gorgeous creature you'd ever want to meet. She was very funny, and very good with kids. She had a very sweet personality. We all knew that she had a drinking problem. That was obvious. And [she had] an eating problem. Sandy would eat like a bird.

"Unfortunately, being part of the studio system, if you put on two pounds, it shows," he said. "So she was always very conscious of her weight, for good reason. If she was doing a photo session, or a movie or whatever, she had to be conscious of her appearance. And her mother was always on top of her. 'You can't have that, Sandy.' So she would go and throw it up."

Sandra's drinking had grown progressively worse and was driving a wedge into the marriage. There were whispers that Mary Douvan, who was living with Bobby and Sandra, was the major cause of the friction. Sandra and Bobby still went out together in public—and Sandra continued to give her feel-good interviews to the gossip magazines—but it was apparent there were problems behind the closed doors at Toluca Lake.

"I think that this was going to be Bobby's version of the All-American kind of family," said friend Tom Mankiewicz. "The kind of family that he never had, that he was going to build for everybody, and he was going to be the father. I never knew Sandy all that well, but I know the drinking problem just short-circuited the whole idea that this was going to be that kind of family.

"I mean, the truth was, no, it was going to be a kind of fucked-up family," Mankiewicz said. "And I think that disappointment must have been tremendous for him."

Sandra had talked openly of having another child just the year before; now, with her marriage in trouble, she talked around the subject when asked directly by insensitive gossip columnists. "I'm not ready for another baby now, I have my hands full with Dodd," she told Wanda Hale. "He's a wonderful little boy, strong, built like an ox, tough and can be a hellion. He needs a lot of attention from both Bobby and me."

Dodd was in his first year of nursery school, where he found a friend in John Clark Gable, the late Clark Gable's son. "We were beginning to wonder why we were sending Dodd to this exclusive, expensive nursery school when all he did was play in the sand pile with John Clark," Sandra said. "After Christmas, our doubts were dispelled.

"We were visiting my grandmother in New Jersey. Dodd and his two cousins were whooping it up in the living room when suddenly he jumped on a chair and in a loud, clear voice recited, 'I pledge allegiance to the flag' from beginning to end. We were flabbergasted.

"At home Dodd is always on, mimicking comics he sees on television," Sandra said. "We thought he would grow up to be a comedian but now we are sure he will be an orator so we will keep him in that exclusive, expensive nursery school."

Sandra's seven-year contract with Universal ended in December, marking a milestone in Hollywood history. She had been the last of the big-name movie stars still under contract to a major studio; now, the expiration of her contract drove the final nail into the coffin of Hollywood's rigid studio system. Sandra's next movie, *Kaleidoscope*, would be her first "independent" feature. She seemed genuinely surprised, and hurt, that all those years at Universal meant nothing more than dollar signs to the studio executives.

"I thought they were my friends," Sandra said of the Universal executives. "But I found out on the last picture [*A Man Could Get Killed*] that I was simply a piece of property to them. I begged them not to make me do the picture. But they insisted."

Bobby returned to live performing in early 1966. In January, he was back at the Flamingo in Las Vegas for the first time in two-and-a-half years, opening to terrific reviews.

"Darin is one of the few nitery performers who click with all age groups. Despite his youth, he's a real pro with a song delivery, his stage presence, and his entertaining patter," *Variety* opined. "He's one of the better mimics and devotes a funny ten minutes to impreshes of such celebs as Cagney, Grant, Brando, Martin and Lewis. His well-paced turn at one point features a medley of all his top platters, and he does an interestingly dramatic (without music) version of 'Brother Can You Spare a Dime?' with a topical segue into 'King of the Road.'

"Ringsiding Groucho Marx, when introduced, summed up the first-nighter reaction to Darin; 'When I first saw you, you were only a singer. Now you're a singer and an actor.'"

The actor part would have to wait a while, at least on the movie screen. Bobby's next movie, *Gunfight at Abilene*, wouldn't start filming until later in the year, but Bobby kept busy on television, making his second appearance on *The Andy Williams Show.*

"He brought an awful lot to the table and, when he came to the show, everybody knew how to write for him," Williams said. "They knew what to say, they knew his attitude. It would be like writing for Jack Benny—you know exactly what you can say with Jack Benny that's going to be funny. And that's what Bobby had.

"Other singers that I've worked with were great singers and great people," Williams said. "If I worked with, say, Vic Damone, we knew Vic and I were going to be pretty bland. But we knew Bobby was going to be interesting. He was somebody to play off of."

Bobby followed his appearance on *The Andy Williams Show* with a guest-starring role on NBC's *Run for Your Life* (starring Ben Gazzara as a lawyer with two years to live). The show's title was an apt metaphor for Bobby's battle with his rheumatic heart. He always seemed to be on the run, always moving, afraid to keep still—as if he was trying to cram every life experience he could into a finite amount of time.

In essence, that's what he *was* doing. He had been telling friends for years now that he didn't expect to live very long, that it was a fucking miracle that he'd lived as long as he had with this bum ticker. Still he pushed himself to the limit, astounding nightclub audiences with his balls-to-the-floor energy—mixing musical numbers with imperson-ations, pounding away on a drum kit, dancing like there was no tomorrow.

"Bobby Darin's got a great new act at the Copacabana . . . that's where the Charlie is now, at the Copa," noted *The New York Post.* "Bobby's non-arrogant, mellow, hard-working, gifted, does 'King of the Road' with his jacket off and collar open, and introduces 'Mame,' from the forthcoming musical, which could be his new hit record."

In April, Atco released *Bobby Darin Sings the Shadow of Your Smile* and followed that up quickly in June with *In a Broadway Bag* which did, indeed, include the song "Mame." Neither album did particu-larly well.

With his thirtieth birthday fast approaching, Bobby dropped the bomb on Sandra: He wanted a divorce. "He just woke up one morning and didn't want to be married anymore," Sandra explained later. They waited a few days, and on May 17, 1966, three days after Bobby's birthday, they announced their separation to the press. By that time, Bobby had already packed his bags and moved out of the house in North Hollywood. Newspaper reports had "friends of Darin's" intimating that Bobby and Sandra had argued over Sandra's mother.

There would be no reconciliation this time. On August 18, Sandra filed for a divorce on charges of extreme cruelty, asking for custody of Dodd. The next night, Bobby hosted a "lawn party" at actor Barry Nelson's house in Bel Air.

"Freedom, it's wonderful!" he said of the impending divorce. "No ties, no bickering. I can go my way, do my job and pursue my career with no worries." Bobby was in a festive mood, getting up and singing a few numbers for his friends—including part of "Happy Days Are Here Again."

Bobby opened at the Flamingo that week, and his good mood over the divorce carried over into his performance. "Darin's current turn is as electric, exciting and strong as ever, he's an outstanding showman, a fact which embellishes his tone versatility," raved *Variety*. "His stage savvy blends neatly with his pleasant patter between songs . . . His impression segment again proves uncanny ability to carbon other celebs.

"Richard Pryor makes his Vegas debut on the bill, and the young comedian scored consistently with first nighters through the Bill Cosby school of reminiscing and identifiable storytelling. His wonderfully kooky style slaughters such subjects as New York, school plays and TV commercials."

Bobby didn't feel the need for a manager anymore, but he still needed a conductor for his live performances. Roger Kellaway was hired.

"I went down to his office to meet him; it was Steve Allen's old office on Vine Street, and he had this throne chair that he used to sit in that had about a twelve-foot back on it, which I found amusing," Kellaway said.

"We were talking and he wanted to hear me play and wanted to do a couple of songs with me and it was successful. That was a Thursday and he was at the Flamingo the following Tuesday. He looked at me for a second and said, 'Go into the files and see if you can find a track for "The Shadow of Your Smile." So I went through the files and I found three or four charts on 'The Shadow of Your Smile' but none the way he wanted and I went back to him a little arrogantly and I said, 'Mr. Darin, there is no chart that has "The Shadow of Your Smile." He cut me off and said, 'Well, there *will* be by Tuesday, won't there?' So that was kind of our beginning together.

"Bobby was always great with the right songs, the right opening for how to put the act together and what kind of ideas should be in the arrangements," Kellaway said. "I basically took dictation for the first year. He told me everything he wanted and he would sing it to me or play it for me on the piano."

Bobby also needed help over at TM Music; someone to organize, to go through the mail, keep his appointments straight, his toupees coiffed. Someone who, on occasion, could provide a shoulder to lean on or simply would be there to bullshit with. When Bobby's valet, Tommy Culla, saw the name "Sandra Dee Garris" on a resume—well, *that* was a no-brainer.

Sandra had been working for Vince Edwards over at Desilu Studios, where Vince was starring in the *Ben Casey* television series. Sammy Davis Jr. told her Bobby was looking for an assistant and she headed over to the ABC building, where Bobby had just moved his offices.

"They sent me up to the *Dating Game* floor, so I sat there for a few minutes before I realized this couldn't be it," she said. "I made a call upstairs and Tommy Culla got me. He told me he thought Bobby had already hired someone; how did I hear about it? I told him Sammy Davis Jr. said he heard Bobby was looking for an assistant.

"But when I handed Tommy my resume—he looked like something right out of *GQ*, he was always dressed to-the-nines—his eyes kind of lit up and he said, 'This is your real name?' And I said yes and he said, 'No kidding? Will you just wait a moment?' And he went up to see Bobby, who wanted to see me so I went to meet him and we sat down and started talking and we just hit it off.

"The moment I walked in, the first thing that hit me was, he's short!" she said. "He had a huge smile and he walked clear around from his desk and he had this guitar propped up on his desk and he had on a pair of Levi's. I can tell you that was the first and last time I ever saw him in a pair of Levi's. He said, 'This has got to be fate, where did you get your name?' and I told him my father was reading a comic book when I was born and there was a Western character named Sandra Dee, so he picked my name out on the spot. Bobby laughed."

BOBBY'S NEXT ALBUM, which he started recording in August before opening in Vegas, marked a return to his folk phase. *If I Were a Carpenter* was the complete antithesis of *In a Broadway Bag* and was rooted in some conversations Bobby had several years before with Charles Koppelman, an associate of Don Kirshner's. After leaving Kirshner, Koppelman went into business with Don Rubin, and they would eventually count The Lovin' Spoonful and The Turtles in their stable of performers.

"When I went into my own business I went to pitch Bobby some songs, and that's when we started to get friendly," Koppelman said. "The first time I called him he answered the phone and I said, 'Hi, Mr. Darin' and he said, 'What's up, kid?' and I said, 'I have a song I think is great for you' and he said, 'Well, come on over.'

"His office wasn't far from mine, so I walked over and played him a song called 'Daydream,' which we were considering whether to put out by the Lovin' Spoonful, but I thought Darin could have a big hit with it," Koppelman said. "He listened to it and he said, 'It's good, but I wrote something just like it' and he went to the piano and played me another song and obviously didn't record 'Daydream.'

"Well, 'Daydream' went on to become a number-one record," Koppelman said. "About four months later, I had another song that I thought would be great for Bobby and I called him, he was in Chicago, and he asked me to play it over the phone . . . and I played him a song called "a younger girl keeps rolling across my mind" and again, he said, 'You know that sounds great' but he passed on 'Younger Girl' and he played me something he had written.

"I played him another couple of songs along the way that he didn't want to do that became hits and then one day, about a year later, I was in Los Angeles and my phone rang and it was Darin and he said, 'Where are you, you've got to come and see me.' He was also in Los Angeles and I went to see him and he said, 'Okay, I give up' and he threw his hands up. He said, 'I'll record whatever song you want me to record.'"

That song turned out to be "If I Were a Carpenter," penned by Tim

Hardin, a young songwriter working for Koppelman-Rubin. Bobby played acoustic guitar on the track, accompanied only by a bass—and insisted that Koppelman and Rubin, who had very little production experience beyond demos, produce the track and the eponymous album on which it appeared.

"What he said was, 'Listen, if I am going to be working with Koppelman and Rubin, you guys have to produce,'" Koppelman said. "I said, Nah, you really don't want us to produce, you want Eric Jakobsen, who was producing the Spoonful, or Joe Wissert, who was producing The Turtles. But he said, 'No, if I'm going with Koppelman and Rubin, I gotta have Koppelman and Rubin.' And so we ended up producing the album."

Recording "If I Were a Carpenter" turned into a marathon session. Bobby, the perfectionist, wanted to get it just right. "It was kind of a 24-hour session and at the end, when we were finished, it was like 7 o'clock in the morning," Koppelman said. "We were leaving the recording studio and I was there with my wife and she said to Bobby, 'You know, everybody says you're really nasty, but you're really such a nice guy.' And he said, 'Do me a favor, honey, don't tell anybody.' He was a cute guy."

If recording the song was difficult, trying to get it on radio-station playlists wasn't exactly a walk in the park. Bobby hadn't had a hit in several years, and DJs weren't exactly keen on this quiet folk ballad. FM radio was still in its infancy, and there weren't many AM stations catering to the folk genre.

"It was a very tough sell," Koppelman said. "When we finished the record, we sent it to Atlantic Records and the guys that ran Atlantic didn't really like it. I had a promotion man on the West Coast at that time and he actually got it played on the radio, and the response was so terrific that Atlantic then had to release it."

"If I Were a Carpenter," released in October, reached #8 on the singles charts and thrust Bobby back into the public consciousness. He got some additional mileage out of the song when he received a Grammy nomination for Best Contemporary Rock and Roll Solo Vocal Performance, eventually losing to Paul McCartney and "Eleanor Rigby."

Not all of Bobby's friends, though, were buying into this immersion into folk. Some figured it was just a phase he was going through; others, like Dick Clark, just thought it made him look silly.

"I felt bad for him at the time because he had such extraordinary success and potential and all of a sudden he was a latter-day hippie," Clark said. "He was going after all sorts of strange thoughts. He seemed to have reverted to being ten years younger when he should have been mature enough to understand what was going on—but, all of a sudden, he was in a dither."

Not so, however, when it came to his live act. Bobby knew exactly what he was doing, and he was still one of the best in the business in wowing 'em in Vegas—every now and then working in "If I Were a Carpenter" or some other folk-influenced tune but never overdoing it. An April 1967 *Variety* review of Bobby at Harrah's in Lake Tahoe was typical of the notices he was receiving.

"Back on the Harrah's Tahoe marquee, after an absence of four years, Bobby Darin reprises basically the same act he showcased in his preem outing at Harrah's Reno last September. He remains a class endeavor with promanship all the way. Musical arrangements are superb and singer has the know-how to sell each tune for ultimate effect. He's also developing high proficiency along comedy lines as evidenced in a session miming other show-biz names.

"He initials on 'Don't Rain on My Parade' and demeanor suggests complete confidence and assurance. It's retained for the full forty-five minutes of variegated song and chatter. The lush, luminous charts . . . provide colorful drops for Darin's discriminating interpretations of 'Got You Under My Skin,' 'Charade,' 'If I Were a Carpenter' and '18 Yellow Roses.' His 'Mack the Knife 'earns big response, ditto for a lilting declination of 'Shadow Of Your Smile' . . ."

Bobby also returned to television that winter as a guest on ABC's *Stage 67*, which devoted an hour to the songs of Rodgers and Hart performed by "contemporary" musicians including Petula Clark and The Supremes. "The participants by and large didn't have the vaguest idea of what Mr. Hart is all about," wrote *New York Times* critic Jack Gould. "The proof lay in the total lack of expression and subtlety in the performances of Petula Clark, Bobby Darin, the Mamas and the Papas and the Supremes. . . . Whether in gaiety or lament, the Mamas and the Papas and the Supremes adhered relentlessly to their one set of repetitious gestures while Mr. Darin and Miss Clark radiated blank stares regardless of what their lips were saying."

Bobby was having better luck on the charts with "Lovin' You," a funky, ragtime-flavored tune written by Lovin' Spoonful leader John Sebastian. The song peaked at #32. It would be Bobby's last Top 40 hit.

DODD, OR "MOOSE" as Bobby affectionately called him, was almost six now, and Bobby tried to see him as much as possible once the divorce from Sandra became final on March 7, 1967. A judge granted Sandra the divorce on grounds of "mental cruelty." Under the settlement, she received the house in North Hollywood. Bobby was ordered to pay $1,200 a month for child support—and up to $3,000 a year for travel expenses if Dodd was to accompany Sandra on trips. Sandra was granted token alimony of $1 a month.

Moose would visit Bobby often in his new bachelor pad in Beverly Hills, or he would come up to the TM offices, where he would sometimes play with Sandra Dee Garris's son, roughly the same age. "There were several times when my babysitter was sick and I would bring my son over and he and Dodd would play," Garris said. "But you know, when Dodd was around, Sandy was constantly calling. Constantly.

"She just drank and she would have fits over the phone. And then Dodd didn't want to go home. He loved his daddy and wanted to stay with his daddy," she said. "I went through a lot with Bobby and Sandy. There were a lot of calls I had to screen and I had to stay with her on the phone to keep her from Bobby. He really loved her, he adored her . . . but she couldn't let Bobby and Moose just have a good time. She had to call up and be upset and she would lock herself in her room. She locked Dodd in the room with her one time with a bottle of booze and she wasn't going to let him out. Bobby had to go to the house. It was just awful.

"Bobby never shared a lot of his personal feelings, but he said that during the time Sandy and he were married, her mother, Mary, would come in to brush her hair before she was put into bed at night," Garris said. "He said her mother had a very strong hold on Sandy, and just wouldn't let go, so when Bobby married Sandy, he married Mary, too. She made sure Sandy's makeup was done properly and Sandy just couldn't get along without her. And Bobby said, 'I just couldn't be married to two women, I just couldn't.' He went with very few women after his divorce that I saw, and I was there constantly.

"He worshipped the ground Ann-Margret walked on but it couldn't be reciprocated," she said. "I think she wanted to be good friends but he would buy her wonderful little presents and she would come up to the office when we moved into Jerry Lewis's old office. They would sit and talk and go over a song and everything just seemed so right between them . . . but her heart was elsewhere."

Bobby returned to the Copa in March, sans the elevator shoes he'd been wearing but still sporting the toupee. It was noted that, at least this time around, patrons were seeing the new, "humble" Bobby Darin, who introduced guest Sammy Davis Jr. as "the world's greatest entertainer." One guest Bobby purposely didn't introduce was Ed Sullivan—and even needled Sullivan in print, saying Ed had only become a television success by mispronouncing the names of his guests.

"I haven't done his show in five years, now I won't do it for another five years," Bobby said. "And now he has a reason." Bobby also announced that he would perform in August at a Red Cross benefit show in Monaco, organized by Princess Grace.

Inside Out, which Bobby recorded in March, was released to little fanfare, and his next release, recorded in July, was a whimsical album that seemed to come out of nowhere. *Bobby Darin Sings Doctor Doolittle* was as advertised—Bobby singing tunes from the hit Leslie Bricusse movie musical starring Rex Harrison as the famous veterinarian who talks to the animals.

It was produced (reluctantly) by Ahmet Ertegun and arranged by Roger Kellaway, Bobby's conductor who was working in the studio with his boss for the first time.

"One day he called me and said, 'Kellaway, get your ass over here' and he handed me the 'Doctor Doolittle' material and he told me when we were going to record, and gave me the instrumentation," Kellaway said. "We were the first ones to do it, and we recorded with thirty-five pieces in what was Western Studios at that time. It had four tracks—three tracks for the orchestra and one for Bobby—so whenever he changed his mind vocally there was no extra track to overdub. We had to wipe out the one he was working on and do it again.

"There wasn't time for Bobby to tell me how he wanted those tracks done," Kellaway said. "He just let me do it because I only had three weeks, tops, to write the whole album. And because I had taken dictation from Bobby, I knew a lot about who he was and how the album should come out.

"He said, 'We're going to do this album in six hours.' And there is no overtime. So we did five tracks per three hours. Our hit single, 'Talk to the Animals,' was only done in one take because there wasn't time to do anything but read through it."

"Roger and Bobby would yell at each other in recording sessions, where Bobby would say, 'That's wrong' and Roger, who had quite an ego, would say, 'Well, listen, if you don't like the way I'm doing it, then let's just not do it,'" said Tom Mankiewicz. "And Bobby would say, 'Fine, let's not.' And they used to quit and fire each other about two or three times a day, but the next morning they were back in again."

Bobby Darin Sings Doctor Doolittle tanked, although "Talk to the Animals" received modest airplay. Bobby loved the tune and incorporated it into his stage act, often singing it a la Rex Harrison and working his impressions of James Cagney, Cary Grant, Clark Gable, Jimmy Stewart, Walter Brennan and Robert Mitchum into the song.

With Bobby's album sales dropping off markedly, he found it necessary to increase his nightclub and concert workload in order to support his affluent lifestyle—which now included an apartment in the East 60s in Manhattan, a house in London, a villa in Rome and a new house on ritzy Rodeo Drive in Beverly Hills. Bobby thought the Rodeo Drive place needed drastic renovations and quickly had the house gutted, putting in a new kitchen and a dining room.

"It was very Beverly Hills, very green and white and wicker and he said, 'Call the Salvation Army and have them come take everything out of here,'" said Bobby's assistant, Sandra Dee Garris. "Being a wine connoisseur, he wanted to have a dining room but he had made a complete mistake because the whole house was very light with lots of windows, and he took this dining room and closed it off all onto its own.

"He had this thing about entertaining and had a huge dining room table," she said. "It was all dark wood in there. It had a chandelier, dark wood, lots of wine and heavy furniture. It was the most mis-placed room I've ever seen in my life, in this beautiful, light house. Bobby said he liked to dine in the dark. He said, 'This is my room. This is what I like.' He never entertained in that room the whole time I was there."

Garris oversaw the renovations that August while Bobby traveled first to Paris, to help open a disco there, and then on to Monaco, where he performed for Princess Grace and her Red Cross Ball.

Bobby wasn't traveling alone, however. He had hooked up with red-head Diane Hartford, the much-younger wife of fifty-seven-year-old A&P heir Huntington "Hunt" Hartford. Diane, a model who hailed from Wilkes-Barre, Pennsylvania, married Hunt in 1962 and the union was a rocky one; they'd been separated for a while the previous year when Diane went to Hollywood seeking a movie career.

Now, Bobby and Diane were involved in a torrid affair that both vehemently denied—despite the fact that Bobby was seen in Diane's limousine taking her to Kennedy Airport the very day Bobby was fly-ing to Paris.

Hollywood writer Tom Mankiewicz became a close friend of Bob-by's around the time of *Le Affair Hartford* after being introduced to Bobby by screenwriter Peter Stone. "Peter said, 'Boy, do I have a new best friend for you. You're going to love Bobby Darin.' And he was absolutely right," Mankiewicz said. "About the time we started hang-ing out, Bobby gave me a key to his house, because I lived at the beach. He said, and this is so typical of Bobby, the kind of instant generosity, he'd say, 'It's such a long drive back there and when you're in town, just stay at my house. The guest room is there. The houseboy knows who you are. Here's the key, here's the combination to the house.'

"He was having an affair at the time with Diane Hartford," Mankie-wicz said. "She was a kind of marginally interesting woman who was very pretty, sort of 'To the manor born.' That horribly overused word 'socialite.' And Huntington Hartford was so pissed that she was hav-ing an affair with Bobby. But Bobby's charm to her, and his charm to a lot of people, was that he was the diamond-in-the-rough. She was just thrilled to be with him because he was just as smart as anybody else in the world, but he had this street quality about him at the same time."

The New York newspapers had a field day with the scandalous tryst. "A&P Heir's Wife Puts Him on Shelf," blared *The New York Post* headline. The accompanying story featured an interview with Huntington Hartford, who phoned from London to complain that his twenty-five-year-old wife was avoiding him.

"She absolutely refuses to talk to me. Tell her to please call me and I'll stop all the publicity," he told *The Post*. Hartford said that Diane had been seen in San Francisco, Los Angeles and Manhattan. The article quoted Bobby as saying "She's a friend of mine, she's a lovely lady. Knowing her is fun, yes. But as far as I know, she's very much married. I know many people who are married who have dinner with other people." Yes, *The Post* reporter wondered, but what about the fact that Diane has been in the same places as you've been lately, Bobby? "I'd say you have a pile of coincidences on your hands," Bobby snapped.

Huntington Hartford claimed that Diane met Bobby that June, when she flew to Los Angeles for a screen test arranged by Hunt. She then followed Bobby to San Francisco, where he performed at the Fairmount Hotel. "She wouldn't answer any of my calls," Hunt said. "That's the way she is when she gets mad." He said Diane had then followed Bobby back to L.A. for his gig at the Melody Club. "I have a friend out there who says they were together practically every day," he said.

Huntington also called *The New York Daily News*, saying Diane left him without even saying goodbye. "She just took her jewelry, packed a few things and went," he said, adding that he looked upon the whole incident as "the wife just having another fling."

Bobby, tracked down by the *Daily News* in Paris, was asked if Diane would join him in Monte Carlo for the Princess Grace performance. "I don't think so, but you can never tell," he said. Huntington had said Bobby was "monopolizing" Diane. "I don't play Monopoly. Hartford does. He has enough money for that," Bobby said, and repeated his "we're just friends" statement. "She's a beautiful, charming, sweet, lovely lady, but there's no romantic involvement between us—just a beautiful platonic friendship."

Back in Los Angeles a week later, rehearsing for an appearance on NBC's *Kraft Music Hall*, Bobby had a more difficult time backing up the "platonic friendship" claim—especially since Diane reportedly was flying in from San Francisco to meet him.

"Make it just plain platonic. Take out the qualification," he snapped, attributing Diane's appearance in L.A. to "another coincidence, it's a whole mess of coincidences."

Columnist Earl Wilson, noting that Bobby was stuttering, asked him directly if his relationship with Diane was serious.

"I have to tell you that it's like a very big, nice, strong, lovely friendship . . . uh . . . uh . . . uh . . . but I wouldn't be able to . . . uh . . . I wouldn't . . . couldn't . . . uh . . . but anyway," Bobby answered, "she's a lovely lady . . . and she's uh . . . married . . . and . . . uh . . . it's fairly platonic."

By September, Diane had filed for divorce, with Bobby the beneficiary of her split with Hunt. In her court papers, Diane cited Hunt's remarks about Bobby as the basis for his "cruel and inhuman conduct" toward her—and Bobby now dropped all pretense of the "platonic" relationship. "She's out of sight," he told columnist Sheila Graham about Diane.

Of course making headlines wasn't the worst thing to happen to Bobby at this juncture—at least it kept his name in the spotlight—and he announced that he would play a "psychotic killer" in *The Bells*, a movie he wrote and would produce under his Darin Films production banner. The movie would be shot in Mexico, Bobby said, and added that he would film another as-yet-untitled project in London.

Bobby showed his old pal Dick Lord the script for *The Bells* which, in a roundabout way, resulted in a reunion of sorts between Bobby and old bandmate Steve Karmen.

"The movie was about this sacred bell and the Americans have stolen it and they're trying to schlep it across Mexico," Lord said. "It's like a four-ton Statue of Liberty. I read the script. It was interesting. Bobby was looking for a producer. I had done a motion picture short called *The Locusts* that Steve Karmen produced and it was very successful. It won an award.

"So I suggested Steve to Bobby," Lord said. "I figured enough time had gone by. Bobby agreed, Steve came to Vegas, we met and they talked. Each one wanted creative control and they both had their egos, as we all do, and it never worked out. And they never stayed friends."

With Diane Hartford in the audience, Bobby opened at the Flamingo in Vegas in October, but their relationship was already starting to cool. Bobby was dating a number of women, including Kathe Brenner, a college student he'd met at the Red Cross benefit in Monaco. Kathe was there with her mother, Tammy, who'd known Princess Grace when they both worked at Paramount (when Princess Grace was still known as Grace Kelly).

"I didn't even want to meet Bobby because I thought he was very uncool," Brenner said. "But he was totally charming. He was bright, he was personable, and he had a great sense of humor. I met him after the show and we sat up in one of those bistros they set up in the street and we talked all night with some other people.

"I didn't see him until we got back to the States," she said. "He had a house on Rodeo Drive then and he liked to entertain a lot. He would have dinner parties every night and he would pick me up, or have his butler pick me up. It was like people had entertained him before, so now he was entertaining them. I know he enjoyed it and it gave him a sense of roots.

"There were some very interesting people coming through," Brenner said. "I remember Rex Harrison and his wife at the time being there with Arthur Jacobs, who was Rex's publicist. And then one night Jeannie Martin came with Mort Viner. Jeannie and Bobby got into a religious conversation and it got very uncomfortable because she was a devout Catholic. Bobby was so bright and got so into this conversation. It was unrelenting."

Brenner said Bobby's sense of humor didn't preclude poking a little fun at himself, and his recent divorce from Sandra. "He had a photo of the picture that was in the *Los Angeles Times* announcing his divorce by his bed," she said. "That was his sense of humor. He had it in a little frame."

By the time the new year rolled around, Bobby and Diane Hartford were no longer an item. Bobby had a short romance with journalist Barbara Howar and continued to date many women, including a stewardess, Lois Kanter, he met on a Bonanza Airlines flight from L.A. to Las Vegas. Bobby was on his way to Vegas to replace Charles Aznavour, who was bombing at the Flamingo, and he struck up a conversation with Kanter, taking her phone number and promising to call.

Kanter figured Bobby was pulling the usual celebrity bullshitting routine and that she'd never hear from him again—until her phone rang a few days later.

"He said, 'I know this is last-minute, but would you be able to go to see Steve and Eydie at the Sands with me? They kept a table for me down in front and want me to come and enjoy the show,'" Kanter said. "He was starting there the next day or the day after. He said, 'I don't have a car, would you mind bringing your car?' and I jumped out of bed screaming 'I'm going out with Bobby Darin!'

"Somehow I got myself together, jumped into a dress, picked Bobby and his valet up at the Flamingo and we went over to the Sands," she said. "We walked into the showroom and this was my first introduction to the limelight. When we walked in, everybody's head turned. I wasn't quite aware of what was going on. The host was walking us down to a table near the front of the stage. Steve and Eydie were talking to Bobby during the show, having him stand up, and the people near us were whispering. I was kind of excited feeling that, wow, this is pretty neat!"

After the show, Bobby brought Lois backstage to meet Lawrence and Gorme, who invited them along to meet Sonny King and Sammy Davis Jr. for dinner in the Sands dining room.

"So we all go into the dining room and here were all these celebrities and me, with Sonny King and Sammy Davis Jr. Richard Pryor was there too," Kanter said. "Richard had done a show where he made some remark about the [Vietnam] War and a woman got up and just ripped him because her son was over there fighting, so he got booed and hissed. It was very traumatic and they were all talking about this.

"Then Bobby turns to me and says, 'One of my very good friends, Juliet Prowse, is over at Caesar's, let's run over there really quickly and catch her second show, we won't stay late.' So we go there and the same thing happens. After the show people would just go crazy getting Bobby's autograph. He was very nice about that. He was very warm and down-to-earth with me. The only thing he had a problem with was that he always wore a toupee and face makeup, and he always had to have a new shirt every day."

Bobby's relationship with Lois lasted the length of his run at the Sands, and was only one of the many fleeting relationships Bobby had during this period. While both he and Lois knew it wasn't going to turn into anything serious, Bobby made a generous gesture toward her that left a lasting impression on the young stewardess.

"At the time there was a big jeweler in Vegas called Thunderbird Jewelers in the Thunderbird Hotel," she said. "Bobby said he needed a new watch, so we go across the street and walk in and their eyes bulged—the people working behind the counter recognized Bobby and started bringing out trays of jewelry and he just bought, bought, bought. He turned to me and said, 'You pick out something, I insist.' They're bringing out trays to show me . . . and I picked a diamond-faced gold watch.

"When we walked out of the jewelry store I turned to him and said, 'I just don't understand how someone can spend so much money in such a short amount of time.' He said, 'I have something to tell you. I've made so much money in my life in show business, I have invest-ments that will always take care of my son and ex-wife. My son will never have to worry. I've got so much money invested because I'm not going to live much longer.' That's when he told me about his heart problem. He said, 'I don't have very much time to live; it could be a year, two years, five years. I have a bad valve and there's not much they can do about it. So that's why I do this and it's okay.'"

Romance beckoned again when Bobby began shooting his role as a gigolo named Franco in a movie called *The Happy Ending*, directed by Richard Brooks and starring his wife, comely actress Jeanne Simmons. Bobby fell madly in love with Simmons, but the attraction wasn't mutual, and Bobby spent much of his time on the set complaining to co-star Shirley Jones about his unrequited love.

"He was very unhappy," Jones said. "She was married to Brooks at the time and Bobby would just lament to me the fact that he was fall-ing madly in love with Jeanne but there was no reciprocation."

"I don't know if they were having sex or what, but Bobby came back from the shoot, called Richard Brooks and he said he and Jeanne were going to run off," Steve Blauner recalled. "That's how honest he was—he talked to her husband about it."

10

President Lyndon Johnson stunned the country when he announced he wouldn't run for reelection in 1968. Bobby had been watching the changing political landscape with keen interest. A tried-and-true Democrat, he'd been outspoken in his opposition to the Vietnam War, had marched for Civil Rights in Alabama, was at the Lincoln Memorial for Dr. Martin Luther King's "I Have a Dream" speech and performed in Montgomery in 1965.

Bobby was also a vocal supporter of Indiana's Democratic senator, Birch Bayh, and had performed at several Bayh fundraisers, most recently with Jimmy Durante. He'd visited Resurrection City, a shantytown located on a fifteen-acre site near the Lincoln Memorial, with other celebrities including Marlon Brando, Barbra Streisand, Eartha Kitt and Bill Cosby. They were trying to call attention to the plight of the country's poor and downtrodden.

But it was Senator Robert F. Kennedy who caught Bobby's imagination. Bobby was an early and enthusiastic supporter of Kennedy's run for the White House. His devotion to RFK was almost slavish, his admiration of the former Attorney General and brother of the slain President John F. Kennedy worshipful.

"My cousin Frank was RFK's press secretary, so I got Bobby all kinds of access to Bobby Kennedy and he was just crazy about him," said Tom Mankiewicz. "And Frank said, 'What an asset this guy is for us.' And Bobby, again, he learned everything, he read every book on politics, he knew every presidential election since the turn of the century. He knew who was what. Historically, he would just sop it up.

"I think he recognized a lot of himself in Bobby Kennedy," Mankiewicz said. "That Bobby Kennedy was quick to anger, was impatient, knew everything about everything, was thirsty to know. I think, whether or not it's true that Bobby Darin and Bobby Kennedy had similar personalities, I think Bobby Darin thought so. Bobby had an immediate affinity to RFK because of that impatience, and Bobby Kennedy was somebody that gave you the impression he would settle for nothing less than perfection. You know, 'There's something wrong here and we're going to fix it' and it wasn't going to be a Band Aid solution. I think Bobby just loved him.

"Bobby Kennedy didn't suffer fools gladly," Mankiewicz said. "I'll never forget Bobby told me he was in an elevator with Bobby Kennedy after he lost the Oregon primary. This was on his way to the California primary; he was the first Kennedy to ever lose an election with that primary. And a woman got in the elevator, and she said, 'So how does it feel to be the first Kennedy to lose an election?' And he said, 'Madam, if I was as ruthless as I'm supposed to be, I'd kick you right in the instep.' And Bobby said, 'What a deal! The instep! Isn't that great!' He kept obsessing about that. That was the kind of thing that really appealed to him."

Bobby himself was growing increasingly ambivalent about a career in politics, inspired by his newest Kennedy idol. He was seriously thinking about running for office now and acting on the beliefs and ideals put forth by RFK. The Democratic Party had come calling, impressed with Bobby's commitment to "the cause" and his ability to communicate this thoughts and ideas, not only through his music but in public forums. Bobby's history as a protestor and activist stretched back to the early '60s; with the dawning of the new decade, perhaps the time was right to seize the moment.

"Bobby had fallen madly and passionately in love with Bobby Kennedy and what he stood for," said his nephew, Gary. "Bobby was a creature where, if he was going to go into a career, he was going to be the best-known for it. The same drive that drove him to other heights would now apply to his political career. He had no doubt about it and he was going to be successful at it."

Bobby was booked for a February engagement at the Latin Casino in Cherry Hill, New Jersey, just outside of Philadelphia. He invited Nina, Vee, and twelve-year-old Gary down to Philadelphia, where he was staying, to see the show. "It was literally weeks from the decision of what office he was going to try for," Gary said.

Nina was aware of Bobby's political aspirations, and now she fretted that a deep, dark secret from the family's past would embroil Bobby in scandal and ruin the career in politics he was planning.

"Bobby says, 'Come down and stay at the Barkley [Hotel] and see the show," Gary recalled. "So we went down to Philadelphia. They took me out of school and we went and saw the show. And in the middle of the week, on Wednesday, my mother went up to Bobby's penthouse and talked to him and told him the truth."

The "truth" was that Nina was not Bobby's sister. She was his mother. His beloved Polly, the woman who had raised him, was not Bobby's mother but his *grandmother*. Vee, Vanna and Gary were not Bobby's nieces and nephews but his half-siblings. His former brother-in-law Charlie Maffia—the man who had carried Bobby around when he was a sick child—had actually been his stepfather.

The Big Lie had been perpetrated for thirty-one years, Nina explained to her stunned son, because Bobby was born out of wedlock when Nina was eighteen—a moral sin in 1936. To cover it up, Nina and Polly put the charade into motion: Bobby would be raised by his "mother," Polly, who had Bobby late in life years after giving birth to Nina, his "older sister." The one piece of information Nina would not divulge to Bobby was the identity of his father. That, she insisted, she would take to her grave.

The news, as expected, sent Bobby reeling. "He was so devastated by it," Gary said. "I remember that my mother went up to see Bobby in his penthouse suite; she was gone for about two hours and when she came down she was very upset. And I remember Vee and my mother going into another room and talking for like two hours. Obviously, Bobby didn't take the news well.

"The beauty of the whole thing is that Bobby never questioned it," Gary said. "Once he heard the words said to him, 'I'm not your sister, I'm your mother,' he knew it was the truth and it made sense, all those little episodes that led up to that point. He knew Nina was speaking the truth and it was like this revelation. Unfortunately, he could never accept it. He was honest when he said to Nina, 'You are the strongest person I've ever met because you denied your own son for thirty-one years.' "

Bobby now knew the truth, but the family decided to keep the news from Gary, who they figured was still too young to handle the situation. Bobby would remain "Uncle Bobby" until Gary was old enough to understand the truth.

"My sister Vee knew. Vana said she knew but it was never discussed," Gary said. "But my mother talked to Vee and that was her stronghold, because now with Polly being long gone, she needed somebody to talk to about it. So she talked to Vee and they weighed it all out and Vee said, 'You know what? You've got to tell Bobby because what will happen is, if he goes into politics, they will uncover the truth. And better that he knows up front than trying to find it out in some other way.' "

The story later told to Gary, and what Nina probably told Bobby in his Philadelphia hotel suite, was that Nina became pregnant at seventeen during her relationship with a college student.

"You can say many things about Nina; however, she wasn't a whore, she wasn't a prostitute, she was my mother and the fact remains that she loved Bobby's father very much," Gary said. "But unlike so many other women before her and after her, she could have taken this guy who was in college and said, 'You knocked me up, you marry me and take care of me.' She didn't do that. The day she went into the hospital was the last time she saw Bobby's father.

"My mother always had a weight problem, even as a teenager," he said. "When she knew she was pregnant, she told her mom. Of course Polly wasn't thrilled about it, but they had seven or eight months to talk about it. There was never an option. Nina must have met this guy—at that time in the 1930s they had social clubs, you go dancing—at one of those clubs. It cost you whatever to come in. She slept with him and she got pregnant.

"Now that she was pregnant, what was she going to do? You could always have an abortion. But they decided the best thing was not to go back to this guy," Gary said. "He has a budding career. Yes, you love him, but what kind of start is that? You're forcing this guy to leave college because now he has to support you and a baby and his mother-in-law, because my mother's relationship with Polly was

unbreakable. And because of the mob connections that my grandfather Sam had, Polly could have easily have gone down that route
and gotten under the blanket of the mob.

"But neither of them wanted that," he said. "So they abandoned
that whole idea. My mother went to work and they found themselves
on home relief."

Bobby somehow managed to pull himself together after his meeting
with Nina. He didn't have much choice; he had club dates and other
commitments to fulfill and he desperately wanted to keep the Cassotto family secret under wraps. He told no one outside of a few close
friends and was forced to carry on as usual, keep up a brave front and
somehow trying to cope with his rage and inner turmoil. His political
aspirations were dead.

Bobby never completely recovered from the bomb Nina dropped on
him and expressed his hurt, and rage, to close friends like Joyce
Becker. Becker happened to be in Philadelphia working on a magazine
story and saw Bobby just after his meeting with Nina.

"We went up to his suite and I never left the suite until the next
afternoon," she said. "We sat, we talked, we reminisced. We talked
about how he felt, how hurt he was about what was done to him as a
child, the lies. I was like his shrink.

"We talked about he missed Polly because she would always be his
mother, about how he was more angry at her than at anyone else for
not telling the truth, about how he kept his promise to Polly about his
education because she was a teacher," Becker said. "And we talked
about how he was a growing man and Polly still didn't tell him the
truth. And he said, 'I will never be the same.'

"He didn't know who he was because everybody had lied to him,"
she said. "He was searching for himself. Was he a figment of Polly's
imagination? Or, if he was raised by his mother/sister, would he have
become, who knows? So he didn't know who he was.

"I think people should know what a heavy heart he had about this,"
Becker said. "I remember very well Bobby saying to me, 'I don't know
who to trust anymore.' And I said, 'The first thing you have to do is
trust yourself and look into people's eyes and you will see.' He said,
'I looked into my mother's eyes and it wasn't the truth.' What do you
say to that?"

Back in New York, Bobby called Dick Lord. "I remember what he said to me. 'I can't even think of anything funny to say.' And he hung up the phone," Lord said. "I think it was a tremendous shock." Bobby began seeing a psychiatrist to help him deal with the emotional trauma.

"He didn't see him for very long and he wasn't very compliant," a friend said of Bobby's time in analysis. "He was in psychoanalysis and he refused to go. I mean, you can't tell Bobby what to do. It was very brief. It was well under a year that he was in treatment."

Bobby also poured his heart out to Shirley Jones. They used the same pediatrician, Dr. Marvin Goodwin, with whom both Bobby and Shirley had become very friendly. Goodwin was known for making house calls on his motorcycle—which appealed to Bobby's sense of the outrageous—and he would often accompany Shirley to events if her husband, Jack Cassidy, was out of town.

"Bobby knew that Marvin was a great friend of mine so that got us closer," Jones said. "One day, Bobby called and asked me to come over. I had been there once or twice before if Bobby wanted to play me something or read me some poetry.

"He said, 'I want to tell you something,' then he proceeded to tell me the whole story of his mother and his grandmother," Jones said. "We sat at a table and he told me that story and said, 'Shirley, how could that happen? Can you imagine any family doing that?' He felt as if his whole life had been a lie and he also talked about his health at that point. He said, 'I don't know how much longer I have to live, and that fact that this could happen to me . . .' He was very bitter at that point and wanted to hide away.

"I feared for him because he was just devastated, but what can you say?," she said. "He was hurt and angry and wanted to strike back, to get even."

The Bobby Darin who opened at the Copa in March 1968 seemed more focused and mature. Bobby wasn't about to reveal the family secret, but the shock of finding out the truth about Nina made him more introspective. "I wanted everything better, faster, quicker," he told columnist Earl Wilson. "I think anybody's young period is ensconced in a bunch of insecurities, which in my case manifested themselves in being too flip, too off the shoulder. The goals have

changed and what I aspire to now is a more meaningful contribu-
tion," he said.

"To be called the greatest entertainer may mean being paid more
than anybody, having four limousines. Those are not essentials to me
anymore. Being accepted universally as an entertainer and human
being are."

Dr. Martin Luther King Jr. came to Bobby's show at the Copa during
the March engagement. Bobby introduced him to the crowd, but the
reception King received was a chilly one, and he immediately left with
his entourage. Bobby was mortified. A month later, King was assassinated in Memphis.

The movie work, meanwhile, was slowing down. Since the final
breakup with Sandra, Bobby had starred in two movies, *Gunfight in
Abilene* (his only Western) and *Cop-Out*, neither of which did much at
the box office. The deals Steve Blauner worked out in the early '60s
were ending, and with Bobby's popularity on the wane, movie studios
weren't eager to throw big money at him anymore.

Bobby was still a big television draw, though, especially for the
variety-type shows on which he thrived. He hosted two *Kraft Music
Hall* specials within a three-month period in late 1967 and early 1968.
The first one, entitled "Give My Regards to Broadway," featured Liza
Minnelli and Jack Benny; on the second show, "A Grand Night for
Swinging," Bobby was joined by comedian George Kirby, Bobby Van
and singer Bobbie Gentry, who would date Bobby on and off for the
next year.

Musically, Bobby was entering uncharted waters. Atlantic dropped
him after the *Bobby Darin Sings Doctor Doolittle* debacle and he sold
TM Records to Commonwealth United. The sale resulted in legal
wrangling that would play itself out for the next several years and
eventually cost Bobby over $1 million in lost royalties.

With none of the major record companies rolling out the welcome
mat, Bobby started his own label, which he called Direction Records.
He also revamped his band for the new push. Roger Kellaway was
leaving to pursue other opportunities, including film and TV work (he
eventually wrote that familiar ragtime-piano piece heard over the
closing credits of *All in the Family*). For Kellaway's replacement, Bobby

tapped pianist Bob Rozario. Rozario had never conducted before, a small fact that didn't seem to bother Bobby in the least.

"I went to a rehearsal hall and in walked Bobby with his music, and Roger Kellaway, who was his conductor at the time, and they threw the music in front of me and asked me to play," Rozario said. "Bobby started to sing and we did about three or four songs and he said thank you and left. So about two weeks later I get a call from his road manager, Marty Singer, and he says, 'Bobby wants you to go to Puerto Rico and rehearse the orchestra for his next engagement there,' which was in a couple of weeks. And I said, hold on, he wants me to do *what*? I said, 'Marty, I thought he was just hiring me as a piano player, I don't know how to conduct. Give me Bobby's phone number, let me call him.'

"So I called Bobby and thanked him for choosing me as his piano player but I said, 'Bobby, I've never conducted an orchestra.' He said, 'You don't tell anybody and I won't tell anybody.' And that was the end of the conversation. So I panicked. I went to every hotel in Las Vegas and watched every show and watched what the conductors were doing and I prepared myself and went to Puerto Rico.

"I was so nervous, because when the curtain went up I saw all these celebrities," Rozario said. "There were actors like Richard Harris and people of that caliber. As it was, everything turned out fine, and as Bobby was taking his bows, he walked by the piano and said, 'See?' And that was it. I became Bobby's conductor."

Bobby decided that he would arrange his first Direction Records album himself for the first time in his career. He laid down some tracks for what he called *Bobby Darin Born Walden Robert Cassotto* but he needed a good engineer. A chance meeting with Brent Maher in a Las Vegas recording studio resulted not only in Bobby finding his engineer, but in rounding out his new backing band.

Maher had arrived in Las Vegas from Nashville along with musician pals Quitman Dennis (bass), Tommy Amato (drums), Billy Aikens (piano) and Bubba Poythress (guitar). "We decided to move out there because we wanted to pursue studio production work," Dennis said. "And Brent being an engineer, we would have access—we could present ourselves as a studio rhythm section with some background of having done that in Nashville."

Maher eventually landed as a recording and mixing engineer at United Recording, and was thrilled one day to see Bobby Darin's name in the studio logbook. Bobby would be coming in the next day with some multi-track tapes that needed work. Maher was a huge Darin fan, but was taken aback when he received a warning from a fellow engineer who'd worked with Bobby before.

"He said, 'Brent, just don't let him get under your skin. I don't want to bring you down, but nothing you can do will please him,'" Maher said. "He said, 'I worked with Bobby three or four times and he's not a bad guy, he's just a perfectionist and no matter what you do it's not quite good enough. That's just the way it is, so know that going in and don't let it bring you down.'

"Well, I was crushed," Maher said. "So sure enough Bobby walks in the next day with an armful of tapes and he walks into the studio and says, 'Hi, I'm Bobby' and drops off a load of multi-tracks he had recorded in L.A. with his band. He said, 'Well, I'll tell you what. The best way to do this is, you just get something up—I'm going to leave and I'll come back in about two hours and I'll just check it out and see where you're at with it.'

"So he leaves, and of course I'm on pins and needles. So I throw this mix up and work with it and do the best I can. Right on time Bobby cruises back in, he was polite and everything, he sits behind the console and he tells me to hit 'play.' So I played this mix for him and I'm standing behind him and I can get absolutely no read on whether this guy is grooving or not. No read. Which makes me believe he's not grooving.

"And so the song's over and he turns around in the chair and looks at me and he says, 'That sounds great, man. In fact, I'm hearing things I never heard before. Let's do the whole record.' I was just floored," Maher said. "So from that point on we just really hit it off and I mixed the whole album for him.

"But there was one track on the *Walden Robert Cassotto* album that just wasn't happening," Maher said. "Bobby had sort of written it off and I said, 'Well, let me take another stab at it.' I think by then he had left and went down to Puerto Rico to work in a nightclub. So I worked on it some more and I sent it to him and it still wasn't grooving him. I said, 'Well, Bobby, I hate to lose this song because I think it's a great tune. I told you about those guys that moved up here with me from Nashville—how about us taking a stab at the track? We'll just do our take on the song and if you dig it, we can move forward.' "

"There were about three of the tracks that Bobby's rhythm section did that were absolute failures,"said Quitman Dennis. "And so we did the tracks to those three tunes without Bobby present and took them to L.A. and met him at Sunset Sound and he heard them for the first time and said, 'You guys are cool, man!' "

Bobby had his new backing band: Drummer Tommy Amato, bassist Quitman Dennis, keyboardist Billy Aikens and guitarist Bubba Poythress—who was eventually fired and replaced by guitarist Terry "T.K." Kellman. "They just plopped me at the Landmark and Bobby was backstage and he said, 'Hey, welcome to the family,'" Kellman said. "He was kind of cavalier about it. I don't think he even heard me before the show, just Quitman did, and I was at the rehearsal for that day."

Bobby campaigned for Robert Kennedy throughout the spring of 1968. In early June, both Bobbys were in San Francisco, Darin opening the new Mr. D's nightclub and Kennedy campaigning in the city before he left for Los Angeles to await the results of the California primary.

"While we were on stage in San Francisco, it said on the television that Bobby Kennedy had been assassinated," Bob Rozario said. "Bobby didn't know yet. He was still on stage. And when he got off stage, he just went into complete shock. Oh, he was devastated. He just couldn't believe it."

"It broke Bobby's heart," Tom Mankiewicz said. "It just cut him in half. Bobby formed such strong attachments, and he was not the kind of guy that could say, 'Well, I'll go after Eugene McCarthy.' He had everything invested in Bobby Kennedy. And it was not just the loss of Bobby Kennedy. It was what it meant to him. He clearly never knew exactly who he was."

"Bobby loved Bobby Kennedy," Steve Blauner said. "Bobby was devastated. He went right from Mr. D's not to St. Patrick's Cathedral, where they had the funeral, but to the gravesite in Arlington. He was at the gravesite and the news media there had nothing to do so they wanted to interview him. He wouldn't let them interview him. And

Resurrection City was up, there had been a big march in Washington and there had been terrible weather and there was a quagmire. And then they come finally, and it's dark and they put the coffin in the ground and they leave. They don't cover it. Bobby wouldn't leave the gravesite. He slept at the gravesite. He had a vision at the gravesite . . . he explained it to me as this massive ball of flame that left his body."

"Suddenly I saw things with a peace and calm I have never seen before," Bobby would say later. "It was as though all my hostilities, anxieties and conflicts were in one ball. That ball was beginning to fly away from me into space. As I stood there, I could feel it getting farther and farther away from me all the time, leaving me finally content with myself."

The change in Bobby was almost immediate. "When Bobby Kennedy was killed, I thought, if a man like that could die, then what can I do for this world?" he told journalist Al Aronowitz. "I only knew him a short time, but in my relationship with him, in committing myself to him, I was seeking my own identity through somebody of courage and conviction. When he died, that void that I was trying to fill in committing myself to him, that void was even greater."

Bobby decided that material possessions weren't important to him anymore. It was spiritual happiness he was now chasing, and to hell with the cars, houses and everything else attached to that lifestyle. The house on Rodeo Drive would have to go, along with everything in it— and most of Bobby's possessions. He was moving to Big Sur in northern California to live in a trailer and commune with nature. He would still perform, but only sporadically now. He needed to get his head together and decide how he wanted to live his life and do more for humanity.

"Bobby calls me one day and he says, 'You and Ellen, do you want to come to my house on your day off?'" said Dick Lord. "So we go to his house and he's sitting there and people are saying, 'Bobby, can I have this?' 'Take it.' 'Bobby, how about the chandeliers?' 'Take it.' I said, 'What are you doing?' He said, 'I don't want any more possessions. I don't need this kind of stuff,' and people are carting things out of his house. Television sets, cameras, chandeliers. He had an old-fashioned gumball machine and he handed it to my wife and he said, 'Here, I know you like this, take it' and she said, 'I can't take it' and he said, 'Okay, it's four hundred dollars.' That's exactly what he said. He always knew how to get you. I still have the gumball machine.

"He called me one night and he said, 'I just spoke to Robert Kennedy,'" Lord said. "I said, 'Robert Kennedy is dead.' He said, 'I know, but he spoke to me.' 'What did he say?' 'I'm going to run for public office.'"

"Bobby was a tortured soul. I can't begin to explain it, but here's a guy who sold all his worldly possessions and lived in a trailer in Big Sur," said Steve Blauner. "I went there with my wife and you had to leave U.S. 1 in the middle of Big Sur and go down this dirt road. It was almost like a rainforest-type of beach and then you came out and there's this farm.

"And Bobby had this ratty old trailer," Blauner said. "We went by the trailer and you walked into this harbor, out onto a beach with the whitest sand in the world and one of those famous rock formations with a hole in the middle of the rock. It was God's country. Bobby went up there and lived in that trailer and he'd go to the library in Carmel everyday."

When he wasn't in Big Sur, Bobby was performing in Vegas, sharing a house there on Russell Road with Quitman Dennis and his future wife, Jeannie (Bobby was best man at their wedding), or bunking with Terry Kellman over at his place, sleeping on a mattress on the floor. Sometimes he'd have Moose with him.

"He'd stay at my house and then the next morning we would get up real early and run out with the rest of the band to Lake Mead, where he had this old boat that he liked fixing up," Kellman said. "I thing it was just something he bought, not because he wanted to fix it up, but because he wanted to hang with Moose and the guys and just kind of bond and sand down the hull or something. The boat never ran. It never started, *ever*," Kellman said. "I think it was towed to Lake Mead."

The good times off-stage, though, were tempered by the changes Bobby now brought to his live act in the wake of RFK's assassination and the move to Big Sur. Hewing to his new commitment to eschew the glitz of show-business in favor of "keeping it real," Bobby replaced his expensive tuxedo with a Levi's version made out of denim. Gone were the lifts he'd been wearing for years, along with the stage makeup and the toupee. He grew a mustache. Bobby now wanted to be known as "Bob" Darin. The transformation from swingin' Vegas entertainer to folk troubador was complete.

"I would talk to him from time to time. Bobby would have times where he didn't talk to anybody, so for a month you'd say, where the hell is Bobby?" said Tom Mankiewicz. "And then somebody would say, 'Oh, he's up in Big Sur. He's not talking to anybody, but he'll be back next Tuesday.' And then you'd get a call."

The change was even more pronounced in Bobby's act, now heavily laden with folk music and protest songs, including "A Simple Song of Freedom," which Bobby wrote in the wake of Robert Kennedy's assassination.

Bobby ended the Big Sur experiment in early 1970, more out of necessity than disappointment. He needed the money, and he would have to return to Vegas and a more rigorous touring schedule. Bobby also realized that running away from reality, rather than facing it head-on, wasn't the solution. "That was a defeatist thing," he said of his time in Big Sur. "A Kafka-esque prison."

"He did some of the old stuff in the act, but he really didn't want to do it," guitarist Terry Kellman said of Bobby's return to Vegas. "He liked the 'Simple Song of Freedom' folk stuff and the protest stuff. And Tommy Amato told me, just before I joined the band, that Bobby had really angered a bunch of people because they had a big General Motors convention at the hotel and the place was packed with ad executives from the company, and Bobby started ranting about how General Motors makes cars designed to last only three years and then you have to buy a new car, and you guys are assholes. Tommy told me there was a line to get out of there."

Bobby marked his return to regular Vegas performing by signing a deal with the Sahara paying him $40,000 a week. Although he wasn't living in Big Sur any longer, he hadn't surrendered the trappings of his folk phase, at least in terms of his physical appearance. The Sahara crowd seemed more shocked than anything else at the balding, Levi's-wearing acoustic guitarist who now greeted them.

"The Copa crowd and the Vegas crowd didn't want that at all," said Bob Rozario. "Bobby did it in gradual steps but it just wasn't going over with the general public."

Brent Maher, who was engineering Bobby's second Direction Records album, *Commitment*, also recorded Bobby's "Return to Vegas" show at the Sahara, which was going to be released as a live album (that never happened).

"It was a mixed review at the Sahara," Maher said. "And it would go from night to night. They came there expecting to see Bobby in his tux doing all the Vegas things and he was in jeans and a denim shirt with a little vest and a guitar.

"You would have some nights where the people were just totally with him. He was so great at being an entertainer he could take any of those environments and switch them around and bring the crowd into his camp," he said. "But having said that, every once in a while there'd be a guy who would yell out 'Hey, "Mack the Knife"!' Some people could be a little uncomfortable with that. They didn't come there to see that. They came there to hear 'Splish Splash,' to rock a little bit . . . and they didn't particularly want to hear politically positioned material. But Bobby could still flip that around and pretty much have the people in the palm of his hand by the time the show was over."

To Bobby's bassist, Quitman Dennis, it was a change for which the public was unprepared, and unwilling to accept.

"At the gig that flopped at the Sahara, Bobby had a full-size cardboard cutout silhouette of himself—Levi's pants, Levi's jacket, a denim shirt and a cowboy hat, holding an acoustic guitar," Dennis said. "That was outside the showroom so people could see that coming in. There was something about Bob Darin. I don't know whether it was the 'new Bob Darin,' but it was Bob Darin, at least. And he said, 'Hey, I let these people know this is not Bobby Darin, it's Bob Darin.' But these people weren't really clued in to his change in focus."

Bobby interspersed political commentary in between songs, talking about "Slicky Dick" Nixon and his vice president, "Zero" Agnew. Journalist Al Aronowitz reported that people were walking out in the middle of Bobby's show, disgusted. Still, Bobby took the high road on his closing night.

"It was fourteen months since I last played this town. It took a lot of guts on the Hotel Sahara's part to try me out doing what I'm doing now," he said. "They pay me a lot of money for something I would do and virtually have done for nothing."

Bobby had a new manager, Don Gregory, who met Bobby back in 1967 when he and Harry Belafonte went to see Bobby perform at the Flamingo. In 1969, Gregory sold Rowan & Martin's *Laugh-In* to NBC and got re-acquainted with Bobby when he appeared on the show.

"He said, 'I want you to understand that I'm 'Bob' Darin, not 'Bobby,' and I just want to work with a guitar and do folk songs'" Gregory said. "'No more tuxes or toupees.' He called me 'D' and I called him 'B.' I said, 'You can't just go into Vegas, into a place like the Sahara, like that. Why not dress in a suit? The hell with the toupee, your hair is fine, do a couple of old songs,' and that's what he did. It was a nice blend. I got him $35,000-a-week at the Landmark for six weeks and he was a big hit there.

"He once said 'I'm high on the natch,'" Gregory said. "I'll never forget that."

Being predominantly a folk singer, however, didn't mean that Bobby's attitude and brashness were mellowing. In the spring of 1969 he was invited to appear on *The Jackie Gleason Show*, which taped in Miami Beach. Bobby reached into the *Bobby Darin Born Walden Robert Cassotto* album for "Long Line Rider," a tune about inmates murdered at an Arkansas prison.

"When we rehearsed the song, Jackie Gleason's producers just wigged out," said Bob Rozario. "They didn't want that song on their show, and I don't blame them, but they promised Bobby that they would allow him to do one of his new songs. They said 'Long Line Rider' was just too much of a downer for the show. But Bobby refused to change, so while the audience was coming in, we were walking out because he refused to do the show."

Bobby also rubbed Jules Podell the wrong way when he opened at the Copa in early 1969. He actually garnered solid reviews—"a workmanlike bout of singing, impressions and patter," said *Variety*—but the denim suit, balding pate and mustache were too much for Podell's old-style sensibilities, not to mention the protest songs and Bobby's refusal to be introduced when he took the stage. Podell was pissed, and made it clear that Bobby wouldn't be welcomed back, *ever*, unless he reverted back to his old form. "He never said a word, but listen with Julie, silence is voluminous," Bobby said.

"I went to see Bobby at the Copa and he came out on stage with his jeans and jeans jacket, with a guitar, and he only had two or three guys backing him," said Tom Mankiewicz. "And he started to sing 'Simple Song of Freedom' and all these drunks at the Copa who had come for a big show—they would come with their hookers and dates for a Saturday-night Copa show—they started screaming 'Sing "Mack the Knife!" "Beyond the Sea!"' and Bobby would just keep going."

"And then I went back with him, either to the Pierre or the Sherry-Netherland where he was staying, and he had to pack quickly because he was getting on a plane the next morning," Mankiewicz said. "And we went into the bedroom, and there on the bed, were like eight or ten pairs of jeans laid out. They were all carefully kind of ripped and bleached and so on. The performer in him was still very much alive. It wasn't like, gee, he came to New York with his only pair of jeans. He knew what he was doing."

Bobby and old flame Diane Hartford were linked again publicly in April 1969 when Diane was called to the stand in the wiretap trial of electronics expert Bernard Spindel. Spindel was allegedly let into an East Side apartment by Huntington Hartford to repair a tapped phone Hunt was using to listen in to Diane's calls to and from lawyer Kenneth Klein. Hunt suspected Diane was having an affair with Klein. Spindel's attorney, in an attempt to discredit Diane, asked her "Did you ever have relations with [Bobby Darin]?" "I refuse to answer," Diane replied.

"Mrs. Hartford admitted that she had met Darin in Los Angeles in the fall of 1965, seen him again in San Francisco, and had occupied a suite in the Regency Hotel here while Darin occupied a suite in the same hotel," reported *The New York Post*. "She admitted that each had visited the other's suite during their stay there." Spindel was later convicted of tapping Klein's phone.

Bobby and the band toured the clubs and fairgrounds throughout the winter, spring and summer of 1969, sometimes playing to half-empty venues. "Bob" Darin's fans were sending him a message.

"That was not what they came there for and those of us who were rather naïve to what was going on in the background with Bobby, we were just having a good time with 'Bob,'" said Quitman Dennis. "We didn't know what was going on with Don Gregory and the issues and the problems with booking more of these shows and I thought, well, it's obvious he will never book any more of them because word gets around real quick. It was like, hey, this isn't going to work."

Bobby himself was coming to the realization that people didn't come to see Bob Darin and his "message" songs. They didn't want that. What they wanted was show-biz glitz and Bobby Darin in a smart tux snapping his fingers, shrugging his shoulders and singing "Mack the Knife" and the old hits. It was a tough nut to swallow.

"I realized that there are certain people who are just not going to accept certain things," he told Al Aronowitz. "I had been too slick. After I put on my denims, my aggressiveness had disappeared. Nobody listened to what I said. People would not let me into places. I knew what it was to be a black man in a white community, to be rejected for nothing you did, to be a victim of that kind of bigotry. I always knew it intellectually but I never knew the pain that accompanies it. People hear what they see."

"He rationalized the folk stuff," said Don Gregory, "but he knew people weren't buying into it. Bobby carried the charisma with him. People were patient. They waited for him to be 'Bobby' again."

He and Sandra attempted a reconciliation after his sojourn to Big Sur. In the rush to unload all his "material" possessions, Bobby had sold the place on Rodeo Drive and now he moved in with Sandra and Moose, attempting to rekindle the romance and start over again.

"Bobby and I are sitting in his front room on the floor, with tapes scattered around, and into the door walks Sandra Dee with an armful of groceries that she had picked up," said Brent Maher, who was engineering the *Commitment* album around that time. "Now, I have to tell you, not only was I a Bobby Darin fan, I was hopelessly in love with Sandra Dee at the age of fifteen.

"She walks into the room and God, she hadn't changed a bit," Maher said. "She just looked precious. She walks in and says, 'Hey Bobby, hey guys, I'll put the stuff in the fridge.' My jaw just hit the floor and Bobby looked at me and says, 'You too?' I was so embarrassed. He said, 'Don't be—everybody's like that.' He had fun with it."

The reconciliation didn't last and Bobby moved out to a place on the beach in Malibu. He also decided to chuck the folk act, which wasn't getting him anyplace, "put the tux back on" and return to being Bobby Darin. He pegged the final decision to a concert in Puerto Rico.

"When I played the El San Juan in Puerto Rico, that was really it. As I walked out on the floor, they walked out of the audience," he said. "That's the key I remember, the total feeling of rejection, like I had come down with the plague.

"So I began to realize the need to be anonymous on the street and somebody on the stage. I had tried to put my street self on the stage, but then I began to look at myself and think, 'No, that's not it. What they want is an actor on the stage.'

"An actor wears a costume and makeup. I'm an actor. There's nothing wrong with that. You go out and you entertain them. If what they hear is what they see, then, indeed, let me put on my tux. I'm comfortable in it. I don't have any inner arguments anymore. And you know what? It's a fact. People hear what they see.

THE NEWS THAT Bobby Darin was "back" spread quickly. Bobby was visibly more comfortable in his familiar on-stage persona, but was nervous he might have permanently damaged his career, which hadn't been going great-guns before the folk phase.

"He was afraid that it might be tough because he burned a lot of bridges when he left, but people were really interested in him. Everybody was curious," said Mimi Greenberg, Bobby's new publicist. "It was like, 'He's back? Oh my God!'"

"We went back to do a followup engagement at the Landmark," said bassist/conductor Quitman Dennis. "And that's when he told us in the rhythm section that we really needed to get out of our casual clothes because he had to upgrade the act a little bit.

"All of us in the rhythm section went back into tuxedoes and suits at that point. But Bobby wasn't happy with moving back and agreeing with the establishment. I think he felt like he was failing because the message songs did carry weight.

"We were at the Landmark when he introduced new arrangements of 'Mack the Knife' and he had Roger Kellaway doing arrangements there," Dennis said. "He was back to being Bobby Darin."

Bobby now called Bob Rozario, who left a few years earlier to conduct the house orchestra at King's Castle in Lake Tahoe. "He said, 'Bob, I'm putting my tuxedo and my hairpiece back on. You want to come back to work for me? I'd love to have you back.' And I said, 'Sure, Bobby, when do you want me to start?' And he said, 'How about tonight?' I was in Tahoe and he was down in Vegas at the Hilton."

Bobby was also putting the finishing touches on *The Vendors*, a movie he wrote, produced and directed. Bobby had been working on the movie, on and off, since the Big Sur days. The plot revolved around a folk singer, his relationship with a hooker and the seamy underbelly of the recording industry. Bobby hired Dick Lord to play the folk singer's scheming manager, and young actor Gary Wood to star as the folk singer. Mariette Hartley played the hooker.

"He wouldn't show it to us," Tom Mankiewicz said of Bobby's *Vendors* script. "I would say, 'Bobby, I'm your friend and I can help you. I don't care. Everybody's first draft is rough.' He'd say, 'Yeah, yeah, I'll show it to you in a couple of days, I've got more work to do on it.'"

Bobby had initially approached Roger McGuinn to play the folk singer. McGuinn, a big hit with The Byrds, would give the movie some star power.

"I agreed to do it but changed my mind," McGuinn said. "I didn't want to be portrayed as a drug dealer or a junkie. Bobby had a camera guy set up and I paid him what it cost to get out of it. He was pissed; he accepted my resignation but didn't like it because he went out of his way to set it up. I gave him my word and changed my mind. I felt badly about that."

"I suppose many of Bobby's thoughts were based on his experience with managers and publishers," said Dick Lord regarding *The Vendors*. "I went to L.A. and stayed at Bobby's house. He worked very hard. We filmed in Nancy Sinatra's house. Nancy was a big fan of Bobby's even though her father wouldn't talk to him. We also filmed in a nightclub somewhere in L.A. My scenes were with the folk singer, played by Gary Wood. One thing I remember, Bobby was so true to himself. He loved Gary Wood. He really did.

"Gary was up for a part in another movie and they said, well, what have you done lately?," Lord said. "He had done Bobby's movie, so he says to Bobby, 'I need a clip of what I've done to show these people.' And Bobby wouldn't give it to him. 'I'm sorry, but nobody sees anything here,' Bobby said. He wouldn't give him the clip."

"Bobby made the movie in 16mm. It was awful," said Steve Blauner. "And when he came to show me the movie, what do you do? That's a pisser, especially with someone you love so dearly. So I told him what I thought. I said, 'Look, I think you can get a deal for this picture if you restructure it and make it the girl's movie.' She was a hooker, played by Mariette Hartley. 'You'll have everybody crying their eyes out.' She was great in the part, the best thing in the movie." *The Vendors* was never released.

Bobby's FBI file grew a bit thicker in May 1970. For years, he'd been an outspoken opponent of the war in Vietnam, and when news broke of the secret bombing in Cambodia, he took out full-page newspaper ads denouncing President Nixon's decision. On May 12, about four hundred USC students marched from the campus to Los Angeles City Hall in an anti-war protest, allegedly carrying fifty-thousand letters addressed to President Nixon and objecting to the military activity in Cambodia.

"This march reached the City Hall at approximately 3:30 p.m., where an estimated crowd of 600 heard anti-war speeches from students, political peace candidates, and Los Angeles City Councilman Thomas Bradley," the FBI noted in its surveillance report. "Entertainer Bobby Darin addressed the crowd and said he was starting a project called 'Phone For Peace.' He urged the crowd to telephone the White House in Washington, D.C., and leave a peace message for President Nixon.

"Darin expressed the hope that a tie-up at the White House switchboard would cause the President to take notice. The crowd dispersed at 5:00 p.m. This demonstration occurred without violence or incident and no arrests were made."

Bobby worked his show-biz commitments in and around his political agenda. "Elvis came to see Bobby all the time, because he was usually scheduled to open after Bobby," said guitarist Terry Kellman. "So he would come in a few days earlier.

"One time I remember we were at the International, where the elevator went from the stage to this long hallway. Elvis was in the audience, and when we came down, the elevator doors opened and way at the other end of the hall, there was Elvis and a girl named Lisa, a beautiful model. She saw the elevator doors open up and saw the band in there and she runs away from Elvis into the elevator and gives us a big hug. Well, this did not sit well with the man. And he makes big strides to the hallway, takes her arm and pulls her away and they go right into Bobby's dressing room.

"I don't think Elvis realized I was going to come into the dressing room because we just walked in there routinely," Kellman said. "And when I open the door, it was a bizarre scene of Bobby and Elvis using the couch as a trampoline and grabbing the light fixtures, bouncing up and down and yelling and screaming at each other like little kids, like they had turned into five-year-olds. Lisa was trying to maintain her composure. It seemed to be a private moment. Elvis was always a weird guy."

Bobby's television appearances were few and far between between 1967, when he guest-starred on three specials, and the spring of 1970. A whole year had elapsed between Bobby's shot on *Laugh-In* in 1968 and his turn on *The Tom Jones Show* in October 1969, where he sang "Distractions" and dueted with Jones on '60s classics "Aquarius" and "Let the Sunshine In." It was time to get busy again, if not in the recording studio—since he was without a recording contract—then at least on television, where he had always shined.

Bobby agreed to co-host *The Mike Douglas Show* in late July, still sporting a thin mustache and without his toupee. The syndicated *Douglas Show* aired in the afternoon in most markets and originated from Philadelphia, where Douglas had moved the show after its beginnings in Cleveland. While Douglas wasn't exactly cutting-edge, he welcomed a wide array of guests, including co-hosts John Lennon and Yoko Ono—a weeklong appearance made even more memorable when Lennon rocked out with guest Chuck Berry.

"The first time I was on the road with Bobby we were having dinner in Philadelphia when he was doing *The Mike Douglas Show*," recalled

Bobby's publicist, Mimi Greenberg. "He verbally asked me, he said, 'I don't want to hit on you or make a pass, if this isn't something that you are comfortable with.' I said, 'Please, don't. I'm in psychotherapy, I see you as a father figure. I really enjoy working for you, I like you as a person, I like my work, let's not muddle this up.' He said, 'Wow! I really respect you for telling me all that.' And that was the end of it. There was never another word and I think he thought I was a character. I know he thought I was cute, but there was never any great interest on his part, it's just that I was something to do on the road and if I wanted to do the same thing, then it would be convenient."

Bobby also became romantically involved with singer Brenda Lee, a situation that soon turned sour.

"He had a one-night stand with her, which Brenda Lee didn't know was going to be a one-night stand," Greenberg recalled. "This was in Las Vegas. Brenda fell madly in love with him and thought he was going to be the love of her life, and that she was going to get divorced and marry Bobby.

"He, I think, was a little scared," Greenberg said. "He didn't realize that he had gotten in over his head. And her thugs were threatening him. She is very redneck and the people around her are very redneck but she was very, very angry at Bobby.

"That eventually died down, but he realized that there were going to be a lot of Brenda Lees in his life," she said. "He realized that if he was going to screw around every time he hit a new town with whoever was there, whoever happened to meet his fancy, that he was going to start either getting bad publicity or getting roughed up by the boyfriends of some of these people."

Sometimes, the sex was anonymous.

"He was into scenes, any kind of sex scene imaginable," said Steve Blauner. "There was a place in Malibu, up in the mountains, called Sandstone. There was group sex going on, or whatever, and he would go in the back way and go in a dark room and nobody would know he was there, and he would partake."

In October, Bobby went to Toronto to film a Canadian TV special, *The Darin Invasion*, with guests Linda Ronstadt and George Burns. He sang "Simple Song of Freedom," "Your Love Keeps Lifting Me Higher" and "Hi Dee Ho," among other numbers, and played Fagin in a scene from *Oliver!* with a cast of kids. But something wasn't right; Bobby wasn't feeling well during the taping. "He was having tremendous pain in his chest and he was sweaty and weak," recalled manager Don Gregory.

It was his rheumatic heart. Just as the doctors predicted when he was a child, the valves of Bobby's heart were wearing away. Bobby was suffering irregular heartbeats, his heart sometimes pumping over six times its normal rate for hours at a time. Bobby's doctors told him that the only option would be for him to undergo open-heart surgery—a fairly new procedure, considered extremely risky and enormously expensive—and to have two of his valves replaced. There were no other options if Bobby planned on living much longer. He took the news stoically and promised to undergo the surgery. First though, he wanted to complete an upcoming engagement at the Desert Inn, where he opened at the end of January 1971.

"Back in his old snappy form, Bobby Darin hits off very well with the assorted junketers and middle-roaders who populate tables here," *Variety* wrote of Bobby's opening at the Desert Inn. "Remembering his 'Mack the Knife' chiefly, they give him a torrent of enthusiastic applause for its inclusion, with other kudos receding in ratio for 'If I Were A Carpenter,' 'I'll Be Your Baby Tonight' and his kindergartner tune 'Splish Splash.'

"The rest of his log has some very current ties in presentation, with a Beatles medley winning plenty of approval and his own 'Simple Song of Freedom' achieving very respectable results."

"We were at the Desert Inn in February, right before he had the open-heart surgery," recalled Quitman Dennis. "We knew that Bobby had a history of rheumatic fever and he had some problems there. So we get this booking at the Desert Inn, and this is cool, you're working twenty-eight days in row, no nights off and it's two shows a night. And we show up there, we all know what we're going to do, but we find out that Bobby's not in good health and that he has no energy and that he's kind of hiding away eating spinach and showing up to do his show and barely making it through.

"And at the end of the twenty-eight days, at the end of that second show on the twenty-eighth day, he goes out backstage, takes a limo to the airport to L.A. and he's in the hospital. A few days later we learned that he's had open-heart surgery.

"What I saw from Bobby during that time at the Desert Inn was that he was very frail," Dennis said. "He would do the show and then go back to his dressing room. He was reluctant to receive people in the dressing room unless they were old friends. And then he's eating spinach and protein and then back to his room to watch Marx Brothers movies until show time the next day."

"Having lived with a damaged heart for twenty-six years, I didn't think there was anything heroic about going in for surgery," Bobby told journalist Al Aronowitz. "I also always felt I was going to kick off by the time I was thirty anyway. The only reason it was time for the operation was that my valves had deteriorated to a point where if it was not now then it would have to be next year and in the meantime I'd have to curtail my activities.

"Because I'm fearless and insane, it was no risk," he said. "I told the doctor, 'You give me these six weeks to work—the first six weeks in 1971—somehow, you keep me alive by remote control, and the moment I close I'll go home, spend four hours with my son and then I'll check into a hospital and give myself to you.

"So I closed in Vegas at the Desert Inn on Feburary 8th, the morning of the earthquake. I spent a few hours with Moose, my son. He was nine years old then. I explained to him I was sure everything was going to be okay but it was very possible I would never see him again and I told him wherever I am you know I love you. And he looked up at me and said, 'Don't worry about it, Dad, everything's going to be fine.' And I checked into the hospital."

Bobby put up a brave front, but he was worried. Dick Lord had become a stand-up comedian after stints working for Don Kirshner and as an agent and elsewhere in the record industry. Now he was opening for Bobby at the Desert Inn, and he noticed a big change in Bobby's mood and demeanor as the heart surgery approached.

"He was really losing his hair, and he hated it," Lord said. "And he said, 'I'm losing my hair because I'm not getting enough oxygen to my brain. And I'm going to die.' And every time he said this, I'd say, 'You're not going to die.'

"I would go with him to the doctor, for his heart. I remember once, coming out of the doctor's office in the garage, he said, 'There's Howard Hughes.' At this time Howard Hughes was holed up at the Desert Inn. And at that moment, I started to think, well, maybe he really *is* losing it. I just refused to believe it, I couldn't accept it. Maybe it was Howard Hughes, but it was the first time I ever thought that what he said was absolutely wrong.

"So at the Desert Inn Bobby would sleep all day and stay in bed," Lord said. "He would get up at 5 o'clock, do the shows, and then get back into bed. And he would say, like a little kid, 'Would you stay with me?' So I would go after the shows sometimes and he would be in bed and we would watch television or talk.

"One night after the show he said, 'Boy, I wish I could have some Chinese food.' He would have a way of getting you like that," Lord said. "There was a Chinese restaurant in the Sands hotel, but you weren't allowed to take food out. And I'm thinking, poor Bobby is lying in bed, I wish I could get him some Chinese food.

"So Jim O'Neil, Bobby's road manager, and I go into the casino and I get two of those big buckets they keep the chips in and we take them back and the waitress comes over and we order the Chinese food. And then, when no one is looking, we're shoveling the food into the buckets. Now, we are very proud that we thought of this. We get to the room and we say, well, here's the Chinese food and Bobby goes, 'It's all mixed together! I can't eat this!'

"At the end of the engagement I walked into his dressing room," Lord said. "There were a lot of people there and he said, 'I would appreciate it if everyone would leave.' He said it very nicely. So they start to leave and he says, 'No, Dickie, you stay.' Everybody leaves and he puts his arms around me and said, 'I'm going to die.' I said, 'You're not going to die. You told me that nine out of every ten of these operations are extremely successful—I called the hospital, I'm the tenth guy.'

"Bobby was leaving that night and he didn't want to fly, so Jim O'Neil had this little truck with a camper top, and he put in a bed and lamp because they were going to drive from Vegas back to L.A. and then Bobby was going into the hospital. And we knew that he loved to have his biggest treat if he could, an ice cream sundae. So after the show one of us handed him the ice cream sundae and he was lying in the bed, with the sundae in his hand, like a little kid, waving goodbye."

THE LOOMING HEART SURGERY couldn't have come at a worse time, not only in Bobby's personal life but professionally as well. In the fall of 1970, Bobby made the first of five appearances spanning two years on NBC's top-rated *Flip Wilson Show*. Wilson, a talented stand-up comedian and monologist, made his Las Vegas debut several years earlier opening for Bobby. The two men became fast friends and enjoyed each other's company; now, with Bobby's career stuck in neutral, Wilson was about to pay back the favor.

"Bobby was grateful for anybody who was willing to take a chance," said Mimi Greenberg. "When he returned, he knew that he had behaved badly and he was very grateful for anybody who was willing to give him a fair shake. Flip had been one of his opening acts and Bobby was always an activist for the black movement.

"They had a good rapport and it started with Bobby just singing on the show, then he started doing some sketches with Flip, then they were talking about wanting to make movies together, reworking the old Bob Hope-Bing Crosby road movies. They really did want to do that," she said. "But Bobby's sickness and Flip's heavy cocaine use certainly prevented that. But because Flip's show was so successful and was seen by so many people, it certainly helped Bobby's comeback because now he was getting nightclub engagements."

"I think Flip Wilson is a brilliant comedian," Bobby told David Frost. "There are many comics and comics can make you laugh with prepared material and once in a while a funny face. Flip is just a generically marvelous funny human being. He is probably the only performer I ever remember getting upstairs early for to listen to, because of his sense of timing, his sense of audience, feel, that marvelous electricity to know when and how to do things.

"I was constantly learning from him," Bobby said. "I was always watching him and we became fast friends. It's a strange kind of thing . . . You do know when that kind of relationship is going to turn around and the other party is going to do something for you . . . when I was a little bit of a difficult sale for television, when Flipper got his own show, he said to the people who were involved in booking it, 'I want Bobby to do the show, I want him to do it not just once, I want him to do it as many times as he wants to do it.' It was a true gesture of a real kind of genuine friendship. I love him very much."

Bobby appeared on the *Flip Wilson Show* in September, November and December then again in January 1971. A month later, at the end of February, he went in for the open-heart surgery in Los Angeles. On February 23, the *Associated Press* moved a one-paragraph story informing the world of Bobby's surgery. "Bobby Darin, 34-year-old singer, actor and songwriter, was in 'very good' condition today after undergoing heart surgery, a hospital spokesman said."

"I didn't see him for a few months and one day he called and asked me if I was going to this gathering, some party outdoors in a garden," recalled Tom Mankiewicz. "I said I wasn't planning on it and he said, 'Why don't you come, I really want to talk to you.' And I thought it was weird. And we sat on this stone bench and he said to me, 'I've got to go back for another operation. They told me if I don't have it, the odds on my dying are one-hundred percent, if I don't have it within six months or a year. They told me if I do have it, I've got a seventy-five percent chance of not making it through.'

"And I stared at him," Mankiewicz said. "And I'll never forget, he just grinned and winked and reached down and cupped my cheek. And we just hugged. That was the last time I ever saw him."

The nine-hour surgery was complicated and required an extremely long recovery time. Bobby spent five days in the Intensive Care Unit, another six weeks in the hospital and another week living in a hotel near his doctor's office.

Bobby was also recuperating with the help of his new girlfriend, Andrea Yaeger, a divorced mother of two young boys, Armen and Alex. Andrea, divorced in 1968, was working in the office of a lawyer Bobby had gone to see about a business deal. They struck up a conversation and began dating. Within three months they were living together.

"Andrea was very beautiful and very compliant," recalled Mimi Greenberg. "It was almost like she had no personality of her own. She really was Bobby's alter-ego. I mean, she would not say mean things to people—she wouldn't act out Bobby's anger—but she made friends with the people that he told her she should be friends with, and she stopped talking to the people that he wanted her to stop talking with."

"Bobby would come over to my house in Bel Air, where I had a projection room, and he would come and watch movies and he would come over with Andrea," said Steve Blauner. "She's a great lady. Had no idea who he was. And she was never enamored with his celebrity or anything. She just loved him for him."

Bobby took the summer off, resting at home and building up his strength. He returned to the stage on September 1, opening at Harrah's in Reno for two weeks "getting the rust out" and did ten days at a nightclub in Columbus, Ohio, before heading back to Harrah's again.

"He picked up from where he was but it was not back to that very spontaneous, energetic, bubbly guy from a year before," said Quitman Dennis. "He wasn't back up to that. It was more like depression than anything else, a kind of lump, like a black cloud around him. I was starting to become more involved in production and being an engineer at a studio in Vegas and I didn't like where this was going with Bobby on the road and I signed off.

"Bobby and I talked about it and he said, 'It's because you're not happy working with me' and I said, 'No, I still like you and I like working with you but I want to do this other work.' So I left."

Bobby spent the fall months busy with television work. He did a few spots on *The Flip Wilson Show* and shot guest-starring roles on *Cade's County*, *Ironsides* and Rod Serling's *Night Gallery* (where he ended up as a can of dog food).

Bobby's relationship with Andrea deepened, and he would now introduce her as his "wife," even though they weren't legally married. "We've been married since the day we met," he told columnist Earl Wilson "But we're not married according to the tenets of legality. We feel that marriage is a state that exists between two people who love each other. She has two wonderful boys, aged eleven and eight. They're always with us. When my ten-year-old son can make it, he's with us, too."

11

Bobby returned to the Copa in February 1972 for the first time in three years. This time, he was clean-shaven and wearing a tux to assuage Jules Podell. But it wasn't easy getting the booking; Podell was still angry about Bobby's folk antics the last time around. Bobby had a third party call Podell to plead his case.

"I told them to tell Julie I wanted to play it and settle the situation," Bobby told Al Aronowitz. "I did a bad thing there last time. One thing I know now is that I'm a saloon singer. There's a certain frame of mind in a saloon that's perfect for me.

"I'm a saloon singer and that's what I'm going to major in."

That didn't mean, however, that the always controversial "saloon singer" didn't court trouble during that Copa engagement. This time, it presented itself in the form of one of the wiseguys who was there with his girlfriend for a good time on a Sunday night.

"Generally they would sit at a long table, with the bodyguard sitting on one end of the table, close to the stage," said Terry Kellman. "There really wasn't much of a stage; it was kind of a floor and behind you on the stage was the orchestra. And one night we were sitting there and I don't really know why, but Bobby didn't like this guy. I think what happened was, Bobby came on in his usual brash self, and this bodyguard who actually looked like Bobby with jet-black hair, kind of showed Bobby his gun that he was wearing. And man, Bobby got pissed off. I was sitting behind Bobby.

"Well, this guy showed him the gun and Bobby laid into this guy and I'd seen Bobby before when there was a guy in the audience who caught his eye who he particularly didn't like, he was merciless," Kellman said. "As a matter of fact, in the Landmark one time, I saw Bobby do a Nazi strut in front of a guy he didn't like.

"But he didn't like this brash guy sitting in front. And the tension became really thick. There was a break where Bobby would run back, and he would take off his shirt and stuff, sort of a mini encore. And by the time that would happen, people all around the club knew something was going on and this guy is showing him his gun.

"I was not too comfortable and I was thinking to myself, boy all these heads of families being killed at the Copa, oh my God, here we go and Bobby is going to leap under a table and I'm going to get shot. It was really bad. So when he went back on stage there was a guy named Tony Lip, who was a maitre'd, a big guy, and another guy named Carmine, two big bodyguards-slash-maitre-d's—Tony Lip went back there and said, 'Hey Bobby, what are you doing? Don't fuck with these guys! Don't screw with these guys, these are big guys!' And Bobby says, 'Goddammit, don't tell me what to do!'

"He runs back on stage and people are wondering how this is going to turn out," Kellman said. "This was like a battle of two Italian egos. The band was skittish to say the least. So what happened was, the next song was 'If I Were a Carpenter,' and at the end of the song, there was a blackout, except for a pin spot on Bobby's hands as he held them out, sort of like Allstate. And it was a real quiet part of the show, and just as the lights are going down and the pin spot is on his hand, some drunk guy was arguing with his wife and everybody burst out laughing. Tony Lip and Carmine immediately ripped the tablecloth off of the table and lifted the table up, and lifted the guy up, because it was so packed, over the crowd and muscled their way through the crowd, with his wife following going 'He didn't mean it! He had too much to drink!'

"Everybody was cracking up and laughing, it broke the tension and the guy in the front row held out his hand to shake Bobby's and Bobby shook his hand, and there was big applause. And the rest of the evening went fine."

The press welcomed Bobby back to the Copa with open arms. "Effusive though his style may be—folky-humble at some points, Vegas-flashy at others—Darin is still a first-class performer," noted *The New York Times*. "He sang, played the guitar, drums and piano,

tied things together with a virtually nonstop and often quite witty patter and managed to pull a lackadaisical first-night audience out of its
lethargy. . . . He clearly is most comfortable with the Frank Sinatra-
Dean Martin style that was the essence of his first musical incarnation."

While he was at the Copa, Bobby also took some time to have an
earnest talk with Gary, who hadn't yet been told the truth about his
half-brother. Gary was almost seventeen now, and wanted to drop out
of high school. It was a decision that enraged Bobby, who always had
a special place in his heart for Gary—even more so now that he knew
the truth about their mother.

"It had come up at the table that I had decided to leave school, and
he was pissed," Gary said. "He was outraged. So we went from one
side of the restaurant to the other and as I look back on it, what it was
was an older brother talking to a younger brother, a 'You've got to do
something with your life' kind of talk.

"At the time I didn't know, but of course he knew, so he was going
to give me the benefit of his years of experience. It was a brother talking to a brother."

Bobby also signed with a new record label. It had been three years
since his last release, *Commitment*, which Bobby put out on his own
Direction Records, and six years since his last hit, "If I Were A Carpenter." The offers weren't exactly rolling in.

Berry Gordy's Motown label, however, was willing to take a chance.
What might have seemed an odd choice on the surface really made a
lot of sense; "saloon singer" Bobby was an R&B aficionado who, after
all, had put out an entire album of Ray Charles songs. Motown had
already released Bobby's first single, "Melodie," the previous April,
two months into Bobby's recovery from the heart surgery. "Melodie"
did absolutely nothing on the charts and received even less airplay.
Bobby's first Motown album, *Bobby Darin*, failed to do much better
when it was released in August.

NBC HAD TAKEN NOTICE of Bobby's interaction with Flip Wilson on
its own airwaves the past several years. *The Dean Martin Show* was taking the summer off, and NBC needed something to fill the timeslot.
Network executives approached Bobby about hosting his own show.

To quote a line from that year's Oscar-winning movie, *The Godfather*, it was an offer Bobby couldn't refuse.

To produce *The Bobby Darin Amusement Company*, as it was being called, NBC tapped veteran producers Saul Ilson and Ernest Chambers. Ilson had written for Danny Kaye and, with Chambers, had produced *The Smothers Brothers Comedy Hour* in 1967 and the Brothers' summer replacement show the following year.

"It was called 'The Bobby Darin Amusement Company' because Saul and I felt that it was very tough for a music show to be successful, so we had to couch it in comedy," Chambers said. "And Bobby, although he had not done comedy, was an experienced actor who'd been nominated for an Academy Award. So we put together a repertory company of comedians."

Ilson had worked with Bobby years before on *Coke Time*, the show on which Pat Boone told Paul Anka how to get even with Bobby for the constant ribbing. "I liked him," Ilson said. "To me, Bobby was extremely gifted. Conflicted, but gifted. To play comedy you have to be a good actor. A lot of actors can't play comedy and he was able to do that because he was just so natural."

Bobby didn't want to let this golden opportunity slip away, and was determined to be a hands-on participant in the television show. He knew that networks often gave full-season orders to summer-replacement shows if they proved themselves worthy in the ratings department. With his record sales nearly non-existent and the movie roles drying up, Bobby was hell-bent on making sure his prime-time television exposure would pay off.

"It's the first time that anyone spoke to me about doing a TV show utilizing all the different things I like to do," Bobby said. "I would not be satisfied with a series featuring just songs and small talk with my guests. Saul and Ernie hit all the right nerve centers in talking to me, and by the end of the meeting with them I was already committed."

One of the young writers Ilson and Chambers hired for the summer show was Alan Thicke, the son of Ilson's personal physician in Canada. Thicke would eventually host his own talk/variety show, *Thicke of the Night*, and found fame as the star of the ABC sitcom *Growing Pains*. Ilson and Chambers briefly considered hiring Bobby's former publicist Mimi Greenberg as a writer, but passed on the idea even though Greenberg had experience writing for *Hollywood Squares*. Bobby put in a good word for Mimi, but there was only so much he could do.

Bobby also brought Dick Lord back into the fold. Lord, who had established himself as a standup comedian, sometimes opening for Bobby in Vegas, was hired as the creative consultant for *The Bobby Darin Amusement Company*. He created the show's opening and contributed some writing suggestions, but felt shut out and ignored and eventually left the show before the end of its summer run.

"Bobby was very much involved. He really wanted the summer show to be special," Ilson said. "He and I worked very closely with Ernie Chambers and I spent a lot of time with him. Sometimes Bobby knew what he wanted and sometimes he didn't know what he wanted. We always had our conflicts but I always had great respect for him.

"Sometimes he could drive you crazy, but when you got to know him . . . we would end up arguing a lot, but at the end of the day I kind of understood him a little bit," Ilson said. "I remember once I picked him up at the Beverly Wilshire Hotel and we went over to the studio and he was very tired. I remember him saying to me, 'You know, I got up this morning and I looked in the mirror and it's getting harder and harder to be Bobby Darin.' I thought, wow, that's pretty deep. What I liked about him was that he really cared and he wanted to work hard."

Comedian Steve Landesberg, a gifted dialectician, had appeared several times on *The Tonight Show* and hit it big with his main characters, a crazy German psychiatrist and his patient. Landesberg was hired by Ilson and Chambers to play the "NBC Psychiatrist," who would open every show by coming out and "analyzing" Bobby. It was Landesberg's first job in a long Hollywood career highlighted by a starring role on the classic ABC sitcom, *Barney Miller*.

"I did other sketches, too, but that was the main one," Landesberg said of his German psychiatrist. "One day, to Bobby's credit in the rehearsal hall in NBC, he said, 'Why don't you let this guy go?' So we got up in the rehearsal and I improvised with him and I had my tape recorder going. So I went home and listened to it and tried to keep the best of it in my head. When we went onstage in front of the audience we did it but I really roughed him up," Landesberg said. "I was like a German [Don] Rickles. I really went after him.

"But I think it was six weeks into the eight weeks we had that I said to Ernie, 'Where is the psychiatrist?' And he said, 'Well, you know, Bobby was uncomfortable and he saw that you were uncomfortable,' which of course wasn't true. And that was the end of it. I did other sketches the last two weeks."

"We had come up with the idea to cast Steve as Bobby's psychiatrist because Bobby was notorious for his fits of ego and for being temperamental and having the chip on his shoulder," Chambers said. "It was a technique that was used a lot in television, which is to have the star denigrate himself and thereby win the audience. It worked really well.

"But Bobby said, 'I want to get rid of that psychiatrist. I am not going to go out there every week and have him come out and humiliate me.' And we tried to explain to him that what it did was actually ingratiate him to the audience . . . But he wouldn't hear of it, so we had to get rid of Steve."

Ilson and Chambers also hired Geoff Edwards, a local Los Angeles radio personality, to work on the summer show in the comedy sketches.

"I was at my house playing a tennis match when the phone rang and it was my agent, saying that Bobby Darin wanted to interview me about being on his show," Edwards said. "I went down to NBC and Bobby walks out of his office and says, 'Walk with me.' We're walking down the hall and he says, 'This is the character I want to do. I want to be a shoeshine guy and you're coming to get a shoeshine' and then he got into character and I started in character and we did this bit all the way down the hall. And then he says, 'You're hired. See you tomorrow at rehearsal,' and that was that."

Edwards joined the ensemble cast, which included comic Rip Taylor playing a helicopter traffic reporter named Skyway Silverman, and Dick Bakalyan, who had a small role opposite Bobby in *Pressure Point*.

"Dick was a friend of Bobby's, and Bobby created this concept of the front stoop, because Bobby had grown up in the Bronx," Chambers said. "So every week on the show, he and Dick played these two neighborhood guys on the front stoop, and they would do humor—

but it was more humor than comedy. And it was something that Bobby liked very much."

Bobby enjoyed working on the show that summer and seemed to enjoy the ensemble feel of the show.

"Bobby liked to be the godfather because when we first started out he always wanted everybody to join him at a restaurant after we taped the show," Ilson recalled. "He'd sit at the head of the table and he liked that feeling and if you didn't show up he'd say, 'Why aren't they here?' For example, he started 'The Bobby Darin Amusement Company First Annual Picnic.' He wanted it to be good. That was all Bobby.

"I remember he wanted a camel wraparound coat for a thing we were doing about Broadway and I went to talk to him and I said, 'Why does it have to be camel hair and why does it have to be wraparound?' And he said to me, 'Jolson used to wear wraparounds.' And we made it for him. Because there was a child in him, too."

Bobby opened at the Hilton in Las Vegas in September and returned to the Copa in October, accompanied by his "valette," Andrea's twenty-three-year-old sister, Terri Koenig.

He joked about his hairpiece and the elevator heels in the act now. "I felt I was vertically inadequate and I went to a bootmaker," he said. "I got me a three-inch adjustment and thought I was John Wayne. Then Steve Lawrence went around town saying, 'Did you hear about Bobby Darin's accident at the Copa? He fell off his shoes.' I loved that. But November 15, it'll be nine years since I've spoken to him."

NBC rewarded Bobby's hard work on the summer-replacement show by announcing in November that it was canceling the long-running series *Bonanza* and the freshman drama series *Banyon*—which would be replaced on Friday nights by *The Bobby Darin Show.*

That good news was followed by the announcement that Steve Blauner was back in the picture.

"Bobby shows up at my office one day in December of '72 and he says, 'Steve, I'm out of the business. I haven't sold a record. I need you,'" Blauner recalled.

"I loved Bobby and he was the brother that I had but didn't have . . . and I said, look, I'm going to Jamaica for the holidays. I'll call you when I get back. I come back and I'm at the office and I get a phone call from somebody saying, 'Bobby is at NBC doing his show and he can't understand; he knows you're back and you haven't called him.' So I'm trapped now. I make an appointment to meet him on a Sunday at a deli in Beverly Hills.

"I don't want to say no to him so I come up with a deal that I know he can't live with so he'll say no to me," Blauner said. "And the deal was very simple: You have to guarantee me a million dollars, whether you work another day or not, against twenty percent. And I don't travel and you don't call me after 6 o'clock at night and you can't call me on weekends. And you're not number-one anymore—I've got a wife and a kid. And if your lawyer accepts this deal, we gotta fire him. Now let's sit down and figure out who to get [to manage] you.

"And as only Bobby could, he looks up and says, 'You got it.' Now what was I going to do, tell him I was kidding? I'll never forget this. I went back to my wife and I said, 'We're managing Bobby again.' She wasn't with me the first time. I remember her putting her arms around me and saying, 'Well, only you know when to quit.'"

That same month Bobby began taping new episodes of *The Bobby Darin Show*, which would return to the air in January. Geoff Edwards, Dick Bakalyan and Rip Taylor returned, along with Bob Rozario and the band. Drummer Tommy Amato was often featured in skits, including thumping the bongos in support of "Dusty John Dustin," Bobby's beatnik character. Bobby also tried convincing Dick Lord to return for the new series.

"He said, 'What do you want?' and I said, 'This is what I want. Ilson and Chambers come to me for this and that, but when they have the meeting, they don't want me to be in the room. I have to be in the room, that's my job,'" Lord recalled. "'And secondly, I have to be on the show. I love the show, I love you, I love being part of the show, but I'm a comedian. I'm not saying I have to be on every week, but after we do the Carmine and Angie segment, I gotta do my stuff about stickball and Little League baseball. It helps me immensely if I have three or four shots on your show.'

"And Bobby said to me, 'Hey, I'm going for ratings. If it says in *TV Guide* that this week's guest is Alan King or Dick Lord, what do you think I have to do?'" Lord did not return.

Production on the show resumed, and Bobby threw himself into the work, spending more and more time at the NBC studios.

"I had this tiny little window of opportunity after lunch where I could rehearse with Bobby and pick his tunes for the next show," said Bob Rozario. "And I was walking by his dressing room to go to rehearsal with him and I hear him having a meeting, and I didn't want to disturb him so I came back in ten minutes and I still hear him having a meeting.

"And I said, what-the-hell, I'm going to disturb him because we've got to do it. So I knock on the door, he says come in, and I looked in and he was all by himself," Rozario said. "He had been rehearsing his lines and he was such a good actor I thought he was actually talking to someone."

But Bobby was also complaining to Blauner that he wanted to wriggle out of his NBC deal. The show wasn't creative enough, he said, and he wasn't satisfied with the results.

"He calls me down to the Beverly Wilshire Hotel and he said, 'This TV show is not very good, it's not creative and I want out,'" Blauner recalled. "So out of my mouth came the following, 'You know, all your life you throw tantrums and have gotten away with it, when you were a kid probably because you were sick and everybody felt sorry for you. For once, see something through to the end, and you will be a man,' and I left the room. I didn't know what was going to happen the next day, but he showed up at NBC."

Part of Bobby's unhappiness stemmed from network interference. It's an age-old truth—or at least a truth hearkening back to the birth of television—that network suits can't help themselves when it comes to meddling in the on-air product. They always know better and are *much* smarter, of course, than the people actually writing the shows and performing them every week. It wasn't any different on *The Bobby Darin Show*.

"The network, as always, was telling Bobby what to do and what not to do and Bobby's attitude was, 'Screw 'em, I'm going to do it my way. If I fail, I'll fail my way, not theirs,'" recalled co-producer Ernest Chambers. "He said, 'If I do what they say and I fail, they're not going to forgive me anyway.'

"Bobby was two people," Chambers said. "He was the tough, villainous kid from the streets of the Bronx who had no principles and was a street fighter. But on the other hand, he was an extremely sensitive guy who had tremendous admiration for art, music and literature. He was well-read and had high aspirations. He was very conflicted that way.

"But you never knew which Bobby you were going to be with that day," Chambers said. "He could be the desperate, threatened street fighter or he could be the comfortable gentleman. He was like a caged animal. He would just get into that and then suddenly he would be this other guy who was at ease in the world and confident in his talent and confident in his place. Of all the people that I've worked with over the years, and I've worked with a helluva lot of them, I have a personal sense of loss about Bobby."

The Bobby Darin Show premiered in January to mediocre ratings but good reviews. There was still plenty of comedy—Bobby's characters included a Jonathan Winters-type grandmother, "The Godmother," and Carmine and Angie—but this incarnation of the show included a stronger musical element than the summer series.

"What lifts the Darin show a notch above its category is the genuine talent of its star," Robert Berkvist wrote in *The New York Times*. "I say this without, I confess, really *liking* Bobby Darin. I *admire* the many different things he can do, the professional way he does them, and the way he spends lavishly on himself to give the customers their money's worth.

"He also has a flair for comedy. On his first show, for example, there was a quick bit of zaniness in which Darin, made up to look uncannily like Groucho Marx, and sounding like him as well, sparred with guest star Dyan Cannon. She: 'Would you like to check my racing form?' He, with a Marxian leer: 'I'd rather check your Maidenform.' And so forth, in a funny and all-too-brief routine."

TV Guide's Cleveland Amory hadn't been a fan of *The Bobby Darin Amusement Company*—he'd predicted in fact, that the show wouldn't return—but he changed his tune with the revamped version of the show.

"His show is a lot better than it was last summer," Amory wrote. "Now that doesn't mean we love it or that we haven't seen some episodes which, when it comes time to rerun them, will find us rerunning too—in the opposite direction.

"But Mr. Darin has more going for him this time out, for which credit should go not only to him but to his imaginative team of producers, Saul Ilson and Ernie Chambers. Mr. Darin is kind of a cross between an older early Frank Sinatra and a younger later Dean Martin."

What Amory and the rest of the viewing public didn't know—and *couldn't* know, as far as Bobby was concerned—was the precarious state of his health now, which made his strenuous production schedule on *The Bobby Darin Show* all the more remarkable. It had been a little over a year since Bobby's open-heart surgery and, as his doctors had warned him, the beneficial effects were short-lived.

"We were sitting around Tommy Amato's house, he was living with Telma Hopkins at the time, and Bobby was in bad shape," recalled Terry Kellman. "I guess we were going to open the next day or something and Bobby just came right out and said, 'Guys, this is my last year, I'm going to die this year.' And we all kind of poo-poohed it, we were just like, 'Come on, boss, that's not going to happen.' But inside I don't think any of us were poo-poohing it."

The new strength and optimism Bobby felt after recuperating from the first heart surgery was slowly evaporating; walking up the steps was a chore now, and Bobby was often listless and depressed during rehearsals. He was forgetting things and repeating himself which was the result, perhaps, of not enough oxygen reaching his brain.

"To me, it had gotten bad," Steve Blauner recalled. "It was like he was senile. He'd be walking down the street and walk into the wall. He didn't drink, he didn't do drugs. He once took Dodd into Westwood to buy a bike and he told Dodd he'd be right back. He never came back. He forgot. That's how bad it was. It was just awful."

Bobby couldn't hide his condition from the cast and crew of his television show. There was an oxygen tank backstage, allowing Bobby to run back, strap on the mask, and take some deep breaths before continuing. He was dropping weight from his already slight figure, giving the appearance of a man much older than his thirty-six years. With his toupee off, Bobby easily looked twenty years older.

"I used to go into his dressing room and he'd be sitting there on oxygen," said Geoff Edwards. "And I would say something and he would say—taking a deep breath—'Yeah, that's funny'—and take another deep breath. He was not a well guy.

"The last show we did was with Peggy Lee and they were standing on two podiums. Bobby would sing and they'd go to break and he would drop his head down with his chin on his chest and his hands down and just stand there like that until they were ready to come up and then he'd be back on."

"We would program little breaks into the show after Bobby would do his comedy bits; he would come back and do 'Midnight Special,' for instance," recalled guitarist Terry Kellman. "He'd walk off and he'd come back on with, say, like a tie off or his jacket off. And then he went backstage, and he would suck on a big oxygen tank. His color was horrible. He was gray. But the audience didn't seem to know, which is just amazing. What he must have been going through as a singer, trying to breathe, is unbelievable."

The change was evident to Quitman Dennis, Bobby's former conductor, who'd played a few gigs with the band and stopped by the NBC studios to say hello.

"I went to visit him on the NBC lot and went to his dressing room and said, 'Hey, how ya doing?' and he was just sitting there," Dennis said. "He looked up at me and said, 'Okay' and looked back down at the floor. And I'd sit there and there was no conversation to be had. We did that a couple of times and I realized something had changed and things were not what they used to be. I didn't really understand what was going on."

In early April NBC cancelled *The Bobby Darin Show*, which got the axe along with *Madigan, Search, Cool Million* and *Circle of Fear*. "This was how self-destructive he could be," said Ernest Chambers. "Bobby insisted on doing more and more music because that's what he was, a musician. But the trouble is, even in those days you couldn't do a [musical] number that ran more than two minutes maximum. And he would like to do things like that and he wouldn't give a damn."

Peggy Lee was the guest for the final show. Bobby, already fed up with the network's interference, especially toward his musical numbers, took a "fuck you" attitude toward NBC and decided he would do the final show his way. Besides, what was there to lose?

Bobby decided the final show would be an hour of solid singing, a concert of sorts in which he'd sing alone, with Peggy Lee and essentially perform his stage act. Part of this final show would later be shown on public television and came to be known as Bobby's last recorded "live" concert.

"We never even rehearsed for it," Bob Rozario said. "Peggy Lee was on the first half of the show but she rehearsed first and she took a lot of Bobby's time, so we were running out of time and he started to feel very badly. And he looked at me and said, 'Bob, we've just got to wing it.'

"We didn't have time to rehearse and I couldn't have rehearsed even if I wanted to. So Bobby went back to his dressing room and we just came out and winged the show. I told the musicians to stay on their toes, because anything could happen.

"It was one of Bobby's better performances. You'd never know he was sick," Rozario said. "He was so thrilled by this performance that when he got offstage, he cried because his son was not in the audience. Bobby wanted him to have caught the show but, for some reason, Sandy didn't allow Dodd to come and see the show that day."

BOBBY'S DEPRESSION DEEPENED with the cancellation of his show and his progressive physical deterioration. Steve Blauner, thinking ahead, made a major push to land Bobby a Vegas deal. Blauner went to Bobby's agents at William Morris and convinced them to let him go to Vegas, visit the hotels, and sell Bobby.

"I told them, 'You'll get the commission but no one can sell Bobby like I can sell him,'" Blauner said. "I said, 'I don't want any of your agents around with me. Just let me do it.' And they said yes and set up these meetings and I went to every hotel up and down the strip. I wanted a three-year deal, twelve weeks a year, because I said to Bobby, 'I'm going to Vegas, and between Vegas and Tahoe you won't have to work another day if you don't want to. From then on, you pick and choose. If you want to work, we'll get work. But I'll get you enough money.'"

The Sands couldn't commit to Blauner's twelve-weeks-a-year demands, but the Hilton and the new MGM Grand, which was under construction, were receptive to the idea.

"Little did I know who I was dealing with . . . they were gangsters out of Detroit, whatever," Blauner said of the MGM Grand management. "And I made the deal for nine weeks a year. I couldn't believe the deal that I made. It stuns me to this day. $75,000 a week, plus they paid for Bobby's four musicians that he carried on the road, plus the regular band, plus the singers. And he had the power of the pencil, which means we could sign for anything. We could have fifty people and all these suites and rooms for friends to come visit."

On top of the MGM Grand deal, Blauner worked out deals for Bobby at the Sahara hotel in Lake Tahoe—two weeks in the winter, two in the summer—that brought the deal close to $1 million a year.

The MGM Grand, though, wasn't scheduled to open until Christmas of that year. Blauner, aware of Bobby's illness, built a disability clause into the MGM Grand contract, ensuring that if Bobby couldn't make a date, those weeks would be tacked on to the end of the deal to recoup the lost money. But the disability clause became a sticking point with MGM Grand management, leaving the deal up in the air.

In the meantime, Bobby opened at the Hilton in Vegas during Easter week under a separate eight-week deal (four weeks now, four weeks in July). The crowds, though, were sparse, and Blauner worried that news of Bobby's trouble drawing an audience would get back to the MGM Grand management.

"On Sunday I call the girl at the reservation desk and say how are we doing? And she says, 'only . . .' and when I hear 'only,' I die. It was a disaster," he said. "Now I know I'm in trouble with the MGM Grand because everybody gets the information."

Blauner's instincts were right. The MGM Grand wanted to "move in another direction" and did an about-face on signing Bobby. The Hilton management also got nervous and backed out of committing to Bobby in July (although they later changed their minds).

"I got in the car and the next thing I find myself halfway to San Francisco. I didn't know how I got there; I just drove," Blauner said. "I ended up turning around, going home and getting into bed in the fetal position and just lying there."

The next morning, Blauner called a friend of his whose father-in-law owned the biggest laundry service in Vegas, and whose clients included some of the strip's biggest hotels—including the MGM

Grand. While making his rounds at the MGM Grand, Blauner's friend just happened to mention that Bobby was about to sign a huge deal with the Hilton, and wouldn't it be a shame if the MGM Grand lost out?

"So the guy at the MGM Grand says, 'You can't trust anyone anymore,' picks up the phone and the contracts arrive at the lawyer's office the next morning," Blauner said. "To have made it, lost it and gotten it back again was probably the high point of my business life. Nothing was like Bobby."

The new deals did little to brighten Bobby's mood. With the cancellation of *The Bobby Darin Show* he sank further into a depression that was deepened by his worsening physical condition.

"It was ominous and I was very upset by it," said Mimi Greenberg. "He was in one of his depressions and it was after the winter show had not been picked up. He called me and said, 'I'm thinking about going into radio. Why not? I failed in every medium. The only one I haven't failed in is radio because I haven't tried it yet.' His plan was to do some kind of talk show on a daily basis or maybe do something where he would have like five minutes at the end of an hour, like Paul Harvey or one of those guys, and he wanted to know if I would write the material.

"I said of course I would and he said, 'Okay, I just want to make sure I have people who I can trust and who will work with me.' He was always a little paranoid, but he got very paranoid in the end. And that was my very last conversation with him."

Bobby did, in fact, host a syndicated radio show around that time which was underwritten by the American Dairy Association. "They wanted him to do a show five days a week, five minutes a day, where he would spin a record and talk about the song," Blauner said. "But he said he wouldn't do that because it wouldn't be fair to the disk jockeys. But he would do it live, he would sing live. So he did twenty-six weeks worth of shows, five shows a week, where he actually sang with a trio or a quartet, sang a song and a half or whatever, a short version."

SINCE THE BEGINNING of their relationship, Bobby and Andrea always told people they were married, if not legally then spiritually.

"We've just dispensed with the bureaucratic involvement," Bobby once said. They changed all that on June 27, 1973, when Bobby and Andrea legally married in Walnut Grove, California. They honeymooned on a rented houseboat in the Sacramento-San Joaquin delta area.

"She was really a nurse toward the end, especially when the series ended because that was when he really went downhill fast and she was trying to keep him together," Mimi Greenberg said of Andrea. "She knew he wasn't taking the medicine and she couldn't get him to take his medicine. Sometimes you can say, 'Oh well, they forgot to take the medicine because they were busy doing this and that,' but she was there in the picture and she kept reminding him and he still didn't take it.

"So it wasn't that he absentmindedly forgot to take it," she said. "He was deliberately not taking it."

Whether or not that was the case, there was no doubt that Bobby's medical condition was spiraling out of control. Bobby didn't help his own cause when he went in for some extensive dental work that spring, knowing full well that he needed to take preventative antibiotics to head off the risk of infection. Bacteria loosened during the dental work could break off, enter his bloodstream and infect his already damaged heart. It was an often fatal scenario.

For some reason, Bobby didn't take the antibiotics before his visit to the dentist and contracted blood poisoning shortly thereafter, spending six weeks in the hospital just prior to marrying Andrea. To someone like Bobby's pal Mimi Greenberg, who would later become a psychotherapist specializing in patients with debilitating illnesses, Bobby realized what he was doing all along.

"I can tell you this—Bobby wanted to die," Greenberg said. "There was no question. He wanted to die. He flirted with the idea of death and dying and he was enough of a daredevil that he would take it to the edge—and he took it to the edge and he went over.

"He was a hypochondriac who was acutely aware of every symptom and every medical thing that was going on with him, and his not taking his medication and then having dental work done was not accidental," she said. "He knew. Now, he didn't know that he was going to get the infection, but he figured there was a pretty good chance."

Bobby returned to live performing in July, opening at the Hilton and somehow getting through the shows with his usual athleticism and hard-charging style. But his behavior off-stage was beginning to alarm Andrea. He would lay in bed for days with the shades drawn, refusing to get out of bed, and he was forgetting things.

"Once, Andrea called me and I came over and threw the blinds open and I started to yell at him," said Blauner. "I said, 'What the hell are you feeling sorry for yourself for? What do you mean you'll never work again? You can direct, you can write, you can publish.' He looked at me and said, 'Thanks, Steve, now close the blinds when you leave.' It was awful and Andrea put up with it."

That wasn't the only problem. The piece of paper that made Bobby and Andrea's marriage legal now seemed to throw the couple for a loop. They had gotten along famously before, or at least seemed to keep the fighting to a minimum. Soon after their "official" marriage, however, their relationship started to sour.

"Within a week Andrea had told him everything that he had ever done wrong for the last three years," said Bobby's brother, Gary. "Bobby called my mother and said, 'I can't believe this. For the last three years I've been the most wonderful person. We get married, now all of a sudden I'm the biggest SOB that ever lived on the face of the earth. What did I do wrong?'"

Gary himself was hit by a double-whammy that summer. Nina figured he was old enough, at seventeen, to handle the delicate family situation, which turned out to be much more complicated than Gary could ever have imagined. Charlie Maffia, it turned out, wasn't Gary's real father. Nina had been having a long-term affair, while she was still married to Charlie, with Gene, the friendly cop who spent so much time in the Maffia apartment in New York. Gene was Gary's father. Charlie knew the truth, but never said a word.

"We were talking in the kitchen one day and I found out who my real father was," Gary said. "I was seventeen and I was with my mother. You could ask her a direct question, but be prepared because you would get a direct answer. And I asked her one day if Gene was my father. And she turned to me and said, 'Yes.'

"Then, about a month later, we happened to be in the kitchen again and we're talking because now it's out in the open and I would see

Gene all the time, and he looks like me and one ear is attached and the other isn't attached—just like me.

"So anyway, it seemed like now was the appropriate time and my mother said, 'I want to let you know that Bobby is not your uncle, Bobby is your half-brother.' I was thrilled because I didn't have a brother and I always loved him, I always looked up to him, so now, instead of being an uncle, he was even closer, he was my half-brother. I was thrilled to death. Vana, who was sitting at the table said, 'Well, I've known for fifteen years.' But now it was spoken."

In the meantime, Bobby hoped that getting Andrea and Steve Blauner to visit his psychiatrist might shed some light on his personality which might, in turn, help his marriage and his deepening depression. Dick Lord turned down a similar request. "Bobby said, 'I want you to tell the shrink how I've changed,'" Lord recalled. "I said, 'I'm not going. The dues would be too high.'"

Andrea and Blauner agreed, however, and accompanied Bobby to his psychiatrist. "He says, 'You'll go in and do ten minutes and she'll go in and do ten minutes, then I'll come in and he'll know all about me,'" Blauner said. "I said fine. So we went down there, I met the man and he took Andrea in first. Bobby and I went for a walk around the block, came back, the shrink opened the door and told both of us to come in.

"The shrink had arranged for Bobby to be admitted to UCLA, I think he said to the psychiatric ward, but he would be going in as a heart patient," Blauner said. "I sat there and I said, 'This is not the way to handle Bobby.'

"Bobby said, and I knew he was bristling, 'Is that the way you feel, Steve?' And I choked on it but I said, 'Yes.' Then he asked Andrea, and she said yes. He got up, left the shrink's office and I followed him out to the elevator and said, 'What's the matter with you?'

"Now I knew he thought we were trying to railroad him into the hospital," Blauner said. "I said, 'Bobby, this was your idea. You're in control. You asked us to come here.' But he pulled away from the curb and he called Andrea's sister, who at one point had been his valet on the road. The next day, Andrea found out she was getting a divorce.

"That same night I was home and Bruce Dern and his wife were over for dinner," Blauner said. "I had been upstairs showing Bruce the bedroom or something and I'm coming downstairs and there's Bobby, looking like death warmed over. I asked Bruce to excuse us and we went to talk. Bobby had come up and explained to me, in his words, that our relationship was through. My daughter was sitting on my lap and she was trying to get into my belt, she was so frightened of this man, the way he looked, someone she had seen a hundred times.

"And I started to play with him, because I wasn't going to let this become serious," Blauner said. "So I said, 'Now listen, let me understand this Bobby, if I'm walking down the street and I see you coming toward me, do I have to walk across the street because I don't want to be embarrassed?' But he left and got into his car and I leaned into the window and I kissed him and I said, 'Bobby, you can't legislate love. I will always love you, you do what you have to do.' That's when his doctors sent him out of town. They wanted him away from everything and he went to his house in Vegas."

Bobby called Nina, who had moved with Gary and the girls to a house trailer in upstate New York.

"When he got home from the doctor's office he called my mother and he was crying on the phone and he said, 'Can you believe this is what my wife and supposed best friend want to do?'" Gary recalled. "They thought he was incompetent, that he was losing it. He had a heart condition. He had a heart condition since he was seven years old.

"He got off the phone with Nina, and she went in and talked to Vee and said, 'Get your stuff in a suitcase, we're going out to see Bobby.' They went all over the place, cashing checks so they had money to make the trip. They hopped in the car and when they were halfway there, they called Bobby and said, 'We just want to tell you we're on . . .' and he said, 'I knew as soon as I got off the phone that you'd get in the car and come out.' He had a house in Las Vegas at the time and he went home.

"Now, Bobby wanted no part of my mother. He was still angry. But he found solace in Vee," Gary said. "True, there was seven years difference in age between them but the fact remained that he felt close to Vee. They had had numerous discussions and arguments over the years, because my sister had no problem telling him exactly what an SOB he was, and how he had mistreated his family, how he would do anything for a stranger but would walk all over his family. So he knew he was going to get straight talk from her, but he also knew that she loved him desperately.

"They stayed in Vegas and Bobby got to the point where he didn't want my mother around," Gary said. "Bobby never got over the fact that he was lied to. He never accepted Nina as his mother. And said to her, 'There's a person inside of me that hates you for what you did. And if I die before I can reconcile that hatred, so be it.' And he never did.

"So Nina called and said, 'I'm sending you an airline ticket, I want you to fly to Vegas and drive back with me and Vee is going to stay.' And the day I got there Bobby decided to go to Los Angeles and change his will. What the old will was I don't know, I never found out. If there were ten wills before that I don't know. But he changed the will. Vee stayed with Bobby and we drove back."

The tough kid from the Bronx was a shell of his former self now. All the fight—all the brashness and cockiness that coursed through Bobby's veins—was rushing out of his body like air from a pricked balloon. His wife was gone. His best friend was gone. His recording career was non-existent. He hadn't starred in a movie in six years. The walls were closing in, and there was no work to help ease the pain.

"I was driving with Bobby Rozario and a car pulls up next to us and it's Bobby Darin," recalled Tony Orlando. "And Bobby looks over and motions for us to pull over. So we pull over and he gets out and, I mean, Bobby is about as skinny as I'd ever seen him.

"And he said, 'Bobby, listen to me. I'm not feeling all that great. I'm not taking my medicine and I'm not going back to the doctor as often as I should. I just want you to know that if anything ever happens to me, I want you to go with Tony and I want the whole rhythm section to be with Tony.'

"He was bequeathing his whole rhythm section to me," Orlando said. "Now, I'm standing there in total awe of what I'm hearing, that this man who I've idolized all these years is now bequeathing the band to me. I said, 'Bobby, come on, don't be talking so negatively like that. I don't want to hear that. You're going to be fine. We're going to work together, do some dates together.' He said to Bobby, 'If I go, I want you to give me your word because Tony is going to need you because he's going to be a big star, he's going to need your expertise and what you know about nightclubs and what you know about the stage.'"

THERE WAS ONE MORE VISIT with Steve Blauner, to whom Bobby had apologized after returning from Las Vegas. "He came up to the house; he was having trouble with his heart and we went down to Westwood to buy some stuff to counteract it," Blauner said. "He announced that he was not working anymore and that he was letting everybody go and right in front of his lawyer he looked at me and said, 'Timing is everything, Steve.'

"He owed me a million dollars and I said, 'Look, Bobby, you knew I'd never take [the money] if I didn't earn it. All I want is, this past month I didn't get paid for what I was supposed to, which amounts to $25,000. I want protection if you ever go back to work, that even if I'm not around I'm protected on the MGM Grand deal.'

"His attitude was, 'Well, what did Steve think I would do?' and so he came out and played hardball. His lawyer called me and said, 'He'll make that decision when the time comes' and I said, 'Well, then we're in a lawsuit.' And so I was going to sue him. And we never talked again, ever. And the lawyer said to me, 'Steve, look, you're entitled to $25,000. You're entitled to the cash. Don't sue Bobby. There is no statute of limitations,' and all of this. I said, 'What if he dies?' And he said, 'I guarantee you the $25,000.'"

Bobby began experiencing heart fibrillations, and in October he suffered congestive heart failure. By December, he was back in Cedars of Lebanon Hospital. His doctors told him he needed a second heart operation to repair the two valves implanted the first time. There was no alternative. If he didn't have the surgery, he would die. Even if he did have the surgery, there was no guarantee he would survive.

Vee had stayed with Bobby, and moved into his hospital room as he prepared himself for the open-heart surgery.

"He really didn't want to see anybody but Vee," Gary said. "They talked at length. Bobby didn't want to die and he didn't think he was going to die. He figured he was going to cheat death one day at a time. He had it all planned out, that he would get out of the hospital and he would come home and stay with us. My mother would make manicotti for him to build up his strength and he wouldn't have all these phony people around. Because he realized everyone was in it for the buck . . . he went back to his family because no matter how much you dump on the family, they still love you. Whether you're Bobby Darin or you're a very sick man, we'll take care of you."

Some of Bobby's old friends came by the hospital to visit. Dick Behrke, Bobby's old press agent David Gershenson and Don Gregory all showed up to visit their frail, weak friend.

"He said, 'I told you, D.,'" said Gregory. "He knew he wasn't getting out and said so. He was in bed with a sheet over the blanket and had his head resting on a pillow. It was tender and nice and left me with a good feeling for him. My last moments with him were sweet."

Steve Blauner was conspicuous by his absence. "When he went into the hospital I sent him a note telling him I loved him and I wished him well," Blauner said. "I will go to my grave feeling guilty that we never talked after that night at my house."

Bobby underwent the six-hour open-heart surgery on December 19. He pulled through the surgery for a few short hours, but slipped away around 12:15 a.m. Pacific Time on December 20, 1973. "He never really came around after the operation," said a hospital spokesman. "He was just too weak to recover." He was thirty-seven.

Bobby's will stipulated that his body be donated to medical science, and it was transported to the University of California in Los Angeles for use in research. There was no funeral.

In upstate New York, Nina's phone rang.

"The phone rang and you just knew," Gary said. "Nina answered the phone. Vee told her and my mother just went through the house screaming, 'He didn't make it!' So I went to the phone. My mother was running back and forth. And I started to cry. Nina wanted to talk to Vee. She was inconsolable. So I was holding Nina and we were both crying. It was over."

Bob Rozario, who Bobby had "bequeathed" to Tony Orlando, did, indeed, become Orlando's conductor. They were down in New Orleans with Terry Kellman, Tommy Amato and the rest of the band, working at the Fairmount Hotel, when the news of Bobby's death broke over the radio.

"Bob was a spiritual kind of guy; you never heard him complain or whine and you never expected him to lose control," Orlando said. "Well, when the word came over the radio that Bobby passed away, I ran down to Bobby Rozario's room and as I approached the room, I'll never forget the wailing that was coming from behind his door.

"It was the kind of wailing that you knew you better not knock on that door," Orlando said. "It was the kind of a cry that was coming from the depth of this man. He was a wreck. I went to knock on the door, and I thought no, so I stood outside the door and I started to pray. And I prayed as hard as I could that Bobby would go to heaven and then Bobby Rozario would be okay. He kept saying in his wailing and crying, 'Bobby, I love you. Oh no, I love you.' He was really crying hard.

"I don't think that Bobby Rozario ever really recovered from that," Orlando said. "I think that had an impact on him all of his life. I think it nailed him to a point where he really felt a brotherly loss. That was really deep."

"We had to work that night. We were just devastated and Tony knew that," recalled Terry Kellman. "We couldn't even function. I don't know how we did it. I don't even remember working that night."

Dick Lord heard the news that morning.

"I hadn't seen Bobby in a while but we had spoken," he said. "The night before, I was working in Lancaster, Pennsylvania at a place called Host Farms. I usually stayed over; I don't know why but I said to my wife, 'We have to go home.' I don't know why I did that. I went home and went to sleep and at 7 o'clock in the morning someone called and said, 'Bobby's dead. Who should we invite to the funeral?' I suggested Flip Wilson and some other people. But there was no funeral."

"I got a call from the hospital that he was dead," Steve Blauner recalled. "It was in the middle of the night and I remember getting out of bed, going upstairs, putting on the radio and being pissed off. Nancy Sinatra called me about a funeral. I said, 'Look, Nancy, I'm not second-guessing. I can't do something he didn't want. But if you want to, great, I'll be there. You do whatever you want to do. He said he didn't want a funeral, I'm not going to go against his wishes.'"

Joyce Becker hadn't seen Bobby since their long talk in 1968 when Bobby found out the truth about Nina.

"As fate would have it, one of my best friends had a baby at Cedars of Lebanon in Los Angeles and I was in the hospital when she had the baby," she said. "I had come out and sat on a bench and there were a lot of reporters and photographers and people I knew. I said, 'What the hell is going on here?' Did somebody just die?' And one of the guys turned around and looked at me and said, 'Yeah, Bobby Darin just died.'"

The New York Times ran a three-column obituary on December 21— "Bobby Darin, Pop Singer, Dies at 37"—along with a picture of a serious-looking Bobby wearing his hairpiece and tux, almost scowling at the photographer.

"Of course it was front-page news and it was the lead story on the news and we had to sit through all of that—my mother wanted to see it, visually," Gary said. "She had to see Bobby's picture on the screen. Bobby, of course, donated his body to science so there would be no finalization, no grief. This was the end. And that was a difficult thing.

"It was horrible to lose somebody, to go through the process of a viewing and a funeral . . . but Bobby didn't want that," he said. "He didn't want a parade, he didn't want a show, he didn't want this whole routine of grieving with Sandy. Nothing. He just wanted to disappear and that's basically what happened. It made it hard for everybody because there was no way to say goodbye."

Bobby's old friend, Tom Mankiewicz, heard the news on the radio like so many others. In his mind, he flashed back to the image of his old friend who'd come rocketing into his life and then left—much too quickly.

"I always thought Bobby would be fabulous casting for *The Great Gatsby* because Gatsby was the guy with bootlegging in his past who didn't quite fit in with the big swells on Long Island, but yet, Daisy fell in love with him," he said.

"Gatsby had that million dollar charm. And that was Bobby. You can talk about the Bronx High School of Science or whatever, but the impression you had from Bobby was that he came from the wrong side of the tracks, but he had this unbelievable personality, this million-dollar charm. And I think that's why women were very attracted to him. There was something wonderfully cocky about him, but not arrogantly cocky. It was a generous kind of cockiness."

Epilogue

Bobby Darin in death proved to be as controversial as he had been in life. He foiled any plans for a funeral by donating his body to science, almost daring someone to go against his final wishes. No one did. There was no memorial service. In his will, he left nothing to his immediate family but established a generous trust fund for twelve-year-old Dodd—who couldn't touch the bulk of the inheritance until much later in life.

"Unfortunately, as much as I loved him, he was a very cruel individual as far as his family was concerned," said Bobby's brother Gary, who later changed his surname from Maffia to Walden. "He seemed to enjoy inflicting pain on people who loved him, especially his family. I mean, you die, you're a wealthy individual—you're the highest-paid nightclub performer in the world—how can you not leave something to your mother?

"I understand the others, your nieces and nephews, half-brothers and half-sisters . . . but my mom was never well," he said. "She got diabetes in 1971, she had a weight problem, she lost half of her body weight in six months. She wasn't a well person. How can you do that to your mother? I don't understand it to this day. It's thirty years later and I still don't understand it.

"But that was Bobby."

Bobby's legacy extended itself in other ways, as Tony Orlando discovered a year after Bobby's death. Bobby had "bequeathed" his band and its leader, Bob Rozario, to Orlando, and they remained a cohesive unit for many years thereafter. But, from beyond the grave, Bobby seemed to have even more in store for Orlando—in whose bright future Bobby had always believed.

"How amazing is this? Bobby Rozario brings Saul Ilson and Ernie Chambers, who produced Bobby's TV show, to meet me," Orlando said. "And he brings them to meet me at Disney World. Why? Because Freddie Silverman's babysitter sees me on *The Merv Griffin Show* and is the same babysitter that tipped Freddie off to seeing Sonny and Cher on *The Merv Griffin Show*. And who does Freddie tell to go check me out? Ilson and Chambers. So who do Ilson and Chambers call? Bob Rozario. How do they know Bob Rozario? They produced *The Bobby Darin Show*.

"Do they know my affiliation with Bobby Darin? No. So it was almost like Bobby, after he died, going 'Hey, Ernie and Saul, go with Tony. Take care of him.' It was so strange. I mean it was such an amazing thing. And sure enough they became producers of *The Tony Orlando and Dawn Show*."

Bob Rozario, who had been decimated by Bobby's death, also felt the grasp of Bobby from beyond, but in a different way.

"When I first joined Bobby, it was about six months later and we were flying to Australia to do a date in one of the hotels in Sydney," he said. "On that flight, he called me over and said, 'Bob, as long as I'm alive, you have a job with me.' And I just realized that I still have a job with him. People are always asking me to talk about him, what he was like, what his music was like. So, in a way, I'm still working for him.

"Like Steve Blauner," Rozario said. "Steve tells the story of whenever he goes to a record store, he always looks for Bobby's albums and he'll put them in the front of the bin. I said, 'See, Steve, we're still working for Bobby.'"

It took a long time for Nina to deal with the reality of her son's death.

"She came to terms with it, and it took years for her to even hear Bobby singing," son Gary said. "It wasn't that you couldn't mention Bobby, she just couldn't hear him sing. We couldn't watch. I mean there was no such thing at that time as videos. But for whatever reason, if one of Bobby's movies came on, if you wanted to watch it you had to go in another room. She couldn't take seeing his image or hearing his voice. And then things started to change where she wanted to hear him again."

In the late 1970s, Nina was approached by Al DiOrio, a New York-based writer and Bobby Darin aficionado who was writing Bobby's biography. It was in DiOrio's book, published in 1981 and called *Borrowed Time*, that Nina disclosed she was, in fact, Bobby's mother and not his sister.

"The only thing she wouldn't tell Al was the fact of who the father was, because everybody wants to know," Gary said. "She said she would take that with her to her grave and she did. I'm sure my mom would have told me but I'm not a curious person. And I never bothered to ask because we had a wonderful relationship. I took care of her until the day she died. I bought her a brand-new house close to the water and she was thrilled with that."

DiOrio's book, and Nina's startling revelation therein, ignited Hollywood's interest, and the scramble was on turn Bobby's life into a movie. It wouldn't be easy. Producer Steve Metz coughed up $75,000 for the rights to *Borrowed Time*, and planned to produce a $4 million movie. To find his Bobby Darin, Metz hired the same casting agents who cast an unknown Gary Busey in *The Buddy Holly Story*, for which Busey won an Oscar. Metz, along with co-producers Lee Miller and Bob Reno, wanted Tom Mankiewicz to write the screenplay.

There was one stumbling block, however: Sandra Dee.

Sandra was said to be "fuming" over plans to turn Bobby's life into a movie, and she clashed with Metz and company from the get-go. "We offered Miss Dee script approval and a consultancy on the film if she'd agree to work with us," Metz said at the time. "But Sandy has been very negative, very uncooperative. She won't have anything to do with the film."

Sandra, Metz said, feared she would be portrayed in "a bad light." To get around that problem, Sandra would be called "Allison Wade" in the movie, which was now going to be written by Al Giardino, who envisioned Allison as a compulsive gambler.

Metz and company still hadn't found their Bobby, although George Burns agreed to play himself and actress Brenda Vaccaro was being considered for the role of Vee. Dodd would make a decision on whether or not he wanted to participate in the movie after he turned twenty-one in a few months. George Scheck, still representing Connie Francis, refused approval of the film script.

The hassles proved too much for Metz and his associates, and they eventually abandoned the project. But the idea of a Bobby Darin movie biography kicked around Hollywood for the better part of the next twenty years—and was given further juice when Bobby was inducted into the Rock and Roll Hall of Fame in 1990. At the time, director Barry Levinson and his partner, Mark Johnson, were attached to the movie at Warner Bros. Through the years, that list would also include Dick Clark and husband-and-wife Marty Ingels and Shirley Jones.

The dormant Bobby Darin movie project got a huge kick-start when actor Kevin Spacey got involved. Spacey, a Bobby Darin fanatic, had long wanted to make the movie and star as Bobby. And, with the power of Oscar-winning performances in *The Usual Suspects* and *American Beauty* behind him, Spacey was finally able to put together financing for the project, which was entitled *Beyond the Sea*. In addition to starring as Bobby, Spacey would direct the movie.

Spacey fancies himself a credible singer and impressionist, and was intent on singing Bobby's songs himself. That decision didn't sit well with Bobby's estate, notably Dodd and Steve Blauner, who had to give permission for Spacey to use Bobby's songs. They battled back and forth, and Spacey eventually won. He would sing Bobby's songs in the movie.

Spacey was intent on getting it right, and he wanted to meet with some of Bobby's former arrangers before the movie went into production. One of those calls went to Roger Kellaway.

"He's Juilliard-trained and the guy can sing," Kellaway said of Spacey. "He does a fabulous imitation of Bobby. He's very good at that. So when he does 'One for the Road,' which was the song I heard him do, he was excellent."

Beyond the Sea began shooting in Europe in the late summer/early fall of 2003. The movie, written by Paul Attanasio and Lorenzo Carcaterra, is scheduled to be released in late 2004. Besides Spacey in the starring role, the cast includes Kate Bosworth as Sandra; John Goodman as Steve Blauner; Bob Hoskins as Charlie Maffia; Brenda Blethyn as Polly; and Caroline Aaron as Nina.

Postscript by Gary Walden

My brother Bobby was many things to many people, but to me he was truly a great performer in every sense of the word.

Anyone born into a show-business family sees what a wacky world it can be. It's a world in which you must be ready for anything that comes your way.

My grandmother, Polly Cassotto, was a great singer in vaudeville, and with Bobby Darin as my brother, you could say that our household was filled with music. I grew up watching the Grammy Awards, which, in our house, was a must-see event. This was particularly true in 1959, when Bobby won for Best New Artist and also for "Mack the Knife."

Years later, in 1971, Bobby was asked to be a presenter at the Grammys. He did his usual terrific job, and a few days later I called Bobby to ask him if there was any way I could possibly go with him the next year if he was asked to present again. "Of course," Bobby said. "I'd be glad to take you along." My dream came true in 1972, when Bobby was asked to be a presenter at the Grammys because he had been such a hit the previous year!

The 1972 Grammy telecast was scheduled for March in the Felt Forum in New York City. The original plan was for Bobby to fly into New York at 9 a.m., get to the Felt Forum for the run-through at 1 p.m., then spend the rest of the day with me until showtime at 8 p.m. that night.

Bobby was due to arrive in New York from London after the last leg of a European tour. But due to adverse weather conditions in both cities, his flight didn't arrive at JFK Airport until 7 p.m.—one hour before the Grammy telecast. Bobby had to change into his tux in the limo, and then we got stuck in traffic!

When we finally got to the Felt Forum it was 8:30. Upon entering the backstage door, Bobby was handed the envelope for his category, which was coming up in the next half-hour segment. In the meantime, I was brought down to my front-row seat during a commercial break and seated next to Charlie Pride and Freda Payne. It was such a thrill to be there. Sixteen years old and at the Grammy Awards! It didn't matter to me that my plans to spend the day with Bobby didn't work out. But Bobby was upset for me, because the situation certainly wasn't what he had intended.

Within minutes, my brother came out with Aretha Franklin to present the award for Best Jazz Performance. No one could have guessed that Bobby hadn't rehearsed his segment and, once again, he was a big hit as a presenter. And when Bobby came off-stage, he was asked to host the post-Grammy Awards show at the Americana Hotel!

In those days, it was commonplace to air the main awards and to have performers showcase their songs for the public to enjoy. But there was also a huge show after the telecast at which all of the other awards were distributed. This second ceremony was not shown on television.

Andy Williams had hosted the Grammy Awards for the last few years and was supposed to have done the post-Grammy show as well. However, during the telecast of the main show, Williams became ill. He decided that he would finish the show as planned but was unable to do the second event at the Americana.

Both shows had been planned, staged, set up and rehearsed far in advance. Williams, who had been at all the rehearsals for both shows, was well-prepared and well-rested, but my brother was not.

Bobby had been up all day and half the night before—at a London airport, on a plane, circling the airport, and then in a limo stuck in New York traffic. He had had no time to prepare for the first show, much less for a second show as the host. Yet he accepted this tremendous, last-minute responsibility without hesitation.

Bobby and I were both driven to the Americana Hotel. What a joy to be seated at a table next to Karen and Richard Carpenter on one side, Three Dog Night across from me and The Fifth Dimension on the other side. They were all favorites of mine. Then Bobby stepped on stage for two and a half hours of perfect hosting. I was simply amazed at this man who could walk in ice-cold, with nothing, and give a an outstanding performance. It was just another example of what Bobby could accomplish with that God-given talent of his.

To say that the Grammy Awards Committee was grateful to Bobby for what he did is bittersweet for me. Even though Bobby pulled them out of a very big jam, Andy Williams was brought back to host the 1973 Grammy Awards—and, tragically, Bobby died several months later.

What a shame that my brother never got the chance to shine as host to the millions who watched the Grammys each year. I will always remember that day and cherish it, for I witnessed what a real, true showman is.

And he was my brother, Bobby Darin.

Gary Walden, July 2004

Index